COPYRIGHT CLASS STRUGGLE

Earning an income in our time often involves ownership of creative assets, or control over them. Employing the law and philosophy of economics, this illuminating book explores the legal controversies that emerge when authors, singers, filmmakers, and social media barons leverage their rights into major paydays. It explores how players in the entertainment and technology sectors articulate claims to an ever-increasing amount of copyright-protected media. It then analyzes efforts to reform copyright law in the contexts of (1) increasing the rights of creators and sellers, and (2) allocating these rights after employment and labor disputes, constitutional challenges to intellectual property law, efforts to legalize online mashups and remixes, and changes to the amount of streaming royalties paid to actors and musicians. This work should be read by anyone interested in how copyright law – and its potential reform – shapes the ownership of ideas in the social media age.

Hannibal Travis is Professor of Law at Florida International University College of Law where his research focuses on the universal accessibility of digital libraries, the rights of authors and performers to compensation from streaming sites under international and domestic law, privacy and the surveillance of Facebook or YouTube activity, and copyright and patent reform. Previously he practiced technology and entertainment law at Debevoise & Plimpton LLP in New York and at O'Melveny & Myers in San Francisco.

Copyright Class Struggle

CREATIVE ECONOMIES IN A SOCIAL MEDIA AGE

HANNIBAL TRAVIS

Florida International University College of Law

CAMBRIDGE
UNIVERSITY PRESS

University Printing House, Cambridge CB2 8BS, United Kingdom

One Liberty Plaza, 20th Floor, New York, NY 10006, USA

477 Williamstown Road, Port Melbourne, VIC 3207, Australia

314–321, 3rd Floor, Plot 3, Splendor Forum, Jasola District Centre, New Delhi – 110025, India

79 Anson Road, #06-04/06, Singapore 079906

Cambridge University Press is part of the University of Cambridge.

It furthers the University's mission by disseminating knowledge in the pursuit of
education, learning, and research at the highest international levels of excellence.

www.cambridge.org
Information on this title: www.cambridge.org/9781107193635
DOI: 10.1017/9781108147958

© Hannibal Travis 2018

First published 2018

Printed and bound in Great Britain by Clays Ltd, Elcograf S.p.A.

A catalogue record for this publication is available from the British Library.

Library of Congress Cataloging-in-Publication Data
NAMES: Travis, Hannibal, author.
TITLE: Copyright class struggle : creative economies in a social media age /
    Hannibal Travis, Professor of Law, Florida International University College of Law.
DESCRIPTION: Cambridge [UK]; New York : Cambridge University Press, 2018. |
    Includes bibliographical references and index.
IDENTIFIERS: LCCN 2018031521| ISBN 9781107193635 (hardback: alk. paper) |
    ISBN 9781316645031 (pbk.: alk. paper)
SUBJECTS: LCSH: Copyright. | Copyright–Economic aspects. |
    Copyright–Audio-visual materials. | Copyright and electronic data
    processing. | Copyright–Interactive multimedia. | Patent laws and
    legislation. | Copyright infringemnet.
CLASSIFICATION: LCC K1420.5 .T73 2018 | DDC 346.04/82 — dc23
    LC record available at https://lccn.loc.gov/2018031521

ISBN 978-1-107-19363-5 Hardback
ISBN 978-1-316-64503-1 Paperback

To Bianca

Contents

Figures

Figures

Tables

Tables

1

On Owning Ideas in Our Time

1.1. STATEMENTS OF INTEREST

On February 18, 2009, Dr. Marc Maurer, President of the National Federation of the Blind, wrote that more ebooks should be posted to Google for use by Americans who are visually disabled or otherwise in need of accessible ebooks. Copyright cases dragging on for half a decade had kept out-of-print books away from the public, limiting access to ebooks for the blind, the physically handicapped, the dyslexic, and other readers.[1] A settlement between Google and authors' and publishers' representatives created a vast new digital service for reading and marketing books, subject to the right of authors and publishers to control whether they participated in it at all. A coalition of publishers, technology companies, and nonprofit organizations had come together to resolve to their mutual benefit the most important copyright dispute of our lifetime.[2]

The settlement would have delivered millions of books to the 30 million Americans affected by visual impairment. The primary source of book lending for the blind, prior to the settlement, was the 70,000 books available through the National Library Service for the Blind and Physically Handicapped of the Library of Congress. Out of the millions of Americans who are blind, fewer than 41,000 used the digital download service of the National Library during the period when the Google settlement

---

[1] Press Release, National Federation for the Blind, National Federation of the Blind Supports Google Settlement in Court, PRNewswire-USNewswire (February 18, 2009), www.prnewswire.com/newsreleases/national-federation-of-the-blind-supports-google-settlement-in-court-84708377.html.

[2] Jonathan Band, The long and winding road to the Google Books settlement, 9 *John Marshall Review of Intellectual Property Law* 227 (2009) at 233; Settlement Agreement, *The Authors Guild v. Google, Inc.*, No. 05 Civ. 8136 (S.D.N.Y. filed Oct 28, 2008); US Department of Justice, Statement of Interest of United States of America with Respect to Amended Settlement, *Authors Guild v. Google, Inc.*, No. 05 Civ. 8136 (S.D.N.Y. statement filed February 4, 2010) at 2–3, 21–3; US Department of Justice, Statement of Interest, Authors Guild (S.D.N.Y. statement filed Sept 18, 2009).

was being considered.[3] Fewer than 50 percent of blind Americans graduated from high school. Estimates of the unemployment rate in the blind community were greater than 70 percent.[4]

Although digitization of major library holdings and the creation of audiobooks from them would not be a cure-all, these steps might help close skills gaps for the visually impaired. Unlike printed books, websites are accessible by the visually impaired using voice-navigation, voice-dictation, and magnification software.[5] Aging populations in developed countries like the United States will increase the numbers of the visually impaired, who may suffer from dementia and depression more often.[6]

Authors' groups also defended the settlement. It would benefit authors because they would have a new outlet for selling books that are no longer carried on store shelves, and that may only exist in a few libraries at elite colleges and universities. Even authors of chapters or other portions of larger works could each earn hundreds of additional dollars. Scholarly works would receive an outsized benefit, as the lack of marketing and shelf space for these titles could be corrected by an online presence.[7] Meanwhile, authors retained the right to tell Google to remove their books from the service.[8] Readers would benefit tremendously from terminals at public and university libraries where large numbers of out-of-print

[3] *NLS implementing advances in its digital talking-book system*, 43 NLS News No. 4 (October–December 2011), http://loc.gov/nls/newsletters/news/2011/oct-dec.html.

[4] National Federation for the Blind, Letter to the United States District Court for the Southern District of New York Re: The Authors Guild ..., *Authors Guild* (S.D.N.Y. letter filed January 19, 2010) at 2–3, www.thepublicindex.org/wpcontent/uploads/sites/19/docs/amended_settlement/NFB_request_appear.pdf.

[5] *Access Now, Inc.* v. *Southwest Airlines*, Co., 227 F. Supp. 2d 1312, 1315 (SD Fla. 2002).

[6] Oriel Spierer, et al., Correlation between vision and cognitive function in the elderly: a cross-sectional study, 95 *Medicine* e2423 (2016), http://journals.lww.com/mdjournal/subjects/Ophthalmology/Fulltext/2016/01190/Correlation_Between_Vision_and_Cognitive_Function.13.aspx; Verena Cimarolli, et al., Anxiety and depression in patients with advanced macular degeneration: current perspectives, 10 *Clinical Ophthalmology (Auckland, NZ)* 55 (2016). Vision loss may cause dementia or cognitive impairment by making reading (and other mental and physical activities) more difficult.

[7] Michael Hirschorn, The hapless seed: publishers and authors should stop cowering; Google is less likely to destroy the book business than to slingshot it into the twenty-first century, *The Atlantic Monthly*, June 1, 2007, at 134.

[8] Society of Authors, Letter to the United States District Court for the Southern District of New York Re: The Google Book Settlement, *Authors Guild* (S.D.N.Y. letter filed Jan. 22, 2010), www.thepublicindex.org/wpcontent/uploads/sites/19/docs/amended_settlement/Society_of_authors.pdf; Plaintiffs' Supplemental Memorandum of Law, at 12–22, *Authors Guild* (S.D.N.Y. brief filed Feb. 11, 2010), www.thepublicindex.org/wp-content/uploads/sites/19/docs/amended_settlement/Supplemental_memorandum_of_law.pdf; Declaration of Tiffany Allen, ¶ 10, *Authors Guild* (S.D.N.Y. declaration filed Feb. 10, 2010); Competition and Commerce in Digital Books: Hearing Before the House Committee on the Judiciary, 111th Cong., 1st Sess. (Sept. 10, 2009) (statement of Paul Aiken, Authors Guild), http://judiciary.house.gov/f_files/hearings/pdf/Aiken090910o.pdf.

books could be searched, browsed, and perhaps printed out or saved to mobile devices.[9]

In 2010, a judge postponed this promising future of greater knowledge accessible to all. Microsoft, leading a rival group of data licensing corporations, wanted to block the settlement, as did the Obama administration, foreign publishers and their governments, and allied nonprofit organizations. Legal briefs deluged the judge with claims that Google would monopolize knowledge and block competition for out-of-print books.[10] Various technicalities and international foreign/law issues emerged, often treated summarily.[11]

The judge accepted the argument that the digital library would give Google too much economic power in the Internet search market. He ignored the arguments of many antitrust and copyright experts that there was little to no existing competition regarding these books, which had largely been abandoned by publishers and companies like Microsoft that focus on selling current titles at a considerable mark-up, along with many public domain books, leaving a gap for copyrighted but out-of-print volumes.[12] Several decades would pass before something akin to Google's search engine, but for most published books, could exist lawfully. The government claimed that it would table legislation to provide the public with access to these books, and their authors with new markets for them, but it did not do so.[13] In Chapter 7, I will return to this case and the theories and evidence underlying various interest groups' positions on the settlement.

1.2. CLASS STRUGGLE IN THEORY AND PRACTICE

The varying interests that vied for recognition in the Google Books settlement included, on both sides, representatives of different economic sectors and strata.

---

[9] Einer Elhauge, Why the Google Books settlement is procompetitive, Harvard Law School John M. Olin Center for Law, Economics and Business Discussion Paper Series No. 629 (2009) at 43, http://lsr.nellco.org/harvard_olin/629.

[10] Brief Amicus Curiae of the French Republic, *Authors Guild* (S.D.N.Y. brief filed Sept. 8, 2009); Memorandum of the Federal Republic of Germany in Opposition to Proposed Settlement, *Authors Guild* (S.D.N.Y. brief filed Sept. 1, 2009); Objections of Amazon.com to Proposed Settlement, *Authors Guild* (S.D.N.Y. objections filed Sept. 1, 2009); Objections of the Japanese Publisher's Association on Book Distribution (Ryutaikyo), *Authors Guild* (S.D.N.Y. objections filed June 5, 2009); Objections of Microsoft Corporation to Proposed Settlement, *Authors Guild* (S.D.N.Y. objections filed Sept. 1, 2009); Objections of Open Book Alliance to Proposed Settlement, *Authors Guild* (SDNY objections filed Sept. 4, 2009). Cf. Letter of Academic Authors in Opposition to Settlement, *Authors Guild* (S.D.N.Y. objections filed Sept. 3, 2009). All of these documents may be available at www.thepublicindex.org/filings/ag-v-google/original-settlement.

[11] Plaintiff, Supplemental Memorandum, note 8, at 80–137, 158–68.

[12] *The Authors Guild, Inc., et al. v. Google, Inc.*, 770 F. Supp. 2d 666, 683 (S.D.N.Y. 2011). See also Amicus Brief of Antitrust Law and Economics Professors, *Authors Guild* (S.D.N.Y. brief filed Sept 8, 2009).

[13] US Department of Justice, Statement of Interest, note 2, at 2–3, 18, 20–1.

This book is about the ways in which different communities within an economy articulate their interests in new creative possibilities, and in controlling new expressions of ideas.

In sociology, classes initially represented distinct economic roles, such as (1) wage laborers, (2) small business and proprietors of small farms (the petty bourgeoisie), (3) the managerial and technical experts (the intelligentsia), and (4) the owners of valuable aggregations of capital (the elite). Society, in this way, is divided into economic tiers, or strata.[14] A class difference is a process of humans experiencing and expressing their differences with other strata in society, notably those with opposing interests.[15]

The most influential extended analyses of social class may have been those of Simon Kuznets from an economic point of view, and those of E. P. Thompson from a historian's vantage point. Kuznets portrayed class distinctions as a temporary phase of capitalism that results from nascent, frustrated, and imperfect competitive environments. The French economists Thomas Piketty and Emmanuel Saez point to a cleavage in the upper class between the "working rich" and the "rentier", or the purely ownership-based class.[16] The rise of the corporation on the one hand, and the increased income share of business executives and lawyers on the other, has "blurred" the labor–capital dynamic.[17]

Thompson's work portrayed another overlap between labor and capital: the artisanal or elite laborer, often better-paid, routinely owning at least some means of production.[18] Similarly, Richard Florida grouped together seemingly disparate workers in globalized capitalism into a "creative class" of 38 million highly educated people who come up with ideas and expressions, from "designs" to texts, products, and music:

> The super-creative core of this new class includes scientists and engineers, university professors, poets and novelists, artists, entertainers, actors, designers, and architects, as well as the "thought leadership" of modern society: nonfiction writers, editors, cultural figures, think-tank researchers, analysts, and other opinion-makers ...
>
> Beyond this core group, the creative class also includes "creative professionals" who work in a wide range of knowledge-based occupations in high-tech sectors, financial services, the legal and health-care professions, and business management.

[14] Nicholas Gane, Max Weber as social theorist: "class, status, party", 8 *European Journal of Social Theory* 211 (2005) at 213, citing Stephen Edgel, *Class: Key Ideas* (Abingdon and New York: Routledge, 1993) at 13.
[15] E. P. Thompson, *The Making of the English Working Class* (New York: Vintage, 1963).
[16] Thomas Piketty and Emmanuel Saez, Income inequality in the United States, 1913–1998, 118 *Quarterly Journal of Economics* 1 (2003) at 3; Simon Mohun, Class structure and the US personal income distribution, 1918–2011, Paper Presented at the 2013 Analytical Political Economy meeting at the University of Massachusetts Amherst, updated 2015 version, at 4–5, https://thenextrecession.files.wordpress.com/2015/09/classstructure1918to2011wmf.pdf.
[17] Mohun, note 16, at 17.
[18] E. P. Thompson, *The Making of the English Working Class* (Pantheon, 1966) at 234–68.

These people engage in creative problem-solving, drawing on complex bodies of knowledge to solve specific problems.[19]

In analyzing capital and wealth formation, economists often use the division of households into three categories based on their place in the economy, called classes for shorthand rather than based on a conceptual definition. The "lower class" is the group containing the bottom 20–50 percent of households by income or wealth, the "middle class" contains the next 40–75 percent, and "upper class" the remaining 5–10 percent.[20] Within classes, moreover, there are gender and age differentiations, with women and children frequently being denied control of resources available to the household as a whole.[21] There are also racial disparities, creating "extreme case[s]" of exploitatively low wages.[22]

Marx and Engels conceived of class struggle as a relationship of domination based on differentials in power. They refer to this struggle as an "uninterrupted, now hidden, now open fight, a fight that each time ended, either in a revolutionary reconstitution of society at large, or in the common ruin of the contending classes."[23] Max Weber argued that economic power grows out of other sources of inequality, such as the power to allocate land or to conquer a territory and establish its form of government.[24] Thus, Native American and African Diaspora enslavement and dispossession contributed to disparate economic power across populations seen historically as "races."[25]

Socialist theory predicted that inequality of condition between the owners of capital and those selling their labor would grow. To this theory's pioneers, private property was a system of "class antagonism" forged so that the owners of land could exploit the landless classes.[26] The idea went back at least to the Digger movement in

[19] Richard Florida, Cities and the creative class, 2(1) *City and Community* (2003) at 8.
[20] Thomas Piketty, *Capital in the Twenty-First Century* (Harvard University Press, 2014) at 250–1. Piketty states that class is measured by "level of wealth or income."
[21] E.g. Richard America, *The Wealth of Races: The Present Value of Benefits from Past Injustices* (Greenwood Press, 1990); Harriet Fraad, Children as an exploited class, in Antonio Callari, Stephen Cullenberg, and Carole Biewener (eds.), *Marxism in the Postmodern Age: Confronting the New World Order* (Guilford Press, 1994) at 375–84; Lisa Vogel, *Marxism and the Oppression of Women: Towards a Unitary Theory* (Brill, 2013); Andre L. Smith, *Tax Law and Racial Economic Justice: Black Tax* (Lexington Books, 2015).
[22] Patricia Hill Collins, Learning from the outsider within: the sociological significance of Black Feminist thought, 33 *Social Problems* S14 (1986) at S27–S28; Guadalupe Luna, The dominion of agricultural sustainability: invisible farm laborers, 2014 *Wisconsin Law Review* 265 (2014) at 269–81.
[23] Alvin So and Suwarsono, Class theory or class analysis? A reexamination of Marx's unfinished chapter on class, 17 *Critical Sociology* 35 (1990) at 39, citing Karl Marx and Friedrich Engels, *The Communist Manifesto* (Penguin, 1967) at 79.
[24] Max Weber, *Economy and Society: An Outline of Interpretive Sociology* (University of California Press, 1978) at 926.
[25] Smith, note 21, at 69, 71–2, 82, 91, 94; Robert Wesley, Many billions gone: is it time to consider the case for Black reparations? 40 *Boston College Law Review* 429(1998).
[26] Karl Marx and Friedrich Engels, *Manifesto of the Communist Party,* Marxists.org (1848), https://www.marxists.org/archive/marx/works/1848/communist-manifesto.

England, and to Pierre-Joseph Proudhon's *What Is Property?* The Norman conquest of England turned the natives into virtual slaves, enclosing their common lands and forcing them into servitude under tyrannical laws implemented with jails, torture, and hangings.[27] The eloquent Digger, Gerrard Winstanley, theorized that:

> A ruling class began violently to appropriate what had hitherto been common property. The earth was bought and sold ... So the earth ceased to be a common treasury and became "a place wherein one torments another." Private appropriation was "the cause of all wars, bloodshed, theft and enslaving laws that hold people under misery."[28]

Two centuries later, Proudhon predicted that as economies developed, inequalities in the ownership of land dating to violent conquest and racial struggle would translate into vast wealth gaps. Proudhon explained that the first-occupation principle in land law leads to injustice, extreme poverty, and struggle on the part of the poor, who risk starvation and may resort to selling their children to other families.[29] In between Winstanley and Proudhon, the American Enlightenment writer and publicist, Thomas Paine, wrote of a capitalist regime as "government by terror," and to the poor as a "class dispossessed of their natural inheritance" by the private property system.[30]

For both sociology and Marxist economics, class cuts across societies, and carries the potential of changing history through class struggle.[31] In the early nineteenth century, most famously, the capital-trading or bourgeois class achieved the disenfranchisement of the workers and marginalization of the feudal lords and hereditary monarchs.[32] The modern state wields an "all-embracing" power, penetrating and shaping family life as well as associations formed for purposes of political, religious, or cultural speech or action.[33]

Marx wrote that his own innovations involved theorizing class struggle as being related to eras in the relations of production, and as requiring transitions from one

---

[27] Gerrard Winstanley, John Barker, and Thomas Star, *An Appeal to the House of Commons, Desiring their Answer; Whether the Common-People shall have the Quiet Enjoyment of the Commons and Waste Land* (n.p., 1649) at 6–7, 14–15; Gerrard Winstanley, *Fire in the Bush* (Giles Calvert, 1650) at 25.

[28] Christopher Hill, *Winstanley's "The Law of Freedom" and Other Writings* (Cambridge University Press, 2006) at 36 (quoting ibid., at 77–80, 99–101, 281–2, 290). My block quote is from Hill's introduction, a passage which quotes from Winstanley's works, *The True Levellers' Standard Advanced, A Declaration from the Poor Oppressed People of England,* and *The Law of Freedom in a Platform.*

[29] Pierre-Joseph Proudhon, *What Is Property? An Inquiry Into the Principle of Right and of Government* (Benjamin Ricketson Tucker trans., John Wilson & Son, 1876) at 87, 118, 133, 178–83, 192, 200–1, 309, 327–31, 336–9, 341, 344–5, 425.

[30] Thomas Paine, *Agrarian Justice, Opposed to Agrarian Law, and to Agrarian Monopoly, etc.* (R. Folwell, 1800) at 23. See also Thomas Paine, *Rights of Man, Common Sense, and Other Political Writings* (Oxford University Press, paperback reissue ed. 1998) at xix, 209 304, 410–11, 470.

[31] So and Suwarsono, note 23, at 40.

[32] So and Suwarsono, note 23, at 43, citing Marx and Engels, note 26, at 94.

[33] So and Suwarsono, note 23, at 47 (quoting Karl Marx, The Eighteenth Brumaire of Louis Bonaparte, in Karl Marx (ed.), *Surveys from Exile* (Pelican, 1973) at 143–249).

system of production to the next due to contradictions between classes that develop within each era of development.[34] Antiquated relations of production, or political economies, must be abandoned when the means of production becomes too powerful for them and requires new social patterns.[35] Marx argued that Proudhon's proposal for equality of wages, meanwhile, did not go far enough to challenge the property relation.[36]

Analytical Marxism begins with the observation that there is a conflict of interests between the owners of the means of production (capital) and those employed by them (labor).[37] A neo-Marxian analysis of law and legislation deals with struggles relating to class, in which members of a social stratum coalesce in rivalry with members of another stratum or strata. Thus, it is not reducible to the "vulgar" observation that every law is written for the benefit of the dominant class, or that every legal controversy will end in a capitalist victory whether in the court or in legislatures.[38] One or more classes may choose to reach an accommodation with other classes, even when the class that surrenders in this way sacrifices its short-term interests. A class may grow more organized and "militant," or be deradicalized or dispersed because of prior victories, collective action problems, propaganda and "double consciousness," etc.[39]

Class struggle is therefore often a struggle between those who own little or no property and those who own the product of labor as property to a degree that their ownership rights serve as a bottleneck on further labor, because labor requires capital to thrive.[40] Class struggle may also occur between laborers and those consuming the produce of their labor. In media studies, scholars construct a model of "receiving" and "transmitting" classes struggling as "consumers" and "producers,"

---

[34] Karl Marx, Social classes in America: Letter to Joseph Weydemeyer, Mar. 5, 1852, *in* Frank Mecklenburg and Manfred Stassen (eds.), *German Essays on Socialism in the Nineteenth Century* (Continuum, 1990), 65–6. See also Marx and Engels, note 26, at 3–14.

[35] Marx and Engels, note 26, at 7. See also Friedrich Engels, *The Origin of the Family, Private Property and the State* (Charles Kerr & Co., 1902) at 56–217.

[36] Marx and Engels, note 26.

[37] Philippe van Parijs, *Marxism Recycled* (Cambridge: Cambridge University Press, 1993) at 110.

[38] "Vulgar Marxism" is described as an economic reductionism that rejects the influence of non-economic factors on history, culture, or politics, or that deterministically discounts the possibility of a free or collective response to economic and historical forces that might shape their trajectories (or, as the flip side of the same process, deterministically predicts that the working-class will be radicalized by the contradiction between capitalist economic forces and relations of production into greater class consciousness, so that it would be impossible to tame its energies with beguiling rhetoric, the threat of brute force, or government largesse). Gyorgy Lukács, History and class consciousness, *in* Robert Daniels (ed.), *Documentary History of Communism* (I.B. Tauris, 1986) at 39–40; Alasdair Macintyre, *Herbert Marcuse* (Viking Press, 1970) at 45; Herbert Marcuse, The foundations of historical materialism, *in* Andrew Feenberg and William Leiss (eds.), *The Essential Marcuse: Selected Writings of Philosopher and Social Critic Herbert Marcuse* (Beacon Press, 2007) [1930] at 101.

[39] Adam Przeworski, *Capitalism and Social Democracy* (Cambridge University Press, 1985) at 28, 47, 53, 77, 99–102.

[40] Herbert Marcuse, *Reason and Revolution* (Routledge, 2013) at 381.

in a "social division of labor" that makes economies of mass communication and cultural production possible.[41]

The existence of "classes" is a theory that may help explain changes in infrastructures, machines, and legislative frameworks characteristic of a productive system. At contrasting times, class theory may indicate that government policy serves as an instrument of one class at the expense or against the wishes of another, as in Marx's analysis of labor legislation in England (1530–1871). At other times, the state may maintain its distance and freedom of action with respect to the most powerful class or classes. At still others, the state may exploit the tension among classes, and balance various classes' political forces so as not to be vulnerable to a dominant class.[42]

Twentieth-century legal and political theory has echoed Marx and Proudhon on some occasions. "Critical legal studies" (CLS) was a movement that gained prominence in the 1980s for its analysis of legal rules and cultures, and of their relationship to economic and social inequalities. For Singer, CLS is a theory that modern law works by "creating and legitimating configurations of economic and political power."[43] This book will draw on CLS as explicated by Singer and other scholars to examine key controversies in copyright law, especially as they impact digital media.

In the late 1990s, political science developed its own version of CLS. Thomas Ferguson's "investment theory of politics" argued that the two major political parties are mechanisms for wealthy elites to buy friendly politicians in order to seize and deploy government agencies for class purposes.[44] As three scholars recently explained, "In our new Gilded Age," campaign contributions, the revolving door between corporations and government agencies, stock speculation by and the rising private incomes of members of Congress, etc. suggest "the dominance of the superrich" over politics.[45] The accumulated capital of the upper class or classes constitutes a barrier to effective political participation by the poor and middle-classes, because the latter may not generate the liquid savings needed to mobilize politicians to serve them.[46] Such a theory would not have to posit that there can never

---

[41] Alexander Galloway, *Protocol: How Control Exists After Decentralization* (Massachusetts Institute of Technology Press, 2004) at 56.

[42] Paul Wetherly, *Marxism and the State: An Analytical Approach* (Springer, 2015) at 17–22. See also Karl Marx, Capital, in Robert Hutchins et al. (eds.), *Great Books of the Western World*, vol. 50: Marx (Samuel Moore et al. trans., Encyclopedia Britannica, Inc., 1964) at 364–7.

[43] Joseph William Singer, The player and the cards: Nihilism and legal theory, 94 *Yale Law Journal* 1 (1984) at 7.

[44] Thomas Ferguson, *Golden Rule: The Investment Theory of Party Competition and the Logic of Money-Driven Political Systems* (University of Chicago Press, 2nd ed. 2011) [1995].

[45] Thomas Ferguson, Paul Jorgensen, and Jie Chen, How money drives US congressional elections: more evidence. Paper Presented to Institute for New Economic Thinking Annual Conference (April 2015), at 1–2, www.ineteconomics.org/uploads/papers/How-Money-Drives-US-Congressional-Elections-More-Evidence.pdf.

[46] Ferguson, note 44, at 24–30, 36, 41–3, 52, 99, 362, 382–4; Ferguson et al. note 45, at 16. Eric Williams also pointed to the disproportionate access to Parliament enjoyed by the British planters, beneficiaries of the slave trade. Eric Williams, *Capitalism and Slavery* (University of North Carolina Press, new ed.

be political outcomes that aid labor against capital or the poor against the rich. Initiatives like the abolition of US slavery (or its transformation into convict labor and sharecropping), Reconstruction, the New Deal, and the Great Society served many investors' interests as well.[47]

The "investment theory of politics" may help us understand why 80 percent of Americans surveyed in the 1990s opined that government is "run for the benefit of the few and the special interests, not the people," why a similar proportion called the economic order "inherently unfair," and why most of them concluded that "[b]usiness has gained too much power over too many aspects of American life."[48] In 2003, the US Supreme Court concluded that large donations to political parties cause corruption.[49] By the summer of 2012, two-thirds of Americans surveyed stated that "elections are usually for sale to the candidate who can raise the most money," while an even higher share stated that most decisions by Washington politicians result from influences by "campaign contributors."[50] By 2015, three-quarters of Americans told pollsters that corruption in government was "widespread," compared with only 14 percent in Sweden.[51] In law-and-economics terms, on the other hand, these perceptions may flow from the fact that the general public confronts higher costs in organizing, compared with small interest groups.[52]

2014) [1944] at 94. Ferguson's "Golden Rule" is "to see who rules, follow the gold." Ferguson, note 44, at 391. See also James Galbraith, The importance of being sufficiently equal, *in* Ellen Frankel Paul et al. (eds.), *Should Differences in Income and Wealth Matter?*, vol. 19, pt. I (Cambridge University Press, 2002) at 218.

[47] Eric Williams argued that the slave trade and eventually slavery itself began to be seen as inefficient by some capitalists in the nineteenth century. See Williams, note 46, at xvi, 6, 49, 92, 94, 149, 154, 189. The US economy grew more rapidly after the Thirteenth Amendment, Reconstruction, and the New Deal, including in the South. Robert Friedland and Laura Summer, *Demography is not Destiny*, revisited, Commonwealth Fund No. #789 (2005), at 94, http://ccp.ucr.ac.cr/creles/pdf/georget.pdf (about 5 percent growth in real GDP per capita in United States, 1933 to 1939, and more than 12 percent growth averaged from 1939 to 1944); Angus Maddison et al., *New Maddison Project Database* (2013), www.ggdc.net/maddison/maddison-project/data.htm; Clayne Pope, Social mobility, free labor, and the American dream, *in* Stanley Engerman (ed.),*Terms of Labor: Slavery, Serfdom, and Free Labor* (Stanford University Press, 1999) at 248 (1.7 percent growth of GDP per capita in South, 1840 to 1860, and only 1.3 percent in North). The Great Society may in part have grown out of the near-recession of 1959 through 1961, and the fear that the Vietnam War and Civil Rights Movement could have resulted in revolutionaries seeking alternatives to capitalism itself. Ferguson, note 44, at 151–3, 348; Melvin Small, *Johnson, Nixon, and the Doves* (Rutgers University Press, 1988) at 103.

[48] Noam Chomsky, "Consent without consent": reflections on the theory and practice of democracy, 44 *Cleveland State Law Review* 415 (1996) at 416–17. See also Noam Chomsky, *Hopes and Prospects* (Penguin, 2010) at 32, 108, 208.

[49] *McConnell v. Federal Elections Commission*, 540 U.S. 93, 154 (2003).

[50] CNN Opinion Research Corporation, Poll: June 3–7, 2012, CNN.com (June 9, 2011) at 2, http://i2.cdn.turner.com/cnn/2011/images/06/09/rel10d-2.pdf.

[51] Gallup, 75 percent in US. See Widespread Government Corruption (September 19, 2015), www.gallup.com/poll/185759/widespread-government-corruption.aspx.

[52] Richard Posner, Economics, politics, and the reading of statutes and the constitution, 49 *University of Chicago Law Review* 263 (1982) at 265; Rachel Sachs, The new model of interest group representation in patent law, 16(3) *Yale Journal of Law and Technology* (2014), at 348–52, 388–9.

Class antagonism is fueled by the growing ranks of those who sell their labor to earn a living grow resent the outsized incomes of those who buy labor with accumulated capital. At times, the productive forces in an economy will be held back, at least in part, by relationships developed to protect and promote the interests of a class that may not represent the economy's future. There is some macroeconomic evidence to support this theory from twentieth-century Russia, China, and the Middle East regions where economic growth was much faster in socialist times than under feudalism or early capitalism.[53] More recent theories focus on how democratic processes may be hijacked to satisfy the dictates of economic elites, contrary to the public interest.[54]

1.3. CLASS STRUGGLE AND INTELLECTUAL PROPERTY

Reflecting on several decades of copyright legislation starting in 1976, L. Ray Patterson observed in 2001 that the system censored the freedom of speech.[55] The system was irrationally prioritizing corporations over employee – authors, and creating monopolies lasting three or four generations.[56] In both the copyright and trademark areas, courts and legislatures often dispensed with careful balancing of the

---

[53] During the first half of the Soviet period in Russia, economic output per person grew by an average of 4.6–6 percent, as compared with less than one percent per year from 1880 to 1885. E.g. Alex F. Dowlah and John E. Elliott, *The Life and Times of Soviet Socialism* (Greenwood Publishing Group, 1997) at 29–135; Vitali Meliantsev, *Three Centuries of Russia's Endeavors to Surpass the East and to Catch Up with the West: Trends, Factors, and Consequences,* Paper presented to Havighurst Colloquium in Russian and Post-Soviet Studies, Miami University, Oxford, Ohio (2002) at 2, 6, 11, 16–19, 23–4, 39, 42, www.cas.miamioh.edu/havighurstcenter/; Manuel de Molina Navarro and Victor Toledo, *The Social Metabolism: A Socio-Ecological Theory of Historical Change* (Springer, 2014) at 11; Adam Szirmai, *Socio-Economic Development* (Cambridge, 2nd ed. 2015) at 30. China, which had not only been stagnant, but which had lagged behind Russia in the nineteenth century, exceeded Soviet economic growth rates after the 1949 revolution, hitting growth of 7 or 8 percent per year. E.g., Chris Bramall, *Chinese Economic Development* (Routledge, 2009) at 292; US National Intelligence Estimate, NIE 13-2-59 (February 10, 1959), in Foreign Relations of the United States, 1958–1960, vol. XIX: China (US Government Printing Office, 1996) at 523; World Bank, Reshaping Economic Geography (World Bank, 2009) at 113. Iraq, Libya, and Syria experienced unprecedented growth under socialism or a mixed economy. Their output increased by more than 300 percent between 1974 and 1999. Levant: Modern Syria in Joel Mokyr (ed.), *The Oxford Encyclopedia of Economic History,* vol. 1 (Oxford University Press, 2003) at 321; Matthew Shane, Real Historical Gross Domestic Product (GDP) and Growth Rates of GDP, US Department of Agriculture (November 2, 2009), www.ers.usda.gov/data-products/internationalmacroeconomic-data-set.aspx; Bassam Yousif, *Human Development in Iraq: 1950–1990* (Routledge, 2013), at https://books.google.com/books?id=LXTe9l-f1VEC&pg=PT21.

[54] Ferguson, note 44; Fred McChesney, *Money for Nothing: Politicians, Rent Extraction, and Political Extortion* (Harvard University Press, 1997) at 41; Fred McChesney, Rent extraction and rent creation in the economic theory of regulation, 16 *Journal of Legal Studies* 101 (1987) at 101–2; David Yosifon, The public choice problem in corporate law: corporate social responsibility after Citizens United, 89 *North Carolina Law Review* 1197 (2011) at 1209.

[55] L. Ray Patterson, Copyright in the new millennium: resolving the conflict between property rights and political rights, 62 *Ohio State Law Journal* 703 (2001) at 704, 706–7, 723.

[56] Patterson, note 55, at 723.

evils of free-riding against the evils of monopolistic censorship, in favor of bromides which support the claims of IP owners.

The term "property" could be used to short-circuit thought, and provide a means of ignoring the burdens and distortions that exclusive rights create. The Enlightenment-era critique of royal prerogative and other mercantilist measures to inhibit competition and enrich elites culminated in the US Sherman Act, which was used to reduce power in IP sectors.[57] Yet distortions of the market threatened to return with the use of IP to suppress modern technologies or creative works.[58]

Since Patterson and Lemley published their research, studies of "class war" in the context of copyright have referred primarily to the struggle between the recording industry and the legions of primarily young and impecunious people downloading popular songs for free on services like Napster. Other studies focused on the struggle between incumbents and upstarts in the music industry.[59] While cases involving digital downloads have received a great deal of press, they arguably are not as important in the long term as those involving ebooks, sequels, characters, actors' rights, and due process in enforcement. Even though artists like Chuck D, Prince, and Dave Matthews who wanted to use Napster to publish music directly to their fans had that option (partially) blocked, those wanting to sample or collect music for free found other download services.[60]

The degree of corporate lobbying for greater intellectual property rights is such that some speak of a "political economy" of these rights.[61] Political economy analyzes these and other trends in the distribution of the fruits of production in light of supply and demand as influenced by systems in which states, international trade,

---

[57] E.g. Jennifer Porst, Hollywood and antitrust law, in Paul McDonald, Emily Carman, and Eric Hoyt (eds.), *Hollywood and the Law* (Palgrave Macmillan, 2015) at 103, 110–22.

[58] E.g. Joel M. Cohen and Arthur Burke, An overview of the antitrust analysis of suppression of technology, 66 *Antitrust Law Journal* 421 (1998); John Flynn, Antitrust policy, innovation efficiencies and the suppression of technology, 66 *Antitrust Law Journal* 487 (1998); David McGowan, Regulating competition in the Information Age: computer software as an essential facility under the Sherman Act, 18 *Hastings Communication and Entertainment Law Journal* 771 (1996); Hannibal Travis, Free speech institutions and fair use of copyrighted work: a new agenda for copyright reform, 33 *Cardozo Arts and Entertainment Law Journal* 673 (2016) at 696–722; Hannibal Travis, Google Book Search and fair use: iTunes for authors, or Napster for books?, 61 *University of Miami Law Review* 87 (2006) at 151–9.

[59] Niels Schaumann, Copyright class war, 11 *UCLA Entertainment Law Review* 247 (2004); see also Siva Vaidhyanathan, *Copyrights and Copywrongs: The Rise of Intellectual Property and How it Threatens Creativity* (New York University Press, 2001) at 133–4.

[60] Schaumann, note 59, at 277. See also Rebecca Giblin, Physical world assumptions and software world realities (and why there are more P2P software providers than ever before), 35 *Columbia Journal of Law & the Arts* 57 (2011) at 96–103. On artists speaking out in support of Napster's promise, see Amy Jensen, Copy protection of CDs: the recording industry's latest attempt at preventing the unauthorized digital distribution of music, 21 *John Marshall Journal of Computer & Information Law* 241 (2003) at 265; Robert Levine, *Free Ride: How Digital Parasites are Destroying the Culture Business, and How the Culture Business can Fight Back* (Anchor Books, 2011) at 39.

[61] E.g. Michael Perelman, The political economy of intellectual property, *Monthly Review*, January 2003, at 29.

money, and the division of labor operate.[62] In the case of copyright, lobbying helps perpetuate and expand the system of works made for hire, nonliteral rights, controlled performances, and similar issues that characterize the relations of production governing the "creative class."

Arguably, there were no pro-user copyright reforms after the early 1990s, despite the introduction of several reforms that made copyrights broader, more confusing and difficult to comply with, and more punitive for disfavored or "unproductive" users.[63] Although the most important reform, the Digital Millennium Copyright Act (DMCA) of 1998, is seen as pro-user or pro-infringer to the extent that it creates a safe harbor for online service providers from infringement claims (as does its European counterpart), it may in fact have benefited the IP-producing or -owning classes. The DMCA may be less favorable to users than the courts' use of analogies and policy-based reasoning would have been in immunizing conduits, intermediaries, and Internet service providers (ISPs) who transmit, store, or index infringing works.[64] Absolving ISPs of liability for user conduct would liberate ISPs to permit users to say and publish whatever they might like. Case law prior to the DMCA suggested that an ISP is not liable for its users' conduct if it maintains a system providing Internet access to any user, or if it restricts access in certain ways but without monitoring what users do, while charging a fee to users that does not vary with how much a user's material is accessed or visited.[65]

As a balanced, limited codification of portions of this early case law, the DMCA was not an unequivocal victory for users, and may have benefited rightsholders to the extent that the safe harbor deflected courts' efforts to protect Internet freedom.[66] The DMCA does not provide much more of a defense to ISPs who do not purposefully

[62] E.g. Karl Marx, *A Contribution to the Critique of Political Economy* (N.I. Stone trans., Charles H. Kerr & Co., 1904) at 284–94, 297–8, 302–3.

[63] Center for Democracy and Technology, Comments in Response to the Department of Commerce Internet Policy Task Force's Inquiry on Copyright, Creativity, and Innovation in the Internet Economy (November 19, 2010) at 2, 11–13, www.cdt.org/files/pdfs/CDT%20Comments%20to%20NTIA%20 Copyright%20Task%20Force.pdf; Greg Lastowka, Innovative copyright, 109 *Michigan Law Review* 1011 (2011) at 1025–6; Jessica Litman, *Digital Copyright* (Prometheus Books, paperback ed. 2006) at 80; Rochelle Cooper Dreyfuss, TRIPS-round II: should users strike back?, 71 *University of Chicago Law Review* 21 (2004).

[64] Electronic Commerce Directive of the European Communities, articles 12–15, 2000/31/EC, passed 8 June 2000; Lilian Edwards, *Role and Responsibility of Internet Intermediaries in the Field of Copyright and Related Rights*, World Intellectual Property Organization (2011), www.wipo.int/export/ sites/www/copyright/en/doc/role_and_responsibility_of_the_internet_intermediaries_final.pdf.

[65] *Religious Technology Center* v. *Netcom On-Line Communication Services., Inc.*, 907 F. Supp. 1361, 1375–7 (N.D. Cal. 1995); *Marobie-FL, Inc.* v. *National Association of Fire Equip. Distributors*, 983 F. Supp. 1179 (N.D. Ill. 1997); Nathan Lovejoy, Standards for determining when ISPs have fallen out of section 512(a), 27 *Harvard Journal of Law and Technology* 256 (2013) at 264.

[66] E.g. *Rosen* v. *Global Net Access, LLC*, No. CV 10-2721-DMG, slip op. at ¶ 5 (C.D. Cal. June 20, 2014). As the most important opinion in the field stated this concern, "it does not make sense to ... would hold the entire Internet liable for activities that cannot reasonably be deterred ... [and that are] practically impossible to screen out [as containing] infringing bits." *Netcom*, 907 F. Supp. at 1371–3.

infringe, but who benefit from or facilitate others' infringements than the early case law did. Its safe harbor is limited to ISPs that expeditiously remove infringing material that they store on behalf of users upon receiving notice of infringement, and imposes hurdles even to that defense.[67] Courts routinely find ISPs liable, but there were only a few such decisions prior to the DMCA, despite many years of infringement enabled by ISPs.[68]

For my purposes, copyright class struggle is the fight to define the relations of creative production insofar as they shape the distribution of the fruits of creativity, including ideas. The struggle may be more likely to arise or intensify when the productive forces outstrip the prevailing laws and norms for production or distribution.[69]

As the terms capitalism and socialism imply, there is a dialectic between private ownership of wealth as a means of maximizing productive investment and use, and social or public control to maximize surveillance and political regulation, including

[67] Compare, e.g. 17 U.S.C. § 512(b)–(d), with *Netcom*, 907 F. Supp. at 1373–6; see also 17 U.S.C. § 512(i)–(k); *Viacom International, Inc.* v. *YouTube, Inc.*, 676 F.3d 19, 31 (2d Cir. 2012); Eric Raymond (ed.), *The New Hacker's Dictionary* (Massachusetts Institute of Technology Press, 1996) at 478–9. One area in which the DMCA may be more helpful to potential infringers than the common law might have been is in the area of the liability of so-called "conduits," providers of transmission lines and wires who do not control or select the content that they transmit, like the telephone companies (and, by analogy, like toll roads with respect to illegal cargo in cars and trucks). While *Netcom* stated that such services might be liable for infringement as intermediaries unless they qualified for the exemption in the Copyright Act for passive carriers of secondary transmissions, which the ISP in *Netcom* did not, the DMCA exempts them if they satisfy § 512(i)–(k) even if they do not expeditiously remove infringing material. Compare *Netcom*, 907 F. Supp. at 1369 & n.12, with 17 U.S.C. § 512(a). See also *In re Charter Communications., Inc.* v. *Subpoena Enforcement Matter*, 393 F.3d 771, 776–7 (8th Cir. 2005); *Recording Industry Association of America, Inc.* v. *Verizon Internet Services, Inc.*, 351 F.3d 1229, 1237–8 (D.C. Cir. 2003).

[68] Compare, e.g. *EMI Christian Music Group, Inc.* v. *MP3Tunes, LLC*, 840 F.3d 69 (2d Cir. 2016); *Viacom*, 676 F.3d at 41; *Columbia Pictures Industries, Inc.* v. *Fung*, 710 F.3d 1020, 1043–4 (9th Cir. 2013); *BMG Rights Management (US) LLC* v. *Cox Communications, Inc.*, Civil Action No. 1:14-cv-1611 (E.D. Va. February 14, 2017), https://scholar.google.com/scholar_case?case=15797577648169022214; *MGM Studios, Inc.* v. *Grokster, Ltd.*, 454 F. Supp. 2d 966, 985 (C.D. Cal. 2006), with Lawrence Kenswil, Executive Vice President of Business and Legal Affairs, Universal Music Group, Testimony before the House Committee on the Judiciary, Subcommittee on Courts and Intellectual Property (September 16, 1997), https://web.archive.org/web/20021018012914/; www.house.gov:80/judiciary/4003.htm ("To date, we count only a dozen or so decisions dealing with copyright liability on the Internet – and only a couple of them have involved [Internet access providers]. And the one decision dealing directly with the issue of IAP liability came out on the side of the IAP."), Marjorie Heins and Tricia Beckles, *Will Fair Use Survive? Free Expression in the Age of Copyright Control* (Brennan Center for Justice, 2005) at 5 ("Section 512 is misguided because ISPs should not be liable for copyright infringement in the first place ...," being "akin to telephone companies or highways" without committing users' "wrongs" themselves).

[69] For Marx, relations of production are the legal, social, and political forms and norms that correspond to a mode of production, as feudal estates, the family, Catholicism, and monarchy may have corresponded to the agricultural-feudal mode of production. Karl Marx, *Capital: A Critique of Political Economy, vol. 1* (Ben Fowkes trans. Vintage Books ed., 1977) at 175–6; Ira Katznelson, *Marxism and the City* (Oxford University Press, 1992) at 28.

regulation that might increase production more rapidly.[70] Capitalism, as the engine of wealth, inspires and calls up socialism, which promises to accelerate the economic engine. The struggle between these possibilities transforms the people itself.[71]

Copyright, as the engine of creative expression, provokes a move towards copyright socialism or communism, the declaration of a common property or redistribution scheme in valuable ideas, characters, plots, melodies, beats, pictures, videos, and the like. Switching metaphors, capitalism in general, and creative copyright-based capitalism in particular, triggers an immune response in the body politic, because people fear that they are being exploited for capital's benefit. In struggles over copyright, the fear is that creativity is being sacrificed to licensing and corporate control.

Unlike conventional narratives of copyright class war, I do not limit my attention to digital downloading or other turn of the twenty-first-century events. In contrast to some writers, I also explore ways in which *weaker* copyright or patent protections from the standpoint of the individual author or inventor experiencing infringement by large corporations could devastate middle-class bargaining power, exacerbating income inequality. Moreover, my account surveys international law as well, and touches on coalitions across national borders that may wage similar struggles.

1.4. CLASS STRUGGLE IN THE SOCIAL MEDIA ERA

The stakes are high in the struggle to redefine copyright in the social media era. A company's future can be secured or lost based on what would seem like obscure doctrines to many Americans. Entrepreneurs are making fortunes by cloning the works of others on social media or online video sites, while avoiding just enough expression to stay on the right side of the law. Meanwhile, changes in copyright laws threaten to deny many persons their dreams of building on similar ideas, even when those dreams involve almost entirely new words, film, sounds, or computer code.

The year 2007 represented a bit of an inflection point as products like the iPhone and services like Facebook became more accessible. These and other platforms for publishing and selling literary works, videos, songs, and applications unleashed enormous amounts of creativity, innovation, and connectivity powered by the Internet. The social media era is also linked to political struggle when new technologies help to "blow up weak countries" and stress the institutions of more powerful ones.[72] The

---

[70] Micharl Hardt and Antonio Negri, *Multitude: War and Democracy in the Age of Empire* (Penguin, 2004) at 203.
[71] Hardt, note 70, at 101.
[72] Thomas Friedman, *Thank You for Being Late: An Optimist's Guide to Thriving in the Age of Accelerations* (Farrar, Straus, and Giroux, 2016); Seth Rowe, Thomas Friedman reveals themes of upcoming book at St. Louis Park High School, *Minneapolis Sun*, May 24, 2016, https://www.hometownsource.com/sun_sailor/; ParkTV St. Louis Park, Thomas Friedman, writing for *The New York Times; Always looking for Minnesota*, YouTube (2016), www.youtube.com/watch?v=gv9gGgLODOsl. See also Nathaniel Persily, Can democracy survive the Internet?, 28 *Journal of Democracy* 63 (2017).

"end of the beginning" of the social media era may be near as Facebook and Twitter engagement have begun declining, perhaps to be replaced by more private applications like Snapchat, Telegram, and WhatsApp, which promise some of the benefits of the early years of social media in which user commoditization, clunky advertising, public shaming and scapegoating, and mass surveillance were less prominent.[73] The shape of the era is being contested as governments, including the US government, attempt to control sites like Facebook, and as publics seek alternatives like Telegram, Tor, and the Dark Web to evade states' gaze and reach.[74] The transition of Internet governance from a model dominated by the US Department of Commerce to a more global model potentially housed within the United Nations would be the structure undergirding this trend.[75]

The initial chapters of this book will argue that there are conceptual indeterminacies within the statutory frameworks for copyrights and patents in the United States. This is as predicted by CLS.[76] The indeterminacy surfaces at major decision points such as vesting copyrights as an initial matter, defining their duration and ownership

---

[73] Libby Plummer, How private is YOUR messaging app? Charity rates WhatsApp as the most secure – but experts aren't so sure, *Mail Online*, October 21, 2016, www.dailymail.co.uk/sciencetech/article-3859412/How-private-messaging-app-Charity-rates-WhatsApp-secure-experts-aren-t-sure.html.

[74] E.g. Matthew Cooper, Can Congress keep Russia off Facebook? Bill aims to force disclosure for political ads, *Newsweek* (October 19, 2017), www.newsweek.com/can-congress-keep-russia-facebook-bill-aims-force-disclosure-political-ads-688930; Jason Pontin, Transparency and secrets, *MIT Technology Review*, February 22, 2011, www.technologyreview.com/s/422854/transparency-and-secrets/; Maria Shirts, Brazilians will always remember the Great WhatsApp Blackout of 2016, *MIT Technology Review*, May 4, 2016, www.technologyreview.com/s/601393/brazilians-will-always-remember-the-great-whatsapp-blackout-of-2016/; Tom Simcrite, How cops could wiretap encrypted iMessage and WhatsApp chats, *MIT Technology Review*, 2016, www.technologyreview.com/s/601039/how-cops-could-wiretap-encrypted-imessage-and-whatsapp-chats/; David Talbot, Dissent made safer, *MIT Technology Review*, April 21, 2009, www.technologyreview.com/s/413091/dissent-made-safer/.

[75] *Cf.* A job for Rubio-Cruz: save the web, *The Wall Street Journal*, May 22, 2016.

[76] CLS theorizes two phenomena relevant to this book: the indeterminacy of statutory and judge-made law and the influence of social class on the application of vague or ambiguous concepts in concrete cases, and law as superstructure to its material basis in economic modes and modalities of production. E.g. Raymond Belliotti, Marxist Jurisprudence: historical necessity and radical contingency, 4 *Canadian Review of Law and Jurisprudence* 145 (1991); James Boyle, The politics of reason: critical legal theory and local social thought, 133 *University of Pennsylvania Law Review* 685 (1985); Morton J. Horwitz, *The Transformation of American Law, 1870–1960: The Crisis of Legal Orthodoxy* (Oxford University Press, 1992) at 102–17, 160–210; Alan Hunt, The theory of critical legal studies, 6 *Oxford Journal of Legal* 1 (1986); Lawrence Lessig, Plastics: Unger and Ackerman on transformation, 98 *Yale Law Journal* 1173 (1989); Akbar Rasulov, The nameless rapture of the struggle: towards a Marxist class-theoretic approach to international law, in J. Klabbers (ed.), *Finnish Yearbook of International Law* (Hart, 2010) at 243–94; Roberto Mangabeira Unger, The critical legal studies movement, *Harvard Law Review* 561 (1983) at 570–2, 592–9, 663–9. More recently, Hardt and Negri argue that postmodern globalized sovereignty evades the will of publics by subdividing and dispersing its operations in order to manage resistance efficiently. See also Michael Hardt and Antonio Negri, *Empire* (Harvard University Press, 2000) at 138, 160–203, 325–50, 393–413. Apparent legal clarity dissolves at a global scale.

decades after authorship, and determining their scope. It surfaces again when deciding which patents are valid, and which are "abstract" or "obvious."

A series of books published over the past two decades proposed several reforms to bring copyright law up-to-date and into line with society's needs for education, scholarly research, and freedom of expression in the digital age.[77] Many of them appeared in the period between the negotiation of the WIPO Copyright Treaty in 1994–6 and the decision in the *Viacom v. YouTube* case in 2012. For that reason, few of these books could trace the extended trajectories of the struggle over the ownership of superhero copyrights (especially in 2004–14), US patent reform and its implications for social media firms (2007–17), the scope of copyright from the standpoint of characters or thematic ideas (2008–17), the motion picture industry's campaign to seek the pretrial forfeiture of domain names and websites (2010–17), a treaty concluded in Beijing about reforming copyright law to prohibit imitating or changing unwritten performances (2013–17), and the evolution and outcome of the Google Books cases (2005–14).

This book uses class struggle as a lens through which to view the politics of Internet and media governance in the early twenty-first century. The notion of economic class suggests that there are differences in how public policy will respond to activism and demands for reform. Thus, Congress and the courts may ignore blind individuals or their representatives, who appeal for greater access to ebooks for the visually impaired. On the other hand, judges and policymakers may rapidly come to the aid of owners of vast aggregations of cultural and technological wealth, including copyright catalogs and social network infrastructure. Courts and lawmakers will often ignore persons who are charged with infringing on copyright but who appeal for judicial rulings, due process and trials by constitutional procedures, as they might ignore the independent inventor demanding a jury trial in a fight against a corporate goliath that is infringing the inventor's patent. By contrast, the leading firms of the entertainment and technology industries sometimes obtain rapid judicial resolution in their favor of relatively strong legal claims against them. The resulting system of inquisitorial justice for some, adversarial decisions for others, is consistent with what critical theories of law and social structures would predict.

---

[77] James Boyle, *The Public Domain: Enclosing the Commons of the Mind* (Yale University Press, 2008); Manuel Castells and Gustavo Cardoso (eds.), *Piracy Cultures* (Xlibris, 2013); Gaëlle Krikorian and Amy Kapczynski, *Access to Knowledge in the Age of Intellectual Property* (Zone Books, 2010); Lawrence Lessig, *Free Culture: How Big Media Uses Technology and the Law to Lock Down Culture and Control Creativity* (now interactive ed., 2017) [2004] at ch. 1, http://download.nowis.com/index .cfm?phile=FreeCulture.html&tipe=text/html; Lawrence Lessig, *Remix: Making Art and Culture Thrive in the Digital Economy* (Penguin, 2008); Litman, note 63; Neil Weinstock Netanel, *Copyright's Paradox* (Oxford University Press, 2008); John Tehranian, *Infringement Nation: Copyright 2.0 and You* (Oxford University Press, 2011); Siva Vaidhyanathan, *The Anarchist in the Library* (Basic Books, 2005); Vaidhyanathan, note 59.

The story of the struggle to own ideas in the social media era goes through three stages. In Part I, I explore trends towards the unequal treatment of idea owners that accelerated in the 2009–11 period. This part deals with "IP Disparities," and includes the foregoing discussion of copyright and class, the for-hire concept in copyright (Chapter 2), and the crisis of the small inventor due to a series of Supreme Court decisions and new Acts of Congress including the America Invents Act (Chapter 3).

In Part II, entitled "IP Liberties," the scope of copyright is the focus. The law generates or reflects a dialectic in which (1) those creating content without access to capital, who apply their labor to what has come before, argue for narrower rights; (2) those who have transitioned to owners of capital in the form of IP assets seek and enjoy broader rights, while strategically exploiting and denying the rights of the creators they imitate; and (3) an accommodation is reached between these ideal types, a peace which is threatened with unraveling due to licensing and royalty disputes, among others. At stake is literary freedom. What creative liberties may a writer or filmmaker take? Those most at risk of having their labor discounted and their products disqualified in the marketplace, it seems, are authors whose literary freedom is not backed by accumulated capital.

The law's solicitude for profit may have overridden its care for authorial rights in some cases. While there are certainly limits to US law's de facto exemption for profitable works from claims of content theft, the courts seem highly deferential to how copyright conglomerates such as Disney, Viacom, or Time Warner explain and justify the origin of their creative ideas and expressions. In theory, the law guarantees a right for anyone to protect, license out, and grow rich from ideas, images, and genre archetypes. Digital technology and legal gymnastics severely curtail this right in practice.

In Part III, the book's analysis turns to "Pirates' Dilemmas," and to debates arising out of cases of relatively clear copying of protected expression, especially high-quality digital copies. While the imminent death of high-technology innovation serves to justify eviscerating patent rights, the impending death of music and film paradoxically serves to justify *supercharging* copyrights while abandoning constitutional limitations on corporate copyright enforcement. The case for automatic copyright enforcement, my analysis suggests, is based on economic and legal myths that cast the ordinary Internet user as a destructive "pirate." Upstart creators and ambitious authors seem to benefit from a broader scope of copyright, and from guarantees that their rights will be respected in the digital environment. The dilemma is that individual creators are often frustrated when they invoke the generous rights that are advertised. Problems persist in remedying content theft by copyright conglomerates, ensuring impartial treatment of distinct types of creators, and guaranteeing due process to the poor or middle-class author.

1.5. ON POSSIBILITIES OF CREATION

Some brief notes of thanks are warranted. The FIU College of Law supported this research, by awarding me generous summer research funding. My colleagues there have provided feedback on my research over the years. The assistance of Matt Gallaway of Cambridge University Press was important to getting the book published. Jessica Ciminero provided helpful research assistance on social norms in IP and Internet law. Ashley Allison, Christian Sanchelima, Lancena Bizune, and Roger Notario aided the research process involving copyright infringement and fair use for Chapter 4 in particular.

PART I

IP Disparities

2

Authors As Hired Hands

2.1. INTRODUCTION

Assigning copyright rights should be easy. The person who actually puts pen to paper, or finger to keyboard, should be the author. Surprisingly, there is a "glaring exception" to this simple rule, designed for persons working "for hire." Their works, if prepared within the scope of employment, are owned by their employer(s).[1]

The struggle of Stan Lee and Jack Kirby's widow for control of dozens of beloved Marvel characters may have been the most important copyright dispute in years.[2] Kirby's artwork for *Iron Man, The Incredible Hulk, The Avengers*, and *The X-Men* changed the course of comic-book and world-cinema history.[3] Kirby and Lee worked together to forge the Silver Age of comics, featuring more complex heroes, interstellar adventures, and an occasionally critical view of postwar American history.[4]

---

[1] Ryan Vacca, Work made for hire – Analyzing the multifactor balancing text, 42 *Florida State University Law Review* 197 (2014) at 198 (quoting *Community for Creative Non-Violence v. Reid*, 490 U.S. 730, 737 (1989)).

[2] In 2009, the heirs of Jack Kirby served Marvel with forty-five notices purporting to terminate Kirby's assignment of his copyrights in comic books published between 1958 and 1963 (and the character images and stories they contained). *Marvel Worldwide, Inc. v. Kirby*, 777 F. Supp. 2d 720 (SDNY 2011), *aff'd sub nom. Marvel Characters, Inc. v. Kirby*, 726 F.3d 119 (2d Cir. 2012), *cert. dismissed*, 135 S. Ct. 42 (2014); Brent Staples, *Marvel superheroes and the fathers of invention*, The New York Times, June 26, 2011, at SR11. The characters included the Avengers, the Hulk, Iron Man, the Mighty Thor, the X-Men, Spider-Man, Dr. Strange, and The Fantastic Four. In addition to books named after these characters, it was said that Kirby co-authored comic book issues entitled *Amazing Adventures, Amazing Fantasy, Journey into Mystery, Strange Tales, Tales of Suspense*, and *Tales to Astonish*.

[3] Scott Rosen, Gods and fantastic mortals: The superheroes of Jack Kirby, *in* B. J. Oropeza (Ed.), *The Gospel According to Superheroes: Religion and Pop Culture* (Peter Lang, 2005) at 113.

[4] Rosen, note 3, at 114–15; *Marvel Worldwide*, 777 F. Supp. 2d 720, *aff'd sub nom. Marvel Characters*, 726 F.3d 119; Petition for Certiorari at 10–11, 28–37; *Kirby v. Marvel Characters, Inc.*, No. 11–33-v (April 2014), www-deadline-com.vimg.net/wp-content/uploads/2014/04/KIRBY-HEIRS-SCOTUS-PETITION-MARVEL-DISNEY-WM__140403023608.pdf; see also Scott Bukatman, X-Bodies:

They sought additional remuneration for their creative work, which had generated millions of dollars in new value.[5]

The work-made-for-hire doctrine divests thousands or millions of copyrights that vested between 1909 and 1966 from the actual authors thereof.[6] Jack Kirby, for example, repeatedly "assign[ed]" rights vested in him under the Copyright Act of 1909 to Marvel, only to learn in 2012 that he never enjoyed authorial rights while he was working at Marvel's direction and expense.[7] Since 1978, the work-made-for-hire doctrine has treated post-1977 works as being authored by someone other than the "writer," for example when the writer is an employee, or when he or she contributes to a commissioned work and the parties agree in writing on its for-hire status.[8] As for works created prior to 1978, courts have extended the work-made-for-hire doctrine so far that authors of works produced prior to that date have been divested of what they

The torment of the mutant superhero, *in* Rodney Sappington and Tyler Stallings (Eds.), *Uncontrollable Bodies: Testimonies of Identities and Culture* (Bay Press, 1994) at 92–129; Tim Perry, Mutants that are all too human: The X-Men, Magneto, and original sin, *in* Rodney Sappington and Tyler Stallings (Eds.), *Uncontrollable Bodies: Testimonies of Identities and Culture* (Bay Press, 1994) at 172, 177–80. Contrasted with the Golden Age of comic books from 1938 to 1954 or so, the Silver Age may have spanned from the appearance of *Green Lantern* in 1959 to Jack Kirby leaving Marvel Comics in 1970. Craig Shutt, *Baby Boomer Comics: The Wild, Wacky, Wonderful Comic Books of the 1960s* (Krause Publications, 2d ed. 2011) at 9, 15–16, 22, 103–9, 202.

5   Staples, note 2, at SR11.
6   Petition for Certiorari, at 3–4, 28–37, *Kirby*, No. 11–33-v; *Brattleboro Publishing Co. v. Winmill Publishing Corp.*, 369 F.2d 565, 567–68 (2d Cir. 1966) (holding, as matter of first impression in Second Circuit, that "employer" concept in Copyright Act of 1909, Act of March 4, 1909, ch. 320, section 26, 35 Stat. 1075 (1909), could include commissioning party at whose "instance and expense" work is produced); *Lin–Brook Builders Hardware v. Gertler*, 352 F.2d 298, 300 (9th Cir. 1965) (holding, as matter of first impression, that term "employer" could include *commissioning* party in cases involving independent contractor authors); see also *Martha Graham School and Dance Foundation, Inc. v. Martha Graham Center of Contemporary Dance*, 380 F.3d 624, 641–2 (2d Cir. 2004) (reiterating broad interpretation of "work for hire" standard from *Brattleboro*, and applying it to work in relation to which employer did not supervise employee, who had "creative freedom" to make works); *Easter Seal Society v. Playboy Enterprises*, 815 F.2d 323 (5th Cir. 1987) (similar), citing *Murray v. Gelderman*, 566 F.2d 1307 (5th Cir. 1978); *Picture Music, Inc. v. Bourne, Inc.*, 457 F.2d 1213, 1217 (2d Cir. 1972) (reiterating that right to control production of work by independent contractor may make commissioning party an "employer"). The abrogation of a heretofore valid copyright for public purposes arguably constitutes a taking of "property" for Fifth Amendment purposes. Jay Dratler and Stephen McJohn, *Intellectual Property Law: Commercial, Creative, and Industrial Property* (Law Journal Press, 2006) at 5–60.8; Daniel Saunders, Copyright law's broken "Rear Window": Assessment of damage and estimate of repair, in Hon. Stanley Birch et al. (Eds.), *Copyright Law Symposium*, vol. 41 (Columbia University Press, 1997) at 35–41; Dorothy Schrader, Copyright restoration for public domain works, in John V. Martin (Ed.), *Copyright: Current Issues and Laws* (Nova Publishers, 2002) at 37. *Cf.* 17 U.S.C. § 201(e); H.R. Rep. No. 94-1476, http://uscode.house.gov/view.xhtml?req=granuleid:USC-prelim-title17-section203&num=0&edition=prelim.
7   Petition for Certiorari, at 26–7, 29–30, 32, *Kirby*, No. 11-cc-v.
8   17 U.S.C. § 101 (2012) (defining a "work made for hire" as a work prepared by an employee within the scope of employment, or as "a work specially ordered or commissioned ... if the parties expressly agree in a written instrument signed by them that the work shall be considered a work made for hire").

reasonably regarded as their property rights.[9] The contemporary work-made-for-hire doctrine has retroactively classified numerous works created by independent contractors between 1909 and 1966 as being vested in employers, whereas the doctrine did not apply to independent contractors in cases decided in the 1940s and 1950s.[10]

The labor unions for America's creative workers stepped into this debate by filing their arguments with the US Supreme Court. They stated that commissioned works were traditionally owned by the actual producer, that works-made-for-hire require an "employment relationship," and that freelance artists like Kirby would have had no reason to reserve their rights by contract because there was no case law equating parties with employers:

> By retroactively deeming commissioned works as ones "made for hire," the Second Circuit has given the purchaser all of the copyright benefits of the employment relationship, without any of the associated burdens or obligations. The "expense" prong of the test assumes that the acquiring party has borne the risk in a work's ultimate success by paying value to acquire it and then to market and distribute it, thereby completely disregarding the risk borne by the freelance creator attendant a work's creation in a relationship such as the one between Jack Kirby and Marvel.
>
> Many creators, like Kirby, bear all the initial risk in their works – they invest time, resources and effort in creating a work requested or preferred by the purchaser, with no guarantee that the work will be accepted or that they will be paid … . Until it has accepted and paid for the work, the purchaser bears no risk – it pays the creator nothing, it has no costs for the supplies or materials used in the work's creation, and it shoulders none of the employee benefits or taxes associated with an employment relationship. To give purchasers the benefit of the employment relationship, without the concomitant burdens and expenses, results in an unjustified boon to the purchaser at the creator's expense.[11]

The PEN Center USA, a group representing famous authors of novels, plays, film scripts, and poems, chimed in with a similar argument: "With little or no financial

---

[9] *Cf. Marvel Characters*, 726 F.3d 119 (collecting cases). Calling copyright "property" does not necessarily require its duration to be perpetual, its scope to be infinite, or its misappropriation to be a theft or crime. The Copyright Act of 1976 and its legislative history refer to copyright protection as a "property right" while strictly limiting its duration and scope in various ways, E.g. 17 U.S.C. § 201(d); H.R. Rep. No. 94-1476, http://uscode.house.gov/view.xhtml?req=granuleid:USC-prelim-title17-section304&num=0&edition=prelim; *White-Smith Music Publishing Co. v. Apollo Co.*, 209 U.S. 1 (1908).

[10] The Petition for Certiorari From note 4 at 3–4, 17–19, 21, 31; *Tobani v. Carl Fischer, Inc.*, 98 F.2d 57, 59 (2d Cir. 1938); *Shapiro, Bernstein, & Co., Inc. v. Bryan*, 123 F.2d 697, 698–700 (2d Cir. 1941); *Shapiro, Bernstein, & Co. v. Jerry Vogel Music Co.*, 221 F.2d 569, 570 (1955).

[11] Brief of Screen Actors Guild-American Federation of Television and Radio Artists, Directors Guild of America, Inc., and Writers Guild of America, West, Inc. as Amici Curiae in Support of Petitioners, at 10, 18–21, *Kirby*, No. 13-1178 (U.S. brief filed June 13, 2014), https://cfmedia.deadline.com/2014/07/kirby-marvel-sag-aftra-amicus-brief.pdf; see also *500 greatest songs of all time*, Rolling Stone, April 7, 2011, www.rollingstone.com/music/lists/the-500-greatest-songs-of-all-time-20110407.

security, the prolific Kirby created a wealth of material featuring novel storylines and characters, while Marvel alone has reaped the benefits of Jack Kirby's most valuable creations."[12] In addition to plays, scripts, and the like, the "instance and expense" doctrine may affect songs and albums, because the vast majority of the most popular songs of all time were released before 1978.[13]

The changes are so dramatic as to present a possible Takings Clause problem.[14] If courts viewed the loss of at least some authors' rights pursuant to the work-made-for-hire doctrine as retroactive, then additional compensation could be due to many authors for taking their "property."[15] On the other hand, the Supreme Court and other courts have held that the government does not owe just compensation for altering or abrogating IP rights.[16] Likewise, it has been said that no one "[n]o person has a vested interest in any rule of law, entitling him to insist that it shall remain unchanged for his benefit."[17]

Longer copyright terms heighten the impact of broader corporate copyrights. Prior to the Copyright Act of 1976, some courts had concluded that once the initial copyright term of twenty-eight years has expired, the copyright returned to the author or his or her family "clear of all rights, interests or licenses granted" thus far.[18] Congress declared that: "If the work proves to be a great success and lives beyond the term of twenty-eight years … it should be the exclusive right of the author to take the renewal term, and … the author could not be deprived of that right."[19]

In the 20th century, if a court had found that Kirby was the co-author of the character Spider-man, then Kirby and his family may have enjoyed the renewal term copyright in the character, spanning from 1990 or 1991 until 2018 or 2019. Kirby

---

[12] Brief of Amici Curiae Mark Evanier, John Morrow, and Pen Center USA in Support of Petitioners, at 22, *Kirby*, No. 13-1178, quoted in Eriq Gardner, Comic book legend Jack Kirby's lawsuit could have big implications for music, *Billboard*, June 19, 2014, www.billboard.com/biz/articles/news/legal-and-management/6128502/jack-kirby-lawsuit-marvel-x-men-termination.

[13] Brief of Screen Actors Guild et al., note 11, at 19–20.

[14] The abrogation of a heretofore valid copyright for public purposes arguably constitutes a taking of "property" for Fifth Amendment purposes. Dratler and McJohn, note 6, at 5–60.8; Saunders, note 6, at 35–41; Schrader, note 6, at 37. *Cf.* 17 U.S.C. § 201(e); H.R. Rep. No. 94-1476, http://uscode.house.gov/view.xhtml?req=granuleid:USC-prelim-title17-section203&num=0&edition=prelim.

[15] *Cf. Zoltek Corp.* v. *United States*, 442 F.3d 1345, 1350 (Fed. Cir. 2006) *reh'g en banc denied*, 464 F.3d 1335, 1370–4 (Fed. Cir. 2006) (Plager, J., dissenting from the denial of reh'g en banc) (arguing that patents are constitutional property under the Patent Act of 1952 because that law provided a right to exclude in 35 U.S.C. § 154(a)(1)), *vacated in part*, 672 F.3d 1309 (Fed. Cir. 2012); Ibid., at 1335–7 (Newman, J., dissenting from the denial of reh'g en banc) (arguing that patents are constitutional property under *Ruckelshaus* v. *Monsanto Co.*, 467 U.S. 986, 1002–3 (1984)).

[16] *Schillinger* v. *United States*, 155 U.S. 163 (1894); *Zoltek*, 464 F.3d 1335.

[17] *New York Central R.R.* v. *White*, 243 U.S. 188, 198 (1917). See also *Stop the Beach Renourishment, Inc.* v. *Florida Department of Environmental Protection*, 560 U.S. 702, 7285 (2010) (plurality opinion).

[18] *G. Ricordi & Co.* v. *Paramount Pictures, Inc.*, 189 F.2d 469, 471 (2d Cir.), cert. denied, 342 U.S. 849 (1951); Benjamin Kaplan, *An Unhurried View of Copyright* (1967) at 112. See also 17 U.S.C. § 24 (1975 ed.).

[19] H.R. Rep. No. 2222, 60th Cong., 2nd Sess. (Government Printing Office, 1909) at 14.

may have prepared the original drawings for Spider-man, working together with Joe Simon and Stan Lee, later collaborating with Steve Ditko under Lee's leadership.[20] The renewal term of the copyright now stands at sixty-seven years, so that unless Kirby was the author of the drawings, Marvel need not share the windfall profits associated with exclusive exploitation of the character in the additional nineteen years tacked on to the copyright in 1978, and the additional twenty years tacked on in 1998. The copyright will last well into the 2000s, indeed into the 2050s.[21] The same goes for *the X-Men, Iron Man,* and *The Incredible Hulk,* released in 1962–3.[22] While Kirby might have assigned the renewal term in his copyright interests starting in 1973 by signing checks with a legend containing assignment language, it is not clear that such an assignment would have been valid as to characters created in the 1960s or earlier.[23]

This chapter contends that there is no constitutional basis to subject authors to a broad and automatic transfer of rights to commissioning parties (prior to 1978) or to payroll employers (both before and after 1978).[24] While Congress has the power to

---

[20] Christ Gavalier, *Superhero Comics* (Bloomsbury, 2017) at 277; Rob Steibel, The never-ending "who created Spider-man" debate, Jack Kirby Museum Kirby Dynamics Blog (November 22, 2011), http://kirbymuseum.org/blogs/dynamics/2011/11/22/the-never-ending-who-created-spider-man-debate/. See also *Shapiro, Bernstein, & Co.* v. *Jerry Vogel Music Co.* 221 F.2d 569, revised 223 F.2d 252 (2d Cir. 1955); M. William Krasilovsky, *This Business of Music* (Billboard Books, 1995) at 249–50.

[21] 17 U.S.C 304, note (1999 ed.) ("Renewal registration will be required during the 28th year of the copyright but the length of the renewal term will be increased from 28 to 47 years."); The Sonny Bono Copyright Term Extension Act, Pub. L. 105–298, § 102, October 27, 1998, 112 Stat. 2827 (Government Printing Office, 1998) at 2828. The difference between 75 years (28 plus 47) and 95 years is 20 years.

[22] Brief of Amici Mark Evanier et al., note 12, at 10–11, 18–21. See also Marc H. Greenberg, *Comic Art, Creativity and the Law* (Elgar, 2014) at 90; Amazing Fantasy No. 15 (Marvel, August 1962); The Avengers No. 1 (Marvel, September 1963); The Incredible *Hulk* No. 1 (Marvel, May 1962); Tales of Suspense No. 39 (Marvel, March 1963); X-Men No. 1 (Marvel, September 1963).

[23] Plaintiffs' and Counterclaimant-Defendants' Reply Local Rule 56.1 Statement of Undisputed Material Facts in Support of Their Motion for Summary Judgment, at 124–130, *Marvel Worldwide, Inc.* v. *Kirby,* No. 10 Civ. 141 (S.D.N.Y. statement filed April. 8, 2011), https://cases.justia.com/federal/district-courts/new-york/nysdce/1:2010cv00141/356975/108/0.pdf. Kirby died in 1994, and before that time a Marvel company filed renewal copyright registrations for the disputed comic books. However, Kirby's heirs claim that it was common for authors to rely upon companies to process such renewals. Whether such an assignment of all "related" renewal copyrights to a company in 1973 or thereafter was valid might depend on whether consideration was adequate and whether there was coercion, deception, oppression, overreaching, or unconscionability involved. *Fred Fisher Music Co.* v. *M. Witmark & Sons,* 318 U.S. 643, 656–657 (1943) (coercion, oppression, or unconscionability); *Rossiter* v. *Vogel,* 134 F.2d 908, 910–12 (2d Cir. 1943) (deception or unconscionability); Paul Goldstein, *Goldstein on Copyright* (Aspen Publishers, 2005) at 6-44–6-45 (overreaching or "grossly inadequate consideration"; noting that consideration that is adequate at time of creation may not be adequate years later).

[24] Many prior articles have maintained that the doctrine is unconstitutional, without necessarily presenting an argument or an overview of its history. E.g., Alina Ng Boyte, The conceits of our imagination: Legal fictions and the concept of deemed authorship, 17 *New York University Journal of Legislation and Public Policy* 707, 745–6, 752–3; Jane C. Ginsburg, et al., The constitutionality of copyright term extension: How long is too long?, 18 *Cardozo Arts & Entertainment Law Journal* 651

define and limit copyright interests, it lacks the power to grant copyrights to persons the Framers would not have regarded as "Authors," or to otherwise alter the traditional contours of copyright.

In the US Congress, there has been reluctance to revisit the work-made-for-hire rule because this would disrupt settled expectations and create licensing chaos, upending a system of vesting copyright that has prevailed for the last century. In response, this chapter outlines some ways that doctrines of implied assignment or license are sufficient to prevent disaster for media conglomerates, copyright licensees, and online repositories of literary or audiovisual works. Other options for achieving this aim include principles of beneficial ownership, joint authorship, and license/waiver of rights. Amending section 201 of the Copyright Act could also vindicate the intention behind the Copyright Clause while protecting the interests of those who commission, originate, or employ authors.

2.2. THE ORIGINAL UNDERSTANDING OF AUTHORSHIP

An original intentions view of the Constitution focuses on the Framers' intent.[25] The Supreme Court has taken such an approach on numerous occasions.[26] A purist form of textualism, as opposed to originalism, would dispense with intentions in favor of the plain meaning of textual provisions.[27] An originalist approach might shape our understanding of the copyright system, and illuminate the ambiguous phrases in the Constitution's text.

At common law, prominent judges described copyright as a right of individual authors, transferred only with some difficulty to publishers.[28] A receipt for money

---

(2000) at 698; Marci Hamilton, The constitution and your CDs, *Findlaw's Writ*, September 19, 2000, http://writ.findlaw.com/commentary/20000919_hamilton.html; Roberta Rosenthal Kwall, Authors in disguise: Why the Visual Artists Rights Act got it wrong, 2007 *Utah Law Review* 741, 749–50; Lawrence B. Solum, Congress's power to promote the Progress of Science: *Eldred v. Ashcroft*, 36 *Loyola Los Angeles Law Review* 1 (2002) at 39; Edward Walterscheid, Divergent evolution of the patent power and the copyright power, 9 *Marquette Intellectual Property Law Review* 307 (2005) at 351.

[25] E.g., Larry Alexander and Saikrishna Prakash, "Is that English you're speaking?" Why intention free interpretation is an impossibility, 41 *San Diego Law Review* 967, 976 (2004); Richard S. Kay, Adherence to the original intentions in constitutional adjudication: Three objections and responses, 82 *Northwestern University Law Review* 226, 245–84 (1988); Timothy Sandefur, Liberal originalism: A Past for the future, 27 *Harvard Journal of Law and Public Policy* 489 (2004) at 491.

[26] Richard S. Kay, Original intent and public meaning in constitutional interpretation, 103 *Northwestern University Law Review* 1 (2009) at 3. See also *Medellin v. Texas*, 552 U.S. 491, 541 (2008) (Breyer, J., dissenting).

[27] Alexander and Prakash, note 25, at 976.

[28] George Ross, A *Treatise on the Law of Vendors and Purchasers of Personal Property* (Butterworth, 2nd ed. 1836) at 94, citing *Clementi v. Walker* (1824) 2 B. and C. 861, 2 Law J.K.B. 176). Although statutory replaced common-law copyright sometime in the eighteenth century, the phrase "at common law" is often used to refer to both decisional and statutory law of Great Britain as of 1789 or some decade not too far from that.

paid for a work was insufficient to show transfer of rights.[29] Transferring rights to another party required a document attested by two witnesses, like a deed.[30] It was not until 1911 that Britain codified the employer's claim to the copyright of a work made during a contract of employment or apprenticeship, or made on commission for the hiring party.[31]

In 1710, the Statute of Anne adopted a theory of "romantic authorship" developed in part by the journalist Joseph Addison and the novelist Daniel Defoe to oppose the London booksellers' control over copyright. Their writings opposed the parental love between author and book to the coercion practiced by publishers, which they described as being situated towards books as kidnappers are to their captives, as robbers are to their loot, and as invaders are to occupied lands.[32] The "Author" is a solitary type who "has separated himself from the rest of Mankind, and studied the Wonders of Creation ... and the Revolutions of the World."[33] A friend of Addison introduced what became the first copyright act, and the House of Commons focused it closely on authors' interests.[34] An amendment substituted "Authors, or Purchasers" of books as the beneficiaries of protection, for "the Rightful Owners" of books in the drafts.[35] The booksellers themselves described the booksellers' interest as being derivative of the authors, who transfer their rights for money.[36] Even the language used for copyrights, "Copies," implied a physical item handed over by a human author.[37]

In the romantic view, either authors must be free to sell or give away their writings, or they will become hacks exploited by publishers who monopolize learning and knowledge. The great cases of *Millar* v. *Taylor* and *Donaldson* v. *Beckett* distinguished between authorial copyright, as a beneficial limited monopoly, and publisher's broader monopolies, which led to abuse.[38] In *Donaldson*, twenty-two members of the House of Lords reversed a common-law injunction against the publication of

---

[29] *Kyle & Cook* v. *Jeffreys* (House of Lords, 1859), in George Dingwall Fordyce (Ed.), *The Scottish Jurist*, vol. 31 (Thomas Constable & Co., 1859) at 566 (wherein appellants cite *Davidson* v. *Bohn* (Ct. of Common Pleas 1848) 6 Com. Ben. Rep. 455–6, and other cases for this proposition).

[30] George Ticknor Curtis, *The Law of Copyright* (Charles C. Little and James Brown Eds., 1847) at 226, 232–33 (several courts stated that a deed, and not merely a writing, was needed to transfer a copyright from author to publisher or purchaser); Assignment of copyright under Stat. 54 Geo. 3, c. 156, *in* The Jurist, vol. 26, pt. 2 (1863) at 149 (similar). See also Act of February 3, 1831, 4 Stat. 436.

[31] William Benjamin Hale, *A Treatise on the Law of Copyright and Literary Property* (The American Law Book Co., 1917) at 1045, citing Copyright Act, 1911 (1 & 2 Geo. V, c. 46 §§ 5(1), 19(1). See also Eaton Sylvester Drone, *A Treatise on the Law of Property in Intellectual Productions in Great Britain* (Little, Brown, & Co., 1879), at 247–48, citing 5 & 6 Vict. C. 45, § 18).

[32] Mark Rose, *Authors and Owners: The Invention of Copyright* (Harvard University Press, 1993) at 35–9, 41.

[33] Ibid., at 36 (quoting Addison, *The Tatler* 101, 1 December 1709).

[34] Ibid., at 42, 46.

[35] Ibid., at 46.

[36] Ibid., at 42, 44, 45.

[37] Ibid., at 58.

[38] Edward Walterscheid, *The Nature of the Intellectual Property Clause: A Study in Historical Perspective* (W.S. Hein & Co., 2002) at 231.

a book without the consent of its proprietor.[39] Lord Camden objected that if the
decree be upheld: "All our learning will be locked up in the hands of the [London
booksellers], who will set what price upon it their avarice chooses to demand, till the
public become as much their slaves, as their hackney compilers are."[40] Within the
memory of the parents and grandparents of his generation, publishers had conspired
with the crown to censor the books of human authors.[41]

Judges and legislators, in *Millar* and in its wake, emphasized the rights of the
person whose actual thoughts are embodied in the manuscript.[42] In 1774, publishers
appealed for legislative relief from the rule announced in *Donaldson v. Beckett*. The
House of Lords rejected a bill that had passed the House of Commons, vesting copyright in "the purchasers" of works as well as their authors.[43] Opposition in the House
of Commons had been fierce, based on "appeals to prejudice against the booksellers, as a class of monopolists ... ."[44] The booksellers of London, like the employers
and commissioners of our time, argued that "large sums had been invested in the
purchase of ancient copyrights ... ."[45] They were unsuccessful.

Some booksellers, theater owners, and designers of maps and engravings argued that
they were the "authors" of works that they had designed and left to other author(s) to
execute. In one line of cases, the courts held that although a reporter of judicial cases
may receive a salary as an employee of the court or the British government, he could
still secure a copyright in his reports of a case's factual background, the arguments of
counsel, annotated footnotes to opinions, and headnotes.[46] If the government desired
the copyright, it had to contract with the reporter for an assignment of the copyright,
even though the reporter was already its employee. For such reasons, a theater owner
was not the author of a play written by an author on a weekly salary at the theater,
who had been hired for the very purpose of writing plays to be performed.[47] Likewise,
the courts held that it was insufficient to develop the "subject" of a "picture" to be

---

[39] Ibid., at 58–9, 62–3.
[40] Ibid., at 62 (quoting 17 Parl. Hist. 999, 1000).
[41] Ibid., at 27, 29, 39.
[42] Curtis, note 30, at 84–5 (quoting *Millar v. Taylor* (1769) 4 Burr. 2303, 2398, 98 Reprint 201, and 1
   Bell's Comm. p. 68).
[43] Curtis, note 30, at 66–7.
[44] Curtis, note 30, at 67.
[45] Curtis, note 30, at 66.
[46] Hale, note 31, at 1059, citing *Callaghan v. Myers*, 128 U.S. 617 (1888); *Gray v. Russell*, 10 F. Cas.
   1035, 1 Story (U.S.) 11 (C.C.D Mass. 1839) (No. 5,728); *Lewis v. Fullarton* (Ch. 1839) 2 Beav. 6, 17
   EngCh 6 (Eng.); *Sweet v. Benning* (1855) 16 C. B. 459, 81 Eng. Com. L. Rep. 459; *Cary v. Longman*
   (K.B. 1801) 1 East 358, 7 ERC 78, 102 Eng. Rep. 138; *Hodges v. Welsh* (1840) 2 Ir. Eq. 266 (Ir.);
   Jarrold v. Houlston (1857) 3 Kay & J. 708; *Saunders v. Smith* (Ch. 1838) 3 Myl. & C. 711, 14 EngCh
   711 (Eng.); *Mawman v. Tegg* (Ch. 1826) 2 Russ. 385, 3 EngCh 385, 38 Eng. Rep. 380; *Buttersworth
   v. Robinson* (1801) 5 Ves. Jr. 709, 31 Eng. Rep. 817).
[47] *Shepherd v. Conquest* (1856) 17 C. B. 427, 443, 84 ECL 427, 139 Reprint 1140; Evan James
   MacGillivray, *A Treatise upon the Law of Copyright in the United Kingdom and the Dominions of the
   Crown, and in the United States of America* (John Murray, 1901) at 63–4.

engraved. Instead, the author "must have designed or represented the subject in some visible form, from which the engraver who executes it must have taken the picture."[48] Similarly, an author claiming copyright after "procuring a drawing to be made" was not the copyright owner unless he "has made the design [of it] himself."[49]

Other cases involving encyclopedias, maps, and theatrical works recognized the authorship of those who handed a plan or design to others to perform some creative or mechanical labor such as engraving or writing. One court held that by designing a map, and delegating the drawing of it to a draftsman employed for that purpose, the designer became its author.[50] At the time, the language of the British and American statutes governing engravings and prints referred in the alternative to those making and designing such productions as the copyright owners.[51] Also, a theater manager had the right to own or use the music his predecessor had employed a composer to create for a play, even after the engagement ended.[52] The author had the right to restrain the publication in finished form of a work that a publisher requested that an author produce. In a suit against infringers, the publisher or planner of a work written by several contributors could claim to be the author in an equitable sense as the result of creating the "scheme of the work."[53] The notion of authorship in the "scheme of the work" was reportedly limited to collective works, and did not transfer authorship of individual contributions to the collective work's editor or former.[54]

The US Constitution contains an Authors and Inventors Clause, which contains no reference to copyrights, patents, or property as such, but contemplates rights governing the "Writings and Discoveries" of "Authors and Inventors."[55] Although there was at least one potential meaning of "Author" at the time it was drafted that was consistent with employers or commissioning parties, the meaning most likely meant was that of "writer"[56] or "first writer of any thing."[57] The other meaning, that

---

[48] Curtis, note 30, at 146, citing *Binns v. Woodruff*, 4 Washington's Rep. 48, and Act of April 29, 1802, ch. 36).

[49] Curtis, note 30, at 140–1, citing *Jeffreys v. Baldwin* (1798) Ambl. 164, 27 Eng. Reprint 109; Richard Godson, *Godson on Patents and Copyright* (Joseph Butterworth & Son, 1823) at 403–4.

[50] Drone, note 31, at 254, citing *Stannard v. Harrison* (1871) 24 L. T. x. § 570, 19 W.R. 811).

[51] Drone, note 31, 178citing 7 Geo. III. C. 38).

[52] Drone, note 31, at 249–53, citing *Hatton v. Kean* (1859) 7 C. B. n. s. 268; *Wallenstein v. Herbert* (1867) 15 L. T. n. § 364, on appeal, 16 L. T. n. § 453).

[53] Curtis, note 30, at 228, 230, citing *Planche v. Colburn* (1831) 5 Car. & P. 58, 172 Eng. Rep. 876, *The Times*, June 15, 1831 (C.P.), and quoting *Barfield*, 2 Law Journ. Oh. O. S. at 90, 102). A theater employee case was cited in *Barfield*, but was perhaps seen as distinguishable because the employer did not design or execute the play at issue. *Shepherd v. Conquest* (1856) 17 C. B. 427, 443, 84 ECL 427, 139 Reprint 1140, cited in Barfield v. 2 L. J. Oh. O. S. at 90, 102).

[54] Walter Arthur Copinger, *The Law of Copyright* (Stevens & Haynes, 1870) at 110–111.

[55] Walterscheid, note 38, at 1 (quoting US Constitution, art. I, § 8, cl. 8).

[56] Noah Webster, *A Dictionary of the English Language: Compiled for the Use of Common Schools in the United States* (George Goodwin & Sons, 1817) at 24.

[57] Samuel Johnson, *A Dictionary of the English Language*, vol. 1 (4th ed. Strahan & Rivington, 1773), at 99.

of cause, producer, or beginner of an effect or thing, would help justify a congressional power to create work-made-for-hire copyrights, but it seems to be out of place with respect to writings, and more relevant to usages of "author" in reference to the origin of events, ideas, or other non-writings.[58]

Distrust of monopolies and their history may have motivated the focus on authors. James Madison, tasked with defending the clause before the public, agreed that "Monopolies ... are justly classed among the greatest nusances [sic] in Government."[59] In *The Federalist* No. 43, Madison explained that: "The copyright of authors has solemnly adjudged in Great Britain to be a right at Common Law. The right to useful inventions seems with equal reason to belong to the inventors. The public good fully coincides in both cases with the claims of individuals."[60] This was a reference to the great cases of *Millar* v. *Taylor* and *Donaldson* v. *Beckett*.[61] Monopolies, on the other hand, Madison saw as liable to "abuse."[62]

The first attempt at a federal copyright regime included *publishers* within its scope.[63] Rather than granting such a power to Congress to secure copyrights "to the authors or publishers of any new books," the Constitution grants the power to "secur[e] ... to Authors ... the exclusive right to *their* respective Writings ... ."[64] Publishers are out of the picture.

The Authors and Inventors Clause was designed to preclude exclusive rights from being enjoyed by someone other than the true author or inventor. Federal district court judges required inventors to show that they were the first inventor in the world, not merely an importing agent or assignee of a foreign inventor.[65] Scholars of copyright have recognized the parallel focus on natural persons in the Authors and Inventors Clause.[66]

Commentators have observed that the Copyright Clause "underscores the value of ... individual contributions to our public discourse."[67] It represents a decision to disfavor "the publishers who reprint long-existing works, as was the

---

[58] Ibid., at 99.
[59] Ibid., at 6 (quoting *Letter from James Madison to Thomas Jefferson (October 17, 1788)*, in *The Republic of Letters* 566 (James Morton Smith ed., 1995)).
[60] James Madison, The Federalist. no. XLIII, 267, in Lionel Bently and Martin Kretschmer (Eds.), *Primary Sources on Copyright (1450–1900)* (University of Cambridge, 2014), http://copy.law.cam.ac.uk/cam/tools/request/showRecord.php?id=record_us_1788.
[61] Walterscheid, note 38, at 231.
[62] Walterscheid, note 38, at 226 (quoting James Madison, Aspects of monopoly over one hundred years ago, 128 *Harper's Magazine* 489 (1914) at 490).
[63] Walterscheid, note 38, at 73 (emphasis added) (quoting *Journals of the Continental Congress*, vol. XXIV (May 2, 1783) at 326–27).
[64] Walterscheid, note 38, at 1 (emphasis added) (quoting US Constitution., art. I, § 8, cl. 8).
[65] Walterscheid, note 38, at 330, citing *Reutgen* v. *Kanowrs*, 20 F. Cas. 555, 556 (D. Pa. 1804) (No. 11,710); *Dawson* v. *Follen*, 7 F. Cas. 216 (D. Pa. 1808) (No. 3,670).
[66] E.g. Ginsburg, et al., note 24; Solum, note 24, citing Act of May 31, 1790, § 1); Walterscheid, note 38, at 351 (collecting cases).
[67] Neil Netanel, *Copyright's Paradox* (Oxford University Press, 2005) at 105.

case in England through the seventeenth century."[68] The privileging of authors had the purpose of creating a "limited term statutory copyright," which would make creative economies more dynamic than a perpetual booksellers' protection regime.[69]

The copyright legislation drafted for the independent United States divided owners into two categories: those who create a work, and those who acquire it by contract, will, or intestacy.[70] The first copyright act copied the renewal term from the Statute of Anne (1709/1710).[71] The "Purchasers" that commissioned works were not treated as independent owners of copyright.[72] Reviewing state law precedents for the federal renewal term, Patterson observes that most of them manifested a suspicion of monopolistic booksellers, and clarified "that copyright was granted only to the author."[73]

The language of the first US copyright act followed Maryland's statute in granting copyright only to authors, their assigns, and administrators/executors, for a term of fourteen years with a renewal term of equal duration if the author was then living.[74] It did not recognize the copyrights of "the Bookseller or Booksellers, [or the] Printer or Printer," who may have "acquired" the rights in a work published before the US Act's effective date, as the Statute of Anne did. Instead, it required that such a bookseller, printer, or publisher be an assignee who had purchased the copyright from the author.[75]

Courts under the Copyright Act of 1790, as amended in 1831, held that the author of a book, print, or engraving was the person who produced it.[76] The Supreme Court stated that the author of a photograph was the person who took it, and not the employer who planned its taking, based upon a decision of the British common-law court of Queen's Bench in 1883. Under that decision, sending an artist or photographer to make a picture, which is then finalized in an "establishment" that employs him or her, does not make the sender or the establishment the author of the picture, because the author must be the person "who really" makes it, who "actually formed the picture by putting the persons in position, and arranging the

---

[68] Ibid., at 105

[69] L. Ray Patterson & Stanley Birch, Jr., A unified theory of copyright, 46 *Houston Law Review* 215 (2009) at 244.

[70] 1 U.S. Stat. 124, 1; see also *Burrow-Giles Lith. Co. v. Sarony*, 111 U. S. 53, (1884). at 56–7; Theodore Megaarden, Copyright, *in The American and English Encyclopaedia of Law*, vol. 7 (David Shephard Garland et al., Eds., Thompson Co., 1898) at 508, 542.

[71] Anne, c. 19, quoted in L. Ray Patterson, Copyright in the new millennium: Resolving the conflict between property rights and political rights, 62 *Ohio State Law Journal* 703 (2001) at 145–6.

[72] Patterson, note 71, at 147.

[73] Ibid., at 188.

[74] Ibid., at 188, 197.

[75] Patterson, note 71, at 145, 197.

[76] Curtis, note 30, at 142–3, 145–6, citing Act of February 3, 1831, § 1); Hale, note 31, at 1047, citing *De Witt v. Brooks*, 7 F. Cas. No. 3,851 (CCSDNY 1861).

place where the people are to be – the man [sic] *who is the effective cause of that.*"[77]
The employment relationship as the motive for the work is not its effective or actual
cause.[78]

Prior to the 1880s, the federal courts had held that the author of an engraving was
the person who etched or implemented the design, and not the one who inspired
or commissioned it.[79] Similarly, the author of a play owned the copyright in the play
despite being employed by a theater.[80] The court held in one such case that employment did not alter an author's rights:

> In *Boucicault* v. *Fox*, it appeared that the plaintiff, while employed as an actor and
> stage-manager at the Winter Garden Theatre in New York, of which William Stuart
> was owner, had written [a play] under an agreement with Stuart that it should be
> performed as long as it would run at that theatre. It was afterward claimed that
> Stuart had become the owner of the play by virtue of such employment.
>
> But the court properly held that he had acquired no property in the piece, for the
> reason that there was no agreement, and nothing in the circumstances of the case,
> to create an implied understanding to that effect.[81]

---

[77] *Burrow-Giles Lith. Co.* v. *Sarony*, 111 U. S. 53, 60–1 (1884), *aff'g* 17 Fed. 591 (C.C. 1883) (emphasis and ellipses added) (quoting *Nottage* v. *Jackson* [1883] 11 Q. B. D. 627). The court noted that British law allowed the author of a photograph, after registering it under the copyright act of 1882, to enjoy the exclusive right of reproducing and multiplying it. Ibid., citing Act of 25 and 26 Victoria, chap. 68).

[78] *Nottage* v. *Jackson* 11 Q.B.D. 627. In Aristotelian philosophy, an effective cause is the "intentional action" that brings about an effect, while a final cause is the goal (or telos) sought to be achieved, a material cause is the physical domain in which the action is undertaken, and a formal cause is the category that contains the goal sought. M.S. Watanabe, Causality and time, in J.T. Fraser and N. Lawrence, Eds., *The Study of Time II: Proceedings of the Second Conference of the International Congress for the Study of Time* (Springer Verlag, 1972) at 269. An effective, or an "efficient," cause is a more direct (in legal terms, proximate) cause of an effect, as a doctor may be an efficient cause of "being healthy," although the perpetuation of life may be the final cause or goal of health, and although the form of health may be the formal cause (in a Platonic sense, health may be caused by a being partaking in the form of health). Aristotle, *The Eudemian Ethics* (Anthony Kenny, Ed., Cambridge University Press, 2011) at xxiii. To use another analogy, the palate and the wine are the efficient causes of drinking wine, while pleasure may be the final cause and the form of wine as being suited to a certain form of pleasure (as opposed to vinegar or gasoline) may be the formal cause. The efficient cause is the immediate "source of the motion" towards the cause, or in some formulations the prompt or inspiration to pursue it in action. John Burnet (Ed.), *Aristotle on Education: Extracts from the Ethics and Politics* (Oxford University Press, 1967) at 76.

[79] *Binns* v. *Woodruff*, 3 F. Cas. 421 (C.C.D. Pa. 1821) (No. 1,424). The court declared that "the courts saw it as self-evident that the person entitled to original ownership was the actual creator of the work– the author," and not the person "who commissioned various craftsmen to execute the design, drawing, and engraving ...." Oren Bracha, *The ideology of authorship revisited: Authors, Markets, and liberal values in early American copyright*, 118 Yale Law Journal 186 (2008) at 269–70 and accompanying text.

[80] *Boucicault* v. *Fox*, 3 F. Cas. No. 1,691, 5 Blatchf. 87, 95 (1862); Megaarden, note 70, at 541–2.

[81] Drone, note 31, at 258, citing *Boucicault*, 5 Blatcf. 87). The circuit court of the United States, which I refer to as the US Circuit Court for brevity, had original jurisdiction of all suits arising under the patent or copyright laws. Rev. Stat., 1878, tit. XIII, pp. 110, 111; Library of Congress, *Report of the Librarian of Congress for the Fiscal Year Ending June 30, 1903*, at 508–9.

In that case, Justice Shipman held that "a man's intellectual productions are peculiarly his own, and although they may have been brought forth by the author while in the general employment of another, yet he will not be deemed to have parted with his right and transferred it to his employer unless a valid agreement to that effect is adduced."[82] He added: "The title to literary property is in the author whose intellect has given birth to the thoughts and wrought them into the composition, unless he has transferred that title, by contract, to another."[83]

The United States had its own versions of the British case about the author of case decisions employed by the publisher. When a professor prepared a work of literature while working for a college and using its facilities, the court held that the professor rather than the college was the copyright holder.[84] In another case involving a ghostwriter of memoirs, the court held that the employer was not the "author," even though the book "was written by a person in the employment of another, who furnished him with the facts and incidents of a person's life, and a copyright in the book was taken out in the name of the person so furnishing the facts."[85]

There was case law suggesting that after the Act of 1870, employment by another divested an employee-author of copyright, because the law permitted the "proprietor" to recover damages for copyright infringement.[86] These cases arguably ignored the possibility that Congress intended "proprietor" to replace or summarize the categories of "executors, administrators, or assigns" used in the Act of 1790, rather than to add "employers" to that list of categories.[87] The Act of 1870 declared that the "author or proprietor" of the copyright could seek damages for infringement.[88] It gave the sole liberty of printing, selling, or copying a work to the "author, inventor,

[82] Drone, note 31, at 258 (quoting *Boucicault*, 5 Blatchf. at 95).
[83] Drone, note 31, at 258.
[84] Drone, note 31, citing *Peters v. Borst*, 24 Abb. N. Cas., 9 NYS 789, 798 (N.Y. Sup. Ct., 1889).
[85] Drone, note 31, citing *DeWitt v. Brooks*, 7 Fed. Cas. No. 3851.
[86] *Dielman v. White*, 102 Fed. 892 (C.C.D. Mass. 1900); *Press Publ. Co. v. Falk*, 59 Fed. 324 (CCSDNY 1896); Hale, note 31, at 1046–8 (an employer may become a copyright owner "under the later statutes in which the 'proprietor' of a work is expressly mentioned as a person who may obtain a copyright therein."), citing *American Tobacco Co. v. Werckmeister*, 207 U.S. 284 (1907); *Dielman*, 102 Fed. 892; *National Cloak, etc. v. Kaufman*, 189 Fed. 215 (M.D. Pa. 1911); *Colliery Engineering Co. v. United Correspondence Schs. Corp.*, 94 Fed. 152 (CCSDNY 1899); *Mutual Adv. Co. v. Refo*, 76 Fed. 961 (DSC 1896); *Black v. Henry G. Allen Co.*, 56 Fed. 764 (CCSDNY 1893); *Carte v. Evans*, 27 Fed. 861 (CCD Mass. 1886); *Schumacher v. Schwencke*, 25 Fed. 466 (CC 1885); *Heine v. Appleton*, 11 F. Cas. 1031 (CDSDNY 1853).
[87] For example, the Act of 1790 stated that infringers must "forfeit and pay" damages to authors, executors, and assigns, while the Act of 1870 (through 1897) stated that damages could be recovered from the infringer "by such proprietor." Thomas Edward Scrutton, *The Law of Copyright* (John Murray, 3rd ed. 1900) at 237 (quoting U.S. Rev. Stat. § 4964).
[88] Act of 1870 (16 U.S. Stat, at L. 198); Scrutton, note 87, at 233–237 (quoting U.S. Rev. Stat. §§ 4952–4967). Congress reenacted the copyright chapter of the US statutes with similar language in 1874, 1891, 1895, and 1897. Scrutton, note 87, at 233.

designer, or proprietor" thereof.[89] Already, between 1851 and 1869, federal trial courts had held that authors were not the statutory proprietors of the copyright, if they had agreed that the commissioning party (such as an employer) would enjoy the copyright interest, even without a formal assignment as the pre-1850 decisions required.[90] This did not mean that commissioning parties were authors, but that they could "become the owners by [oral] transfer of whatever right [the author], prior to the taking of the copyright, had to convey," or that an employer could become the equitable enforcer of a copyright.[91] Whether under oral or written assignment, a proprietor was a purchaser rather than an author, under such a reading of the cases.[92]

Both British and American courts had found by 1870 that employers were *not* the proprietors of a copyright unless they had bought it. The Act of 1790 itself used "proprietors" to refer to executors, administrators, and assigns as litigants.[93] The intention was no doubt to make clear that if an author died after the act of publication, the administrators of his or her estate or executors of his or her will could obtain damages or injunctive relief notwithstanding the disappearance of the "author."[94] Moreover, the use of the term "proprietors" aided assignees in enforcing their rights, and in granting consent to other persons or entities to publish or republish the work.[95]

Courts between 1790 and 1870 generally did not read the term "proprietors" as giving copyrights to employers.[96] The Supreme Court decided one of the first cases under the 1870 act, involving write-ups of Ohio case law published by a person employed by the State of Ohio for this purpose after 1882, by analyzing whether the author of the case reports had written any original material that he had "assigne[d]"

---

[89]   16 U.S. Stat. at L. 212; see also Library of Congress, note 82, at 481–6 (comparing language of Act of 1870 to that of Revised Statutes of 1873).

[90]   *Little* v. *Gould*, 15 F. Cas. 604, 2 Blatchf. 165, 362 (C.C.N.D.N.Y. 1851) (No. 8,394); *Lawrence* v. *Dana*, 15 F. Cas. 26, 51, 4 Cliff. (U.S.) 1 (C.C.D Mass. 1869) (No. 8,136); Drone, note 31, at 255.

[91]   *Callaghan* v. *Myers*, 128 U.S. 617, 658 (1888); *Black* v. *Henry G. Allen Co.*, 42 Fed. Rep. 618, 625 (CCSDNY 1893) ("An inchoate right to a copyright may, prior to the taking of the copyright, be transferred by parol."), citing, inter alia, *Callaghan*, 128 U.S. 658).

[92]   James Neu, Rights of a copyright holder, 17 *Notre Dame Lawyer* 373 (1942) at 385.

[93]   An Act for the encouragement of learning, by securing the copies of maps, charts, and books, to the authors and proprietors of such copies, during the times therein mentioned, May 31, 1790, §§ 1–4, 6.

[94]   See Act of 1790, §§ 4, 6.

[95]   See Act of 1790, § 2.

[96]   The Act of 1870, and the cases decided after it on employee copyrights, evoked the notion that a "proprietor" may own the copyright in the first instance even though it did not author the work. This idea was prevalent prior to the Statute of Anne and the Authors and Inventors Clause, for example in the Printing Press Regulation (Licensing) Act of 1662 and a series of royal decrees, which provided that printers owned patents or "copies" in particular books or classes of books, rather than each author having a "copy-right." Kaplan, note 18, at 3–13, citing, inter alia, An Act for Preventing Abuses in Printing Seditious, Treasonable, and Unlicensed Books and Pamphlets, and for Regulating of Printing and Printing Presses (Licensing Act) (1662), 13 & 14 Car. 2, c. 33). See also Act of 1662, quoted in Henry Dunning Macleod, *A Dictionary of Political Economy: Biographical, Bibliographical, Historical, and Practical*, vol. 1 (1859) at 554.

to the State, not whether the State itself was the author due to hiring the writer.[97] Under a similar case decided under the 1831 act, the Supreme Court held that a copyright could "be taken out for or in the name of the state, as the assignee of such proprietary right" of an author of headnotes or syllabi of case reports, because:

> Even though a reporter may be a sworn public officer, appointed by the authority of the government which creates the court of which he is made the reporter, and even though he may be paid a fixed salary for his labors, yet ... [he] can obtain a copyright for it as an author ... [of] the parts of the book of which he is the author.[98]

The contemporary work-made-for-hire doctrine, in equating the hiring party and actual author, is contrary to what the Framers intended, because it revives this aspect of English law prior to 1710. One late nineteenth-century treatise clarified the distinction between the author, who produces a writing by creativity and mental labor, and the "proprietor" of a writing:

> While one person by employing another to produce a work may become the proprietor of the production, it seems that he is not the "inventor" or "designer" within the meaning of those terms as used in the statute.... [I]t has been held that one who procures another to arrange a piece of music is not entitled to copyright as author.[99]

Thus, one creator who has employed or procured another to write a specific book did not own the copyright or have standing to sue by having done so.[100] As late as 1900, a court treated a question of a commissioner's ownership of a work which it paid for and specified the materials of, as one of contract interpretation, not of the commissioner's authorship.[101]

The term "author," to eighteenth- and nineteenth-century writers, typically referred to the creative worker. As a prominent treatise stated, the author "creates *both* the ideas *and the particular combination of characters* which represents those

---

[97] *Banks* v. *Manchester*, 128 U.S. 244, 252–3 (1888). See also *Banks* v. *Manchester*, 23 Fed. 143 (C.C.S.D. Ohio 1885), citing *Gray* v. *Russell*, 10 F. Cas. 1035 (C.C.D. Mass.) (Story, J.).

[98] *Callaghan* v. *Myers*, 128 U.S. 617, 647, 650 (1888).

[99] Megaarden, note 70, at 542, citing *DeWitt* v. *Brooks*, 2 Fed. Cas. No. 3,851; *Atwill* v. *Ferrett*, 2 F. Cas. 195, 2 Blatchf. (U.S.) 39 (C.C.S.D.N.Y. 1846) (No. 4,747); *Pierpont* v. *Fowle*, 19 F. Cas. No. 11,152, 2 Woodb. & M. (U.S.) 23, 46 (C.C.D. Mass. 1846) (No. 11,152). Cf. also *Aalmuhammed* v. *Lee*, 202 F.3d 1227, 1232 (9th Cir. 2000) (term "author" is "taken from the traditional activity of a person sitting at a desk with a pen and writing something for publication.").

[100] Megaarden, note 70, at 542 (collecting sources); Drone, note 31, at 257–8, citing *Atwill*, 2 F. Cas. 195; Hale, note 31, at 1047, citing *De Witt*, 7 F. Cas. 757.

[101] *Dielman*, 102 Fed. at 894–5 (where artist was commissioned to produce a cartoon to be turned into a mosaic in specified material, the question was whether artist could "prov[e] that he retains a copyright in the work of art executed, sold, and delivered under the commission" as a matter of "plain and necessary meaning of the [parties'] original contract").

ideas upon paper ... ."[102] The author therefore creates a "volume," and not simply the idea for the volume.[103]

2.3. LIMITS TO CONGRESSIONAL DISCRETION TO DEFINE THE "AUTHORS" OF "WRITINGS"

Courts largely developed the "instance and expense" test of authorship-for-hire after the 1909 Act. This line of cases did have some roots in cases decided under the 1831 and 1870 acts, and in their British counterparts.[104] The Second Circuit adopted "a presumption in the absence of an express contractual reservation to the contrary, that the copyright shall be in the person at whose instance and expense the work is done."[105] Subsequent cases explained the test as assessing whether there was control over the work's content or style, and a supply of capital for making of the work.[106] Melville Nimmer described the test as only "a presumption in the absence of an express contractual reservation to the contrary ... ."[107] Congress apparently considered but rejected using the phrase "instance and expense" for a provision on *collective* works in the 1909 Act.[108] The Second Circuit essentially adopted as law by judicial construction the language of legislation that had been proposed – but not passed – in Congress.[109]

---

[102] Curtis, note 30, at 11–13 (emphasis added).

[103] *Maxwell* v. *Hogg* (1867) 2 Ch. App. 307, 36 L. J. Ch. 433 (Lord Cairns).

[104] One of the first cases arguably adopting this approach could also be read being as consistent with a theory of an employee obligation to assign copyrights vesting initially in himself or herself, because under his contract, the employee had a duty while earning a salary to write and revise educational materials. *Colliery* v. *Schools*, 94 Fed. Rep. 152, 153 (C.C.S.D.N.Y. 1899). In another case, the court stated that an artist was not the author of certain prints and engravings "made for the government," and for which "he received pay," but emphasizing the parties' transfer of rights by "distinct understanding that the sketches and drawings which he might make were to be the exclusive property of the government of the United States." *Heine* v. *Appleton*, 11 F. Cas. 1031, 1032 (C.C.S.D.N.Y. 1853). The Second Circuit has opined that the first use of the phrase "instance and expense" was in 1887. *Martha Graham School*, 380 F.2d at 634 and n. 17. See also *Lin–Brook Builders*, 352 F.2d at 300, citing *Dielman*, 102 F. 892.

[105] *Brattleboro Publishing*, 369 F.2d at 567–8.

[106] E.g. *Epoch Producing Corp.* v. *Killiam Shows, Inc.*, 522 F.2d 737, 740–1, 744 (2d Cir. 1975) (rejecting work made for hire status in absence of showing that plaintiff, the assignee of director D. W. Griffith's copyright in *The Birth of a Nation*, "actually supervised or paid any money for the making of the motion picture," or that it had "requisite power to control or supervise Griffith's work, which is the hallmark of 'an employment for hire' relationship").

[107] *Brattleboro Publishing*, 369 F.2d at 567 (quoting Melville Nimmer, *Nimmer on Copyright* (Mathew Bender, 1964) at 238).

[108] *Martha Graham School*, 380 F.2d at 634 and n. 17 (although the phrase was used in 1905 draft bill, the next draft dropped the phrase, and 1909 Act contained no definition of employer or work made for hire), citing Library of Congress, *Memorandum Draft of a Bill to Amend and Consolidate the Acts Respecting Copyright*, Copyright Office Bulletin No. 10 (1905); S. 6330, H.R. 19853, 59th Cong., 1st Sess. (1906).

[109] *Martha Graham School*, note 108, at 634 and n. 17. See also *Report of the Register of Copyrights on the General Revision of the Copyright Law*, 87th Cong., 1st Sess. 1 (Committee Print, 1961).

While it is easy to see how the work-made-for-hire doctrine evolved into its current form, this evolution is constitutionally suspect. If a proprietor of a copyright could become its owner, and if this could occur by oral transfer, the impulse is: why not do away with the formality of transfer and make the commissioning or employing party the author in the first instance? The answer is that this threatens to vest copyrights in persons or corporations who did not make writings themselves, but only provided the idea, occasion, or facilities for their being made. Such a move subverts the intentions of the Framers to privilege the working author over the more enduring, prosperous, and acquisitive publisher. While an employer may be a but-for cause of a work's creation, the audience might equally be considered as a but-for cause.[110] For this reason, courts originally looked to the originator of the particular form of an expression in all its richness and uniqueness as the constitutional and statutory author.

There are two arguments with deep roots in Supreme Court precedent that defenders of the work-made-for-hire doctrine employ. One argument, adopted by the Supreme Court in dicta in *Bleistein* and *Goldstein*, is that "Author" is a capacious term that may include a commissioning or employing author.[111] Another potentially meritorious argument is that there was a rational basis for Congress to vest copyrights in employers for works produced by employees acting within the scope of their employment under section 26 of the 1909 Act and sections 101 and 201 of the 1976 Act. The Supreme Court has suggested that, if it acts rationally, Congress has the discretion to change the copyright system.

The Supreme Court has rejected the "narrow literal sense" of the term "Authors" as writers of books, in favor of the broad notion of an "Author" as a writing's "originator."[112] An "Author" in the constitutional "sense is 'he to whom anything owes its origin; originator; maker; *one who completes a work of science or literature.*'"[113] An author of a picture, for example, must "produce" it, by "selecting and arranging" its imagery, coloration, etc.[114]

The Supreme Court stated in 1907 that *proprietors* may be copyright holders due to "the intention of Congress to vest in 'assigns,' before copyright, the same privilege of subsequently acquiring complete statutory copyright as the original author, inventor, designer, or proprietor has."[115] The underlying dispute related to statutory interpretation, not construction of the constitutional clause. Moreover, it is consistent with the view that Congress must vest copyright in authors, subject to transfer to proprietors.[116]

---

[110] *Wooderson* v. *Tuck* (1887) 4 T. L. R. 57.

[111] *Bleistein*, 188 U.S. at 248; *Goldstein* v. *California*, 412 U.S. 546, 561–2 (1973).

[112] *Goldstein*, 412 U.S. at 561–2, citing *Burrow-Giles Lithographic Co.* v. *Sarony*, 111 U.S. 53, 58 (1884).

[113] *Burrow-Giles*, 111 U.S. at 57–8 (quoting Worcester) (emphasis added).

[114] Ibid., at 60 (emphasis added).

[115] *American Tobacco Co.* v. *Werckmeister*, 207 U.S. 284, 297–8 (1907).

[116] E.g. Act of 1870, § 89, 16 Stat. 198 (1870) (copyright shall be assignable by any instrument of writing); Act of 1909, § 28 (similar). The proprietor could record his or her name with the Copyright Office as rightsholder. E.g. Act of 1870, § 91; Act of 1909, § 32.

These decisions should not preclude the Court from reaching a fresh ruling on the constitutionality of the work-made-for-hire doctrine. The court's reference to "originators" as "Authors" did not necessarily represent a holding that an employer may constitutionally be vested with authorship of works executed by an employee. In the case first relying on this definition, a photographer sued after infringement of his own photograph, rather than one taken by an employee.[117] The photographer at issue in that case "formed the picture by putting the persons in position," not simply by inspiring or financing its execution.[118] The mere fact that the dictionary definition of the constitutional term "Authors" is copious enough to embrace other "originators" does not end the inquiry. Thus, the Supreme Court also examined the practice of the first Congress, and of subsequent congresses in revising the copyright law in 1802 and 1831, to decide that a photograph could be a writing and the maker its author, by analogy to maps, prints, and engravings.[119] For this reason, the meaning of "Author" must be informed by the "'practice of legislation in England and America,'" and by "instructive decision[s]" from England, as well as by the dictionary.[120]

It would be wrong to regard the work-made-for-hire doctrine's constitutionality as having been resolved for all time, because that question has not been "investigated with care, and considered in its full extent."[121] In *Bleistein* and *Goldstein*, there was no "general expression" of a rule, which the Supreme Court's jurisprudence originally required for its precedents to bind later courts, as to the identity of the author for constitutional purposes.[122] Authorship as between the employees and the employer was not the question presented, so the employer's ownership was not a premise of the court's reasoning in disposing of the case.[123] Where the Court assumes such a finding without deciding it, and the parties have not "crossed swords" on the issue, stare decisis arguably does not require adherence to the finding in later cases.[124]

---

[117] *Sarony*, 111 U.S. at 54–8.

[118] Ibid., at 58, 61 (quoting *Nottage* v. *Jackson* (1883) 11 Q.B.D. 627 (Brett, M.R.)).

[119] *Sarony*, note 117, at 56–7 , citing Act of 1790, 1 Stat. 124, 1; Act of April 29, 1802, 2 Stat. 171, 2; Act of February 3d, 1831, 4 Stat. 436, 1).

[120] *Sarony*, note 117, at 56 (quoting John Bouvier, *Law Dictionary*, vol. 2 (J.B. Lippincott Co., 1879) at 363, and citing *Nottage* v. *Jackson*, 11 Q.B.D. 627 (1883)). See also *Sarony*, note 117, at 57–8 (quoting "Worcester") (author as "an 'originator,' 'he to whom anything owes its origin.'")

[121] *Sarony*, note 117, at 56. See also *Payne* v. *Tennessee*, 501 U.S. 808, 828 (1991) (quoting *Helvering* v. *Hallock*, 309 U.S. 106, 119 (1940)).

[122] *Cohens* v. *Virginia*, 19 U.S. (6 Wheat.) 264, 399–400 (1821).

[123] *Bleistein*, 188 U.S. at 248 (lower courts ruled that such chromolithographic posters were not copyrightable at all); Ibid. at 252 (Harlan, J., dissenting) (same).

[124] *Arbaugh* v. *Y & H Corp.*, 546 U.S. 500, 512 (2006), citing *Steel Co.* v. *Citizens for Better Environment*, 523 U.S. 83, 91 (1998). See also *Brecht* v. *Abrahamson*, 507 U.S. 619, 630–1 (1993); *Edelman* v. *Jordan*, 415 U.S. 651, 670 (1974). Under some theories of precedent, the authority of a case depends on the particular facts and circumstances involved therein. *Cf.* William Eskridge Jr., *Overruling statutory precedents*, 76 Georgetown Law Journal 1431 (1987–88) at 1432–4 (collecting several cases confined to their facts, and whose reasoning was subsequently ignored).

Even had the issue been central, but more "careful analysis" proved it to be decided wrongly, it may be decided differently today.[125]

Is Congress entitled to construe "Authors" as it wishes, if it has a rational basis for the distinctions it draws and rules that it codifies? Such a theory was successful in upholding retrospective term extension and restoration for copyrights on works that had fallen into the public domain.[126] The Supreme Court stated that in *Eldred* v. *Ashcroft*[127] that Congress is owed substantial deference in "defining the scope of the limited monopoly" known as copyright.[128]

Eldred does not fully immunize the work-made-for-hire doctrine from further scrutiny, however. Despite the term extensions in *Eldred* and *Golan* being rational in the sense of benefiting some members of society, albeit at potentially large cost, the Court insisted on examining whether the extensions were consistent with the practice of the first Congress, whose construction of its constitutional authority is entitled to "'almost conclusive' weight" as respects later congresses.[129] Moreover, the Court in *Eldred* analyzed the Authors and Inventors Clause to determine whether its language enumerated a power sufficient for Congress to extend copyrights, despite the rationality of doing so. This process of ensuring fidelity to text and constitutional history was what the Court called the "traditional contours of copyright" limitation on the discretion of Congress to rationally define copyright.[130] Legislation that varies or destroys those contours would threaten a violation of the First Amendment, for example, if fair use was narrowed unduly.[131]

Legislation in conflict with the constitutional text and its early history of a clause is a proper subject of heightened judicial inquiry. After *Eldred*, the question concerning the constitutionality of parts of the Copyright Act depends on the "historical record," and "congressional practice."[132] Part of the record is made up by societal expectations.[133]

2.4. FEAR OF AN AUTHORIAL PLANET

Turning from constitutional to public-policy concerns, the contemporary work-made-for-hire doctrine creates some inequities. For example, inventors are in a

---

[125] *Lawrence v. Texas*, 539 U. S. 558, 577 (2003). But *cf. Payne*, 501 U.S. 808, 827 (1991) ("Adhering to precedent 'is usually the wise policy, because in most matters it is more important that the applicable rule of law be settled than it be settled right.'") (quoting *Burnet v. Coronado Oil & Gas Co.*, 285 U.S. 393, 406 (1932) (Brandeis, J., dissenting)).
[126] *Golan v. Holder*, 132 S.Ct. 873, 883, 889 (2012).
[127] 537 U.S. 186 (2003).
[128] Ibid., at 204–5, citing *Sony Corp. of Am. v. University City Studios, Inc.*, 464 U.S. 417, 429 (1984).
[129] 537 U.S. 186, note 127. at 197–98 (quoting *Sarony*, note 117, at 57).
[130] Ibid., at 221.
[131] Ibid.
[132] Ibid., at 890, 891.
[133] Cf. Elizabeth Townsend Gard, A tale of two Ginsburgs: Traditional contours in Eldred and Golan, 62 *DePaul Law Review* 931 (2013) at 940.

different position than authors even though similar works, such as software interfaces or three-dimensional designs, may be either patented or copyrighted, or both.
An employee–inventor is vested in the first instance with patent rights, with the
employer obtaining in exchange for the inventor's salary either a right to an assignment or a "shop right" to use the invention in its trade or business.[134] Moreover,
some independent contractors who create commissioned copyrighted works are in a
similar position to inventors, obtaining by statute the permission to transfer authorship by a signed writing with respect to the IP that they create to the parties that
commissioned it, but not suffering a transfer by default.[135] The work-made-for-hire
doctrine goes further that the law of assignment, by adopting the fiction, which
some commentators find "philosophically indefensible," that a commissioning party
authored a work that in many cases it did not have the skills, tools, talents, or time
to produce.[136] This fiction contradicts the clear terms of the Copyright Act, which
defines the "authors" of "works made for hire" as "employers," the definition of
which plainly excludes commissioning parties.[137] Perhaps most importantly, the rule
may have a deleterious impact on creativity by concentrating ownership in copyright conglomerates.[138]

Litigants, scholars, and amici curiae such as trade associations may argue that
changing ownership rules that prevailed for decades would disrupt settled expectations and create chaos. Many copyright registrations would have been issued in the
name of the wrong author. Countless copyright transfers could be terminated by

---

[134] *Duman v. Gommerman*, 865 F.2d 1093, 1099, 1102 (9th Cir. 1989), *rev'd on other grounds*, *CCNV*,
490 U.S. 730. See also *United States v. Dubilier Condenser Corp.*, 289 U.S. 178 (1933); *Standard Parts
Co. v. Peck*, 264 U.S. 52 (1924); *Hapgood v. Hewitt*, 119 U.S. 226 (1886).

[135] 17 U.S.C. §§ 101, 201(a) & (b); *Easter Seal Society*, 815 F.2d at 329; *Baltimore Orioles v. Major
League Baseball Players Association*, 805 F.2d 663, 669 (7th Cir. 1986).

[136] Melville Nimmer, Comment and views submitted to the Copyright Office on works made for
hire and on commission, in Borge Varmer (Ed.), *Copyright Law Revision: Studies Prepared for the
Subcommittee on Patents, Trademarks, and Copyrights of the Committee on the Judiciary*, U.S. Senate,
86th Cong., 2d Sess., Pursuant to S. Res. 240 (Government Printing Office, 1960), at 153, www
.copyright.gov/history/studies/study13.pdf. See Varmer, Copyright Law Revision, at 139

> (On the other hand, it may be argued that the concept of designating the employer as the author
> of an intellectual creation of another person is artificial; that the actual creator is intended to
> be the primary beneficiary of copyright; that since copyright works may be used commercially
> in a number of ways beyond their use in the employer's business, the employee-creator should
> ordinarily be the beneficiary of such other uses; and that the burden of contracting otherwise
> should be placed on the employer.);

ibid., at 149–50.

[137] 17 U.S.C. § 26 (1975 ed.) [section 26 of the Copyright Act of 1909]; *Clackamas Gastroenterology
Assocs., P.C. v. Wells*, 538 U.S. 440, 445 n. 5 (2003) (employer does not include a commissioning
party); *Estate of Burne Hogarth v. Edgar Rice Burroughs, Inc.*, 342 F.3d 149, 160 n.14 (2d Cir. 2003).

[138] John Schulman, Comment and views, *in* Borge Varmer (Ed.), *Copyright Law Revision: Studies
Prepared for the Subcommittee on Patents, Trademarks, and Copyrights of the Committee on the
Judiciary* (Government Printing Office, 1960), at 150.

their authors under sections 203 and 304 of the Copyright Act.[139] Individual authors would enjoy holdup or holdout power over employers and their licensees to extract additional rents for works that had been paid for and prepared for hire past decades. The public domain could shrink as copyright terms measured from publication as a work-made-for-hire were recalculated using the life of the author plus seventy years as the term, retrospectively extended. Enormous quantities of work may fall into orphan work status because individual writers or artists are dead or unavailable for licensing, while their employers or their successors continue to exist.

The danger of licensing chaos does not justify maintaining the work-made-for-hire doctrine in its current form. First, practical concerns are not always sufficient to deflect arguments from constitutional text, intentions, and history.[140] Second, industry practices under the copyright term extensions of 1976 and 1998 have shown that the rents extracted by authors from commissioning and purchasing parties may not be very large, as a share of a work's value. Third, the public domain may expand as well as contract, embracing more clearly a universe of works produced more than seventy years ago. The orphan works problem may improve, rather than getting worse. Individual authors may be more likely in many instances to offer open-access or licensed versions of their work than employers are, some employers being defunct, litigious, tough to deal with, or hopeful that they will someday revive works.

The practical implications of constitutional rules arise in several situations. The Supreme Court might reverse a constitutional precedent that it found to be "unworkable" in practice.[141] It might decline to issue a ruling on a constitutional

---

[139] Section 203 lets authors of non-works-made-for-hire works copyrighted after 1977 terminate grants about thirty-five years after assignment or license, or forty years if publication was involved. 17 U.S.C. § 203. Section 304 applies to a work published or otherwise copyrighted prior to January 1, 1978, other than a copyright in a work made for hire. It states that an exclusive or nonexclusive grant of a transfer or license of the renewal copyright or any right under it, executed before January 1, 1978, by the author or inheritors (other than by will), may be terminated by authors or heirs after 56 years from copyrighting, or in 1978, if 56 years happened before that date, by serving a notice in writing. Ibid., § 304(c). The termination right does not affect the continued exploitation of a derivative work prepared under authority of the grant before its termination. Ibid., §304(c)(6). A termination right that was not timely exercised by 1998 may be exercised within five years after seventy-five years passed from copyrighting. Ibid., § 304(d).

[140] Cf. *Mincey* v. *Arizona*, 437 U. S. 385, 393 (1978) ("[T]he mere fact that law enforcement may be made more efficient can never by itself justify disregard of the Fourth Amendment."); *Youngstown Sheet & Tube Co.* v. *Sawyer*, 343 U. S. 579, 587, 590–1 (1952) (rejecting executive action in national emergency because it exceeded executive power under Constitution); ibid., at 593–614 (Frankfurter, J., concurring) (although prompt executive action may be more effective, it had to be rejected as in excess of executive power under Constitution); ibid., at 615–34 (Douglas, J., concurring) (although president may act more speedily, Constitution did not authorize his action); *ibid.* at 635–655 (Jackson, C.J., concurring) (despite "defects, delays and inconveniences" of government by Congress using laws, domestic presidential action in an emergency to ensure supplies to troops in the field could not be justified under text of Constitution).

[141] *Payne*, 501 U. S. 808, 827 (1991) (Court may overrule a decision that seems "unworkable"); *Montejo* v. *Louisiana*, 556 U.S. 778 (2009).

question or right because no "judicially manageable standards" were known to exist on which such a ruling could be based.[142] Finally, the Court might withhold a remedy available in an analogous situation in cases where "considerations of institutional competence" lead to judicial modesty, as in foreign affairs.[143]

Doing away with the work-made-for-hire doctrine need not have consequences that are unworkable in practice, or that involve a ham-handed judiciary ruining an industry well-treated by a competent Congress. For one thing, authors have been terminating transfers to corporations and other commissioners or users of their work for centuries, and the resulting disruption has been relatively minor. Moreover, recent disputes between authors seeking to reclaim highly valuable copyrights on the one hand, and corporate or conglomerate users of the copyrights on the other hand, have been settled for very small sums relative to the overall value of the copyright. It is possible that repeal of the work-made-for-hire doctrine could increase authors' bargaining power, but various limiting doctrines described below may make it difficult for authors to reclaim copyright interests in their work. These doctrines, taken together, indicate that the practical effect of repeal will be modest.

One justification for creating work made for hire exceptions to personal authorship or termination rights in the case of collective works is to reduce holdout power of the actual authors.[144] Transaction costs would be high as diverse contributors to collective works such as films or sound recordings jockeyed for co-author status or a share in termination rights.[145] Judge Richard Posner and William Landes defend the work-made-for-hire doctrine in general on the grounds that it minimizes on transactions costs by vesting authorship in a single entity by default, subject to renegotiation.[146] A similar justification surfaced in the Ninth Circuit's opinion, sitting en banc, reversing a panel decision concluding that actors or other performers could author distinct works of authorship comprised of performances intended for inclusion in a film or television program.[147] The en banc opinion reasoned that actors' copyrights would be a "logistical and financial nightmare."[148] Similarly, Landes and Posner maintain that

---

[142] *Baker* v. *Carr*, 369 U.S. 186, 223 (1962) (collecting cases).

[143] *Sanchez-Espinoza* v. *Reagan*, 770 F.2d 202, 205, 208–9 (D.C. Cir. 1985) (withholding, in covert military action context, the Fourth and Fifth Amendment rights to be free from terrorism, murder, kidnapping, torture, rape, maiming, and the destruction of private property and public facilities, and the remedy of damages under *Bivens* v. *Six Unknown Named Agents of the Federal Bureau of Narcotics*, 403 U.S. 388, 396 (1971)).

[144] Cf. Jessica Johnson, *Application of the copyright termination provision to the music industry: Sound recordings should constitute works made for hire*, 67 *Miami Law Review* 661 (2013) at 670–1 ("Distributing ownership of a work that is meant to be unified could create a holdout problem because it would allow each contributor to have a say in the collective work's use and promotion, causing decisions about its exploitation as a single work to become extremely difficult or impossible.").

[145] Johnson, note 144, 671.

[146] William Landes and Richard Posner, *The Economic Structure of Intellectual Property Law* (Harvard University Press, 2003) at 271–2.

[147] *Garcia* v. *Google, Inc.*, 786 F. 3d 733 (9th Cir. 2015) (en banc).

[148] Ibid., at 742–3.

"transactions costs would be prohibitive if each artist employed by Disney owned the copyright to his work and so could block or delay publication of a project such as a movie or comic book that involved the efforts of many creative employees."[149]

The extent of authors' holdout power has been overstated in this area. Employers today routinely make their employees sign written employment agreements, which could include detailed assignments of copyrights in specific projects on which their employees labor for hire.[150] Standard-form contracts assigning employee rights are widely available.[151] In the patent context, most employers of inventors used prein-vention assignment agreements by the 1970s to ensure that companies owned the vast majority of issued patents.[152] While such agreements may be unenforceable in some circumstances, courts generally respect and apply them.[153] There is little rea-son to abandon constitutional provisions in order to bail out employers who ignore standard-form agreements out of indifference to their legal rights.

Actual experience with renewal and termination rights has shown that authors cannot command even a fraction of a work's market value in a renegotiation with publishers. The co-creators of Superman and *Action Comics* settled their first suit with DC Comics for only $94,000, clarifying the rights to the character for the period from the late 1940s until the 1990s.[154] A subsequent suit initially settled for payments of more than $8.5 million between 2001 and 2013, a period in which the Superman character earned hundreds of millions of dollars in revenue.[155] As the *Captain America Comics* copyright came up for renewal in 1968–9, the character's co-creator Joe Simon reportedly settled with Marvel for a modest $7,500.[156] In 2003, Marvel Enterprises settled with the Simon family yet again, securing all rights to the

[149] Landes, note 146, at 274.
[150] Michele Roth-Kauffman, *The Physician Assistant's Business Practice and Legal Guide* (Jones & Bartlett Publishers, 2006) at 393 ("Written employment agreements are becoming more common. Employment agreements can be very complex.").
[151] Stephen Fishman, *Copyright Your Software* (Nolo Press, 2nd ed. 1998) at 11–16; Inphonic, Inc., Form of Assignment of Invention, Nondisclosure and Noncompetition Agreement (2015), http://contracts .onecle.com/inphonic/noncomp.shtml.
[152] Steven Cherensky, Comment. A penny for their thoughts: Employee-inventors, preinvention assignment agreements, property, and personhood, 81 *California Law Review* 595 (1993) at 627.
[153] Ibid., at 599, 619–20.
[154] Stewart Bishop, Superman heirs claim settlement with DC Comics isn't valid, *Law360*, March 5, 2013, www.law360.com/articles/420941/superman-heirs-claim-settlement-with-dc-comics-isn-t-valid; *Superman movies at the box office*, Box Office Mojo (August 26, 2015), www.boxofficemojo.com/ franchises/chart/?id=superman.htm (*Superman Returns* earned $248 million at box office, adjusted for ticket price inflation, starting in June 2006); Alex Ben Block, Which superhero earns $1.3 billion a year?, *Hollywood Reporter*, November 13, 2014, www.hollywoodreporter.com/news/superhero-earns-13-billion-a-748281 (Superman-licensed products earned about $277 million per year in 2012–13).
[155] *Larson v. Warner Bros. Entertainment, Inc.*, No. 2:04-cv-08400-ODW, Docket No. 709-2 (C.D. Cal. objection filed March 4, 2013), www.scribd.com/doc/128611632/Settlement-rejection-by-Siegel-heirs-March-4-2013.
[156] Kristen Acuna, Erin Fuchs, and Aly Weisman, This genius helped create The Avengers, X-Men, Captain America, Hulk, and Thor – And his family wants to get paid, *Business Insider*, June 7, 2014, http://finance.yahoo.com/news/heirs-co-creator-avengers-x-125733275.html.

character, which then appeared in a string of blockbuster films.[157] These disputes were a blip on Marvel's ascent from a company valued in the millions in the mid-1980s to one valued in the billions in the mid-2000s.[158] In 2014, Marvel Comics settled with the family of Mr. Kirby, as co-creator of *Captain America* as well as *The Incredible Hulk*, Iron Man, and *The X-Men*, on terms that were reported as "amicabl[e]" and which apparently did not prevent Marvel's parent Disney from earning record profits in 2014.[159]

There is no reason to fear a "nightmare" in film and television markets if authors get their copyrights back. Despite uncertainty about the assignability of the renewal right under the 1909 Act, a market for the renewal rights of authors and heirs existed even then.[160] Since then, the courts have repeatedly held that assignments of future interests in copyrighted characters are valid despite strong language in the Copyright Act to the contrary.[161] As George R.R. Martin, author of the epic fantasy novels in the series *A Song of Ice and Fire*, has pointed out, authors do not currently have the power to make excessive demands on producers: "if you're not J.K. Rowling, and you

---

[157] Bloomberg News, *Dispute over Captain America is settled*, The New York Times, September 30, 2003, www.nytimes.com/2003/09/30/business/media/30MARV.html.

[158] Adam Bryant, Pow! The punches that left Marvel reeling, The New York Times,May 24, 1998, at 4; Brooks Barnes and Michael Cieply, Disney to buy Marvel and its 5,000 characters for $4 billion, The New York Times, August 31, 2009, www.nytimes.com/2009/09/01/business/media/01disney .html; Jonathan Hicks, Marvel comic book unit being sold for $82.5 million, The New York Times, November 8, 1988, www.nytimes.com/1988/11/08/business/the-media-business-marvel-comic-book-unit-being-sold-for-82.5-million.html; MacAndrews & Forbes Holdings Inc. History, *in International Directory of Company Histories*, vol. 28 (1999), www.fundinguniverse.com/company-histories/ macandrews-forbes-holdings-inc-history/.

[159] Ethan Sacks, *Marvel, Jack Kirby estate settle bitter legal feud over character copyrights*, The New York Daily News, September 26, 2014, www.nydailynews.com/entertainment/movies/ marvel-jack-kirby-estate-settle-bitter-legal-feud-character-copyrights-article-1.1954408.

[160] US Copyright Office, Library of Congress, *Copyright Law Revision: Report of the Register of Copyrights on the General Revision of the U.S. Copyright Law* (Government Printing Office, 1961), at 539, www.copyright.gov/history/1961_registers_report.pdf [hereinafter 1961 Revision Report]. Some uncertainty was arguably resolved in 1943. Fred Fisher Music Co. v. M. Witmark & Sons, 318 U.S. 643 (1943) (holding renewal right to be assignable). Some uncertainty remained because under the Court's opinion, publishers or other assignees still needed the author who executed an assignment of the renewal term to survive until that time. Ibid., at 950–2 & n.3, citing Fox Film Corp. v. Knowles, 261 U.S. 326 (1923).

[161] Penguin Group (USA) Inc. v. Steinbeck, 537 F.3d 193, 200–4 (2d Cir. 2008) (holding that the 1994 agreement prevented heirs of author from terminating the 1938 transfer of rights under copyright, despite language in Copyright Act indicating that heirs may terminate such transfers notwithstanding an agreement to the contrary), citing 17 U.S.C. § 304(c)(5); Classic Media, Inc. v. Mewborn, 532 F.3d 978, 984 (9th Cir. 2008) (reaffirming that: "The Supreme Court [has] held that the assignment of the contingent renewal right was valid and enforceable, despite the rationale underlying the renewal structure itself of providing a second chance for authors."), citing Fred Fisher Music, 318 U.S. 643; Milne ex rel. Coyne v. Stephen Slesinger, Inc., 430 F.3d 1036, 1048 (9th Cir. 2005) (holding that 1983 agreement prevented heirs of author from terminating the 1930 and 1961 transfers of merchandising and film rights, respectively, despite language in Copyright Act indicating that heirs may terminate such transfers notwithstanding an agreement to the contrary), citing 17 U.S.C. § 304(c)(5).

insist on all those things, the studios are not going to be very interested or less studios will be interested in it so you'll get less money or none at all."[162] Authors may very well feel compelled to "sell them the book and what [the producers] do with it is what they do with it and you have to live with it."[163] Hollywood contracts use stand-ardized terms to transfer all ancillary rights, all future derivatives, etc., regardless of whether the rights are exploited or completely abandoned.[164]

Abrogation of the work-made-for-hire doctrine would simplify the assessment of public domain status, and bring some authors' entire oeuvres out of copyright. It would and reduce of the number of works subject to fixed terms of ninety-five years from publication, or an initial term of twenty-nine years and renewal term of sixty-seven years. The benefit of the life-plus term of copyrighted works that are not for-hire works is that all of an author's works enter the public domain at the same time, unless they were co-authored or published anonymously.[165] The existence of the work-made-for-hire doctrine introduces a great deal of variation in copyright terms.[166] Works made for hire may be renewed more frequently.[167] This is vital because most works that entered the public domain between about 1923 and 2019 were those that were published before 1964 but not renewed in a timely manner pursuant to the 1909 Act.[168]

It could be that in some cases, public-domain status would arrive sooner when authors retain their authorship. In cases when an author died long before twenty-five years have passed since publication of a work, public-domain status would arrive sooner with individual authorship than under the current test of ninety-five years

---

[162] Quoted in Dave Hoffman, George R. R. Martin on copyright, inheritance, and creative control, *Concurring Opinions* (April 2, 2014), http://concurringopinions.com/archives/2014/04/george-r-r-martin-on-copyright-inheritance-and-creative-control.html.

[163] Ibid.

[164] American Bar Association, Option and purchase agreement – underlying rights (2011), www.americanbar .org/content/dam/aba/migrated/2011_build/entertainment_sports/option_and_purchase_agreement. authcheckdam.pdf; Martin Fern, *Warren's Forms of Agreements: Fern's Desk Edition* (LexisNexis, 2017), https://books.google.com/books?id=X3CgkPG-4gC&pg=PT1408#v=onepage&q&f=false; Todd VanDerWerff, Daniel Knauf tells us his plan for the end of Carnivàle, *AV Club* (February 22, 2013), https://tv.avclub.com/daniel-knauf-tells-us-his-plan-for-the-end-of-carnivale-1798236491/.

[165] US Copyright Office, note 160, at 53; US Copyright Office, Library of Congress, *General Guide to the Copyright Act of 1976* (Government Printing Office, 1977) at 2:4.

[166] US Copyright Office, note 160, at 54; Melanie Dulong de Rosnay and Juan Carlos De Martin (Eds.), *The Digital Public Domain: Foundations for an Open Culture* (Open Book Publishers, 2012) at xvii. European and U.S. law has been harmonized, however, for copyrights in works authored by individual natural persons, at life plus seventy years. 17 U.S.C. § 302(c) (2003); Directive 2001/29 on the harmonization of certain aspects of copyright and related rights in the information society, OJ L167/10, June 22, 2001.

[167] *Eldred*, 537 U.S. at 269 (Breyer, J., dissenting), citing Edward Rappaport, *Copyright Term Extension: Estimating the Economic Values* (Congressional Research Service, 1998) at 13–14.

[168] Ibid., at 241 (Stevens., J., dissenting); U.S. Copyright Office, Library of Congress, *Renewal of Copyright Circular* (2012), www.copyright.gov/circs/circ15.pdf (renewal now automatic for works published since 1964).

from publication.[169] The Copyright Office estimated in 1961 that the typical author of a popular musical composition dies within twenty years of publication.[170] On average, authors who died between 1930 and 1955 lived only four years after their last book was published.[171] Holding the work-made-for-hire doctrine unconstitutional may therefore increase the size of the public domain in copyright, and save consumers and new creators millions in licensing fees.[172]

Respecting individual authorship may enable many more creators to enjoy the renewal and termination rights designed for them by Congress, thereby furthering legislative intent. Courts embracing the "instance and expense" test to do away with the renewal rights of employees have arguably disrespected legislative intent under the 1909 Act. Similarly, they have blunted the congressional purpose to enable authors to terminate transfers to publishers and others so that authors may share in the windfall created by the extending the term of copyright to life plus 50 or about seventy-five years under the 1976 Act, and to either life plus seventy or about ninety-five years under the 1998 Act.

The expanded work-made-for-hire doctrine nullifies the renewal copyright interest in many cases, thereby altering the structure of every copyright issued until 1978. Copyrights reverted to the author from the purchaser of an assignment or license, for the second half of the maximum fifty-six-year term under the 1909 Act.[173] The reversion was automatic prior to 1978, but the 1976 Act (effective in 1978) required service of "advance notice."[174] Under both the traditional framework and the 1976 Act, the renewal right (subsequently the termination right) offered authors the chance to escape licenses or assignments, which had been made for small sums relative to a work's value over the long term.[175]

---

[169] 17 U.S.C. § 302(c) (2003) (copyright term of seventy years after death of author in case of a natural person claiming authorship, life plus ninety-five years from publication in case of published work made for hire or anonymous or pseudonymous work, and 120 years from creation in case of unpublished work made for hire or anonymous work); Copyright Term Extension Act (CTEA), Pub. L. 105-298, §§ 102(b) and (d), 112 Stat. 2827–8 (amending 17 U. S. C. §§ 302, 304) (containing these amendments to 1976 act).

[170] US Copyright Office, note 160, at 55.

[171] Ibid.

[172] *Eldred*, 537 U.S. at 248–9 (noting that extension of copyrights to cover copyrights between fifty-five and seventy-five years old generates $400 million in additional royalties to copyright holders, for an average of $20 million for each year that public domain shrinks in scope, while "many billions of royalties" would be saved by limiting duration of copyright to either life plus fifty or seventy-five from publication). Justice Breyer (at 266) has argued that a longer copyright term restricts the accessibility of works that could be widely disseminated at low cost using new technologies such as Web sites and digital libraries.

[173] 1909 Act, § 24; H.R. Rep. No. 94–1476, http://web.archive.org/web/20141210072853/http://uscode.house.gov/view.xhtml?req=granuleid:USC-prelim-title17-section203&num=0&edition=prelim.

[174] Ibid.

[175] Ibid. "A provision of this sort is needed because of the unequal bargaining position of authors, resulting in part from the impossibility of determining a work's value until it has been exploited. Section 203 reflects a practical compromise that will further the objectives of the copyright law while recognizing

Section 203 of the 1976 Act stated that an author, or a majority of two or more co-authors, could terminate a copyright transfer beginning at the end of thirty-five years from the date of the transfer by serving and recording a written notice between 2 and 10 years before termination is due to occur.[176] The termination rights under sections 203 and 304 do not apply to works made for hire.[177] Narrowing the work-made-for-hire doctrine would revive the renewal and termination rights of authors working at another's expense.

Moreover, an originalist view of authorship may reduce the scope of the orphan works problem and expand the accessibility of out-of-print works. The orphan works problem refers to the inaccessibility of works under copyright, particularly due to extended copyright terms since 1978 and 1998, which created a twilight zone in which works are not in the public domain but are out of print and very difficult to license for use.[178] The problem is greatly exacerbated by the fact that bankruptcy or dissolution of the corporate owner of a work made for hire may result in licensing being more difficult that it would have been had the author been the individual author of a work, who might have been found.[179] If the author was a human person, directories of people and probate records could be used to trace

the problems and legitimate needs of all interests involved." (emphasis added in original) (quoting legislative history of 1909 Act); U.S. Department of Justice, Copyright – Renewals and extensions, 6057 *Congressional Edition* 136, 141 (1910) (It not infrequently happens that the author sells his copyright outright to a publisher for a comparatively small sum. If the work proves to be a great success and lives beyond the term of twenty-eight years your committee felt that it should be the exclusive right of the author to take the renewal term and *the law should be framed as is the existing law so that he could not be deprived of that right.*) (emphasis added in original) (quoting legislative history of 1909 Act).

[176] 17 U.S.C. § 203. Section 203 permits termination of grants about thirty-five years after assignment or license, or forty years if publication involved. It applies to post-1978 copyrights only.

[177] Ibid. See also H.R. Rep. No. 94-1476, http://uscode.house.gov/view.xhtml?req=granuleid:USC-prelim-title17-section203&num=0&edition=prelim.

[178] US Copyright Office, *Report on Orphan Works* (Government Printing Office, 2006) at 15 (orphan works is a "term used to describe the situation where the owner of a copyrighted work cannot be identified and located by someone who wishes to make use of the work in a manner that requires the permission of the copyright owner"). A broader and arguably more useful definition of "orphan works" should include other works that are not commercially viable to distribute or to license for lawful distribution, although they could be very useful to researchers, teachers, technological innovators like Google, and transformative users. Katharina de la Durantaye, Orphan works: A comparative and international perspective, *in* Daniel Gervais (Ed.), *International Intellectual Property: A Handbook of Contemporary Research* (Elgar, 2015) at 212–13, citing French and German laws on out-of-print works, French Intellectual Property L., art. L.134-1, and German Act on Collective Rights Management, §13d-e & I-II). Digitization of orphan works makes it easier to research a region's cultural heritage and use it productively. Directive 2012/28/EU, art. 6(1)-6(2).

[179] Dennis Khong, Orphan works, abandonware, and the missing market for copyrighted goods, 15, *International Journal of Law & Information Technology* 54 (2007); Dennis Khong, Abandonware, *in* Aaron Schwabach (Ed.), *Internet and the Law: Technology, Society, and Compromises* (ABC-CLIO, 2014) at 1–2.

ownership down to the current address of the author or his or her heirs.[180] Records on the windup of a business by private contractual means or repossession of property may be more difficult to find, and held as trade secrets or other confidential information.[181]

The work-made-for-hire doctrine could reduce the market and monopoly power of corporate aggregations of copyrights, which have repeatedly been used to fix prices, suppress digital output, and exclude retail competition.[182] Collections of copyrights may confer monopolies upon their collectors.[183] The record labels, for example, argued in the process leading to the 1976 Act that a compulsory license for cover songs (more formally, the making of musical compositions into new recordings) is necessary to ensure "a variety of recordings of any musical work," which would otherwise be monopolized by companies owning exclusive licenses.[184] Between 1970 and 1972, some motion-picture studios and television networks accused one another of conspiring to monopolize film and television production, and to inflate prices wrongfully.[185] Today, companies like Amazon, Apple, and Google are sometimes charged with abusing market power.[186]

Fragmenting and distributing the power created by copyrights may provide more options to startups and sole proprietors. For example, the termination right under section 203 may boost the availability of ebooks by up to 50 percent, as many scholars expected.[187]

---

[180] Maria-Daphne Papadopoulou, The issue of "orphan works" in digital libraries, *in* Ioanni Iglezakis (ed.), *E-Publishing and Digital Libraries: Legal and Organizational Issues* (IGI Global, 2010) at 230.

[181] See ibid.

[182] Hannibal Travis, Free speech institutions and fair use of copyrighted work: A new agenda for copyright reform, 33 *Cardozo Arts and Entertainment Law Journal* 673 (2016) at 718–9.

[183] US Copyright Office, note 160, at 5 ("The real danger of monopoly might arise when many works of the same kind are pooled and controlled together.").

[184] US Copyright Office, note 160, at 34.

[185] Kerry Segrave, *Movies at Home: How Hollywood Came to Television* (McFarland, 1999) at 108.

[186] *United States v. Apple, Inc.*, 791 F.3d 290 (2d Cir. 2015) (alleging that Apple's agreements to license eBooks for iBookstore led to conspiracy to raise and fix new-release and bestseller eBook prices sometime between 2009 and 2012); Press Release, European Commission, Antitrust: Commission Sends Statement of Objections to Google on Comparison Shopping Service; Opens Separate Formal Investigation on Android (April 15, 2015), http://europa.eu/rapid/press-release_IP-15-4780_en.htm (European Commission opened investigation into whether proprietary interest in Google's Android operating system and Google applications was abused to maintain market power in smartphone operating system software); Greg Bensinger and Jeffrey A. Trachtenberg, *Authors group seeks DOJ probe of Amazon*, The Wall Street Journal, August 20, 2015, www.wsj.com/articles/authors-group-seeks-doj-probe-of-amazon-1440090438?tesla=y; Farhad Manjoo, *Tech's 'frightful 5' will dominate digital life for the foreseeable future*, The New York Times, January 20, 2016, www.nytimes.com/2016/01/21/technology/techs-frightful-5-will-dominate-digital-life-for-foreseeable-future.html.

[187] Paul Heald, *Copyright reversion to authors (and the Rosetta effect): An empirical study of reappearing books*, Social Science Research Network (2017) at 4–5, 24, 42, https://ssrn.com/abstract_id=3084920.

2.5. POLICY RESPONSES TO PROBLEMS OF CREATIVE COLLABORATION

The work-made-for-hire doctrine is often justified by reference to its convenience.[188] "This rule may be said to have in its favor simplicity and definiteness in result, once an employment relationship is established." Its operation is welcomed by producers and is said to be consistent with what would be achieved in its absence by "contract or trade custom."[189] A study conducted by the US Patent Office in the 1950s indicated that corporations already by then claimed to be the "authors" of the vast majority of magazines and motion pictures.[190] The reliance interests of these parties may persuade judges not to do away with the doctrine, despite its conflict with the Constitution.[191]

Reliance on doctrines of corporate or other organizational authorship does not necessarily justify the unconstitutional aspects of the work-made-for-hire doctrine. In one famous case, a commissioning party had apparently relied upon the for-hire status of a sculpture in filing a copyright registration for the work in its own name, but the Supreme Court held that the statutory requisites for its authorship had not been satisfied, because: "Strict adherence to the language and structure of the Act is particularly appropriate where, as here, a statute is the result of a series of carefully crafted compromises."[192] It is even more "appropriate" to insist upon "strict adherence" to a constitutional provision such as the Authors and Inventors Clause, which formed part of the compromise that created Congress itself.[193]

Doctrines other than work-made-for-hire, particularly in its sweeping "instance and expense" form, may vindicate reliance interests of proprietors. Implied assignment, joint authorship, and equitable ownership could provide

---

[188] H.R. Rep. No. 94-1976, http://web.archive.org/web/20141210072853/ http://uscode.house.gov/view .xhtml?req=granuleid:USC-prelim-title17-section201&num=0&edition=prelim (rejecting authors' objections to the doctrine in desire to avoid "uncertainties" or "reopen[ing] a number of other issues"). See generally Borge Varmer, Work made for hire and on commission, *in* Borge Varmer (Ed.), *Copyright Law Revision: Studies Prepared for the Subcommittee on Patents, Trademarks, and Copyrights of the Committee on the Judiciary*, U.S. Senate, 86th Cong., 2d Sess., Pursuant to S. Res. 240; Study 13 (Government Printing Office, 1960), www.copyright.gov/history/studies/study13.pdf [hereinafter Varmer].

[189] Ibid., at 149.

[190] Ibid., at 144–5.

[191] Cf. *United States* v. *Gaudin*, 515 U.S. 506, 521 (1995) (suggesting that force of stare decisis is greatest where private parties may have adjusted their primary conduct based on precedent); *Payne* v. *Tennessee*, 501 U.S. 808, 828 (1991) ("Considerations in favor of stare decisis are at their acme in cases involving property and contract rights, where reliance interests are involved.").

[192] CCNV, 490 U.S. at 749 n.14, citing *Rodriguez* v. *Compass Shipping Co.*, 451 U.S. 596, 617 (1981); *United States* v. *Sisson*, 399 U.S. 267, 291, 298 (1970).

[193] Cf. *Payne*, 501 U.S. at 842 (Souter, J., concurring) ("[O]ur 'considered practice [has] not [been] to apply stare decisis as rigidly in constitutional [cases] as in nonconstitutional cases ... .'") (quoting *Glidden Co.* v. *Zdanok*, 370 U.S. 530, 543 (1962)); *Edelman*, 415 U.S. at 671 ("Since we deal with a constitutional question, we are less constrained by the principle of stare decisis than we are in other areas of the law.").

most employers with more than sufficient control over and rewards for employee works.

In patent law, despite the vesting of inventions in their actual producers rather than the employers of inventors, many employers have successfully used implied license theories as a shield from litigation. In 1843, the Supreme Court held that employment for wages creates a presumption of a license to the employer.[194] This implied license could stop employees from alleging patent infringement on the part of their employers.[195] Moreover, an employer enjoyed an implied assignment of an invention that a person was hired "to invent."[196] This rule differs from the work-made-for-hire-doctrine in that invention simply within the scope of employment does not suffice.[197]

An employment agreement was not only a shield against employee suits, but a potential basis for offensive suits against employees or infringers under the theory of implied assignment. "Where there is no agreement *or implied understanding* that what is produced shall belong to the employer, it is clear that the latter acquires no title to the copyright."[198] If literary property vests in employee–authors, they yet may be under an obligation to permit an employer to use the property for the purposes for which it was created. The employer might then be able to sue the author for breach of contract if he or she did not permit the work to be used.[199] Similarly, an employer could sue third parties under a theory of equitable title.

Prior to 1909, it was not difficult to obtain a license, so the default vesting of authorship in the individual writer did not impede the growth of literature. A license could be oral, but an assignment had to be in writing.[200] These assignments could entitle employers to copyright interests without pretending that they were the "authors" of the litigated works.[201] Courts held that a pre-term assignment of a copyright was valid under common-law principles.[202]

The necessity of an assignment of some kind accords with the resolution of prominent recent cases involving new ventures like Carter Bryant's Bratz and Mark Zuckerberg's Facebook. The latter case forms part of the inspiration for the book *The Social Network*, in which Zuckerberg, the Winklevoss twins, and Divya Narendra battle for ownership of the concept and code that allowed a Harvard University-based

---

[194] *McClurg v. Kingsland*, 42 U.S. (1 How.) 202 (1843).
[195] *Gill v. United States*, 160 U.S. 426 (1896).
[196] *Dubilier Condenser Corp.*, 289 U.S. 178, 188 (1933).
[197] Ibid.; Cherensky, note 152, at 617.
[198] Drone, note 31, at 258, citing *Boucicault*, 5 Blatchf. at 95 (emphasis added).
[199] Drone, note 31, at 258.
[200] *Magnuson v. Video Yesteryear*, 85 F. 3d 1424, 1428 (9th Cir. 1996); Curtis, note 30, at 222–4, citing *Storace v. Longman*, 2 Campb. 27, n.; *Latour v. Bland*, 2 Starke's N.P.C. 382; *Power v. Walker*, 4 Campb. 8; *Rundell v. Murray*, Jacobs R. 311).
[201] Megaarden, note 70, at 542.
[202] Hale, note 31, at 1051.

social network to go global.[203] In part, the lawsuit foundered, and perhaps settled, because of uncertainty about the terms of the parties' contract, and Zuckerberg's independent contractor status with respect to ConnectU and thefacebook.com.[204] Had the ConnectU parties been able to produce a clear contractual entitlement to Zuckerberg's work product, the judge might have ruled in their favor and set the stage for a different ending to the film *The Social Network*.[205] The suit settled amid charges of legal malpractice, misrepresentation, and nondisclosure of documents in the period leading up to the negotiations.[206] In the Bratz case, an initial crushing victory for Mattel on the grounds that Bryant's designs of new dolls while he worked for the company were its property gave way to a Ninth Circuit decision that the ownership of the dolls depended on the terms of his assignment agreement with Mattel, not on the mere fact that they were produced by an employee.[207] The opinion did not doubt that copyrighted expression produced by an employee within the scope of the employment relationship belongs to an employer, but underlined uncertainties in the interpretation of the employment agreement and evidence that creating new dolls was not within the scope of Bryant's employment as a Barbie Collectibles fashion and hair designer.[208] There is something appealing to common sense or societal expectations, it seems, in a commissioned worker like Zuckerberg or a paid designer like Bryant being able to negotiate the terms of their rights. On the other hand, the instance and expense rule is arguably at odds with social mores.[209]

The idea of implied contracting as a solution to the problem of for-hire works is not new.[210] In enacting a revised work-for-hire doctrine in the Copyright Act of 1976, Congress noted that composers and screenwriters proposed an alternative that would

---

[203] Sony Pictures, Screenplay for The Social Network (2010), http://flash.sonypictures.com/video/movies/thesocialnetwork/awards/thesocialnetwork_screenplay.pdf.

[204] Jason Pontin, *Who owns the concept if no one signs the papers?*, The New York Times, August 12, 2007, www.nytimes.com/2007/08/12/business/yourmoney/12stream.html?_r=1 (noting that judge seemed inclined to agree that there was no binding written contract in evidence three years into the suit, while an IP attorney opined that had Zuckerberg been an employee, more of thefacebook.com's and ConnectU's source code would have belonged to the ConnectU owners).

[205] Pontin, note 204 (describing how at a key hearing, federal judge hearing ConnectU's case was concerned with its "inability to provide documentary evidence" of a binding agreement).

[206] Miguel Helft, *Twins' Facebook fight rages on*, The New York Times, December 30, 2010, www.nytimes.com/2010/12/31/business/31twins.html?src=me&ref=homepage.

[207] *Mattel, Inc.* v. *MGA Entertainment, Inc.*, 616 F.3d 904, 912–13, 917 (9th Cir. 2010).

[208] Ibid.,at 912 n. 7. In a footnote, the court rejected Mattel's argument that "because employers are already considered the authors of works made for hire under the Copyright Act, 17 U.S.C. § 201(b), the agreement must cover works made outside the scope of employment. Otherwise, employees would be assigning to Mattel works the company already owns."

[209] My intention here is not to say that the result in these cases necessitates a ruling that the work-made-for-hire doctrine is unconstitutional, merely to say that business and investment goes on amidst uncertainty about it, and alongside a significant role for written contracts assigning rights in creative expression.

[210] Cf. *Dielman*, 2012 Fed. at 894 (where artist sells a work on commission, courts will imply "unrestricted right" to reproduce it as a result of "sale," not authorship by commissioning party).

have much the same effect. As in patent law, an employer could be regarded as the beneficiary of an implied contract to permit the use of the employee's work within the scope of the employer's business, but all other rights would remain with the actual author.[211] Congress rejected this proposal as being contrary to then-existing law, and as having "highly conjectural" benefits from employees' point of view.[212] Yet Congress changed existing law, and extended these "conjectural benefits" to authors of commissioned works of sculpture, literature, or music.[213]

Corporations owned most patents issued in a seventeen-year period leading up to a mid-1950s survey, but there was no work-made-for-hire doctrine in patent law.[214] Instead, the doctrine of implied assignment or the implied duty to assign in consideration for employment to invent the device or innovation often resulted in corporate ownership of the patent.[215]

A commissioning or employing party that desired to retain an authorship interest in work fixed by a contractor or employee need only merge its own contributions with the other party to become a joint author and guarantee the status of co-owner.[216] A joint author obtains the right to issue licenses and a share in the profits flowing from exploitation of the work.[217] All that a commissioning or employing party must put into the work to become a co-author is a significant amount of creative expression.[218]

With joint author status, the commissioning or employing party would be immune from suit for infringement by a co-author.[219] If a work is truly prepared at the instance of another, it should not be too difficult for that inspiring or ordering party to insist on a certain level of creative contribution and control.[220] In 1976,

---

[211] Copyright Law Revision, H.R. Rep. No. 1476, 94th Cong., 2d Sess. 120–1 (1976).

[212] Ibid.

[213] 17 U.S.C. §§ 101, 201(b).

[214] Barkey Sanders, Joseph Rossman, and L. James Harris, Patent acquisition by corporations, 3 *Patent & Trademark Office Journal of Research and Education* 217, 217 (1959).

[215] Varmer, note 188, at 140 ("However, if an employee is hired specifically for the purpose of making a particular invention, or if during his employment he is specifically assigned to work on an invention, the employer is considered to be entitled to ownership of the patent and may compel the employee to assign to him the patent secured by the employee.").

[216] 17 U.S.C. § 201(a).

[217] *Brownstein v. Lindsay*, 742 F.3d 55, 68–9 (3d Cir. 2014); *Davis v. Blige*, 505 F.3d 90, 99–100 (2d Cir. 2007).

[218] *Brownstein*, 742 F.3d at 64–5; *Childress v. Taylor*, 945 F.2d 500, 504–8 (2d Cir. 1991).

[219] *Brownstein*, 742 F.3d at 68–9; *MacLean Associates, Inc. v. Wm. M. Mercer-Meidinger-Hansen, Inc.*, 952 F.2d 769, 778 (3d Cir. 1991); *Cortner v. Israel*, 732 F.2d 267, 271 (2d Cir. 1984).

[220] Indeed, the exercise of this control used to be part of the test for work-made-for-hire status under the 1909 Act, for a time. *Easter Seal Society*, 815 F. 2d 323, 331–336 (5th Cir. 1987) (describing "actual control" test regarding for-hire status of independent contractors' works under *Aldon Accessories Ltd. v. Spiegel, Inc.*, 738 F.2d 548 (2d Cir.), *cert. denied*, 469 U.S. 982 (1984)); *Evans Newton Inc. v. Chicago Sys. Software*, 793 F.2d 889, 894 (7th Cir. 1986) (affirming finding of work-made-for-hire status where trial court found that programmers "merely used their programming skills to produce the work according to [employer]'s specifications"). But see *Easter Seal Society*, 815 F.2d at 335–6

Congress defined joint authors as those who intend to merge their respective creative expression into an interrelated whole.[221] Meanwhile, joint authorship avoids the travesty that the author "who did all that was done in the way of drawing [or other expression] can be excluded from all participation in the authorship of the thing drawn by him [or her]."[222]

Joint authorship is a workable framework for producing copyrightable works. In 1988, the D.C. Circuit found joint authorship to exist as between the commissioning party who provided the outlines of a sculpture project, and the sculptor who did the work for the most part using his own skills, tools, and time.[223] All that a joint author needs to do to avoid the obligation to account for profits earned from a joint work is to buy out the actual authors' interests, just like proprietors do when an author exercises termination rights under the 1976 or 1998 Acts.[224]

Equitable ownership is another solution. Section 506 of the Copyright Act of 1976 confers standing on either the legal or the "beneficial" owner of an exclusive right.[225] Beneficial ownership results from a relationship of trust, as in situations when a trustee is supposed to act for the benefit of a person.[226] The underlying intuition or policy objective – that a person may have a duty to administer a property interest or legal right on behalf of another – seems to have influenced the copyright and patent jurisprudence of the nineteenth century.[227] It may be well suited to accommodating the interests of employing or commissioning parties with those of authors, short of using the "instance and expense" test.

According to a helpful discussion in a case addressing situations in which one person dictates the outline of a work to another person who executes it, a relationship of trust is thereby created. The collaboration leads to a shared interest in a work, with

---

("[T]he lack of actual control over the production of a given work – and perhaps even the right to control production – will not make an independent contractor out of an employee."); *Murray*, 566 F.2d at 1310 ("Actual exercise of [the] right [to direct and supervise the manner in which the work was being performed] is not controlling, and copyright is vested in the employer who has no intention of overseeing the detailed activity of any employee hired for the very purpose of producing the material.").

[221] H.R. Rep. No. 14-1476. See Copyright Law Revision, note 211.

[222] *Kenrick v. Lawrence* (1890) 25 Q. B. D. 99, 106.

[223] *Community for Creative Non-Violence*, 846 F.2d 1485, 1494–8 (D.C. Cir. 1988).

[224] Neu, note 92, at 385.

[225] 17 U.S.C. § 501(b) (2013) ("The legal or beneficial owner of an exclusive right under a copyright is entitled ... to institute an action for any infringement of that particular right committed while he or she is the owner of it.").

[226] William Blackstone, *Blackstone's Commentaries on the Laws of England*, vol. 3 (St. George Tucker, (Ed.), Birch & Small, 1803) at 203, citing *Bowerman v. Sybourn* (1796) 7 T. R. 2, 4 R.R. 363 (Lord Kenyon); Jeremy Bentham, Observations on the Actual State of the English Law of Real Property, with the Outline of a Code. By James Humphreys, of Lincoln's Inn, Barrister. 8vo. Murray. London, Westminster Review, Oct. 1826, at 446, 503–4.

[227] *Independent Wireless Tel. Co. v. Radio Corp. of Amer.*, 269 U.S. 459,468–9 (1926); *Litchfield v. Perry*, 88 U.S. 205, 227 (1875).

the person named on the copyright application becoming "a trustee for all the true owners."[228]

In extreme circumstances, a federal court could compel an author to assign a copyright to prevent an inequity being done. In one case, the court concluded that "equitable title may vest in one person to the labors of another, where the relations of the parties are such that the former is entitled to an assignment of the production," for example when the widow of an author hired an editor/writer to prepare a text for publication, which was then infringed.[229] Another court stated that the legal and equitable interests in a work may be divided among several parties, with courts protecting equitable title as "proprietorship."[230] Likewise, a judge declared that a plaintiff who reached an agreement concerning a publication with the defendant "would have been the author ... although a court of equity might have called on him to transfer the copyright to [defendant]."[231] This line of cases seems to date back to the English chancery courts prior to 1814.[232] Finally, a federal court sitting in equity declared that authorship and ownership may be divided, and that equity may compel the parties to abide by the terms of their contracts.[233]

Key players in Congress may come to believe that a new copyright statute is needed. A new section of the Copyright Act could better protect authors as the Framers intended. It could treat authors and inventors in similar ways, thereby respecting the decision of the Framers to recognize their rights in a common constitutional provision.

Six decades ago, entertainment industry practitioner and copyright expert Melville Nimmer proposed an exclusive license solution for works made for hire. The solution would have codified existing collective bargaining practices in the US television industry as a statutory allocation of the benefits of authorship. Four principles of the solution were: (1) employers would enjoy exclusive licenses to exploit works in the industry or medium in which they do business; (2) an employee would be prohibited from granting competitive licenses for a reasonable time assessed by reference to the marketability of the employer's works; (3) authors of commissioned and for-hire works as well as independent contractors would be protected from contracts divesting them in their interest in stories they devised on their own as opposed to being created and dictated to them by an employer or a commissioning party; and (4) where the employer created and dictated the idea of a story to an employee,

[228] *Maurel*, 220 F. at 215–16, *aff'd*, 271 F. 211 (2d Cir. 1921). See also Richard Spencer and Wildred Stone, Creating and preserving a copyright, 14 *Notre Dame Law Review* 362 (1939) at 366–74; J. L. Plattner, Who may secure a copyright?, 37 *Notre Dame Law Review* 362 (1961).
[229] *Lawrence*, 15 F. Cas. at 50–1; Megaarden, note 70, at 548.
[230] *Little*, 15 F. Cas. at 613.
[231] *Hazlitt v. Templeman* (Q. B. 1866) 13 Law Times New Series 595, 1866 Eng. Rep. Ann. 3241, 3244.
[232] Drone, note 31, at 302.
[233] *Pulte v. Derby*, 20 F. Cas. 51, 51–3 (C.C. S.D. Ohio 1852).

the parties could agree in writing to ownership by the employer, thereby overriding default rules (1)–(3).[234]

An amended section 201 of the Copyright Act could give employers an exclusive license to employee works for a reasonable period, subject to reversion to the actual author as contemplated by Congress in the 1909 and 1976 Acts. Given the rise of copyright conglomerates, measures to rebalance power relations in the industry are timely.[235]

---

[234] Nimmer, note 136, at 153.

[235] Cf. James Gaskin, *Corporate Politics and the Internet* (Prentice-Hall, 1997) at 208 ("'Copyright conglomerates' such as Time Warner and Disney-ABC are attempting to redefine the laws of copyright in new and aggressive ways."); Stephanie Haney, Total domination! Disney and Fox films accounted for 90 PERCENT of this weekend's box office take as their combined power is revealed to Hollywood, The Daily Mail, December 18, 2017 (update), www.dailymail.co.uk/news/article-5189153/Disney-Fox-films-90-percent-weekend-box-office.html; William Kunz, *Culture Conglomerates: Consolidation in the Motion Picture and Television Industries* (Rowman & Littlefield, 2007) at 1–4, 28–34. See generally James Gilmore & Matthias Stork, *Superhero Synergies: Comic Book Characters Go Digital* (Rowman & Littlefield, 2014); Patti McCarthy, *The Lucas Effect: George Lucas and the New Hollywood* (Tenco Press, 2014); Janet Wasko, *How Hollywood Works* (Sage, 2005).

3

Independent Invention and Its Discontents

3.1. PATENT LAW IN THE SOCIAL MEDIA AGE

Even during the heyday of social media innovation, underwritten by the patent system that facilitated the rise of Silicon Valley, big companies began attacking that very system. Too many patents had been granted and the cost of dealing with them was too high for investors, a coalition of technology companies told the Supreme Court in mid-2006, just as the social media explosion of the past fifteen years was accelerating.

An alliance of multinational technology corporations, including Google, Microsoft, and Verizon, made five key points about patents in a filing with the Supreme Court. First, while making more inventions patentable appears to benefit inventors, it harms those who want to own patents while denying their competitors the same privilege. Second, "important" patents are threatened by "minor" ones. Third, the owners of "important" patents do not want to "share revenues with the improvers" of their technologies. Fourth, there is a risk of subsidizing "less socially valuable innovation where patents are not needed." Finally, "trolls" or persons and companies that do not sell an invention "are free to ambush companies" that invest in socially-valuable products and services, using bogus patents that proliferate when patentability standards are low.[1]

The patent system's growth came at a "significant" cost, so it had to be rolled back.[2] The Supreme Court agreed, issuing a ruling that contributed to patents being

[1] Brief of Amicus Curiae Computer & Communications Industry Association in Support of Petitioner, at 16–20, *KSR International Co.* v. *Teleflex, Inc.*, 550 U.S. 398 (U.S. brief filed Aug. 22, 2006) (No. 04-1350) (citations omitted), judgment on remand affirmed by 228 Fed. Appx. 988 (Fed. Cir. 2007) (quoting Markus Reitzig et al., On sharks, trolls, and other patent animals – 'being infringed' as a normatively induced innovation exploitation strategy, *Social Science Research Network* (February 2006), http://ssrn.com/abstract=885914, and U.S. Federal Trade Commission, To promote innovation: The proper balance of competition and patent law and policy (2003) at 31 n. 220, www.ftc.gov/os/2003/10/innovationrpt.pdf).
[2] Brief of Amicus Curiae The Electronic Frontier Foundation in Support of Petitioner, at 15, 20, *KSR*, (U.S. brief filed August 22, 2006).

found invalid because they were "obvious" roughly six times as frequently at the trial court level.[3] The decision, known popularly as *KSR*, was based largely on circular reasoning, and led to vague standards being employed in later cases.[4]

The dispute in *KSR* involved an improvement to adjustable pedals, using an electronic throttle control. The Federal Circuit refused to find the improvement obvious, pointing out that the alleged infringer had provided no evidence that a person skilled in the art would know how to solve the problem at hand by combining various designs in the prior art, or that there was any motivation to do so.[5]

The Supreme Court concluded that such evidence was not required, because "market pressure" to solve a problem and the presence of a "finite" number of solutions, would mean that "common sense" would select one of those solutions. If a solution that combines prior art elements is what common sense would select, a patent based on that is invalid.[6] Of course, most inventions result from combining prior art elements to respond to the market's needs.[7] The Court therefore acknowledged the tension between its statement that any "claimed discoveries almost of necessity will be combinations of what, in some sense, is already known," so that there must be "a reason that would have prompted a person of ordinary skill in the relevant field to combine the elements in the way the claimed new invention does," and its seemingly circular decision that a "motivation" to combine elements in a certain way (which the Federal Circuit demanded) is not needed when "there existed at the time of invention a known problem for which there was an obvious solution encompassed by the patent's claims."[8]

The *KSR* decision came only a few years after the Court, again acting in accordance with several appeals from industries incurring costs due to alleged patent infringement, made it much harder to enforce a patent through an injunction, as Congress had intended.[9] This new ruling on injunction standards led to fewer than

---

[3] Ali Mojibi, *An empirical study of the effect of KSR v. Teleflex on the Federal Circuit's patent validity jurisprudence*, 20 *Albany Law Journal of Science and Technology* 559 (2010) at 583. See also Gregory Mandel, *A nonobvious comparison: Nonobviousness decisions at the PTAB and in the federal courts*, 24 *Texas Intellectual Property Law Journal* 403 (2017) at 428 (district courts found patents to be invalid 58 percent of time, versus between 6 percent and 31 percent of time before *KSR*; new rate was 1.8 to 9.66 times higher).

[4] R. Polk Wagner, Lecture 08 – nonobviousness 2, The University of Pennsylvania School of Law/ YouTube (2015), www.youtube.com/watch?v=g4FD6bl3oXo.

[5] *Teleflex, Inc. v. KSR International Co.*, 119 Fed. Appx. 282 (Fed. Cir. 2005).

[6] *KSR*, 550 U.S. 398, 127 S. Ct. at 1741–3.

[7] Ibid. ("[I]nventions in most, if not all, instances rely upon building blocks long since uncovered, and claimed discoveries almost of necessity will be combinations of what, in some sense, is already known.").

[8] *KSR*, 550 U.S. 398, 127 S. Ct. at 1741–2.

[9] *eBay Inc. v. MercExchange, L.L.C.*, 547 U.S. 388 (2006); Brief of Business Software Alliance, Software and Information Industry Association, Information Technology Industry Council, and Information Technology Association of America as Amici Curiae in Support of Petitioners, *eBay* (U.S. brief filed January 2006).

twenty permanent injunctions being issued each year on average from 2003 through 2013, out of 2,500 patent cases filed each year; computer software patents resulted in only five injunctions per year, out of more than 40,000 patents issued and 175 patent cases filed annually in a $500 billion-plus industry.[10]

The inability to obtain an injunction crippled patent owners' leverage in licensing talks. The threat of an injunction opens a space for licensing negotiations in which to seek an amount higher than the alleged infringer sees as the "market value of the license," which is often a small amount compared to its own profits linked to the infringement.[11]

Claiming "abstract ideas" as patented property is nothing new.[12] The Supreme Court limited the practice in a decision on Alexander Graham Bell's claim to the idea of using electricity to send vocal or other sounds over long distances.[13] The Federal Circuit, despite being more friendly to patents than the Supreme Court of that earlier time, declared a patent to be invalid to the extent that it claimed business techniques such as an auction that maximized revenue from all items rather than the price of any individual item, in part because the patent did not represent significant technological inventiveness in calculating, recording, or tabulating the auction process or its results.[14] Still, the US Patent and Trademark Office (PTO) issued some patents in which relatively standard business techniques were coupled with traditional calculating methods performed on a computer, such as gathering real estate listings or accounting for asset allocations.[15]

[10] Mark Lemley, The surprising resilience of the patent system, 95 Texas Law Review 1 (2016) at 4 (cases filed); Christina Mulligan and Timothy B. Lee, Scaling the patent system, 68 New York University Annual Survey of American Law 289 (2012) at 304 (software patents issued); Christopher Seaman, Permanent injunctions in patent litigation after eBay: An empirical study, 101 Iowa Law Review 1949 (2016), draft, at 24, 40, 42 (injunctions). Software and information industry revenue was $565 billion in 2005. Software and Information Industry Association, Comments in response to the request of the intellectual property enforcement coordinator for comments on the joint strategic plan (March 24, 2010) at 3, www.siia.net/LinkClick.aspx?fileticket=PM-QxHEJSaQ%3d&portalid=0.

[11] Brief of Business Software Alliance, note 9, at 9, citing Adam Jaffe and Josh Lerner, Innovation and Its Discontents (Princeton University Press, 2004) at 112.

[12] In Re Bilski, 545 F.3d 943, 989 (Fed. Cir. 2008) (en banc) (Judge Newman, dissenting) (noting that several patents from era of the founders of the US Constitution "appear to involve financial subject matter, and to require primarily human activity"), citing, inter alia, US Patent No. 1159 (July 14, 1777) ("Securing the property of persons purchasing shares of State-lottery tickets."), and US Patent No. 1197 (July 21, 1778) ("Plan for assurances on lives of persons from ten to eighty years of age."); Anthony William Deller and Albert Henry Walker, Walker on Patents, vol. 1 (Baker, Voorhis, 1937) at 38–50, 62–70.

[13] The Telephone Cases, 126 U.S. 1 (1888).

[14] In Re Schrader, 22 F.3d 290, 291–294 (Fed. Cir. 1994).

[15] E.g. US Patent No. 7,117,175 (October 3, 2006) ("Method and apparatus for managing a virtual mutual fund"); US Patent No. 6,236,977 (May 22, 2001) ("Computer implemented marketing system"); US Patent No. 6,202,051 (March 13, 2001) ("Facilitating internet commerce through internetworked auctions"); US Patent No. 6,125,352 (September 26, 2000) ("System and method for conducting commerce over a distributed network"); US Patent No. 6,049,811 (April 11, 2000) ("Machine for drafting a patent application and process for doing same"); US Patent No. 6,029,141

In 2008, the Federal Circuit concluded that a business method without a machine or transformation of matter is unpatentable, despite broad statutory language indicating that any "method" or "process" should be patentable if otherwise new, not obvious, etc.[16] After receiving briefs from much of the Fortune 500, the Supreme Court crafted an even broader standard favoring elimination of technology patents than the Federal Circuit had done. Without mentioning how the particular patent at issue may have required the use of a computer, the Court emphasized the danger that "courts could be flooded with claims that would put a chill on creative endeavor and dynamic change."[17] Although this part of the Court's opinion did not speak for all justices, four other justices expressed concern that compliance with business-method patents could be "costly and time-consuming," necessitate "complex licensing arrangements," and cause businesses that avoid patent compliance and licensing to "live in constant fear of litigation."[18]

The resulting standard for process patents involving computers or software may be even more difficult to satisfy than the Federal Circuit's "machine or transformation test," which looked to whether an innovative technology is really at work in the claims. The opinion of the Supreme Court endorsed a "high ... bar" on patents

---

(February 22, 2000) ("Internet-based customer referral system"); US Patent No. 6,014,643 (January 11, 2000) ("Interactive securities trading system"); US Patent No. 5,960,411 (September 28, 1999) ("Method and system for placing a purchase order via a communications network"); US Patent No. 5,845,265 (December 1, 1998) ("Consignment nodes"); US Patent No. 5,794,207 (August 11, 1998) ("Method and apparatus [etc.] to facilitate buyer-driven conditional purchase offers"); US Patent No. 5,664,115 (September 2, 1997) ("Interactive computer system to match buyers and sellers of real estate, businesses and other property using the Internet"); US Patent No. 5,032,989 (July 16, 1991) ("Real estate search and location system and method"); US Patent No. 5,309,355 (May 3, 1994) ("Automated sales system").

[16] In Re Bilski, 545 F.3d 943, 951–2, 7, 961–2 (Fed. Cir. 2008) (en banc); ibid., at 969–70 (Judge Dyk, joined by Judge Linn, concurring); ibid., at 977–8, 994–7 (Judge Newman, dissenting); ibid., at 1011–21, 1015 (Judge Rader, dissenting). See also 35 U.S.C. § 273.

[17] *Bilski v. Kappos*, 561 U.S. 593, 608 (2010). Compare, with *Bilski*, 545 F.3d at 995–6 (Judge Newman, dissenting) (noting that because "the process Bilski describes employs complex mathematical calculations to assess various elements of risk, any practicable embodiment would be conducted with the aid of a machine – a programmed computer ... "). See also, Brief for Internet Retailers in Support of Respondent, *Bilski* (U.S. brief filed October 1, 2009) (No. 08-964); Brief for American Insurance Association et al. in Support of Respondent, *Bilski* (U.S. brief filed October 2, 2009); Brief for Microsoft Corporation, Koninklijke Philips Electronics N.V., and Symantec Corporation in Support of Respondent, *Bilski* (U.S. brief filed October 2, 2009); Brief for the Bank of America Corporation, Barclays Capital Inc., the Clearing House Association L.L.C., the Financial Services Roundtable, Google Inc., Metlife, Inc., and Morgan Stanley in Support of Respondent, *Bilski* (U.S. brief filed October 2, 2009); Brief for the Computer & Communications Industry Association in Support of Respondent, *Bilski* (U.S. brief filed October 2, 2009); Brief for the Software and Information Industry Association in Support of Respondent, *Bilski* (U.S. brief filed October 2, 2009). Much of the U.S. patented pharmaceutical industry wrote in support of an outcome that would disfavor business method patents. E.g., Brief for the Pharmaceutical Research and Manufacturers Association in Support of Neither Party, at 8, *Bilski* (U.S. brief filed October 2, 2009).

[18] *Bilski*, 561 U.S. 593, 130 S. Ct. at 3253–6, citing, inter alia, James Bessen and Eric Maskin, Sequential innovation, patents, and imitation, 40 *RAND Journal of Economics* 611 (2009) at 613.

involving the use of computers to automate business tasks, and four justices wrote in favor of a ban on business-method software patents.[19] Thus, some patents involving the transformation into a different state of data fixed on some device or medium – such as a disc or server – have been called into question by post-*Bilski* rulings.[20]

In 2014, the Supreme Court further compressed the narrow window for business method patents and some software patents, leading to a deluge of decisions at the PTO and in the courts invalidating software and e-commerce patents.[21] The more recent cases tend to downplay evidence of incremental invention using computers, such as the manipulation of electronic account records to release funds from escrow to close a transaction, at issue in *Alice Corp. Pty v. CLS Bank International, Inc.*[22]

---

[19] These justices stated:

> The breadth of business methods, their omnipresence in our society, and their potential vagueness also invite a particularly pernicious use of patents that we have long criticized. As early as the 19th century, we explained that the patent laws are not intended to "creat[e] a class of speculative schemers who make it their business to watch the advancing wave of improvement, and gather its foam in the form of patented monopolies, which enable them to lay a heavy tax upon the industry of the country, without contributing anything to the real advancement of the arts."

130 S. Ct. at 3256 (quoting *Atlantic Works* v. *Brady*, 107 U.S. 192, 200 (1883), and Clarisa Long, Information costs in patent and copyright, 90 *Virginia Law Review* 465 (2004) at 487–8).

[20] *Alexsam, Inc.* v. *IDT Corp.*, 715 F.3d 1336, 1349–50 (Fed. Cir. 2013) (Judge Mayer, dissenting) (patent involving transformation of data using a bank card and associated hardware could be invalid under *Bilski* 's "high … bar"); *MySpace*, 672 F.3d at 1264–9 (Judge Mayer, dissenting) (claim involving a computer "database" searched for and modified over a network might fail *Bilski*'s "high … bar"); *Research Corp. Technologies, Inc.* v. *Microsoft Corp.*, 627 F.3d 859, 868 (Fed. Cir. 2010) (*Bilski*'s bar on patentability of abstract ideas is indefinable); Timothy Holbrook, Method patent exceptionalism, 102 *Iowa L. Rev.* 1001 (2017); Christopher Holman, The *Mayo* framework is bad for your health, 23 *George Mason Law Review* 901 (2015) at 904, 910; Joshua Sarnoff, Patent-eligible inventions after *Bilski*: History and theory, 63 *Hastings Law Review* 53 (2011) at 55.

[21] E.g. Reply Brief of Petitioners in Support of Certiorari, at 6–8, *Bilski*; Peter Harter and Gene Quinn, *Rule 36: Unprecedented abuse at the Federal Circuit*, IP Watchdog (January 12, 2017), www.ipwatchdog .com/2017/01/12/rule-36-abuse-federal-circuit/id=76971/; Robert Sachs, #Alicestorm: When It Rains, It Pours … , *BilskiBlog*, January 22, 2016, www.bilskiblog.com/blog/2016/01/alicestorm-when-it-rains-it-pours.html; Rob Sterne and Gene Quinn, PTAB death squads: Are all commercially viable patents invalid?, *IP Watchdog* (March 24, 2014), www.ipwatchdog.com/2014/03/24/ptab-death-squads-are-all-commercially-viable-patents-invalid/id=48642/. Commentators suggest that post-*Bilski* law is vague and undermines the patent system from the standpoint of some innovators. E.g. John M. Golden, *Flook* says one thing, *Diehr* says another: A need for housecleaning in the law of patentable subject matter, 82 *George Washington Law Review* 1765 (2014) at 1765–6; Paxton Lewis, The conflation of patent eligibility and obviousness: *Alice's* substitution of section 103, *Utah Law Review On Law* 1 (2017) at 14, 20, 23, http://dc.law.utah.edu/onlaw/vol2017/iss1/1; Peter S. Menell, Forty years of wondering in the wilderness and no closer to the promised land: *Bilski's* superficial textualism and the missed opportunity to return patent law to its technology mooring, 63 *Stanford Law Review* 1289 (2011) at 1305.

[22] 134 S. Ct. 2347 (2014). See also Jay Kesan and Carol Mullins Hayes, Patent eligible subject matter after *Alice*, in John Rothchild (Ed.), *Research Handbook on Electronic Commerce Law* (Edward Elgar Publishing, 2016) at 239–40, 247–8, 257.

Tens of thousands of patents are at risk of being cancelled if enforcement is so much as attempted.[23] Some practitioners and observers the PTO uses fast-track procedures as "patent death squads."[24] Others would say that the *Alice* case is having its intended effect of thinning a "plague" of locusts, the owners of "generic" patents.[25]

The rate patents are issued to independent inventors has fallen sharply. The rate was down by half in the field of computer memory and data processing/business method patents in 2015 compared to 2010. It was down by two-thirds in the field of computer architecture and processor patents, comparing the same years.[26]

The Supreme Court in its recent decisions arguably codified judicially what were failed attempts at congressional patent reform. Multinational software companies, through their lawyers, had lobbied Congress in 1999 for protection against small inventors' litigiousness when it came to business methods that use computers.[27] For a time, finance, software, and retail industries' lobbying against strong patents was matched by that of the pharmaceutical, biotechnology, and other industries.

In curtailing software patents, limiting injunctions, and narrowing the place where patent suits may be filed (venues), judges have seemingly been modeling their decisions on unsuccessful legislation.[28] Similarly, due to a recent Supreme Court decision regarding patent case attorney's fees, some judges are forcing patent owners

[23] One estimate was more than one million patents. Brief of Koninklijke Phillips Electronics, N.V. as Amicus Curiae in Support of Petitioners, at 11 & n. 6, *Bilski* (U.S. brief filed May 2009). Other estimates were in the tens of thousands. Brief of Boston Patent Law Association in Support of Petitioners, at 24 & n. 11, *Bilski* (U.S. brief filed August 5, 2009); Reply Brief of Petitioners in Support of Certiorari, at 6–7, *Bilski* (U.S. brief filed June 2009). A dissent in *Bilski* mentioned 15,000 patents issued between 1998 and 2007 in PTO Class 705, for business methods. 545 F.3d at 992 (Judge Newman, dissenting).

[24] E.g. Sterne and Quinn, note 21. See also Richard Lloyd, As PTAB nears its fifth birthday, the "death squads" have more than just NPEs in their sights, Iam (June 15, 2017), www.iam-media.com/blog/Detail.aspx?g=f35b5d77-a925-4d81-ac93-8bc88db3e308.

[25] Brief of Google Inc., Amazon.com Inc., American Association of Advertising Agencies, Dell Inc., Facebook, Inc., Intuit Inc., Linkedin Corp., Netflix, Inc., Rackspace Hosting, Inc., Verizon Communications Inc., and Zynga Inc. as Amici Curiae in support of Respondents, at 25–34, *Alice* (U.S. brief filed December 14, 2014).

[26] US Patent & Trademark Office, *Patent counts by class by year – independent inventors: January 1977–December 2015* (March 2016), https://web.archive.org/web/20160506040807/http://www.uspto.gov/ web/offices/ac/ido/oeip/taf/cbcby_in.htm [lines 705–6, 712–13].

[27] Committee Print, The "American Inventors Protection Act," 106th Cong., 1st Sess., March 25, 1999 (statement of Michael Kirk, Executive Director, the American Intellectual Property Law Association), www.aipla.org/Advocacy%20Shared%20Documents/CommitteePrint_AIPLA.pdf; Why I quit the AIPLA (American Intellectual Property Law Association, *Halling Blog* (October 2, 2012), http://hallingblog.com/2012/10/02/why-i-quit-the-aipla-american-intellectual-property-law-association/.

[28] Patent Reform in the Courts and Congress: Hearing before the Senate Committee on the Judiciary, 111th Cong. 1 (2009) (Statement of Mark Lemley), http://judiciary.senate.gov/pdf/09-03-10Lemleytestimony.pdf.

to pay alleged infringers' attorney's fees so often that it is as if proposed fee-shifting legislation had passed, even though it died due to patent holders' opposition in Congress.[29]

Most recently, the Supreme Court gave a major boost to corporations' bid for "home court advantage" in patent litigation.[30] In essence, the Court adopted a rule similar to one proposed in Congress by many corporations' trade associations, a proposal which did not pass. For most of American history, the rule was that corporations had to face the risk of patent litigation wherever they systematically infringed a patent, because "it is but justice to the owner of the patent that he is permitted to seek redress in the [federal] district where the wrong is done."[31] Contracting to do business in the long term with residents of a federal judicial district satisfies the fairness concerns associated with having to defend a lawsuit in a courthouse far from one's headquarters, and related concerns about proper statutory "venue," or the location of the pretrial proceedings and the trial.[32]

In 2017, the Supreme Court issued a decision that leads some observers to conclude that many more lawsuits will have to be filed in Delaware, Northern California, or other "home" jurisdictions of Fortune 500 corporations.[33] The decision emulated the VENUE Act, legislation that would have given patent infringers more of a "home court" advantage in litigation, but which stalled in Congress.[34] Having to enforce their patents in multiple actions across many different and overcrowded jurisdictions, where time to trial is very long, may impoverish patentees.[35] This helps companies enjoy the advantages of global and Internet-based marketing and sales without incurring many of the associated liabilities and compliance issues.[36] In their home courts, companies can more often get patents dismissed as "abstract" or "obvious to try."

[29] Hannah Jiam, Emerging trends post-*Octane* Fitness, Patently O (May 13, 2015), https://patentlyo.com/patent/2015/05/emerging-octane-fitness.html. See also ACT: The App Association, Support the Innovation Act (2016), http://actonline.org/innovation-act-support-letter/.
[30] *TC Heartland LLC v. Kraft Food Group Brands LLC*, 137 S. Ct. 1514 (2017).
[31] *Bowers v. Atlantic G. & P. Co.*, 104 F. 887 (S.D.N.Y. 1900). See also *Stonite, Dover Corp. v. Fisher Governor Co.*, 221 F. Supp. 176 (S.D. Tex. 1963).
[32] E.g. *Centre One v. Vonage Holdings Corp.*, No. 6:08CV467, 2009 WL 2461003 (E.D. Tex. August 10, 2009).
[33] *TC Heartland*, 137 S. Ct. 1514.
[34] S. 2733, 114th Cong. 2d sess. (March 17, 2016); H.R. Rep. No. 114-235, at 1–23 (2015).
[35] Brief Amici Curiae of Biotechnology Innovation Organization and the Association of University Technology Managers in Support of Respondent, at 13–15, 23, *TC Heartland* (U.S. brief filed Mar. 8 2017) (No. 16-341); Brief Amici Curiae of Eighteen Individuals and Organizations Representing Inventors and Patent Owners in Support of Respondent, at 12–15, *TC Heartland* (U.S. brief filed Mar. 8, 2017); Matthew Bultman, TC Heartland could make enforcing patents more expensive, *Law360* (June 2, 2017), www.law360.com/articles/930849/tc-heartland-could-make-enforcing-patents-more-expensive.
[36] Cf. *Orbit Irrigation Products, Inc. v. Melnor, Inc.*, No. 1:16-cv-137 (D. Utah April 3, 2017), https://scholar.google.com/scholar_case?case=15943985895586974085&q=%22tc+heartland%22&hl=en&as_sdt=40006&as_ylo=2017.

The Supreme Court's patent law decisions may have reflected the Chicago School approach to patent law, which emphasizes the "patent holdup" problem. First, drawing on Richard Posner's work on specialized courts, Adam Jaffe and Josh Lerner argued that the Federal Circuit – the unified patent appeals court that replaced the regional federal appeals courts in the 1980s – would have an incentive to be "captured" by patent holders and impose excess costs upon alleged infringers.[37] Second, it attacks "bargaining inequality" between patent holders – empowered by an overgenerous US Patent and Trademark Office and a biased Federal Circuit – and unsuspecting innovators who confront a potential ban on a product or service for which "'the patented technology is only an insignificant part.'"[38] The theory is that to save companies a "substantial expense," the rule commonly allowing injunctions in cases involving patent infringement must be done away with, or at least relaxed.[39] Third, fearing existing patents, the theory predicts that companies producing new products or services will avoid investing in potential improvements, or that they will leave the market altogether.[40] This is the problem of "holdup" by patents.[41] Thus, *KSR* reflected a fear that patents issued "without real innovation retard progress and may ... deprive prior inventions of their value or utility."[42] Likewise, four justices in *eBay* expressed concern that patents "can be employed as a bargaining tool to charge exorbitant fees to companies that seek to buy licenses to practice the patent."[43] As mentioned above, the Court's opinion and the concurrence of four justices in *Bilski* emphasized the floodgates of litigation, and its resulting cost, as harming businesses.

Although many of these same points can and should be made about lawsuits or threats by copyright owners against works quite different from their own, neither the Supreme Court nor the Chicago School approach has concluded that copyright infringement should be made easier for businesses, or that large numbers of copyrights should be wiped out.[44] Instead, the Court has endorsed the costly "restoration"

[37] Jaffe and Lerner, note 11, at 103. See also Richard Posner, Patent trolls, *The Becker-Posner Blog* (July 21, 2013), www.becker-posner-blog.com/2013/07/patent-trollsposner.html.
[38] Brief of Business Software Alliance, note 9, at 9 (quoting Carl Shapiro, Navigating the patent thicket: Cross licenses, patent pools, and standard setting, in Adam Jaffe et al. (Eds.), *Innovation Policy and the Economy*, vol. 1 (The MIT Press, 2000) at 126).
[39] Ibid.
[40] Ibid.,at 10, citing James Bessen, Holdup and licensing of cumulative innovations with private information, 82 *Economics Letters* 321 (2004). See also Posner, note 37 ("It's not just that patent trolls don't do anything that encourages innovation; they impair innovation.").
[41] Bessen, note 40.
[42] *KSR*, 550 U.S. 398, 127 S. Ct. at 1741.
[43] *eBay*, 547 U.S. at 396 (Justice Kennedy, joined by Justices Stevens, Souter, and Breyer, concurring).
[44] There are three exceptions to this statement, dealing with the scope of fair use and the duration of copyright. Judge Posner suggests that "minute excerpts" from a work should be included in fair use, and that copyright holders should pay a periodic renewal fee as the years go by, facing forfeiture of their copyrights if they do not or cannot pay. William Landes and Richard Posner, Indefinitely renewable copyright, 70 *The University of Chicago Law Review* (2003) at 471; William Patry and Richard Posner,

of copyrights in public-domain works via trade agreements, and copyrights on athletic uniform designs that were so simple as to be referred to derisively in a dissenting opinion as being about as valid as a copyright on the shape of a spoon.[45]

The producers of derivative works and other improvements are in an unequal and disadvantageous position regarding copyright holders, and copyright infringers therefore either avoid potentially infringing topics and works or incur substantial expense. Larger corporations benefit from this system—and lobby for it—because they can play numerous authors of initial works off against one another as adaptation or transformation rights are licensed, minimizing the resulting expense, while recouping some or all of that expense from their own lucrative derivative-work licensing deals. Derivative-work authors, meanwhile, may find that there is no ready substitute for the works that they would like to sample, quote substantial extracts from, remix, mash up, or otherwise imitate. In addition, it is possible for large corporations to deny that they imitated a relatively unknown script, song, painting, video, or book, despite their employees' receipt of it. While it might be easier to avoid copying a work than to avoid infringing a patent in it, copyright infringement is often inferred where notable features of a widely-distributed copyrighted work are present in the defendant's work.[46]

Neither the Supreme Court nor the Chicago School has abandoned the derivative work right or the doctrines of "fragmented literal" or "comprehensive nonliteral" infringement.[47] Landes and Posner defended the Court's decision leading to an injunction against the taking of an "infinitesimal part" of a book in a magazine article because even though the book was unpublished at the time of infringement, the expected harm from infringement could be large and might be mitigated by

---

Fair use and statutory reform in the wake of *Eldred*, 92 *California Law Review* 1639 (2004) at 1660; Richard Posner, *Do patent and copyright law restrict competition and creativity excessively?*, Becker-Posner Blog (September 30, 2012), www.becker-posner-blog.com/2012/09/do-patent-and-copyright-law-restrict-competition-and-creativity-excessively-posner.html. Moreover, Patry and Posner urge the extension of fair use to situations in which longer or more substantial uses of portions of a work are made, but the cost of locating the rightsholder for purposes of seeking permission would outweigh the value of the use to the infringer (also known as the "orphan works" problem). Patry and Posner, ibid, at 1650.

[45] *Golan v. Holder*, 565 U.S. 1 (2012); *Star Athletica, LLC v. Varsity Brands*, 137 S. Ct. 1002, 1032–3 (2017) (Justice Breyer, dissenting). Justice Breyer claimed that the restoration blessed in *Golan* would increase costs to the users of millions of works, such as school orchestras, by a factor of seven or more. *Golan*, 565 U.S. at 904–5 (Justice Breyer, joined by Justice Alito, dissenting). Justice Breyer also wrote that the decision to allow copyrights in original designs when they are cut in the shape of an article of clothing may put competition and stability at risk in the clothing industry. *Star Athletics*, 137 U.S. at 1035–36 (Justice Breyer, dissenting).

[46] Cf. *Mazer v. Stein*, 347 U.S. 201, 217 (1954) ("Unlike a patent, a copyright gives no exclusive right to the art disclosed; protection is given only to the expression of the idea – not the idea itself."). *Three Boys Music Corp. v. Bolton*, 212 F. 3d 477 (9th Cir. 2000).

[47] *Dr. Seuss Enters., L.P. v. Penguin Books USA, Inc.* 109 F.3d 1394 (9th Cir.), cert. denied, 521 U.S. 1146 (1997); *Twin Peaks Productions, Inc. v. Publications International Ltd.*, 996 F.2d 1366, 1372 (2d Cir. 1993); *Baxter v. MCA, Inc.*, 812 F.2d 421 (9th Cir. 1987).

copyright law.[48] They argue in favor of protecting copyrighted works from infringing works that are imperfect substitutes or no substitutes at all – for example, a cheap postcard of an artwork auctioned for millions at a prestigious gallery – because a "proliferation of variants" may reduce the income for and delay the release of the original.[49] They also rely on the lower transaction costs of concentrating all relevant IP rights involving one phenomenon in one entity to justify the derivative work right.[50] Their defense of the derivative work right in copyright applies with similar force to patent holders who have not entered a particular industry yet and are therefore "trolls" in it, because extending IP's scope to control over derivatives/improvements (1) rewards "time-consuming" labor finding an improvement on the prior art or public domain, (2) reduces transaction costs by placing control over the original IP and any improvement upon it in one party, (3) simplifies proof of infringement, and (4) encourages sublicenses.[51] Like patent infringement injunctions, the threat of copyright injunctions could encourage rightsholders to demand fees greater than the "fair value" of their work, even for works that are out of print.[52]

3.2. OWNING SOCIAL NETWORKS

Social media and social networking are not concepts that are easy to define. Online social networks such as Facebook, Google+, Linkedin, and MySpace obviously qualify.[53] Blogging sites like Twitter and Blogger, and other collaborative Web 2.0 services such as Wikipedia or the virtual world Second Life are also analyzed as social media.[54] Sites that originated for photo sharing, like Flickr, Instagram, Pinterest, and Tumblr are typically included in the category.[55] Video-sharing sites

---

[48] Landes and Posner, note 44, at 144 (*Harper & Row Publishers* v. *Nation Enterprises*, 471 U.S. 539 (1984), was rightly decided). See also *Harper & Row Publishers*, 471 U.S. at 599–600 (Brennan, J., dissenting) (quotes of less than 1 percent of plaintiff's words were "quantitatively 'infinitesimal,'" and intended to "'convey the facts'" but was held infringing by majority).

[49] Landes and Posner, note 44, at 109–111.

[50] Landes and Posner, note 44, at 109–112; William Landes, *Copyright, borrowed images, and appropriation art: An economic approach*, University of Chicago Law & Economics, Olin Working Paper No. 113 (2000) at 12–14, https://papers.ssrn.com/sol3/papers.cfm?abstract_id=253332; Richard Posner, *Law and Literature* (Harvard University Press, 2009), at 538.

[51] William Landes and Richard Posner, An economic analysis of copyright law, 18 *Journal of Legal Studies* 325 (1989) at 354–7.

[52] Brief of Time Warner Inc., Amazon.com, Inc., Chevron Corp., Cisco Systems, Inc., Google Inc., IAC/Interactive Corp., Infineon Technologies AG, Shell Oil Company, Visa U.S.A., Inc., and Xerox Corporation as Amici Curiae in Support of Petitioners, at 4–7, 12, 27–8, *eBay*, (U.S. brief filed January 26, 2006).

[53] Thomas Koenig and Michael Rustad, Digital scarlet letters: Social media stigmatization of the poor and what can be done, 93 *Nebraska Law Review* 592 (2015) at 604; PewResearch, Internet Project, Social Media Update 2013, http://perma.unl.edu/6WCF-DVS8.

[54] E.g. Andreas Kaplan and Michael Haenlein, Users of the world, unite! The challenges and opportunities of social media, 53 *Business Horizons* 59 (2010) at 59, 63–5.

[55] PewResearch, note 53.

like Vine and YouTube are often thrown in to the mix.[56] By virtue of text and photo publishing capability, communications apps like WhatsApp, Facebook Messenger, Snapchat, and WeChat are also called "social media."[57] A more formal definition of social media for economic analysis might exclude much one-to-one or one-to-small-group communication (e.g. emails and texts), piracy and other mere copies (e.g. Napster or a copy of *The Matrix* uploaded to a website), and digital publishing for profit (e.g. cnn.com). Such a definition would employ User-Generated Content (UGC) or Web 2.0 as part of the definition of "social media," and exclude traditional websites, emails, etc.[58]

Social media became pervasive in business, education, politics, and social life between 2006 and 2013.[59] They are more inclusive than traditional media, which often excluded groups from the airwaves or bylines, such as manual laborers, the poor, the Left, women, racial and ethnic minorities, and atheists and agnostics.[60] After decades of discriminatory FCC and state-level regulation of broadcast licenses, ethnic minorities and women owned fewer than six or seven percent of broadcast stations, respectively, in the United States.[61] By contrast, about two-thirds of Americans used some form of social media by 2015, including people from all groups.[62] Politicians are rising to high office using social media. The Occupy Movement mobilized activists and published statements on blogging platforms, Facebook,

---

[56] Ibid. See also Kaplan and Haenlein, note 54, at 59.

[57] *Social media*, Wikipedia (2017), https://en.wikipedia.org/wiki/Social_media.

[58] Kaplan and Haenlein, note 54, at 61.

[59] Koenig and Rustad, note 53, at 599.

[60] Carole Ashkinaze, A matter of opinion: Female pundits are still missing from the media, Ms. Magazine, Summer 2005, www.msmagazine.com/; The Center for American Progress and Free Press, The Structural Imbalance of Political Talk Radio 1, 7 (2007), www.americanprogress.org/issues/2007/06/pdf/talk_radio.pdf; Chon Noriega and Francisco Javier Iribarren, Hate speech on commercial talk radio: Preliminary report on a pilot study, UCLA Chicano Research Center Latino Policy & Issues Brief No. 22 (February 2009) at 1; Jeff Cohen, Mainstream news coverage of economics, *Fairness and Accuracy in Reporting* (March 1, 2000), www.fair.org/index.php?page=254; Media Matters for America, If it"s Sunday, it's conservative: An analysis of the Sunday talk show guests on ABC, CBS, and NBC, 1997–2005 (February 14, 2006), at 1, http://mediamatters.org; Jennifer L. Pozner, *Missing since 9–11: Women's voices*, Newsday/Lexis Advance, December 13, 2001, http://advance.lexis.com; Jennifer L. Pozner, One of ninety!, 9 *Life and Labor Bulletin* 1 (May 1931); S. Craig Watkins and Rana Emerson, Feminist media criticism and feminist media practices, 571 *Annals of American Academy of Political & Social Sciences* 151 (2000); Jon Whiten, *If news from Iraq is bad, it's coming from U.S. officials*, Fairness in Accuracy and Reporting Extra! (February 2004), www.fair.org/index.php?page=1167; Fairness in Accuracy and Reporting, Who's on the news?: Study shows network news sources skew white, male & elite, *Common Dreams News Center* (May 21, 2002), www.commondreams.org/news2002/0521-03.htm.

[61] Free Press, Five things you should know about the FCC's Big Media giveaway (November 28, 2012), www.freepress.net/blog/2012/11/28/five-things-you-should-know-about-fcc's-big-media-giveaway.

[62] PewResearch Internet Project, Social media usage: 2005–2015 (October 8, 2015), www.pewinternet.org/2015/10/08/social-networking-usage-2005-2015/; see also PewResearch Internet Project, Social networking fact sheet, www.pewinternet.org/files/2013/12/PIP_Social-Networking-2013.pdf.

Twitter, and YouTube.[63] The AFL-CIO and SEIU, among other labor unions, also rely on digital engagement of existing and prospective union members.[64]

The similarities between social media and existing computer and Internet technology make it difficult to own IP related to new social media ideas. For example, a company called GraphOn claimed to own a method, apparatus, and system for making user-driven database entries to classify and search for material over a computer network.[65] The patents proved to be invalid because an even older computer "bulletin board" system enabled users to add entries to online hierarchical catalogs.[66] The decision finding the user-driven database patents to be obvious displayed a hallmark of post-*KSR* decisions stripping patents from their owners: it failed to fully analyze the prior art, and fell into the "trap of hindsight" that makes anything seem obvious because it uses some known elements that were employed in one or more prior art technologies.[67]

All inventions cobble together known elements from prior inventions, and employ one or more abstract ideas as an objective or framework.[68] Previously, the courts had stated that "objective evidence of nonobviousness includes commercial success, long felt but unresolved need, failure of others, and copying," and that such evidence "must be considered" as the most compelling proof of inventiveness. Practical insights like these are highly relevant when alleged infringers say that an invention was obvious in hindsight.[69]

In the social media age, courts began to dispense with the detailed analysis called for by traditional legal standards for "inventions." A judge could simply point to one

[63] Bing (2017), www.bing.com/search?q=blogspot+occupy&src=IE-TopResult_ and www.bing.com/search?q=wordpress%20occupy&qs=n&form=QBRE; Sky Croeser and Tim Highfield, Occupy Oakland and #oo: Uses of Twitter within the Occupy movement, 19 *First Monday* 3 (2014), www.firstmonday.dk/ojs/index.php/fm/article/view/4827; Benjamin Gleason, *#Occupy Wall Street: Exploring informal learning about a social movement on Twitter*, 57 *American Behavioral Scientist* 966 (2013); Koenig and Rustad, note 53, at 608; Occupy Movement, Tumblr (2011), http://wearethe99percent.tumblr.com; Occupy Movement's use of social media as an organizing method, *Participedia* (March 1, 2012), http://participedia.net/en/methods/occupy-movements-use-social-media-organizing-method and http://perma.unl.edu/B7AR-9HHG; Occupy Social Media, *Facebook*, www.facebook.com/OccupySocialMedia and http://perma.unl.edu/C3EA-VH4E; Occupy Wall Street (2014), http://occupywallst.org/ and http://perma.unl.edu/38M3-2YFH; Occupy Wall Street YouTube Archive, *Internet Archive* (2017), https://archive.org/details/ows-youtube.
[64] Eric Lee, Bandwagons and Buzzwords: Facebook and the unions, *Ericlee.info* (November 16, 2007), www.ericlee.info/2007/11/bandwagons_and_buzzwords_faceb.html; Graham Attwell, The benefits, risks and limitations of Facebook, *Pontydysgu: Bridge to Learning* (November 8, 2007), www.pontydysgu.org/2007/11/the-benefits-risks-and-limitations-of-facebook/.
[65] *MySpace, Inc. v. GraphOn Corp.*, 672 F.3d 1250, 1254 (Fed. Cir. 2012).
[66] Ibid., at 1254–5, 1262–3.
[67] *MySpace*, 756 F. Supp. 2d 1218, 1240–1 (N.D. Cal. 2010), *aff'd*, 672 F.3d at 1263–4.
[68] *Mayo Collaborative Services v. Prometheus Laboratories, Inc.*, 566 U.S. 66, 71 (2012); *KSR*, 550 US at 418–19.
[69] *Custom Accessories v. Jeffrey-Allan Industries*, 807 F.2d 955, 960 (Fed. Cir. 1986), citing *Graham v. John Deere Co.*, 383 U.S. 1, 33–4 (1966).

or more similar methods or systems and conclude that the claimed solution must be an obvious trick or at least "obvious to try."[70] Given the players and the stakes, the resulting indeterminacy and subjectivity in application of patent law's fundamental eligibility standard might have been predicted by Critical Legal Studies scholars.[71]

Patents, to the extent that they could exist on features of or improvements to social networks and digital content platforms, could redistribute power from the most powerful network and platform administrators to other workers in the digital economy. In Europe, it is increasingly common to say that Facebook or Google is too big, and should be strictly regulated or even broken up.[72] In the United States, competition concerns are raised more often by the federal government about Apple, Amazon, and Google, although there has been scattered talk of Facebook needing to be nationalized, or at least regulated.[73] Workers in high-technology fields have

---

[70] *Perfect Web Technologies, Inc.* v. *InfoUSA, Inc.*, 587 F.3d 1324, 1329, 1333 (Fed. Cir. 2009); *Leapfrog Enterprises, Inc.* v. *Fisher-Price, Inc.*, 485 F.3d 1157, 1162 (Fed. Cir. 2007); Wagner, note 4. *See also*, Benjamin Graf, Prognosis indeterminable: How patent non-obviousness outcomes depend too much on decision-makers, 9 *Cardozo Public Law, Policy, & Ethics Journal* 567 (2010); Timothy Le Duc, Apples are not common sense in view of oranges: Time to Reform *KSR's* illusory obviousness standard, 21 *DePaul Journal of Art, Technology & Intellectual Property Law* 49 (2010); Eli Sheets, Arguing secondary considerations after KSR: Proceed with caution, 21 *Federal Circuit Bar Journal* 1 (2011); Natalie Thomas, Secondary considerations in nonobviousness analysis: The use of objective indicia following *KSR* v. *Teleflex*, 86 *New York University Law Review* 2070 (2011) at 2086; David Tseng, Not all patents are created equal: Bias against predictable arts patents in the post-*KSR* landscape, 13 *Chicago-Kent Journal of Intellectual Property* 165 (2013) at 175.

[71] E.g. Graf, note 70; Le Duc, note 70; Tseng, note 70, at 188–91.

[72] *The Bundeskartellamt Competition Authority is investigating Facebook over abuse of market power through breaches of data protection law*, New Europe/GK (March 2, 2016), www.neweurope.eu/article/german-competition-agency-opens-investigation-against-facebook; European Parliament Resolution on Supporting Consumer Rights in the Digital Single Market ([2014/](RSP)) (November 27, 2014), ¶¶ 10–11; Cemal Karakas, Google antitrust proceedings: Digital business and competition, Member Research Service 6 (2015), www.europarl.europa.eu/RegData/etudes/BRIE/2015/565870/ EPRS_BRI(2015)565870_EN.pdf, citing *Washington weighs in on EU Google probe*, ft.com, November 25, 2014, and *France, Germany back MEPs against Google*, EurActiv.com, November 28, 2014; Should Digital Monopolies Be Broken Up?, *The Economist* (November 27, 2014), www.economist.com/news/leaders/21635000-european-moves-against-google-are-about-protecting-companies-not-consumers-should-digital; James Trew, European Parliament passes vote asking for Google to be broken up, *Engadget* (November 27, 2014), www.engadget.com/2014/11/27/european-parliament-google-break-up.

[73] E.g. Rep. David Cicilline, Following Amazon's Prime Day, Cicilline Calls for Hearing on Acquisition of Whole Foods Market (July 13, 2017), https://cicilline.house.gov/press-release/following-amazon%E2%80%99s-prime-day-cicilline-calls-hearing-acquisition-whole-foods-market; US Department of Justice, Justice Department Reaches Settlement with Three of the Largest Book Publishers and Continues to Litigate Against Apple (April 11, 2012), www.justice.gov/opa/pr/justice-department-reaches-settlement-three-largest-book-publishers-and-continues-litigate; Hon. Jon Liebowitz, Chairman, US Federal Trade Commission (November 25, 2012), Google Press Conference – Opening Remarks (January 3, 2013) at 5, www.ftc.gov/sites/default/files/documents/public_statements/opening-remarks-federal-trade-commission-chairman-jon-leibowitz-prepared-delivery/130103googleleibowitzremarks.pdf. See also Ethan Baron, Google, Facebook and Amazon: Monopolies that should be broken up, *Siliconbeat* (April 22, 2017), www.siliconbeat.com/2017/04/22/google-facebook-amazon-monopolies-broken-regulated; David Bloom, Insights: Are Google,

told US courts, with some success, that their wages for delivering computer graphics or software improvements have been suppressed by a dozen or so big companies colluding on the terms of employment.[74]

The high market shares of some Silicon Valley giants are contrary to the trend in the 1990s and 2000s of reduced industry concentration as many startups used patents and venture capital to challenge entrenched monopolies. In the 1970s, a few large firms, notably AT&T, IBM, and Xerox, controlled a disproportionate share of the technology sector, and its research.[75] Biased treatment of small inventors' patents may have enhanced the leverage of these large firms, which combined many patents, including the most foundational ones, into enormous portfolios. Before the Federal Circuit was established in 1982,[76] the rate of invalidation for litigated patents was more than 20 percentage points higher that it was in the mid- to late-1980s and in the 1990s.[77] Private R&D expenditure as a share of GDP, meanwhile, was only 1 percent in the mid-1960s.[78] With the Federal Circuit in place, more patents

Facebook, and Amazon monopolies too big to tackle?, *tubefilter* (March 31, 2017), www.tubefilter .com/2017/03/31/insights-monopoly-google-facebook-amazon/; Phillip Howard, Facebook should be nationalized to protect user rights, *Slate* (August 12, 2012), www.slate.com/articles/technology/ future_tense/2012/08/facebook_should_be_nationalized_to_protect_user_rights_.html; Suzy Kimm, Should Washington begin regulating Facebook? Some lawmakers say yes, *NBC News* (November 23, 2017), https://khanna.house.gov/media/in-the-news/should-washington-begin-regulating-facebook-some-lawmakers-say-yes; Jeff Spross, Why we should just nationalize Facebook, *The Week,* October 9, 2015, http://theweek.com/articles/582042/why-should-just-nationalize-facebook; Matt Stoller, The evidence is piling up – Silicon Valley is being destroyed, *Business Insider* (April 19, 2017), www .businessinsider.com/the-evidence-is-piling-up-silicon-valley-is-being-destroyed-2017-4.

[74] E.g. In Re Animation Workers Antitrust Litigation, 123 F. Supp. 3d 1175 (N.D. Cal. 2015); In Re High-Tech Employee Antitrust Litigation, 289 F.R.D. 555 (N.D. Cal. 2013), subsequent proceedings *at* No. 5:11-cv-02509-LHK, 2014 U.S. Dist. LEXIS 110064 (N.D. Cal. August 8, 2014) (resolving motion for approval of initial settlement), and at 2015 WL 5158730 (N.D. Cal. Sept. 2, 2015) (approving settlement for $415 million); David Streitfeld, Court rejects deal on hiring in Silicon Valley, *The New York Times,* August 8, 2014, www.nytimes.com/2014/08/09/technology/settlement-rejected-in-silicon-valley-hiring-case.html; High-Tech Employee Antitrust Settlement (2016), www .hightechemployeelawsuit.com/; United States District Court for the Northern District of California, In Re High-Tech Employee Antitrust Litigation (2016), www.cand.uscourts.gov/hk/hightechemployee.

[75] The Role of Non-Practicing Entities in the Modern Patent System: A Debate – Topic I, Case Western Reserve University School of Law/YouTube (February 24, 2012), www.youtube.com/ watch?v=uEoEyTRPE7s [John Duffy, approximately minutes 50:30-52:00]; W. G. Shepherd, The state of the industrial organization field, *in* Peter de Gijsel and Hans Schenk (Eds.), *Multidisciplinary Economics: The Birth of a New Economics Faculty in the Netherlands* (Springer, 2006) at 103, 114; Dan Steinbock, *Wireless Horizon: Strategy and Competition in the Worldwide Mobile Marketplace* (AMACOM, 2003) at 355.

[76] An Act to Establish a United States Court of Appeals for the Federal Circuit, to Establish a United States Claims Court, and for Other Purposes, 96 Stat. 25 (1982); Federal Judicial Center, Federal Circuit Act 1982 – History of the federal judiciary (2016), www.fjc.gov/history/home.nsf/page/ landmark_22.html.

[77] Lemley, note 10, at 8.

[78] Lemley, note 10, citing Editorial: Budgeting for the long run, 10 *Nature Materials* 407 (2011), www .nature.com/nmat/journal/v10/n6/full/nmat3044.html. Meanwhile, federal R&D as a share of GDP had declined. Ibid., at 42–3.

were enforceable, and R&D as a share of GDP doubled.[79] Universities like MIT and Stanford advised their students to file for patents and start their own companies, which many successfully did.[80] Now that the Federal Circuit has been chastened, and part of its role and the roles of the lower federal trial courts usurped in part by the PTO, we may be returning to a time more like the 1970s.

The current system is quite favorable to the interests of already-dominant firms, which no longer require strong patent rights to secure access to capital or protect their market position, and which enjoy more freedom to clone the functions of startups' new services. The startups that might challenge dominant firms' market shares see that the patents their financial backers may look for may be delayed for many years due to growing backlogs and repetitive examinations at the PTO, and extreme difficulties satisfying the standards for enforcement articulated in *eBay* and *KSR*.[81] As the former PTO director explained: "Patents are an equalizer, enabling companies large and small to sustain a competitive balance, ensuring collaboration is a fruitful enterprise for all participants."[82]

The America Invents Act of 2011 (AIA), as small business associations and theorists like John Duffy maintain, rewards the formation of technology conglomerates, unifying research, experimentation, consumer testing, production, and marketing in one corporation or corporate family, and penalizes independent research, invention, entrepreneurship, and licensing.[83]

The tendency of courts to weaken patents in the social media age may eventually kill off many smaller social media firms, as larger firms absorb whatever contribution to social network infrastructure the startups might have made. Manipulating products or prices to harm startup competitors is more viable for diversified firms.[84] If small competitors somehow survive, big firms can buy them out with cash hoards accumulated by strategically charging higher prices where competition is weakest.[85]

Studies of the rise of Facebook, Google, Netflix, and Microsoft document some of these trends. Google's share of general-purpose Internet searches rose from 35 percent to 88 percent between 2004 and 2008, while Facebook's share of mobile

---

[79] Lemley, note 10.

[80] E.g. MIT, An MIT inventor's guide to startups: For faculty and students (2010), http://web.mit.edu/tlo/documents/MIT-TLO-startup-guide.pdf.

[81] Heidi Ledford, High hopes for US patent reform, 458 *Nature* 952 (2009) at 452–3.

[82] David Kappos, Why America's patent system is not killing innovation, *Fortune* (May 8, 2015), http://fortune.com/2015/05/08/why-americas-patent-system-is-not-killing-innovation/.

[83] E.g. American Innovators for Patent Reform, CONNECT, IEEE-USA, IP Advocate, National Association of Patent Practitioners, National Congress of Inventor Organizations, National Small Business Association, Professional Inventors Alliance USA, U.S. Business and Industry Council, and Small Business, Inventors, and Technical Employees, Letter to Harry Reid, Senate Majority Leader, on Patent Reform (February 23, 2011), www.ieeeusa.org/policy/policy/2011/022311.pdf; The Role of Non-Practicing Entities, note 75 [John Duffy, approximately minutes 22:00–25:00].

[84] Liebowitz, note 73; Stoller, note 73.

[85] Stoller, note 73.

social media application usage rose from zero to 77 percent between 2005 and 2016, Netflix's share of all downstream Internet traffic rose from less than 12 percent in 2008 to 33 percent in 2012, and Microsoft's share of all revenue earned by 407 global software companies reached 42 percent in 2006.[86]

Patent owners have alleged that Amazon, Facebook, Google, Microsoft, Netflix, and Twitter have violated a number of social-networking and streaming-related patents.[87] Google became dominant on the strength of its search algorithm, which built on previously patented search techniques, and its Internet crawling ability.[88] In 2010, Google attempted to take a page from Facebook and add status updates to Gmail's chat function, which could be combined with Google's existing profiles to build out a large social network.[89] After other efforts such as Google Buzz, Google launched Google Plus in 2011, prompting Facebook to issue its famous

[86] Jonathan Taplin, *Move Fast and Break Things: How Facebook, Amazon, and Google Cornered Culture and Undermined Democracy* (Little, Brown & Co., 2017) at 6, 21; Sandvine, Global Broadband Phenomena – Executive Summary (2009), https://newmediagr.files.wordpress. com/2009/11/2009global_ broadband_phenomena_exec_sum.pdf; Sandvine, Global Internet Phenomena Report: 2H 2012 (2012), www.sandvine.com/downloads/general/global-internet-phenomena/2012/2h-2012-global-internet-phenomena-report.pdf; Paul Strassman, *The Economics of Corporate Information Systems: Measuring Information Payoffs* (Information Economics Press, 2007) at 188.

[87] E.g. *EasyWeb Innovations, LLC v. Twitter, Inc.*, No. 2016-2066, 2017 WL 1969492 (Fed. Cir. May 12, 2017); *I/P Engine Inc. v. AOL Corp.*, 576 Fed. Appx. 982 (Fed. Cir. 2014); *Parallel Networks, LLC v. Microsoft, Inc.*, No. 1:13-cv-02073 (D. Del. jury verdict for defendant May 11, 2017); *Tele-Publishing, Inc. v. Facebook, Inc.*, No. 09-11686, slip op. (D. Mass. May 11, 2017), www.newenglandipblog.com/files/2017/06/TPI-v-Facebook.pdf; *Profile Protector LLC v. LinkedIn Corp.*, No. 1:11-cv-00665 (E.D. Tex. complaint filed 2016); *Netflix, Inc. v. Rovi Corp.*, 114 F. Supp. 3d 927 (N.D. Cal. 2015), *aff'd*, No. 2015-1917, 2016 WL 6575091 (Fed. Cir. Nov. 7, 2016); *OpenTV, Inc. v. Netflix Inc.*, 76 F. Supp. 3d 886 (N.D. Cal. 2014); *Rembrandt Social Media, LP v. Facebook, Inc.*, 950 F. Supp. 2d 876 (E.D. Va. 2013), subsequent proceedings at 22 F. Supp. 3d 585 (E.D. Va. 2013), *aff'd*, 561 Fed. Appx. 909 (Fed. Cir. 2014); *I/P Engine Inc. v. Microsoft Corp.*, case No. 1:13-cv-00688 (S.D.N.Y. complaint filed January 30, 2013); *EasyWeb Innovations, LLC v. Facebook, Inc.*, 888 F. Supp. 2d 342 (E.D.N.Y. 2012); *Walker Digital, LLC v. Facebook, Inc.*, 852 F. Supp. 2d 559 (D. Del. 2012); *Via Vadis, LLC v. Skype, Inc.*, Civil Action No. 11-507-RGA, 2012 WL 2789733, at *1 (D. Del. July 6, 2012); *Facebook, Inc., et al. v. Skky, LLC*, Case No. CBM2017-00006 (Patent Trial and Appeal Board, April 11, 2017); Jay Fitzgerald, *Phoenix sues online giant Facebook over Web technology patent*, Boston Herald, October 9, 2009, http://bostonherald.com/business/media_marketing/phoenix_sues_online_giant_facebook_over_web_technology_patent; Adam Gaffin, What's left of the Boston Phoenix loses patent lawsuit against Facebook, *Universal Hub* (May 11, 2017), www.universalhub.com/2017/whats-left-boston-phoenix-loses-patent-lawsuit. Cf. also *Smartflash LLC v. Apple Inc.*, No. 16-1059, 2017 U.S. App. LEXIS 3833 (Fed. Cir. Mar. 1, 2017); *Enfish, LLC v. Microsoft Corp.*, 822 F.3d 1327 (Fed. Cir. 2016); *OpenTV, Inc. v. Apple, Inc.*, 2015 W.L. 1535328 (2015), subsequent proceedings at 2016 W.L. 344845 (2016); *Rovi Corp. v. Hulu, LLC*, NO. 1:11-cv-00665, 2012 W.L. 261982 (D. Del. January 27, 2012).

[88] E.g. Ken Auletta, *Googled: The End of the World as We Know It* (Penguin, 2010) at xi–x, xiv, 38–44, 55–6, citing John Battelle, *The Search: How Google and Its Rivals Rewrote the Rules of Business* (Penguin, 2005); see also U.S. Patent No. 8,042,112 (filed June 30, 2004), citing, inter alia, U.S. Patent No. 6,351,755 (filed November 2, 1999); U.S. Patent No. 6,418,433 (filed January 28, 1999); U.S. Patent No. 6,631,369 (filed June 30, 1999).

[89] Ashlee Vance, Google to add social features to Gmail, *The New York Times*, February 9, 2010, www.nytimes.com/2010/02/09/technology/companies/09social.html.

"lockdown" order to clone Google's improved visual interface, photo sharing, and other features.[90] By this time, Facebook had already begun changing its interface to mimic Twitter's instant updates, following system, etc.[91] It later introduced hashtags, disappearing messages, video-sharing, livestreams, and other distinguishing characteristics of competitors such as Twitter, Twitch, or Snapchat.[92] Then it added Stories features to Facebook and Instagram, which observers saw as similar to Snapchat Stories, leading to claims that once Snapchat rejected Facebook's $3 billion offer to buy it, Facebook "spent the intervening years imitating [its] greatest hits."[93]

When the innovation system is open to the sort of lobbying that resulted in the AIA, or in the Supreme Court adopting open-ended rubrics for striking down patents, the accumulated product of human labor turns on the laborer, threatening his or her livelihood. The IP-owning corporation transforms itself from a product of creative labor into the force that defines how labor may be employed, and what its rewards shall be. Starting out as a mere means of production, it arrives at a position where it commands the producer.

In antitrust law, this is referred to as becoming an "autocrat of trade."[94] A corporation with this kind of power can "get hold of the … business," and "command everybody, laborer, consumer, producer, and everybody else … ."[95] A state of affairs may be created, members of Congress feared in 1890, in which "this great aggregated capital is wielded by a single hand and guided by a single brain, or at least by hands and brains acting in complete harmony … , and by this … direction of this immense amount of capital, laborers, vendors, and consumers may be disadvantaged."[96]

At the same time, the dominance of a few large Internet companies should not be overestimated. Contrary to Jonathan Taplin's claims, Facebook, Amazon, and Google

---

[90] Antonio Garcia Martinez, How Mark Zuckerberg led Facebook's war to crush Google Plus, *Vanity Fair*, June 3, 2016, www.vanityfair.com/news/2016/06/how-mark-zuckerberg-led-facebooks-war-to-crush-google-plus?mbid=social_facebook.

[91] Erick Schonfeld, Facebook's response to Twitter, *TechCrunch* (March 4, 2009), https://techcrunch.com/2009/03/04/facebooks-response-to-twitter/.

[92] E.g. Karissa Bell, Facebook is finally bringing live streaming to everyone, *Mashable* (January 28, 2016), http://mashable.com/2016/01/28/facebook-live-video-how-tv-#_IWGgbT2VgqA; Heather Kelly, Vine, Instagram and the rise of bite-sized video, *CNN* (June 21, 2013), www.cnn.com/2013/06/19/tech/social-media/social-video-trend; Justin Lafferty, A closer look at Facebook's hashtags, *Adweek*, June 17, 2013, www.adweek.com/digital/a-closer-look-at-facebooks-hashtags/, citing Brittany Darwell, Facebook releases standalone Poke app for iPhone with Snapchat-like features, *Adweek*, December 21, 2012, www.insidefacebook.com/2012/12/21/facebook-releases-standalone-poke-app-for-iphone-with-snapchat-like-features/, and Facebook, Public Conversations on Facebook (2013), http://newsroom.fb.com/News/633/Public-Conversations-on-Facebook.

[93] Heather Kelly, Facebook's transformation into Snapchat is almost complete, *CNN Money* (March 28, 2017), http://money.cnn.com/2017/03/28/technology/facebook-snapchat-camera-stories/index.html.

[94] 21 Cong. Rec. 2460 (1890) (statement of Senator John Sherman), quoted in William Letwin, *Law and Economic Policy in America: The Evolution of the Sherman Antitrust Act* (University of Chicago Press, 1981) at 91–2.

[95] 21 Cong. Rec. 2726 (1890) (statement of Sen. Edwards).

[96] 21 Cong. Rec. 3147 (1890) (statement of Sen. George).

have not "cornered culture" or driven many newspapers, book publishers, and authors out of the marketplace, while being exempt from taxation, antitrust, or copyright law.[97] Facebook and Google are only two of countless new competitors for US and British newspapers' print advertising revenue. Craigslist and apps such as Zillow or Carvana compete to serve those who might have placed classified ads. Cable television subscriptions and digital video platforms may serve as substitutes for reading or advertising in newspapers, magazines, or broadcast media. Advertising-supported music apps such as Pandora and iHeartRadio vie for the ad spend of those who might have placed ads in the culture and lifestyle sections of newspapers. The online articles of domestic and foreign newspapers and broadcast journalists may compete with local newspapers. Prominent former writers and editors of newspapers and magazines also leave them to start websites and apps, which may divert traffic and advertisers.

There are four million jobs tied directly to the advertising-supported Internet sector, of which Facebook and Google account for fewer than 100,000.[98] Similarly, Facebook, Google, and other sites like Twitter can drive consumers to legacy media offerings, as numerous studies show.[99] The ebooks available with the help of Apple, Amazon, and Google compete for attention with printed books available at Wal-Mart, Walgreens, and other retailers; free ebooks at the Internet Archive and other websites; and free ebook chapters at scholarly Internet archives like SSRN.com and arXiv.org.[100]

3.3. PATENT REFORM AS A STRUGGLE BETWEEN THE RICH AND THE MIDDLE CLASS

Many of the same institutions that have been very active in the movement to weaken patents have also waged class struggle in other economic, social, or military

---

[97] Taplin, note 86, at 6–8, 21.

[98] Michael Coren, Algorithms are helping companies hire more diverse employees, *Quartz* (March 30, 2017), http://qz.com/945342/algorithms-are-helping-companies-hire-more-diverse-employees/; Statista, Number of Facebook employees from 2004 to 2016 (Full-time) (2017), www.statista.com/statistics/273563/number-of-facebook-employees/.

[99] E.g. Gulio Coraggio, A Google snippet tax across Europe, is it the right path?, *Gaming Tech Law* (August 2016), www.gamingtechlaw.com/2016/08/google-snippet-tax/copyright.html; Chong Oh et al., Is Twitter psychic? Social media analytics and television ratings, in IEEE (Ed.), *Second International Conference on Computing Technology and Information Management (ICCTIM)* – (IEEE, 2015) at 150–5; Alice Ju, Sun Ho Jeong, and Hsiang Iris Chyi, Will social media save newspapers? Examining the effectiveness of Facebook and Twitter as news platforms, 8 *Journalism Practice* 1 (2014); Kimberlee Morrison, Facebook, not Google, is now the top referral source for digital publishers, *Ad Week*, August 18, 2015, www.adweek.com/digital/facebook-is-now-the-top-referral-source-for-digital-publishers/; Ravi Somaiya, How Facebook is changing the way its users consume journalism, *The New York Times*, October 26, 2014, www.nytimes.com/2014/10/27/business/media/how-facebook-is-changing-the-way-its-users-consume-journalism.html; Ben Thompson, Facebook and the cost of monopoly, *Stratechery* (April 19, 2017), https://stratechery.com/2017/facebook-and-the-cost-of-monopoly/?utm_source=feedly&utm_medium=webfeeds.

[100] ArXiv.org, https://arxiv.org/; The Berkeley Electronic Press, https://bepress.com; The Social Science Research Network, https://ssrn.com.

domains. In the 1970s, corporate political action committees (PACs) became more prominent, propelled by amendments to the Federal Election Campaign Act in 1971 and 1974, and by an important decision by the Federal Elections Commission in 1975 allowing corporate executives to use their treasuries and to solicit their employees to fund PACs.[101] The US Chamber of Commerce stepped up its political and brief-writing activity starting in 1974, and the year after that the American Legislative Exchange Council (ALEC) was formed to lobby state governments. The Business Roundtable, Heritage Foundation, Olin Foundation, Pacific Legal Foundation, and Law and Economics Center also developed influence over US legislation.[102] The Federalist Society emerged out of efforts by the Olin Foundation to promote conservative ideas on campus in the late 1970s and early 1980s, and its members eventually staffed some of the higher rungs of the legal elite, including Department of Justice positions and Supreme Court clerkships, as well as positions as Supreme Court justice. Groups like the Heritage Foundation and American Enterprise Institute (AEI) achieved a "hard right turn" in economic, social, and military policies, turning government away from ending inequality and towards permanent war.[103]

Moribund in the 1950s and 1960s, starting in the late 1970s and 1980s the AEI revived itself and contributed important officials to presidential administrations.[104] The Heritage Foundation, in turn, wrote the "blueprint" for Reagan–Bush era economic policy.[105]

Since the 1980s, corporate profits have grown very rapidly despite lavish CEO and other executive compensation hikes that widen dramatically the inequalities *within* corporations.[106] Inequality *among* corporations also soared, so that elite corporations

[101] Ted Nace, *Gangs of America: The Rise of Corporate Power and the Dismantling of Democracy* (Berrett-Koehler Publishers, 2003) at 148.

[102] Ibid., at 136–46.

[103] Amos Tevelow, *From corporate liberalism to neoliberalism: A history of American think tanks*, Ph.D. dissertation, University of Pittsburgh, Faculty of Arts and Sciences (2005) at 22–3, 157–8, 181, http://d-scholarship.pitt.edu/9198/1/FinalTevelowETD.pdf.

[104] Ibid., at 172.

[105] Ibid., at 171.

[106] David Harvey, *A Brief History of Neoliberalism* (Oxford University Press, 2005) at 24; Floyd Norris, Corporate profits grow and wages slide, *The New York Times*, April 4, 2014, www.nytimes.com/2014/04/05/business/economy/corporate-profits-grow-ever-larger-as-slice-of-economy-as-wages-slide.html?mcubz=1. See also Josh Bivens, The decline in labor's share of corporate income since 2000 means $535 billion less for workers, *Economic Policy Institute Economic Snapshot Blog* (September 10, 2015), www.epi.org/publication/the-decline-in-labors-share-of-corporate-income-since-2000-means-535-billion-less-for-workers/; Nick Hanauer, Stock buybacks are killing the American economy, *The Atlantic*, February 8, 2015, www.theatlantic.com/politics/archive/2015/02/kill-stock-buyback-to-save-american-economy./385259/; Lawrence Mishel, Economy built for profits not prosperity, *Economic Policy Institute Economic Snapshot Blog* (March 28, 2013), www.epi.org/publication/economy-built-profits-not-prosperity/.

came to earn eight times as much profit as the average one, just as the top 1 percent of income earners seem to hoard wealth.[107]

In 2011, major and minor banks, insurance companies, and retailers urged Congress to enact "patent reform" so that "low-quality business-method patents" could be revoked in light of the prior art.[108] This would save retailers such as Wal-Mart part of their litigation costs.[109] Millions of companies supported reform. Noteworthy supporters included the American Bar Association, the Business Software Alliance, ExxonMobil, General Electric, Visa, Pfizer and the other pharmaceutical companies through their association PhRMA, and the technology companies Apple, eBay, Facebook, Google, IBM, Intel, Microsoft, Netflix, VeriSign, and Verizon.[110]

The Chamber of Commerce supported the AIA as a way to "reduce unnecessary litigation against American businesses ... ."[111] The AEI and the Business Roundtable praised the AIA.[112] The Olin Foundation spent tens of millions of dollars on law and economics programs across the United States, some of which produced papers in favor of patent reform against "trolls."[113] The Heritage Foundation described patent lawyers in much the same terms that think-tanks use for lawyers who represent victims of disfiguring or fatal medical malpractice, employers who disregard workplace safety measures, or companies who use negligent product designs or ads: "frivolous,"

---

[107] Rana Foroohar, The "haves and have-mores" in digital America, *The Financial Times*, August 6, 2017, www.ft.com/content/f6455bb6-7053-11e7-aca6-c6bd07df1a3c; see also Rana Faroohar, The case for higher US taxes, *The Financial Times*, May 21, 2017, www.ft.com/content/a4e01ef4-3c8d-11e7-821a-6027b8a20f23.

[108] 157 Congressional Record S5402 (daily ed. September 8, 2011) at S5423 and S5409.

[109] Ibid., S5410.

[110] Ibid., at S5424–5.

[111] US Chamber of Commerce, Press Release, US Chamber of Commerce Supports Patent Reform (June 14, 2011), https://judiciary.house.gov/_files/news/US%20Chamber%20of%20Commerce%20Patent%20Reform.html.

[112] Innovation, immigration and intellectual property: a forum, Business Roundtable (October 6, 2011), http://businessroundtable.org/media/blog/innovation-immigration-and-intellectual-property-a-forum. See also Jeffrey Eisenach, Trolling for a patent policy fix, American Enterprise Institute (September 16, 2013), www.aei.org/publication/trolling-for-a-patent-policy-fix/.

[113] E.g. Robert Van Horn, How should the Chicago School be explained?, in Warren Samuels, Jeff Biddle, and Ross Emmett (Eds.), *Research in the History of Economic Thought and Methodology* (Emerald Group, 2009), at 300; Lee Anne Fennell, Adjusting Alienability, 122 *Harvard Law Review* 1403 (2009), John M. Olin, Program in Law and Economics Working Paper No. 443 (2008), draft, at 10–13, 32–5, 54, http://chicagounbound.uchicago.edu/cgi/viewcontent.cgi?article=1029&context=law_and_economics; Jonathan Masur, CBA at the PTO, 65 *Duke Law Journal* 1701 (2016) at 1730–2; Eric Posner and E. Glen Weyl, Property is only another name for monopoly, 9 *Journal of Legal Analysis* 51 (2017) at 52, 114. But see Richard A. Epstein, F. Scott Kieff, and Daniel Spulber, The FTC's proposal for regulating IP through SSOs would replace private coordination with government hold-up, John M. Olin Program in Law and Economics Working Paper No. 56 (2011), draft, at 15, http://chicagounbound.uchicago.edu/cgi/viewcontent.cgi?article=1522&context=law_and_economics (Chicago School approach defending patent markets against Obama administration claims of "hold-up").

"[r]apacious," "ambulance chasers."[114] ALEC's website foreshadowed recent moves to get patent owners to pay alleged infringers' legal fees.[115]

The amount spent by corporations on lobbying Congress has grown markedly. The Chamber of Commerce spent more than $200 million lobbying Congress in 2010 and 2011, twice as much as in 2004–2005 and four times as much as in 1998–1999.[116] Overall, companies and other interest groups allocated $20 billion in funds for lobbying Congress in 2009 to 2014, triggering reform efforts in some areas, and stopping them in others.[117] Such figures often do not include money spent to support think-tanks.[118]

Senator Maria Cantwell expressed a rare note of concern before the patent reform bill steamrolled through the Senate in 2011 on a vote of 89-9-2.[119] She remarked:

[T]his is not a patent reform bill, this is a big corporation patent giveaway that tramples on the rights of small inventors. It changes "first to invent" to "first to file," which means if you are a big corporation and have lots of resources, you will get there and get the patent … .[120]

The legislation was therefore a "special giveaway" that said that large corporations could tie up the "little guy's" patent for years and years, imposing high additional costs in the name of allegedly reducing costs. Earlier in the day, she explained what she meant, arguing that (1) "first to file" retards innovation by deterring individual entrepreneurship backed by patents, focusing economic activity on large corporations and their executives; (2) Canada and Europe tried "first to file" and experienced less patenting activity and a slower rate of innovation along with it; (3) the reform legislation granted financial institutions immunity against patents, even those which had already been confirmed valid by a patent examiner and perhaps

[114] Alden Abbott and John Malcolm, A measured approach to patent reform legislation, *Heritage Foundation* (July 14, 2015), www.heritage.org/node/10934/print-display/. See also Marguerite Bowling, Understanding the uninsured numbers, *Heritage Foundation The Daily Signal Blog* (April 14, 2009), http://blog.heritage.org/2009/04/14/understanding-the-uninsured-numbers; Conn Carroll, Morning Bell: The "Buy America" threat to our economic recovery, *Heritage Foundation The Daily Signal Blog*, (February 19, 2009), http://blog.heritage.org/2009/02/19/morning-bell-the-buy-america-threat-to-our-economic-recovery/; Matthew McKillip, Tort reform betrayed in New York, *Heritage Foundation The Daily Signal Blog* (March 28, 2011), http://blog.heritage.org/?p=55716; Hans von Spakovsky, Killing Americans by stifling medical innovation: The Medical Device "Safety" Act of 2009, *Heritage Foundation* (August 4, 2009), www.heritage.org/node/14211/print-display.
[115] Curt Bramble, Patent trolls spell trouble for America's economy, ALEC/Reuters (November 23, 2013), www.alec.org/article/patent-trolls-spell-trouble-americas-economy/.
[116] James Wilson, John DiIulio, Jr., and Meena Bose, *American Government: Institutions and Policies, Essentials Edition* (Cengage Learning, 2016) at 248.
[117] Lawrence Lessig, *Republic, Lost: Version 2.0* (Hachette, 2015).
[118] 2 U.S.C. § 1602 (excluding those who lobby less than 20 percent of the time for any particular client, as a percentage of all services to that client, from definition of "lobbyist").
[119] 157 Congressional Record S5402, note 108, at S5441–2.
[120] Ibid., at S5441.

even by a federal court; (4) amendments to the legislation had been rushed to the Senate floor without hearings in the Judiciary Committee; and (5) mistakes by the PTO in issuing bad patents could easily have been resolved by using patent application and maintenance fees to increase the amount of time spent examining each patent. She added:

> [T]hey have drafted this [legislation] to benefit the big banks of America and screw a little innovator, [and] this is basically drafted so broadly that I am worried that other technology companies are going to get swept up in the definition and their patents are also going to be thrown out as invalid … .
>
> Companies that have revenue streams from royalties that are operating their companies could now have their bank financing, everything pulled out from under them because they no longer have royalty streams. Businesses could lay off people, businesses could shut down … .

The reform legislation gave the PTO greater ability to raise its fees but did not prevent those fees from being diverted to other federal budgetary purposes.[121]

A coalition of engineers, small businesses, and patent law practitioners made similar arguments in a letter to the Senate leadership:

> The "first inventor to file" section of the bill … disadvantages small companies and independent inventors in favor of larger firms – the bill disadvantages companies that must seek outside financing … .
>
> The bill favors multinational and foreign firms over start-up firms seeking an initial foothold in US domestic markets, and favors market incumbents over new entrants with disruptive new technologies. Because S. 23 removes the option to delay patent expenses, the bill advantages established companies, and disadvantages start-ups that must seek and carefully shepherd their capital.[122]

President Obama sold the AIA to the public as helping the next Thomas Edison or Steve Jobs receive patents more quickly. His PTO director, Michelle Lee, touted its provisions for a "lower cost alternative to district court litigation."[123] Some have asked: at lower cost for whom? Not the individual inventor like a young Steve Jobs working with Steve Wozniak in a Palo Alto garage. Instead, AIA provisions are cheaper for large companies who are being sued by small inventors, or by those who bought their patents.[124] Median patent litigation costs rose 10 percent after 2011, as

---

[121] Ibid., at S5407–8; U.S. PTO, Fifth anniversary of the America Invents Act (2016), www.youtube.com/watch?v=bRXx6IRsws4/; Tony Dutra, AIA at 5 years: PTAB's tectonic change in patent litigation, *Intellectual Property on Bloomberg Law* (September 6, 2016), www.bna.com/aia-years-ptabs-n57982077105.

[122] American Innovators for Patent Reform, note 83.

[123] US PTO, note 121. See also Congressional Research Service, *Summaries: S. 23 (112th): America Invents Act*, Govtrack.us (2011), www.govtrack.us/congress/bills/112/s23/summary.

[124] Dutra, note 121.

AIA proceedings added as much as $600,000 to the cost of enforcing a patent against a corporate defendant. The AIA therefore shifted a portion of companies' patent compliance costs to inventors.[125]

The AIA made it much faster and easier to strip patents en masse from individual inventors in the name of helping them and promoting "innovation."[126] Just as doom was predicted if authors rather than employers owned their own works, it was said that financial and technology companies would be devastated and go out of business if the pre-AIA patent system was retained. The cost of patent suits and the number of patents had created a "crisis" that was destroying jobs and the economy, just like Internet piracy in another popular narrative, but from an IP-limiting rather than an IP-expanding motivation.[127] In fact, there was probably no "crisis" for corporate producers.

The AIA forces inventors to file their patents very quickly, often before they would like to or can afford to, and also requires these applications to be more detailed than before, presenting a double-whammy of doing a fast job that must also be complete.[128] Independent inventors may be tempted to file for a provisional patent, which costs less and is easier to do, but this may be a trap, because leaving out important information about the invention could result in an application being rejected, or even worse, competitors or even infringers filing for their own patents containing the missing elements and blocking the initial inventor's use of his or her own technologies.[129]

The market value of patents went into a tailspin with the AIA's changes in 2011, which started to become effective in the spring of 2013.[130] As small technology firms told the Federal Circuit in 2016, an 80 percent fall in patent values had

---

[125] Hannibal Travis, Patent alienability and its discontents, 17 *Tulane Journal of Technology and Intellectual Property* 109 (2014) at 126, citing Cheryl Milone, The America Invents Act "mini-trials" are the next battleground for resolving patent disputes and shifting fees to patent owners, IP Watchdog (December 1, 2013), www.ipwatchdog.com/2013/12/01/mini-trials-next-battleground/id=46514.

[126] Stacy Lewis and Tom Irving, Very few appreciated just how bad AIA Inter Partes reviews would be for patent owners, although IPR denials have been, for patent owners, a glimmer of hope, 11 *Buffalo Intellectual Property Law Journal* 28 (2015) at 35–9, 54–64, 69–70.

[127] E.g. James Bessen, The patent troll crisis is really a software patent crisis, *Washington Post The Switch Blog* (September 3, 2013), www.washingtonpost.com/news/the-switch/wp/2013/09/03/the-patent-troll-crisis-is-really-a-software-patent-crisis/; Paul Edward Geller, An international patent Utopia, 85 *Journal of the Patent & Trademark Office Society* 582 (2003); Roger Milgrim, An independent invention defense to patent infringement, 90 *Journal of the Patent & Trademark Office Society* 295 (2008). See also Colleen Chien, Reforming software patents, 50 *Houston Law Review* 325 (2012); Steven Levy, The patent problem, *Wired*, November 13, 2012, www.wired.com/2012/11/ff-steven-levy-the-patent-problem; Ben Parr, Why the coming patent crisis is inevitable, *CNET Gadgets* (April 4, 2012), www.cnet.com/news/why-the-coming-patent-crisis-is-inevitable/;

[128] E.g. Ryan Davis, 5 tips for 1st-to-file patent applications, 1 year in, *Law360* (March 12, 2014), www.law360.com/articles/517358/5-tips-for-1st-to-file-patent-applications-1-year-in.

[129] Ibid.

[130] Jack Lu, Patent market dynamics and the impact of Alice and the AIA, IP Watchdog (May 17, 2015), www.ipwatchdog.com/2015/05/17/patent-market-dynamics-aia-and-alice/id%3D57728/.

brought average prices down from more than one million dollars to less than $200,000.[131]

Moreover, patent owners are earning less than ever on average from enforcing their rights to inventions in court. Royalty awards were down 75 percent from 2012 to 2014, and 50 percent from 2012 to 2015.[132] The median patent damages award in 2012–2014 was 75–80 percent down from the 1995–2010 period; the average award was also down.[133] There were no years in 2012–2014 in which the median patent award was greater than $2 million, but this happened in five years between 2004 and 2008.[134] Patent damage awards peaked in 2012, with 2014 and 2015 combined not equaling the total for 2012 alone.[135]

The number of patent cases filed, moreover, declined from 3,025 in the first half of 2013, before the AIA took full effect, to 2,238 in the first half of 2016, after its implications had become obvious.[136] Patent case filings fell 40 percent from the AIA's effective date of September 2013 to a year later.[137] Despite all this, it is sometimes said that the AIA did nothing for the software companies that lobbied for it in 2010–2011.[138]

3.4. SUING APPLE, FIGHTING THE GOVERNMENT

The story of Sightsound illustrates the problems with owning ideas in the social media age. Sightsound was the owner of a patent on a method and system for transmitting digital music and movies for sale over the Internet, as told by its co-founder

---

[131] Brief of Amicus Curiae Small Business Technology Council in Support of Petitioner, at 12, *In Re* Trading Techs. International, Inc., No. 2016-120 (U.S. brief filed March 15, 2016).

[132] Ibid., at 29.

[133] PricewaterhouseCoopers LLP, 2011 Patent litigation study: Patent litigation trends as the "America Invents Act" becomes law (2011), at 9, www.pwc.com/us/en/forensic-services/publications/assets/2011-patent-litigation-study.pdf ($5 million median damages in 1995–2010); Owen Byrd and Brian Howard, Lex Machina, 2013 Patent Litigation Year in Review (2014), at 12, http://pages.lexmachina .com/rs/lexmachina/images/LexMachina-2013%20Patent%20Litigation%20Year%20in%20Review .pdf ($1 to $1.25 million median in 2012–2013); Michael Loney, 2014 median US patent litigation damages were second lowest in 20 years, Managing IP (May 27, 2015), www.managingip.com/ Article/3457364/2014-median-US-patent-litigation-damages-were-second-lowest-in-20-years-PwC .html (2014 median had to be lower than 2012 or 2013); see also PWC, note 133, at 9.

[134] Loney, note 133; PWC, note 133, at 9; see also Byrd and Howard, note 133; (stating that 2014 median had to be lower than either 2012 or 2013).

[135] Lemley, note 10, at 29.

[136] Brian Howard, 2015 first half patent case filing trends, Lex Machina (July 14, 2015), https:// lexmachina.com/2015-first-half-patent-case-filing-trends/ (3025 cases filed in first half of 2013); Richard Lloyd, First half US patent litigation down dramatically with new suits falling by almost 1,000, *IAM* (July 5, 2016), www.iam-media.com/Blog/Detail.aspx?g=e6d2dc31-5d07-4e5c-8875-0e6c5eb48bd9 (2238 cases brought in the first half of 2016). *Cf.* also Brian Pomper, In considering patent law changes, don't forget impact on universities, *IP Watchdog* (February 15, 2015), www .ipwatchdog.com/2015/02/15/patent-law-changes-impact-on-universities/id=54690.

[137] Pomper, note 136.

[138] James Bessen, The anti-innovators, *Foreign Affairs*, December 15, 2014, www.foreignaffairs.com/ articles/americas/2014-12-15/anti-innovators.

Scott Sander. The company spent five years seeking a decision from the government on its initial application for a patent in 1998, five more years raising money
and building a business based on the patent, and six years suing the first alleged
infringer, Napster and its parent corporation Bertelsmann, during which time the
record labels, Napster, MusicNet, Microsoft, Apple, and Amazon made tens or hundreds of millions of dollars selling music online. Napster filed for reexamination of
the patent, which was unsuccessful after six years because the closest prior invention
involved using floppy disks to distribute music across computers.

Sightsound sued Apple for patent infringement via the iTunes store in 2011.
When a jury trial on the validity and infringement by Apple of Sightsound's patent was only months away, Apple filed with the Obama administration for post-
grant review of the patent. From Sightsound's point of view, the patent was being
"re-re-examined."

The PTO, through the Patent Trial and Appeal Board established by the AIA,
rejected Apple's arguments in 2014, but raised and accepted another argument for
finding the patents to be invalid.[139] Perhaps the patent truly is invalid. But the process to which Sightsound was subjected in attempting to establish its validity would
bankrupt any company smaller than a Bertelsmann, Warner, Microsoft, or Apple.
One commentator observed: "If patents can be repeatedly challenged on the same
grounds in the same forum, few will take the risk of a major investment in the technology covered."[140]

One of the inventors of social media technologies, David Gelernter, has had more
success than Sightsound, but he may face similar problems in the future. "In his
book 'Mirror Worlds,' published in 1991, he accurately described websites, blogging, virtual reality, streaming video, tablet computers, e-books, search engines and
internet telephony." In the "Mirror Worlds," people could chat electronically with
friends and strangers, and see who agreed with (liked) their comments on various
matters.

Of course, no one can own the catch-all idea of having conversations online,
even if conducted on an iPad using Facebook or YouTube. Like the founders of
Apple, Facebook, Google, and Microsoft, Gelernter and Eric Freeman, his Ph.D.
student at one time, filed for patents on technologies that made an advance over

---

[139] Scott Sander, *SightSound versus Apple, and the death squad for patents, Cuepoint/Medium* (August
    16, 2016), http://medium.com/cuepoint/sightsound-versus-apple-and-the-death-squad-for-patents-
    fe51cc4f9239, citing U.S. Patent 5,191,573 (March 3, 1993). See also *UMG Recordings, Inc. v.
    Bertelsmann AG*, 222 F.R.D. 408 (N.D. Cal. 2004) (Bertelsmann provided Napster with a loan),
    rev'd, 479 F. 3d 1078 (9th Cir. 2007); Anne Urda, Latest Napster deal to cost Bertelsmann $110M,
    Law 360 (April 24, 2007), www.law360.com/articles/23354/latest-napster-deal-to-cost-bertelsmann-
    110m?article_related_content=1 (Bertelsmann later gained an equity stake in the company, making
    it potentially liable for infringement contributed to by Napster's central directory of MP3 files).
[140] William Wells, Letter to the editor, *The Wall Street Journal*, June 23, 2015, p. A12, www.wsj.com/
    articles/new-patent-board-is-a-loose-cannon and www.cormoranttechnologies.com/news.

other inventions in the fields of computing and networking. By combining many computers together and devoting them to common tasks, supercomputers could be built. Gelernter's experiments with this idea at Yale, *The Economist* observes, were the ancestors of the cloud computing resources that are licensed today by Amazon, Google, and Microsoft.[141]

Mirror Worlds the company, which Gelernter sold, sued Apple for patent infringement in 2008, and in 2010 a jury awarded the plaintiff of the largest patent verdicts ever, nearly two-thirds of a billion dollars.[142] The federal courts ruled that Apple's users rather than Apple itself performed one or more of the required steps set forth in the patents, and declined to grant Mirror World the damages it sought.[143]

In 2017, Mirror Worlds sued Facebook on patents claiming a system to organize photos and other user data in chronological feeds rather than the "traditional folder and directory structure."[144] Even though Mirror Worlds settled subsequent suits against Apple and Microsoft in 2015, and collected $47 million in royalties, Facebook may file for PTO review of the patents. This would delay Mirror Worlds' case between about six months and two years, in addition to any time required for an appeal of the PTO's decision to the courts prior to the lifting of any stay on the case against Facebook – assuming that Facebook loses the first phase.[145] Another inventor, Jay Walker of Walker Digital, which has gone through these sorts of proceedings in the past, raises the question of whether, given the growing cost of enforcement, the "big monied interests [will] figure out how to not have to pay any of the small inventors anymore."[146]

Advocates for entrepreneurial and independent inventors predicted that patent owners would find it very difficult to operate in the current environment. Billions of dollars in revenue can be won or lost based on the inclusion or omission of specific technologies or sub-technologies in social media apps and websites.[147] Yet

[141] Seer of the mirror world, *The Economist*, December 3, 2011, www.economist.com/node/21540383.

[142] Ibid. See also Mirror Worlds, *LLC v. Apple, Inc.*, 742 F. Supp. 2d 703 (E.D. Tex. 2010), subsequent proceedings at 784 F. Supp. 2d 703 (E.D. Tex. 2011), aff'd, 692 F.3d 1351 (Fed. Cir. 2014); *Mirror Worlds, LLC v. Apple, Inc.*, No. 6:08cv88 (E.D. Tex. complaint filed March 14, 2008).

[143] *Mirror Worlds*, 692 F.3d 1351; see also, Petition for Certiorari, *Mirror Worlds, LLC v. Apple, Inc.* No. 12-1158, 2013 U.S. S. Ct. Briefs LEXIS 1629 (U.S. Supreme Court petition filed March 21, 2013).

[144] Andrew Denney, Computer scientist sues Facebook, alleging it purloined his ideas, *The New York Law Journal*, May 11, 2017, www.newyorklawjournal.com/id=1202785981845/ Computer-Scientist-Sues-Facebook-Alleging-It-Purloined-His-Ideas.

[145] *PersonalWeb Technologies, LLC v. Facebook, Inc.*, No. 5:13-CV-01356, 2014 WL 116340, at *2 (N.D. Cal. Jan. 13, 2014), citing 35 U.S.C. § 314(a) and 37 C.F.R. §§ 42.100 et seq.

[146] Sam Lane, Inventor behind Priceline bemoans broken patent system, PBS Newshour Making Sense Blog (May 26, 2016), www.pbs.org/newshour/making-sense/inventor-behind-priceline-bemoans-broken-patent-system/. He cites the need to have "spent millions and millions of dollars in lawyers just to make a [patent licensing] deal."

[147] Cf. David Franklyn and Adam Kuhn, The problem of mop heads in the era of apps: Toward more rigorous standards of value apportionment in contemporary patent law, 98 *Journal of the Patent & Trademark Office Society* 182 (2017) at 184.

such incremental innovations in the fields of software and social networking are becoming very easy to disqualify for patent rights as "obvious" or bereft of an "inventive concept."

Without the benefit of even the limited evidentiary discovery that federal courts may order, the Obama-era reviews under the AIA often gave cursory attention to patent holders' arguments.[148] The Obama administration and the PTO began "adding new members" to the AIA panels that did not give the government the result it wanted.[149] If the ability to reshuffle the judges hearing a case was not enough, companies could file multiple administrative challenges to the same patent.[150] Petitioners in the reviews benefit from Congress and Obama administration having "loaded the dice" in favor of alleged infringers, resulting in the procedure being used more than 2,000 times in 2015, versus an average of about 11 times in 1999–2004.[151]

3.5. THE INNOVATION IDEOLOGY

Analytical Marxism predicts that a struggle results when the development and interconnectivity introduced by capitalism alienate the fruits of production from the producers, and elevate the means of production into demigods that govern the laborers who created them.[152] Like these theorists, scholars of copyright and Internet law sometimes emphasize the struggle to reshape the law to suit industry.[153]

---

[148] In Re Cuozzo Speed Technologies, 793 F.3d 1297, 1301 (Fed. Cir. 2015) (Prost, J., dissenting from denial of rehearing en banc). See also Peter Pitts, 'Patent Death Squads' vs. innovation, *The Wall Street Journal*, June 10, 2015, www.wsj.com/articles/patent-death-squads-vs-innovation-1433978591.

[149] Gene Quinn, USPTO admits to stacking PTAB panels to achieve desired outcomes, *IP Watchdog* (August 28, 2017), www.ipwatchdog.com/2017/08/23/uspto-admits-stacking-ptab-panels-achieve-desired-outcomes/id=87206/ (quoting Transcript of Oral Argument, *Yissum Research Development Co. v. Sony Corp.* (Fed. Cir. 2015) (No. 2015-1342)).

[150] Mealey's, Inter Partes Review request filed by Facebook, Instagram, *Lexis Legal News* (January 19, 2017), www.lexislegalnews.com/articles/14036/inter-partes-review-request-filed-by-facebook-instagram.

[151] Roy Strom, Patently dangerous: Rise of the 'death squad', Chicago Lawyer (August 2015), www.chicagolawyermagazine.com/Archives/2015/08/Patent-death-squads-Aug-15 (quoting Ken Adamo, a patent attorney at Kirkland & Ellis in Chicago).

[152] Friedrich Engels, *Feuerbach: The Roots of the Socialist Philosophy* (Austin Lewis trans., Charles H. Kerr & Co., 1908) at 120–4; Clark Everling, *The Dialectics of Class Struggle in the Global Economy* (Routledge, 2013) at 4, 8–9, 34, 65–76, 91, 97–101, 124–52; Jürgen Habermas, *The Philosophical Discourse of Modernity* (Frederick Lawrence trans., The MIT Press, 8th printing, 1995) at 62–9; Ian Hunt, *Analytical and Dialectical Marxism* (Ashgate, 1993) at 145; Herbert Marcuse, *Reason and Revolution* (Routledge, 2013), at 184, 268–70, 398–400; Karl Marx and Friedrich Engels, Manifesto of the Communist Party, *Marxists.org* (1848), www.marxists.org/archive/marx/works/1848/communist-manifesto; Paul Wetherly, *Marxism and the State: An Analytical Approach* (Springer, 2015) at 17–22.

[153] E.g. Jessica Litman, Revising copyright law for the information age, 75 *Oregon Law Review* 19 (1996) at 23; Jessica Litman, Real copyright reform, 96 *Iowa Law Review* 48 (2010) at 53 (arguing that beneficiaries of copyright legislation has obtained virtual veto power over reforms that could reduce cost and improve operation of copyright system); see also Jessica Litman, Copyright legislation and technological change, 68 *Oregon Law Review* 275 (1989) at 312, n. 206; Jessica Litman, Copyright, compromise, and legislative history, 72 *Cornell Law Review* 857 (1987) at 870–9. Cf. also Lloyd L.

Struggle is blunted by ideology. Ideology, within neo-Marxian theory, is an idea or vision that elevates and perpetuates an event or a process.[154] Ideological concepts disappear into the texture of life, forming the field on which the game is played.[155] Ideology seeks to reassure people that there are certainties about social life that are on a par with those of science, such as gravity.[156]

Ideology plays an important role in the relationship among creativity, labor, ownership, and property (capital). Ideology is part of what persuades the creative laborer to part with the full power of that labor, and to recognize the claim of others to own it. Even when the laborer believes that he or she has escaped ideology into dreams of a better life or a society that is fairer, he or she becomes even more entangled in ideology, as the visions, ideals, and propaganda that define life-projects and politics.[157]

Novelty is one ideology of capitalism, which promises to improve everything it touches.[158] Innovation as an abstract concept is arguably becoming an ideology in another sense. In emphasizing change and the march of history, it casts efforts to shape history through collective action or global solidarity as themselves "ideological," even "totalitarian."[159] Innovation therefore joins entertainment as a "hegemonic ideology" of our times; opposing it or its needs would seem radical and tyrannical.[160]

The ideology of innovation is usefully viewed using Analytical Marxism's concepts. Much of the actual work of innovation, reflected in the labor of ordinary innovators, is dismissed as a solution to an existing problem dictated by "market pressure" under the *KSR* framework, supplemented by *PerfectWeb* and *Leapfrog*. Other innovative work is "abstracted" away using the doctrine of *Alice* and *Ultramercial* that a mysterious "concrete idea" or "inventive step" is needed to obtain and enforce a patent. New rules of venue and fee-shifting impose forbidding procedural barriers to obtaining a jury trial on patent rights within the effective life of a patent.

The ideology of "innovation" seems to have inspired much patent reform rhetoric. Unless capital has its way, earning maximal revenue at the lowest possible cost, it will go on strike and refuse to innovate.[161] There is a resemblance to the neo-conservative

---

Weinreb, Custom, law and public policy: The *INS* case as an example for intellectual property, 78 *Virginia Law Review* 141 (1992) at 146–7.

[154] Slavoj Žižek, *In Defense of Lost Causes* (Verso, 2009) at 405.

[155] Ibid., at403, 405.

[156] Slavoj Žižek, *Living in the End Times* (Verso, 2011) at 42.

[157] E.g. Slavoj Žižek, *A Pervert's Guide to Ideology: A Film* (DVD directed by Sophie Fiennes, Channel 4 Films, 2013).

[158] Žižek, note 154, at 338.

[159] Ibid., at458.

[160] Žižek, note 156, at 97.

[161] For example, a bipartisan group of Senators echoed blog posts suggesting that the number of Americans unemployed after the recession had reached the millions in part due to patent lawsuits. Rob Portman, Portman, Udall Lead Bipartisan Effort to Confront Abusive Patent Trolls, Support Main Street Businesses, U.S. Senate (March 14, 2014), www.portman.senate.gov/public/index.cfm/2014/3/portman-udall-lead-bipartisan-effort-to-confront-abusive-patent-trolls-support-main-street-businesses; Vivek Wadhwa, Where are the jobs? Ask the patent trolls, *The Washington Post Innovations Blog*

ideology of labor law, the gist of which is that unless capital has its way in terms of paying very low wages and not contributing more for health insurance, paid leave, or occupational injury prevention, it will retaliate by laying off existing workers and refusing to hire new ones.[162] This ideology also became popular around the time of the patent reform debates, as Republicans predicted that Obamacare and higher minimum wages would result in no hiring as "job creators" declared a "capital strike."[163]

Over the decades preceding the declaration of a "patent crisis" sometime around 2003, individual inventors had been praised frequently by judges, legislators, and PTO officials.[164] This approach – which may itself have devolved into an ideology that patent owners can do no wrong – was gradually replaced post-2003 with a "patent troll" narrative that, in President Obama's phrasing, emphasized the "folks" that "don't actually produce anything themselves" and who are "just trying to ... extort some money ... ."[165] He pledged to consult with "stakeholders" (e.g., lobbyists) so that innovation is not "reduced."[166] This narrative has become dominant in legislative, judicial, and scholarly discourse.[167]

(May 7, 2012), www.washingtonpost.com/national/on-innovations/where-are-the-jobs-ask-the-patent-trolls/2012/05/07/gIQAdIEo8T_story.html?utm_term=.d4od79fac1c2. Cf. Bessen, note 138 (warning that because of patent litigation, contract law, occupational licensing, and defense procurement policy, the "United States may lose what has been the very secret to its success," innovation); Bessen, note 127; James Bessen, Jennifer Ford, and Michael Meurer, The private and social costs of patent trolls: Do nonpracticing entities benefit society by facilitating markets for technology?, *Regulation*, Winter 2011–2012, at 26, www.cato.org/sites/cato-org/files/serials/files/regulation/2012/5/v34n4-1.pdf; James Bessen and Michael Meurer, Lessons for Patent Policy from Empirical Research on Patent Litigation, 9 *Lewis & Clark Law Review* 1 (2005) at 14; Alex Blumberg and Laura Sydell, When patents attack, NPR (July 22, 2011), www.npr.org/blogs/money/2011/07/26/138576167/when-patents-attack; Charles Duhigg and Steve Lohr, The patent, used as a sword, *The New York Times*, October 7, 2012, www.nytimes.com/2012/10/08/technology/patent-wars-among-tech-giants-can-stifle-competition.html?_r=0; Levy, note 127; Parr, note 127. Cf. also James Bessen and Michael Meurer, *Patent Failure: How Judges, Bureaucrats, and Lawyers Put Innovators at Risk* (Princeton University Press, 2009) at 141 (suggesting that patent lawsuits will "inhibit investment").

[162] Michael Adamson, Reagan and the economy, in Andrew Johns (ed.), A Companion to Ronald Reagan (Wiley, 2015) at 149–51, 158. See also Richard Posner, The Economic Analysis of Law (Aspen Publishers, 9th ed., 2014) at https://books.google.com/books?id=o77fDgAAQBAJ&pg=PT484.

[163] E.g. Robert McElvaine, Boehner admits to "capital strike," *HuffPost* (September 16, 2011). www.huffingtonpost.com/robert-s-mcelvaine/capital-strike_b_965407.html; John Miller, Employers go on strike – because they can, *Dollars & Sense* (July 10, 2010), www.dollarsandsense.org/archives/2010/0710miller.html: Joseph Palermo, Capital strike?, *HuffPost* (March 6, 2009), www.huffingtonpost.com/joseph-a-palermo/capital-strike_b_163506.html.

[164] Christopher Cotropia, The individual inventor motif in the age of the patent troll, 12 *Yale Journal of Law and Technology* 52 (2009) at 59–61.

[165] Pres. Barack Obama, Remarks during Google+ Fireside Hangout (February 2013), quoted in Bruce Berman, Obama drinks the kool-aid on weaker patents, "trolls," *IP CloseUp* (February 19, 2013), https://ipcloseup.com/2013/02/19/obama-drinks-the-kool-aid-on-weaker-patents-trolls/.

[166] Berman, note 165.

[167] Cf. Cotropia, note 164, at 61–78. Cotropia suggests that the Supreme Court "ignored" individual inventors in *eBay*, a case in which prominent members of the software and Internet industries argued in favor of the eventual outcome. As Cotropia presciently suggested, the "troll" narrative overpowered the "individual inventor motif" at the White House and elsewhere. E.g. Executive Office of the

For a variety of neo-Marxian writers, including Slavoj Žižek, ideology serves to blunt and redirect movements for economic change by elevating ideas such as freedom or "the Party" – or, for purposes of this chapter, ideas such as innovation or progress – into fetishes more real and vital than mere persons. The critique of ideology is particularly influential among scholars of communications and cyberspace culture, making it well suited to this project.[168] Ideology is not the same thing as falsehood or lies, because truthful information or statements can be incorporated into an ideological frame.

The ideology of innovation predicts that disaster will result from allowing the individual inventor to participate in the high-tech sector on a level playing field with patent conglomerates and multinational manufacturers.[169] However, famous inventors such as Thomas Edison, the Wright Brothers, Charles Goodyear, and others, licensed patents out so that more active firms could use them.[170] The way that many individual inventors seek to maximize their leverage is by alienating their patent rights to aggregators, "patent dealers" who buy patents and enforce them, just like music rights are enforced by Broadcast Music, Inc. or the American Society of Composers, Authors, and Publishers.[171] A rights management organization is said

President, The White House, *Patent assertion and U.S. innovation* (June 2013), www.whitehouse .gov/sites/default/files/docs/patent_report.pdf; Office of the Press Secretary, The White House, Press Release, Fact Sheet: White House Task Force on high-tech patent issues, White House (June 4, 2013), https://obamawhitehouse.archives.gov/the-press-office/2013/06/04/fact-sheet-white-house-task-force-high-tech-patent-issues; Federal Trade Commission, The evolving IP marketplace: Aligning patent notice and remedies with competition (2011), at 3, www.ftc.gov/sites/default/files/documents/reports/evolving-ip-marketplace-aligning-patent-notice-and-remedies-competition-report-federal-trade/110307patentreport.pdf; Sam Graves, Why isn't the Senate taking up innovation bill?, *CNBC* (August 11, 2014), www.cnbc.com/id/101910973; Travis, note 125, at 128, 137. Compare also Jaffe and Lerner, note 11, at 11 (PTO used to grant patents reflexively as a profit center for government raking in application and maintenance fees), with James Edwards, Novel idea: Pick a pro-patent Patent Office chief, *Morning Consult* (June 22, 2017), https://morningconsult.com/opinions/novel-idea-pick-pro-patent-patent-office-chief/ (arguing that PTO began to be suspicious of patents and to invalidate them at high rates in order to reflect bias of Silicon Valley companies against strong patents).

[168] E.g. Christian Fuchs, Information and communication technologies and society: A contribution to the critique of the political economy of the Internet, 24 *European Journal of Communication* 69 (2009).

[169] Travis, note 125, at 124.

[170] Patrick Boucher, *Nanotechnology: Legal Aspects* (CRC Press, 2008) at 30 (Edison); Stephen Haber, Patents and the wealth of nations, 23 *George Mason Law Review* 811 (2016) at 824 (Goodyear); Edward Roach, *The Wright Company: From Invention to Industry* (Ohio University Press, 2014) at 50 (Wright Brothers).

[171] James McDonough III, The myth of the patent troll: An alternative view of the function of patent dealers in an idea economy, 56 *Emory Law Review* 189 (2006) at 199–201, 209–20. ASCAP and BMI say or imply to cities and private companies who want to perform copyrighted music (e.g., by radio, CD, streaming, or live band) that "BMI claims to own the music rights to half of the recording industry," so that "ASCAP owns approximately half of the rights and BMI owns the other half." Austin, Minnesota City Council, Minutes of the Committee-of-the-Whole Work Session (January 19, 2010), www.ci.austin.mn.us/Council/archive/2010/Work%20Session%20Minutes%2001-19-10 .pdf. Technically ASCAP and BMI often assert *nonexclusive* licenses, see *Broadcast Music, Inc. v.*

to be a more efficient way of enforcing rights dispersed among tens of thousands of owners and potentially infringed by hundreds of thousands of users: "ASCAP ... provides the necessary resources for ... enforcement, resources unavailable to the vast majority of composers and publishing houses."[172] Like labor unions, these organizations enjoy an exemption from the antitrust rule against conspiracies and combinations "in restraint of trade," and can build a degree of monopoly power legally due to the courts' belief that individual negotiations may be less efficient, and that collective bargaining may balance out the buying power (or monopsony power) of those who purchase many business inputs, such as labor or music.[173]

As with the neo-conservative or Chicago School theories of labor law, there is reason to doubt that overly strong aggregations of patent rights destroyed innovation prior to the AIA or the *Alice* decision. Several empirical studies have attempted to test the hypothesis that, particularly in software and signally in the smartphone software area, patents will "hold up" innovation. The hypothesis is that patent owners accumulate massive "holdout power" and successfully demand extortionate royalties from "real" innovators due to the sheer number of patents, their vague and ambiguous language, the disparity between the cost of licensing patents versus litigating them in federal court, and related factors.

The empirical studies have shown that even where patent holdup was supposed to be the most common – the Internet and particularly the 3G mobile Internet sector – evidence of it is lacking.[174] The prices of personal computer, smartphones, audiovisual products, and televisions declined much more rapidly than in other industries, and

---

Columbia Broadcasting System, Inc., 441 U.S. 1, 4–5 (1978), but these are referred to colloquially as being song rights that they "own." E.g. *Sixx Gunner Music v. Quest, Inc.*, 777 F. Supp. 2d 272, 274–275 (D. Mass. 2011); *Bourne Co. v. Speeks*, 670 F. Supp. 777 (E.D. Tenn. 1987); Tim Cushing, Restaurant owner ordered to pay BMI $30,450 for 'illegally playing' four unlicensed songs, *Techdirt* (August 17, 2011), www.techdirt.com/articles/20110815/11503015533/restaurant-owner-ordered-to-pay-bmi-30450-illegally-playing-four-unlicensed-songs.shtml.

[172] *Broadcast Music*, 441 U.S. at 21.

[173] *Broadcast Music*, 441 U.S. 1; Donald Dewey, *Monopoly in Economics and Law* (Rand McNally & Co., 3rd printing, 1966) at 265–70, 279–82.

[174] Robert Merges and John Duffy, *Patent Law and Policy: Cases and Materials* (LexisNexis, 4th ed. 2007) at 939 (noting that holdup was expected as of 2005–2006 in Internet services industry), citing Brief of Amicus Curiae Yahoo! Inc. in Support of Petitioner, *eBay*, 547 U.S. 388 (U.S. brief filed January 26, 2006); Mark Lemley and Carl Shapiro, Patent holdup and royalty stacking, 85 *Texas Law Review* 1991 (2007) at 1992, 2025–9 (one might expect holdup to be most common where there are many "essential" patents, such as those covering cell phones, memory devices, Wi-Fi, and the MP3 music format for Internet delivery); Joseph Farrell et al., Standard setting, patents, and hold-up, 74 *Antitrust Law Journal* 603 (2007) at 604–9 (anticipating holdup in industries using cellular, computer, and modem technologies); Daniel Swanson and William Baumol, Reasonable and nondiscriminatory (RAND) royalties, standards selection, and control of market power, 73 *Antitrust Law Journal* 1 (2005) at 3 (one might expect holdup and market power in telecommunications and Internet sectors); Wadhwa, note 161 (smartphone and software industries could be expected to see fewest startups and jobs due to patent trolls).

showed little evidence of reduced holdup power following *eBay*,[175] which legal scholars believed would sap the right to exclude and blunt patentees' power.[176] While the number of standards-essential patents in the cellular device industry rose from 800 to 1600 between 2002 and 2011, the industry grew less concentrated, the number of producers rose by nearly 20 percent, and the average selling price declined more than two-thirds (from nearly $500 to $150).[177]

Despite thousands of new software patents being issued each year, the output of US software publishers rose six times from 1987 to 1999, whereas all industries doubled their output, and communications equipment manufacturers tripled their output.[178] Software publishers' value-added (a measure of production) increased by between a quarter to half between 2005 and 2012, considerably outpacing manufacturing revenue, for example, which stagnated or declined.[179]

Recent economic work has therefore described the possibility of software patent "holdup" as speculative.[180] The former Director of the PTO, David Kappos, argues

---

[175] Alexander Galetovic et al., An empirical examination of patent holdup, 11 *Journal of Competition Law & Economics* 549 (2015) at 551, 570–2, citing Damien Geradin et al., Competing away market power? An economic assessment of ex ante auctions in standard setting, 4 *European Competition Journal* 443 (2008). See also Jonathan Barnett, From patent thickets to patent networks: The legal infrastructure of the digital economy, 55 *Jurimetrics Journal* 1 (2014) at 1–2.

[176] Merges and Duffy, note 174, at 944–5 (collecting sources).

[177] Alexander Galetovic and Kirti Gupta, *Royalty stacking and standard essential patents: Theory and evidence from the world mobile wireless industry* (Stanford University, Hoover Inst. Working Group on Intellectual Prop., Innovation, and Prosperity Working Paper 2016), at 1, 5 and Figures 7–8, 10, http://hooverip2.org/wp-content/uploads/ip2-wp15012-paper.pdf. The 20 percent rise is the difference between about six competitors in 2002 on a firm equivalent basis (which assumes all firms are same size) and nearly eight in 2012.

[178] Jennifer Lee and Andrew Schmidt, Research and development satellite account update: Estimates for 1959–2007, 90 *Survey of Current Business* 12 (2010), at 16, 47, Table 7.1A, https://www.bea.gov/scb/pdf/2010/12%20December/1210_r-d_tables.pdf.

[179] Robert Shapiro, The U.S. software industry as an engine for economic growth and employment, *Sonecon* (2014) at 6, www.sonecon.com/docs/studies/Report_for_SIIA-Impact_of_Software_on_the_Economy-Robert_Shapiro-Sept2014-Final.pdf; Travis, note 125, at 131. If Shapiro's figures are already adjusted for inflation, then software, computer systems design, data processing, and related industries' value-added rose almost 50 percent, from $285 billion to $425 billion from 2005 to 2012, while if the $285 billion needs to be increased by a factor of 1.1756 to 2012 dollars, then the value-added rose by more than a quarter. Manufacturing value-added may have declined from 2005 to 2013, from $1.88 trillion in 2005 (13 percent of GDP of $14.23 trillion in chained 2009 dollars) to $1.84 trillion in 2013 (12.1 percent of $15.6 trillion in chained 2009 dollars). Bureau of Economic Analysis, Current-dollar and "real" gross domestic product (2017), www.bea.gov/national/xls/gdplev.xls; Robert Scott, The manufacturing footprint and the importance of U.S. manufacturing jobs, Economic Policy Institute (January 22, 2015), www.epi.org/publication/the-manufacturing-footprint-and-the-importance-of-u-s-manufacturing-jobs. Compare also U.S. Bureau of the Census, Statistical Abstract of the United States, Table 1020. Value of manufacturers' shipments, inventories, and new orders by industry: 2000 to 2010 (2011), www2.census.gov/library/publications/2011/compendia/statab/131ed/tables/12s1020.pdf.

[180] E.g., J. Gregory Sidak, Holdup, royalty stacking, and the presumption of injunctive relief for patent infringement: A reply to Lemley and Shapiro, 92 *Minnesota Law Review* 713 (2008) at 718–19.

that Microsoft's 2014 R&D budget of $11.4 billion is backed by patent rights and shows that patents do not stop innovation.[181]

Likewise, one might expect that countries with strong rules against software patents, or a "first to file" system that reduces uncertainty, or low damages awards, will have more innovation and more successful technology companies than the United States, which is mired in patent crisis. This core plank of the innovation ideology is also in doubt.

Economic development as measured by GDP per capita is positively correlated with "strong patent rights" across many countries.[182] The direction of causation is unclear, but rapid economic development particularly in high technology industries in countries that expanded patent rights, like Brazil, China, India, and Russia, suggests some causation from strong patents to economic growth.[183] The European Union has begun to overhaul its laws in light of lagging digital markets and less R&D spending than in the United States, even though the United States has many more patents per capita than most European countries, and more than three times as many as Greece, Italy, Ireland, Portugal, or Spain.[184] If patents simply hold up innovators, these Mediterranean nations should have surpassed US levels of R&D and digital invention.

Meanwhile, the incredible growth of the digital economy, smartphone sales, advertising markets, and streaming content has culminated in the success of the FAANG (Facebook, Apple, Amazon, Netflix, and Google) companies in the United States.[185] Along with Microsoft and Intel, these are some of the companies most affected by patent litigation, but they are earning fabulous profits after the corporate media warned that patents could be too costly to them.[186] Facebook was the fastest

---

[181] Kappos, note 82.
[182] Haber, note 170, at 815–16.
[183] Travis, note 125, at 119 (collecting sources).
[184] Fiona Maharg-Bravo, Tech giants don't grow on European soil, *Reuters Breaking Views Blog* (September 16, 2016), http://blogs.reuters.com/breakingviews/2016/09/16/tech-giants-dont-grow-on-european-soil/; Eurostat, R&D expenditure, (February 8, 2017), http://ec.europa.eu/eurostat/statistics-explained/index.php/R_%26_D_expenditure; World Bank, Reaping digital dividends: Leveraging the Internet for development in Europe and Central Asia (March 2017), https://openknowledge .worldbank.org/bitstream/handle/10986/26151/9781464810251.pdf; see also, Patent>Pilot, Patents per one million inhabitants (2015), www.patent-pilot.com/en/wp-content/uploads/sites/2/2016/08/ Patents-per-one-million-inhabitants-823x1024.jpg; Panagiotis Petrakis, *The Greek Economy and the Crisis: Challenges and Responses* (Springer, 2011) at 105.
[185] The FANG companies are Facebook, Amazon, Netflix, and Google, but Apple is often grouped with them as competing with Google and Amazon, so FAANG makes sense as well. E.g. Chuck Jones, FANG stocks and Apple: Cash flows and valuation analysis, *Forbes* (February 7, 2016), www.forbes .com/sites/chuckjones/fang-stocks-and-apple-cash-flows-and-valuation-analysis/#477550366806.
[186] Travis, note 125, at 128–9. Apple and Google make smartphones, as did Microsoft for some time, and Amazon, Facebook, and Netflix market some of the most popular smartphone apps. There are supposedly many patents that cover smartphones and apps for them. Daniel Nazer, Patent trolls vs. app developers, DevCon '13/YouTube (September 5, 2013), www.youtube.com/ watch?v=WzToMcWK3S4.

company in history to reach a stock market valuation of $250 billion, edging out Google's record.[187] Amazon.com's Jeff Bezos became the richest person in the world in 2017, surpassing the $89 billion in assets belonging to Microsoft's Bill Gates.[188] Such Internet companies were initially expected to be prime targets of "holdup."[189] In the case of Apple, one reason for this is that there are many "essential" patents covering standards for making cell phones, memory devices, modems, networking, and compressed data files.[190]

What about small and entrepreneurial companies, are software patents killing them? This is often claimed, and such companies no doubt incur millions of dollars in costs in responding to patent (and employment, contract, and tort) litigation.[191] The fast pace of technological change and the cost of interpreting or inventing around broad and vague software patents would be impossible for startups to bear, one might think.[192] Small software application developers must be going out of business in droves.

While small businesses on Main Street have shuttered across the country, the "app economy" has thrived. It increased its global output from less than $1 billion annually in 2007–2009 to $53 billion in 2013, and increased the jobs created or supported by the sector from probably fewer than 135,000 in the United States in 2009 to 466,000 in 2012.[193] The app economy contributed to nearly 1.3 million more jobs between 2012 and 2017.[194] The number of video games available on the Apple App

[187] Tom Huddleston, Jr., Facebook's stock just stole this record from Google, *Fortune.com* (July 13, 2015), http://fortune.com/2015/07/13/facebook-250-billion/.

[188] Sofia Petkar, Watch out Bill Gates! Amazon's Jeff Bezos could become the richest man on the planet, The Daily Express, July 17, 2017, www.express.co.uk/news/world/829780/amazon-ceo-jeff-bezos-richest-man-on-earth-bill-gates-microsoft-fortune.

[189] Brief of Amicus Curiae Yahoo! Inc. in Support of Petitioner, at 2, *eBay* (U.S. brief filed January 26, 2006), cited in Merges and Duffy, note 174, at 939. See also Brief of Google Inc., Amazon.Com Inc., American Association of Advertising Agencies, Dell Inc., Facebook, Inc., Intuit Inc., Linkedin Corp., Netflix, Inc., Rackspace Hosting, Inc., Verizon Communications Inc., and Zynga Inc. as Amici Curiae in Support of Respondents, at 25–34, *Alice*, 573 U.S. 167 (U.S. brief filed February 27, 2014) (No. 13-298).

[190] Farrell et al., note 174; Swanson and Baumol, note 174.

[191] E.g. Brief of Public Knowledge and the Application Developers Alliance as Amici Curiae in Support of Respondents, *Alice* (U.S. brief filed February 26, 2014). Cf. also, Bessen, note 138; James Bessen, *Learning by Doing: The Real Connection Between Innovation, Wages, and Wealth* (Yale University Press, 2015) at 195–6; Colleen Chien, Startups and patent trolls, 17 *Stanford Technology Law Review* 461 (2013) at 472.

[192] E.g., Brief of Public Knowledge and the Application Developers Alliance, note 191, at 2; Brief of Google Inc. et al., note 189, at 25–34; Wadhwa, note 161.

[193] Brief of Public Knowledge and the Application Developers Alliance, note 191, at 2; Douglas MacMillan and Peter Burrows, Inside the app economy, *Bloomberg* (October 22, 2009), www.bloomberg.com/news/articles/2009-10-22/inside-the-app-economy. The figure of fewer than 180,000 assumes that jobs in the sector are proportional to revenue, so that the $3.5 billion in revenue in 2012 supported 466,000 jobs, while less than $1 billion in revenue in 2009 would support fewer jobs, probably fewer than 135,000, or 29 percent of 466,000.

[194] Progressive Policy Institute, US app economy update (May 2017) at P4, www.progressivepolicy.org/wp-content/uploads/2017/05/PPI_USAppEconomy.pdf.

Store rose from 13,000 games one year after the store was launched, to 90,000 games in late 2011, to 630,000 in 2016.[195]

The weakening of patent rights may be exacerbating inequality within the class of high-skilled workers in technology and telecommunications. In 2014–2015, the US Bureau of the Census and the Bureau of Labor Statistics reported that "74 percent of those who have a bachelor's degree in a STEM major are not employed in STEM occupations."[196] The rate is about 50 percent including master's and doctoral degrees.[197] Including non-engineering employment, the jobless rate for electrical engineers soared to 6.5 percent in early 2013, nearly double the rate in 2010.[198] Black engineers had an even higher unemployment rate, 10 percent in 2010–2012.[199] Electrical engineering saw a decline of jobs, with 85,000 fewer in 2013 than in 2002.[200] Computer programmers could expect 17 percent fewer jobs nationwide in 2015 than in 2005.[201] For the Class of 2014, almost 10.5 percent of electrical engineering graduates were not employed but were seeking employment after graduation, along with 24 percent of graduates in engineering management, 9 percent in computer science, 12 percent in computer and information sciences, 13 percent in information systems, and 14.3 percent in software.[202] Many fewer computer science Ph.D. graduates were employed in 2014 than in 2000 or 2001.[203] Four in ten graduates of the biological and medical sciences and 50 percent of chemistry graduates cannot find work in their field.[204] About two million recent college grads suffered unemployment in early 2013.[205] Figure 3.1 displays the disappointing performance of patent-intensive industries' employment prospects since 2006.

[195] Mike Masnick and Michael Ho, The sky is rising annotated, *Techdirt/Google Docs* (May 15, 2016), https://docs.google.com/document/d/1Qtoe_7a7qMIfmR7L8DueyLqtXxZwMYiRQycoHRyh VkM/edit?pli=1; Statista, *Number of apps from the iTunes App Store 2008–2016*, www.statista.com/ statistics/268251/number-of-apps-in-the-itunes-app-store-since-2008.

[196] Yi Xue & Richard Larson, STEM Crisis or STEM Surplus? Yes and Yes, Monthly Labor Review, May 2015, www.bls.gov/opub/mlr/2015/article/stem-crisis-or-stem-surplus-yes-and-yes.htm.

[197] Department for Professional Employees, AFL-CIO, The STEM Workforce: An Occupational Overview, *Fact Sheet* 2016, http://dpeaflcio.org/programs-publications/issue-fact-sheets/the-stem-workforce-an-occupational-overview/.

[198] Xue and Larson, note 196.

[199] Patricia Cohen, For black college graduates, a tougher road to employment, *New York Times*, December 24, 2014.

[200] Michael Teitelbaum, The myth of the science and engineering shortage, *Atlantic* (March 19, 2014), www.theatlantic.com/education/archive/2014/03/the-myth-of-the-science-and-engineering-shortage /284359/.

[201] Department for Professional Employees, note 197.

[202] National Association of Colleges and Employers, Class of 2014 Bachelor Degree Results – Agriculture Majors (2016), www.naceweb.org/uploadedfiles/pages/surveys/first-destination/academic-program-detail.pdf.

[203] Jordan Weissmann, The stagnating market for young scientists, *Slate* (July 16, 2014), http://slate.com.

[204] Weissmann, note 203.

[205] Ben Casselman, The cost of dropping out, *The Wall Street Journal*, November 22, 2012.

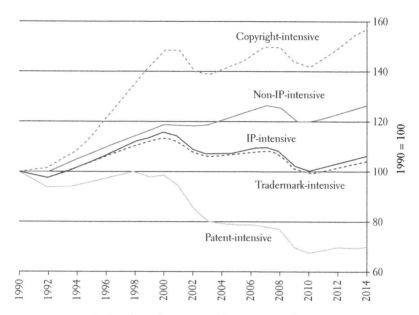

FIGURE 3.1. Indexed employment in IP-intensive industries, 1990–2014
Source: ESA calculations using data from the Bureau of Labor Statistics' Industry Productivity program.
U.S. Economics and Statistics Administration and U.S. Patent and Trademark Office

Perhaps fewer college-educated workers are employed at higher median wages? Not so, it seems. Non-unionized STEM workers earned about $22.82 per hour in 2015, which is less than the wage needed to rent a one-bedroom apartment in many cities, and lower than the median hourly wage for all workers – including retail and restaurant employees, etc. – in Denmark, Norway, and Switzerland.[206] Even scientists who are employed doing research earn relatively low pay after six or more years of study.[207]

A few years after the AIA was passed, the data showed that there has been a 20 percent decline since 1990 in median earnings at young adulthood, adjusted for inflation, despite a 50 percent rise in the share of Americans who are college-educated.[208] Perhaps because of this trend, which may cause some existing or prospective

---

[206] Department for Professional Employees, note 197.; see also Eusebio Bezzina, In 2010, 17% of employees in EU were low-wage earners, Eurostat Statistics in Focus 48/2012, at 2, http://ec.europa.eu/eurostat/documents/3433488/5585412/KS-SF-12-048-EN.PDF/7d87771c-8cc0-4133-a771-56e36ca0903b; National Low Income Housing Coalition, Out of Reach 2015, at 3, http://nlihc.org/sites/default/files/oor/OOR_2015_FULL.pdf.

[207] Weissmann, note 203.

[208] Associated Press, Millennials earn 20 percent less than Boomers did at same stage of life, *USA Today*, January 13, 2017, www.usatoday.com/story/money/2017/01/13/millennials-falling-behind-boomer-parents/96530338/.

students to see the relative rewards of education shrinking, enrolment in higher education fell between 2006 and 2011, with 1.6 million fewer students.[209]

By 1990, wage inequality in the United States had regressed to pre-World War II levels.[210] At the top of the income scale, the list of billionaires maintained by *Forbes* grew from fewer than only thirty names in 1986 to 223 names in 1992, some with over $10 billion in assets.[211] By 2008, there were nearly 500 billionaires and 11 million Americans unemployed, almost twice as many jobless as in 1979.[212]

Recent figures on US and other developed-nation economic inequality are even more stark, if anything. In 2013, two-thirds of all wealth was owned by the top 10 percent of families in the United States.[213] In northwestern Europe, the top 10 percent of households own between 47 percent and 71 percent of the wealth, while in southern Europe, the top 10 percent own 42 percent.[214]

3.6. FROM STARTUP TO CLOSEDOWN

Patent reform may accelerate the concentration of corporate and great-family wealth arising out of technological innovation in fewer hands. It has done little to slow patent acquisition by banks and other multinationals.[215] As Senator Cantwell prophesied, "first to file," or "first inventor to file," works to the disadvantage of the individual inventor, small firms, and new entrants hoping someday to go public.[216] Startup formation fell as the AIA entered into force and was 25 percent lower in

---

[209] Michael Barone, Is college worth it? Increasing numbers say no, *The Washington Examiner*, June 8, 2017, www.washingtonexaminer.com/is-college-worth-it-increasing-numbers-say-no/article/2625304.

[210] Thomas Piketty, *Capital in the Twenty-First Century* (Harvard University Press, 2014) at 20.

[211] Associated Press, Billionaire list expands; average wealth doesn't, *Milwaukee Sentinel*, August 20, 1992, at 26 (citing figure of 232 billionaires worldwide); United Press International, Billionaires in US listed, *Milwaukee Sentinel*, August 28, 1982, at 3 (citing figure of only twelve billionaires in United States in 1981–2); United Press International, Forbes ranks richest people, *The New York Times*, October 13, 1987, at D2 (citing figures of fewer than thirty billionaires in 1986, and forty-nine in 1987).

[212] Larry McShane, Unemployment jumps to 7.2% in December; worst year for layoffs since 1945, *New York Daily News* (January 10, 2009), www.nydailynews.com/money/2009/01/09/2009-01-09_unemployment_jumps_to_72_in_december_wor-2.html (11.1 million in 2008); Larry McShane, *Unemployment up slightly in December*, Sumter Daily Item, January 10, 1980, at 21 (6 million in 1979). See also Andy Geller, Bloomberg cracks Forbes rich list top 10, *New York Post*, September 18, 2008, at 25 (billionaires count).

[213] US Congressional Budget Office, Trends in family wealth, 1989 to 2013 (August 18, 2016), www.cbo.gov/sites/default/files/114th-congress-2015-2016/reports/51846-familywealth.pdf and www.cbo.gov/sites/default/files/114th-congress-2015-2016/reports/51846-supplementaldata.xlsx.

[214] James Davies, Rodrigo Lluberas, and Anthony Shorrocks, Measuring the global distribution of wealth, Paper presented to the 2012 OECD World Forum, New Delhi, India at 13, www.oecd.org/site/worldforumindia/Davies.pdf.

[215] E.g. Susan Decker and Elizabeth Dexheimer, Wall Street is trying to beat Silicon Valley at its own game, *Bloomberg BusinessWeek*, February 11, 2016, www.bloomberg.com/news/articles/2016-02-11/disrupting-banks-go-see-what-they-re-doing-at-the-patent-office.

[216] Cotropia, note 164, at 54.

2014 than in 2005.[217] Lack of funding is a persistent problem, and the percentage of firms that were startups was 20 percent lower in 2016 than in 2006.[218]

Millennials are nearly a quarter less likely to become new entrepreneurs than their counterparts were in 1996, and 40 percent less likely than their older family members, friends, and mentors aged 55–65 are to become entrepreneurs today. Millennials may be less likely to take economic risks than previous generations.[219] They accounted in 2014 for four of every ten officially unemployed Americans.[220]

To critics of the patent reform movement, it seems that after succeeding in the financial markets by leveraging their own patents to go public and the like, software companies are "making sure that start-ups and innovators, even kids in a dorm room working toward the next algorithm that will supplant [them] can't get the patent rights they need to gain funding and build a competitive corporation."[221] As one prominent judge claims, the reformed system works mainly for the 10 or 20 largest firms.[222]

[217] Heather Long, Where are all the startups? U.S. entrepreneurship near 40-year low, *CNN Money* (September 8, 2016), http://money.cnn.com/2016/09/08/news/economy/us-startups-near-40-year-low/index.html.

[218] Ewing Marion Kauffmann Foundation, The 2017 Kauffman Index of Startup Activity: National Trends, at 22–3, 27, 44–6, www.kauffman.org/kauffman-index/reporting/~/media/c9831094536646528abo12dcbd1f83be.ashx; Benjamin Ryan, Starved of financing, new businesses are in decline, *Gallup Business Journal* (September 4, 2014), www.gallup.com/businessjournal/175499/starved-financing-new-businesses-decline.aspx.

[219] Robert Fairlie et al., *The 2017 Kauffman Index of Startup Activity: National Trends* (2017) at 15, www.kauffman.org/kauffman-index/reporting/startup-activity; Derek Ozkal, Millennials can't keep up with boomer entrepreneurs, *The Kauffman Foundation Growthology Blog* (July 19, 2016), www.kauffman.org/blogs/growthology/2016/07/age-and-entrepreneurship.

[220] Leah McGrath Goodman, Millennial college graduates: Young, educated, jobless, *Newsweek* (May 27, 2015), www.newsweek.com/2015/06/05/millennial-college-graduates-young-educated-jobless-335821.html.

[221] Gene Quinn, Our political patent system: Is patent justice for sale? *IP Watchdog* (November 10, 2014), www.ipwatchdog.com/2014/11/10/our-political-patent-system-is-patent-justice-for-sale/id=51951/.

[222] Gene Quinn, Judge Michel says Congress stuck in a time warp on patent reform, *IP Watchdog* (May 12, 2015), www.ipwatchdog.com/2015/05/12/judge-michel-says-congress-stuck-in-a-time-warp-on-patent-reform/id=57648/.

PART II

IP Liberties

4

Hollywood's Copyright Exemptions?

4.1. INTRODUCTION

Hollywood entertainment conglomerates have led the way in seeking copyright protection against quotation or imitation of as little material as a few seconds of music, a snippet of dialogue, a plotline, or an isolated image. The expanded rights enjoyed by movie studios and television brands in these "microworks" do not reliably trickle down to screenwriters, actors, musicians, or songwriters.[1] These creators often find themselves out of luck when big companies copy material that bridges the gap between the overall concept of a work and its precise form.

4.2. SUING THE RICHEST AUTHOR IN THE WORLD

In July of 2010, the New York City federal courts received a complaint alleging that *Harry Potter and the Goblet of Fire* violated the copyright in another book, *Willy the Wizard*.[2] Like Harry, Willy magically transported himself to a fantastic castle, where a global wizard competition was being held, involving the rescue of hostages for about 40 points.

Willy's author, Adrian Jacobs, had died after declaring bankruptcy in the 1980s, but before *Harry Potter* became a global phenomenon. The Jacobs estate claimed that like Willy, Harry obtained an official education in advanced wizardry, relied upon others to research obscure spells, utilized a wand, traveled quickly through space either on a magical train or with magical gizmos and

---

[1] Justin Hughes, Size matters (or should) in copyright law, 74 *Fordham Law Review* 575 (2005) at 578, 614–9.
[2] Plaintiff's Complaint, *Allen v. Scholastic Inc.*, No. 10 Civ. 5335, 2010 WL 2822531 (S.D.N.Y. complaint filed July 13, 2010).

powders, and won the competition's prize of 1,000 shiny things (stars for Willy, galleons for Harry).[3]

There was evidence that the lawsuit had been ill-conceived, including the great disparities of length and style between the two books, and the fact that J. K. Rowling had denied ever having read or heard of *Willy the Wizard*.[4] Years later, the English court ordered the estate to pay £1.5 million as a security to protect Rowling and her British publisher from spending any more money out of pocket on defending a lawsuit that could very well fizzle out.[5] The estate had borne some £800,000 in costs to bring the case to its mid-point,[6] perhaps inevitable when suing the person named by *Forbes* as the world's wealthiest author.[7]

The case was crazy and laughable, according to Rowling and her publisher's attorneys.[8] It was ultimately thrown out, both in downtown New York City and before the High Court of Justice. A federal court in the United States concluded that regularly-occurring international wizard competitions commencing in the great hall of a castle, as well as the education of a modern wizard in "wizard college," and a wizard saving hostages and becoming a type of celebrity were unprotectable or unoriginal ideas.[9] Similarly, the High Court of Justice viewed the "simple and abstract" ideas common to the two works, which contained many differences of detail and presentation, as showing that Rowling and her publisher were innocent of prohibited copying.

Nevertheless, "Willy versus Harry" and cases like it are not so easily pilloried. An English court initially found it to be believable that *Harry Potter* could be based on *Willy the Wizard* if there were twenty-two thematic and story-related similarities between the works. Both books' lead characters diverged from the aged, virtually omniscient, and "all-powerful" wizard like Merlin or Gandalf the White.[10]

---

[3] Plaintiff's Memorandum of Law in Opposition to Defendant Scholastic, Inc.'s Motion to Dismiss, *Allen*, 2010 WL 4972650 (S.D.N.Y. brief filed October 10, 2010).

[4] Benedicte Page, Harry Potter plagiarism case thrown out of US court, *The Guardian*, January 7, 2011, www.theguardian.com/books/2011/jan/07/harry-potter-plagiarism-case-us-court.

[5] Judgment, *Allen v. Bloomsbury Publishing PLC*, No. HC09C01979 (High Court of Justice, Chancery Division, March 18, 2011); Mark Dapin, Max exposure, *Sydney Morning Herald*, November 27, 2010, at Good Weekend-14.

[6] *Allen v. Bloomsbury Publishing PLC*, [2011] EWCA Civ 943 (Court of Appeal, July 14, 2011), at para. 9; Harry Potter plagiarism case dismissed against JK Rowling, *The Telegraph*, July 19, 2011, www.telegraph.co.uk/culture/harry-potter/8645617/Harry-Potter-plagiarism-case-dismissed-against-JK-Rowling.html.

[7] Marjorie Kehe, J.K. Rowling cleared of plagiarism charges in the US, *The Christian Science Monitor*, January 7, 2011, www.csmonitor.com/Books/chapter-and-verse/2011/0107/J.K.-Rowling-cleared-of-plagiarism-charges-in-the-US; The world's billionaires 2011, *Forbes*, October 2011, www.forbes.com/lists/2011/10/billionaires_2011.html [click on tab 12]; Richest authors, *The Richest* (2017), www.therichest.com/celebnetworth/category/celeb/authors/?sort=net.

[8] Harry Potter plagiarism case dismissed, note 6.

[9] *Allen v. Scholastic Inc.*, 739 F. Supp. 2d 642, 659–65 (S.D.N.Y. 2011).

[10] Approved Judgment, *Allen*, No. HC09C01979 (High Court of Justice, Chancery Division, October 14, 2010) at para. 20, 36–74, 86, www.bailii.org/cgi-bin/markup.cgi?doc=/ew/cases/EWHC/Ch/2010/2560.html&query=harry+and+potter&method=boolean.

In the United States, the Supreme Court suggested more than a century ago that a copyright may be violated by using different words, whereby we see a similar "event or story lived."[11] For example, there were only thirteen similarities in plot and character between *Star Wars* and the movie *Battlestar Galactica*, which came out shortly after *Star Wars* proved to be a hit. Still, a US court found infringement to be plausible, despite different visuals, dialogue, and character names in the two movies.[12]

On another occasion, the Supreme Court condemned the copying of a "substantial" aspect of a work's "concrete form," which structures or organizes "circumstances or ideas."[13] Courts declared that even a "series of incidents," which one might call a subplot or plot thread, would receive copyright protection if it had a remarkable "dramatic effect."[14]

British law has a similar structure, with the court in the *Willy the Wizard* case observing that taking the heart of a work without its sundry details, or taking any part of a work amounting to a substantial part of the creativity of its author, can violate copyright law.[15] Looking to the House of Lords for guidance, the court stated: "If one asks what is being protected in such a case, it is difficult to give any answer except that it is an idea expressed in the copyright work."[16]

Had the tables been turned, and had the Jacobs family made tens or hundreds of millions of dollars by publishing a story or producing a film or theme park containing dramatic events or scenes like those in *Harry Potter and the Goblet of Fire*, Warner Bros. or Rowling's publishers may well have filed suit. For example, in 1981 the American Broadcasting Company debuted a television program featuring a schoolteacher who becomes a "Superman" by virtue of an alien suit that enabled him to fly, shrug off bullets, and fight crime with super-speed and super-strength.[17] Warner Bros. sued, claiming that Superman's "costume" and "abilities" were protected by copyright from imitation, even though the alien suit did not share the color scheme of Superman's costume and cape. While the hero of ABC's show did not confidently vanquish evil, but stumbled his way through each episode, Warner Bros. asserted

[11] *Kalem Company v. Harper Brothers L*, 222 U.S. 55, 61 (1911).
[12] *Twentieth Century-Fox Film Corp.* v. *MCA, Inc.*, 715 F.2d 1327 (9th Cir. 1983).
[13] *Holmes* v. *Hurst*, 174 U.S. 82, 86 (1899).
[14] *Nichols* v. *Universal Pictures Corp.*, 45 F.2d 119 (2d Cir. 1930); *Dam* v. *Kirk La Shelle Co.*, 175 F. 902 (2d Cir. 1910), and *Stodart* v. *Mutual Film Co.*, 249 F. 513 (2d Cir. 1918). See also *Eisenschiml* v. *Fawcett Publications*, 246 F.2d 598, 603–4 (7th Cir. 1957); *Dymow* v. *Bolton*, 11 F.2d 690, 692 (2d Cir. 1926) (quoting *Chappell* v. *Fields*, 210 F. 864, 865 (2d Cir. 1914)); *Shapiro, Bernstein, & Co.* v. *P.F. Collier & Son Co.*, 26 U.S.P.Q. 40 (S.D.N.Y. 1934); Ralph Shaw, *Literary Property in the United States* (Scarecrow Press, 1950) at 72–3, 191–2.
[15] Approved Judgment, note 10.
[16] *Designers' Guild Ltd* v. *Russell Williams (Textiles) Ltd* [2000] 1 WLR 2416, at paragraph 24; *Allen*, note 6, at para. 15.
[17] *The Greatest American Hero* (American Broadcasting Network, 1981–1983).

that such scenes as flying through the Earth's orbit in a costume proved copyright infringement, much as the Jacobs estate cited the wizard contests.[18]

The court in the *Superman* case conceded that it does not matter "'that in many respects plaintiff's and defendant's works are dissimilar if in other respects similarity as to a substantial element of plaintiff's work can be shown.'" It emphasized that this rule has a limit, because one may avoid infringement by introducing enough "changes" into a work that would otherwise be too similar to a copyrighted original.[19] Warner Bros. had no claim because the schoolteacher did not act like, look like, or have the talents of Superman. If the television show had copied scenes from *Superman* comics or movies, on the other hand, Warner Bros might have won an injunction or damages.[20]

4.3. THE DEATH OF (ONE KIND OF) COPYRIGHT

In 2013, a group of lawyers for screenwriters and other authors working in Hollywood formed the California Society of Entertainment Lawyers, with an announced aim to "balance the influence of the international conglomerates within the television, film, and music industries."[21] The society claims that individual authors are so disempowered within the federal courts that in most cases that authors file, the film and television studios win on final judgment, often before trial.[22] Notable cases involved Fox's *24*, NBC's *The Apprentice*, Paramount's *Coming to America*, Columbia Pictures' *Groundhog Day*, Warner Bros.' *The Last Samurai*, and Disney's *Sweet Home Alabama*.[23]

As few as two film or television plot-related copyright infringement matters have made it to jury trial without being settled between 1990 and 2010, according to one study.[24] During that period, filmed entertainment revenue increased by many

[18] *Warner Bros., Inc. v. American Broadcasting Companies*, 720 F.2d 231 (2d Cir. 1983).
[19] Ibid., at 241 (quoting Melville Nimmer and David Nimmer, *Nimmer on Copyright*, vol. 3 (Matthew Bender, rev. 1982) § 13.03[B] at 13–38 to 38.2).
[20] *Warner Bros., Inc.*, 720 F.2d 231at 243–4.
[21] Brief of Amicus Curiae the California Society of Entertainment Lawyers in Support of Petitioner, at 1, *Petrella* v. *Metro-Goldwyn-Mayer, Inc.*, (No. 12-1315) (brief filed June 3, 2013), http://sblog.s3.amazonaws.com/wp-content/uploads/2013/08/CSEL-cert-amicus-brief.pdf.
[22] Ibid., at 1–2, citing Steven Lowe, Death of copyright, *L.A. Lawyer*, November 2010, at 32, 34–5, www.lacba.org/docs/default-source/lal-back-issues/2010-issues/november-2010.pdf; Steven Lowe and Daniel Lifschitz, Death of copyright, the sequel, *The Computer & Internet Lawyer*, September 2012, at 1, 7 n. 15, 18. A number of cases settled. After this trend became clear, ABC allegedly circulated a memo regarding the imitation of foreign television programs without seeking copyright licenses. Cf. Nikki Finke, Bombshell ABC studios memo is blatant blueprint to rip off foreign tv series, *Deadline Hollywood* (July 10, 2008), www.deadline.com/2008/07/bombshell-abc-studios-memo-a-blueprint-to-rip-off-foreign-tv-series; Stefan Bechtold, The fashion of TV show formats, 2013 *Michigan State Law Review* 451 at 454–5.
[23] Lowe, note 22, at 32.
[24] Steven Lowe, The death of copyright, 28 *The Computer & Internet Lawyer* 1 (2011) at 1.

billions of dollars. The courts reined in or abandoned several principles that made suing a large company possible for independent and early-career writers and producers, such as the inference of a company's access to a work from the writer's submission of work by mail, the holistic comparison of any work containing a protectable element to the infringing company's entire work, and the reference of cases supported by expert testimony to juries for a community-based evaluation.[25] Lowe argues that the result is that:

> Third parties now have the freedom to steal from screenplays with impunity, provided they cover their tracks by creating sufficient dissimilarities ... . Case law has provided [TV and movie production] defendants with an impenetrable shield of confusing and often contradictory principles that thwart plaintiffs in nearly every instance, with only tiny cracks in the shield [remaining].[26]

The trend might have something to do with the image of the author and the social and economic context of copyright litigation. Copyright scholars and activists have shown over the past twenty years or so that the law's image of the strictly "original" author – the Bachs, Shakespeares, and Disneys – is based upon ignorance of extensive borrowings from other, often unknown predecessors in the relevant genre.[27] The "theft" by acclaimed authors from an even older generation of cultural workers goes unnoticed.[28]

The entertainment lawyers' group calls this trend the "death of copyright." It may simply be the death of a certain type of copyright suit, one that became more viable in the late nineteenth century and matured in the 1930s through the 1950s. For example, courts articulated new rules for copyright in light of allegations that film scripts copied plot ideas from stage plays.[29] Some courts, on the other hand, have

---

[25] Ibid., at 1–9.
[26] Ibid., at 3, 5.
[27] Olufunmilayo Arewa, From J.C. Bach to hip hop: Musical borrowing, copyright and cultural context, 84 *North Carolina Law Review* 547 (2006) at 549, 566–8, 587, 593, 600–12, 16, 644–5; K. J. Greene, Copyright, culture & black music: A legacy of unequal protection, 21 *Hastings Communications & Entertainment Law Journal* 339 (1999); Lawrence Lessig, *Free Culture: How Big Media Uses Technology and the Law to Lock Down Culture and Control Creativity* (now interactive ed., 2017) [2004] at ch. 1, http://download.nowis.com/index.cfm?phile=FreeCulture.html&tipe=text/html; Kembrew McLeod, *Freedom of Expression®: Overzealous Copyright Bozos and Other Enemies of Creativity* (Doubleday, 2005) at 18–29, 74–5; Gary Rinkerman, Sampling unleashed? Migrating visual art fair use principles into the music space, *Social Science Research Network* (December 20, 2014), at 57–61,; Rebecca Tushnet, Copyright law, fan practices, and the rights of the author, in Jonathan Gray, Cornel Sandvoss and C. Lee Harrington (Eds.), *Fandom: Identities and Communities in a Mediated World* (New York University Press, 2007) at 60–71; Rebecca Tushnet, My fair ladies: Sex, gender, and fair use in copyright, 15 *American University Journal of Gender, Social Policy & Law* 273 (2007) at 29–92, 303–4.
[28] *Rip! A Remix Manifesto* (DVD, directed by Brett Gaylor, EyeSteelFilm, 2009). See also Greene, note 27.
[29] E.g. *Universal Pictures Co. v. Harold Lloyd Corp.*, 162 F.2d 354, 361 (9th Cir. 1947); *Sheldon v. Metro-Goldwyn Pictures Corp.*, 81 F.2d 49 (2d Cir. 1936), *aff'd*, 309 U.S. 390 (1940); *Nichols*, 45 F. 2d 119.

concluded that movie and television *plots* are not protectable by copyright, despite the protection extended to simple sequences of notes and beats in music copyright cases.[30] Screenplays, music, and other inputs continue to be licensed for films and television, often at quite lucrative rates.[31] But lawsuits involving film "treatments" often fail.

4.4. MICRO-COPYRIGHTS AND THE UNDEFINED NOTION OF "SIMILARITY"

When a *Harry Potter* superfan attempted to publish an encyclopedia of the novels and movies in the series, Warner Bros. took a position not dissimilar from that of the Jacobs estate. The company successfully argued that copying books "in fragments or in a different order" may be infringing; doctrinally, such copying may qualify as "substantial similarity." Therefore, the fact that the defendant's book was not a novel, but a nonfiction book, did not matter for infringement purposes. The genre distinction also did not result in a fair use finding with respect to the printed encyclopedia. While *Harry Potter* readers were unlikely to avoid the novels because they had seen the encyclopedia, they might not buy a compendium of poems and songs from the novels, because these short works had been included in the encyclopedia, which was a sufficient level of harm to deny fair use.[32]

Moreover, the fact that the encyclopedia differed in style and format and would be "enjoyed for different purposes" did not save it, in contrast to the same court's decision in the *Willy the Wizard* case. *Willy* was not substantially similar to *Harry* due to the former's brevity, simplicity, and lack of "moral" messaging. Still, an insightful reference work was substantially similar to a fictional story, which it described.[33]

Examples from the music world confirm that the Jacobs estate was not entirely off-base in seeking compensation for partial similarities. In the early 2000s, Warner/Chappell Music (part of the same conglomerate as Warner Bros.) claimed that using three words from a song in a documentary film would infringe the song copyright,

---

[30] *Kenney v. Warner Bros. Entertainment, Inc.*, 984 F. Supp. 2d 9, 14 (D. Mass. 2013) (quoting *McGee v. Benjamin*, No. 08-11818, 2012 WL 959377, at *7 (D. Mass. March 20, 2012) (quoting *Franklin v. Ciroli*, 865 F. Supp. 947, 950 (D. Mass. 1994))). Compare this to *Negron v. Rivera*, 433 F. Supp. 2d 204, 216 (D.P.R. 2006) (despite differences in lyrics or tempo, similarities in melody of a song could result in infringement finding).
[31] Mike Fleming Jr., Max Landis is changing things for screenwriters, *Deadline* (May 13, 2016), http://deadline.com/2016/05/max-landis-interview-bright-netflix-cannes-disruptor-1201752; Ellen Killoran, Top Hollywood screenwriter salaries rival studio chiefs, *Forbes* (September 29, 2016), www.forbes.com /sites/ellenkilloran/2016/09/29/top-hollywood-screenwriter-salaries-rival-studio-chiefs/#385c078e1e3d; Peter Tschmuck, The global music publishing market – an analysis, *Music Business Research* (January 31, 2016), https://musicbusinessresearch.wordpress.com/2016/01/31/the-global-music-publishing-market-an-analysis/.
[32] *Warner Bros. Entertainment. v. RDR Books*, 575 F. Supp. 2d 513, 543, 550 (S.D.N.Y. 2008).
[33] Ibid.

even if a subject of the film simply blurted out the refrain so that the tune was not included.[34] By the 1980s, Warner Bros. Records had developed a system of clearing song lyrics or sounds that mimic or sample prior songs, even if the use involved only a few words or seconds of music.[35]

The record labels even developed "parody licenses" for poking fun at pop music's hit records.[36] This practice continued even after the Supreme Court ruled that copyright did not necessarily require parodies to be licensed because "the unlikelihood that creators of imaginative works will license ... lampoons of their own productions removes such uses from the very notion of a potential licensing market."[37] The licensing even of small portions of songs at very high rates contributed to the obscurity of funk and other musical genres of the mid- to late twentieth century.[38] In this way, restrictions on sampling have a similar effect as activism against digital methods of improving the visibility of obscure works, such as Google Books or Napster.

More recently, Warner Music Group and Warner/Chappell Music (now distinct from Warner Bros.) indicated that a song with a similar harmony, but different words, could infringe the copyright in the original song.[39] As part of the Recording Industry Association of America, Warner Music contends that copyright prevents *any* uses of an author's work "that would materially affect the value of his copyright."[40] Under this standard, the alleged use of the twenty-two story elements of *Willy the Wizard* in *Harry Potter and the Goblet of Fire* may appear to "materially affect" the value

[34] Scott Macaulay, Everybody dance now!, *Filmmaker Magazine* (June 25, 2005), http://filmmakermagazine.com/1976-everybody-dance-now/, citing Carrie McLaren and Jason Torchinsky (Eds.), Interview with Amy Sewell, *Stay Free Magazine* (June 2005).

[35] *Grand Upright Music v. Warner Bros. Records, Inc.*, 780 F. Supp. 182, 184–85 (S.D.N.Y. 1991); Kembrew McLeod and Peter DiCola, *Creative License: The Law and Culture of Digital Sampling* (Duke University Press, 2011) at 65, 105, 122.

[36] *Acuff-Rose Music, Inc. v. Campbell*, 972 F. 2d 1429, 1446 (6th Cir. 1992) (Judge Nelson, dissenting), *rev'd*, 510 U.S. 569 (1994).

[37] *Campbell v. Acuff-Rose Music, Inc.*, 510 U.S. 569, 592 (1994). See also Kathleen Doane, Where to catch a visiting artist, *Cincinnati Magazine*, July 2003, at 16; Ben Greenman, *Dig If You Will the Picture: Funk, Sex, God and Genius in the Music of Prince* (Macmillan, 2017) at 57–8; Jeff Vrabel, Revenge of the nerd, *Billboard*, October 28, 2006, at 14. Weird Al Yankovic and other satirists solicited permission for humorous versions of songs because their songs comment on society in general rather than targeting the original music with the critical bite of mockery. Joanna Demers, *Steal This Music: How Intellectual Property Law Affects Musical Creativity* (University of Georgia Press, 2010) at 56. Due to Prince's refusal of parody permissions, Weird Al did not parody Prince as he did Michael Jackson although he did parody a scene from the *When Doves Cry* music video in which Prince emerges from a bath. Greenman, ibid., at 57–8.

[38] McLeod and DiCola, note 35, at 90–5.

[39] Defendants' Memorandum of Points and Authorities in Support of Motion for Summary Judgment, at 17–18, *Skidmore v. Led Zeppelin*, No. 2:15-cv-03462 RGK (C.D. Cal. brief filed February 25, 2016).

[40] Brief of the Recording Industry Association of America and the Association of American Publishers as Amici Curiae in Support of Appellant, at 26, *Oracle America, Inc. v. Google, Inc.* Nos. 17-1118 & 17-1202 (Fed. Cir. brief filed February 27, 2017) (quoting Staff of the House Committee on the Judiciary, 89th Congress, Copyright law revision, Part 6: Supplementary report of the Register of Copyrights on the general revision of the U.S. Copyright Law: 1965 revision bill (Committee Print, 1965), at 13).

associated with uses of Willy's story. Certainly the twenty-two elements were less likely than a musical harmony or progression to be found in virtually identical form in prior copyrighted works.

High-profile lawsuits have refocused our attention on the broad and controversial scope of copyrights, and on potentially inconsistent treatment of plaintiffs such as the Jacobs estate versus musical acts or even video game publishers. In the most famous case, Pharrell Williams and Robin Thicke appealed a judgment finding that they had copied musical phrases from a Marvin Gaye song, "Got to Give It Up," in their hit song "Blurred Lines." In their appeal, they explained that only four or perhaps seven notes were common to both songs, along with a similar inspiration or "groove." Williams and Thicke argued that the court had permitted a jury to award $4 million in damages based largely on public-domain or other unprotected techniques that are often used to write music, such as repeated notes, descending bass lines, or standard sequences.[41]

In an analogous case, a court held that Led Zeppelin had to face a jury trial for about 13 seconds of a bass line, in a descending progression at the same pitch, cut in half by a bridge. The court remarked that a "relatively small" amount of copying music, such as imitating an "arrangement of a limited number of notes," may be "substantial."[42]

McLeod condemns post-1980s copyright doctrine for destroying the freedom of "experimentation" in music typified by Public Enemy's *Fear of a Black Planet* album, or *The Message* by Grandmaster Flash and the Furious Five. In place of these deployments of familiar audible quotations in an explosive, energizing mix, copyright bureaucracies taxed artists and labels to fund other labels and music publishers, leading to the less innovative but doctrinally "original" songs of the late 1990s.[43]

The anti-sampling bias in music law has spread in recent years to the context of film and television. A picture of a Tin Man with his catchphrase "If I Only Had a Brain," used on a t-shirt or mug, was found to infringe *The Wizard of Oz* as a film, even though none of the film negative was used, and both the image of the tin man and the story of his adventures with Dorothy and the cowardly lion are in the public domain.[44] Similarly, the image of the Batmobile enjoys copyright protection apart

---

[41] Plaintiffs-Appellants Opening Brief on Appeal, at 13–14, 17, 26–38, *Williams v. Gaye*, No. 15-56880 (9th Cir. brief filed August 23, 2016), https://assets.documentcloud.org/documents/3034448/ Blurred-Lines-AOB.pdf. On March 21, 2018, the Ninth Circuit rejected this aspect of the appeal from the verdict, concluding that elements common to the two songs supported the jury's verdict of infringement, and the district judge's decision to submit the case to the jury for trial. The common elements included signature phrases, bass melodies, descending bass lines, keyboard notes, musical scales, spoken-word sections, lyrics, and structural components. *Williams* v. *Gaye*, No. 15-56880, 2018 WL 1403577, 2018 U.S. App. LEXIS 7057 (9th Cir. Mar. 21, 2018, petition for rehearing en banc pending.

[42] *Skidmore* v. *Led Zeppelin*, No. 2:15-cv-03462-RGK, 2018 WL 1442461 (C.D. Cal. Apr. 8, 2016), at 16–18, https://arstechnica.com/wp-content/uploads/2016/06/zepjudge.pdf.

[43] McLeod, note 27, at 3, 67–70, 110–16, 133. See also Lessig, note 27, at 6.

[44] *Warner Bros. Entertainment* v. *X One X Productions*, 644 F.3d 584 (8th Cir. 2011).

from the scene in which it appears, and any dialogue or music accompanying it, and even though the Batmobile as an abstract "character" varies in appearance across different comics and films.[45] The phrase "E.T. Phone Home" and the jokes that start out "You might be a redneck if ..." have received protection as against sellers of merchandise.[46] Most recently, a court extended copyright protection to the Vulcan and Klingon races from *Star Trek* television shows and films, as well as to a minor character from the *Star Trek* universe, and other aspects of the *Star Trek* franchise that exist at an abstract level.[47]

One less famous copyright case is so odd, yet full of implications for the future, that it deserves to be mentioned even though it happened years before the era covered by this book. In March 1998, Miramax began marketing a documentary film on corporate crime and outsourcing, called *The Big One*, with posters bearing the tagline "Protecting the Earth from the Scum of Corporate America." The director, Michael Moore, appeared in the poster in a black suit and a black tie, wearing black sunglasses and carrying an oversized metallic microphone. Columbia Pictures, the distributor of the blockbuster science-fiction action-comedy *Men in Black*, sued Miramax for copyright infringement, alleging that the Miramax poster was substantially similar to *Men in Black* posters and trailers. The similarities between the posters boiled down to the tagline and the appearance of a similar sized person "carrying a large object" in front of the New York skyline, with a similar color scheme and layout of the poster. The court enjoined the further use of the poster pending the trial, or any poster containing a New York skyline at night in a similar tint, a man wearing the *Men in Black* outfit with a similar stance and "carrying an oversized weapon or microphone," and the tagline about protecting Earth.[48]

Copyright owners rely on the flexibility of infringement doctrines to assert character copyrights and to suppress new stories based on their characters. The Organization for Transformative Works, a group of law and media studies professors representing creative fans of popular culture in fair use and Internet law policymaking, has fielded a number of requests for help from authors of fan-made works. Creative fans face constant threats that their works will be condemned as derivative and unlawful, even as some of the publishers and entertainment studios doing the complaining get copyright lawsuits dismissed despite arguably more harmful imitation or use.[49]

---

[45] *DC Comics v. Towle*, 802 F.3d 1012, 1019–23 (9th Cir. 2015).
[46] *Foxworthy v. Custom Tees, Inc.*, 879 F. Supp. 1200 (N.D. Ga. 1995); *Universal City Studios, Inc. v. Kamar Industries, Inc.*, 217 U.S.P.Q. (BNA) 1162 (S.D. Tex. 1982); Hughes, note 1, at 583–4, 589–90.
[47] *Paramount Pictures Corp. v. Axanar Prods., Inc.*, No. 2:15-CV-09938-RGK-E, 2017 WL 83506, at *4 (C.D. Cal. January 3, 2017).
[48] *Columbia Pictures Industries, Inc. v. Miramax Films Corp.*, 11 F. Supp. 2d 1179, 1180–6 (C.D. Cal. 1998).
[49] Jeffrey Young, Scholars and pop-culture fans create nonprofit group to fight for creative rights, *Chronicle of Higher Education*, December 18, 2007, www.chronicle.com/article/ScholarsPop-Culture-Fans/40169;

Noncommercial stories or videos are being deterred or prohibited due to micro-level copyright infringement. Such stories and videos are often very different from the original and may exist for a different purpose such as critique or satire, in contrast to competing wizard books or science fiction movies. Notably, Warner Bros. and Scholastic were among those attempting to halt some fan stories' distribution, although sometimes premised on trademark rights in website names or on the presence of "adult" content, rather than on a pure copyright case against fan writing.[50] Confronting a future as "pirates," fans assembled into online pressure groups and won concessions from studios like Warner Bros. and Lucasfilm, as well as publishers like Scholastic, at least as to noncommercial and inoffensive fan works.[51] Still, meekly obeying such limitations on derivative creativity is an incomplete literary freedom and creates a second-class authorship in comparison to publishing and entertainment industry borrowing practices.

The world of nonfiction provides other examples of the breadth and uncertainty of contemporary copyright doctrine. Newspapers and news agencies argue, in both the United States and Europe, that copying headlines from articles, a frequent practice in media of all kinds, violates copyright law because a headline reflects "substantial" creativity and value.[52] This set the stage for laws limiting Internet companies' ability to create or host so-called "news aggregators," which copy headlines and link

Organization for Transformative Works, Comments of the Organization for Transformative Works to the National Telecommunications and Information Administration and U.S. Patent and Trademark Office Internet Policy Task Force (2010), at 62, www.transformativeworks.org/wp-content/uploads/old/Comments%20of%20OTW%20to%20PTO-NTIA.pdf.

[50] Ernest Bond and Nancy Michelson, Writing Harry's world: Children co-authoring Hogwarts, in Elizabeth Heilman (Ed.), Critical Perspectives on Harry Potter (Routledge, 2008) at 319–20; Suman Gupta, Re-Reading Harry Potter (Macmillan, 2nd ed. 2009) at 221–2; Henry Jenkins, Convergence Culture: Where Old and New Media Collide (New York University Press, 2006) at 138, 170, 185–9; Lana Whited, The Ivory Tower and Harry Potter: Perspectives on a Literary Phenomenon (University of Missouri Press, 2004) at 10–11, 362–3.

[51] Bond and Michelson, note 50, at 320; Susan Gunelius, Harry Potter: The Story of a Global Business Phenomenon (Palgrave Macmillan, Paperback ed. 2008) at 99; Emma Keltie, The Culture Industry and Participatory Audiences (Palgrave Macmillan, 2017) at 72; Lessig, note 27, at 209–10, 245–6; Laura Miller, The new powers that be, Slate (September 11, 2016), www.slate.com/articles/arts/the_next_20/2016/09/ online_harry_potter_fans_transformed_what_it_means_to_love_a_story.html; Christina Ranon, Honor among thieves: Copyright infringement in internet fandom, 8 Vanderbilt Entertainment and Technology Law Journal 421 (2005); Aaron Schwabach, Fan Fiction and Copyright: Outsider Works and Intellectual Property Protection (Ashgate, 2016) at 118, 124.

[52] Complaint, Agence France Presse v. Google, Inc., Case No. 1:05-cv-00546-GK (D.D.C. complaint filed 2005); Defendant's Motion and Memorandum for Partial Summary Judgment Dismissing Count II for Lack of Protectable Subject Matter, Agence France Presse v. Google, Inc., Case No. 1:05-cv-00546-GK (D.D.C. brief filed October 12, 2005); Plaintiff's Response in Opposition to Defendant's Motion and Memorandum for Partial Summary Judgment Dismissing Count II for Lack of Protectable Subject Matter, Agence France Presse v. Google, Inc., Case No. 1:05-cv-00546-GK (D.D.C. brief filed October 26, 2005); Her Majesty's Government (U.K.), Modernising copyright: A modern, robust and flexible framework (2012) at 27, www.ipo.gov.uk/response-2011-copyright-final.pdf.

to stories from all over the world that have been posted online.[53] The day may arrive when billionaires such as Rupert Murdoch, Carlos Slim Helú, or Jeff Bezos earn additional profit that they do not need from headline licenses, while individual, family, and small business copyright owners see their considerably more valuable plot and story ideas taken, and earn little income from their literary labors.[54] Highly routine and derivative labor generating headlines out of facts and the statements of public figures will be compensated, while more creative story construction and scene-setting will not be in many cases.[55]

4.5. THE INEVITABILITY OF INFLUENCE

"Blackstonian copyright" is the phrase I have used for doctrines that may prohibit fan fiction and other nonliteral or small literal borrowings from copyrighted work.[56] Neil Weinstock Netanel calls it "bloated copyright," and Lawrence Lessig has referred to an "extreme of regulation" when it comes to creativity and self-expression, especially online.[57] The First Amendment should do more, many scholars argue, for authors who make incidental use of other work, shielding them from copyright sanctions if they use another work in a way that would not have been viewed as an infringement

[53] Act on Copyright and Related Rights, §§ 87f-87h (Copyright Act, as amended up to Act of April 4, 2016) (Germany); Copyright reforms by European Commission would require likes of Google to agree terms, *The Financial Times*, August 24, 2016,; Gulio Coraggio, A Google snippet tax across Europe, is it the right path?, *Gaming Tech Law* (August 2016), www.gamingtechlaw.com/2016/08/google-snippet-tax/copyright.html;; Ian Hargreaves, *Journalism: A Very Short Introduction* (Oxford University Press, 2014) at 117–18; Thomas Hartmann, Eine juristiche agenda für digitale Inhalte, 46 *Recht, Bibliothek, Dokumentation* 21 (2016), http://pubman.mpdl.mpg.de/pubman/item/escidoc:2355452/component/ escidoc:2355451/Hartmann_JuristischeAgendaFuerDigitaleInhalte_InRBD2016.pdf; Tom Hirche, Breiter Wilkderstrand im Europäischen Parlament gegen Presse-Leistungsschutzrecht, *Initiative Gegen ein Leistungsschutzrecht* (April 18, 2017), www.tinyurl.com/leistungs; Laura Oliver, NLA suspends payment of new link charges for aggregators, *Journalism.co.uk* (January 7, 2010), https:// blogs.journalism.co.uk/tag/newspaper-licensing-agency; Texto Refundido de la Ley de Propriedad Intellectual, art. 32(2) (Spain) (2015), https://web.archive.org/web/20170202085301/ and www .boe.es/buscar/act.php?id=BOE-A-1996-8930.
[54] E.g. Gavin Ellis, *Trust Ownership and the Future of News: Media Moguls and White Knights* (Palgrave Macmillan UK, 2014) at 99–136; Des Freedman, Media moguls and elite power, Goldsmiths University of London, Political Economy Research Centre Research Paper No. 2 (February 2015), at 2, 4–6, www.gold.ac.uk/media/documents-by-section/departments/politics-and-international-relations/PERC-2-Freedman-Elites.pdf; Vincent Mosco, The political economy of journalism, *Economia Política/ResearchGate* (2016), at 19, www.researchgate.net/profile/ Patricia_Melo3/publication/311924148_A_imprensa_como_espaco_dos_discursos_de_poder/ links/5862d7e508aebf17d3955b52/A-imprensa-como-espaco-dos-discursos-de-poder.pdf.
[55] E.g. Defendant's Motion and Memorandum note 52. See also Bechtold, note 22, 451.
[56] Hannibal Travis, Pirates of the information infrastructure: Blackstonian copyright and the First Amendment, 15 *Berkeley Technology Law Journal* 777 (2000) at 783; Hannibal Travis, Of blogs, ebooks, and broadband: Access to digital media as a First Amendment right, 35 *Hofstra Law Review* 1519 (2007) at 1558–64.
[57] Neil Weinstock Netanel, *Copyright's Paradox* (Oxford University Press, 2008) at 11; Lawrence Lessig, *Remix: Making Art and Culture Thrive in the Digital Economy* (Penguin, 2008), at 18.

when the First Amendment was ratified in 1791.[58] This would ensure that the freedom of speech is not "abridged," which is what the First Amendment guarantees to every American.

Careful study of literary history, as well as the history of film, music, and video games, raises the question: is any work *not* a derivative work? In neo-Marxist literary theory, there is no originality because every author reworks other authors' works into the text of his or her own, so that every part of a work is a quotation or paraphrase of other works that make up the history or milieu of a work.[59] Similarly, for French post-structuralism and deconstructionism, which were heavily influenced by lines of thought commencing with Hegel and Nietzsche, respectively, every work of authorship is in fact "constructed as a mosaic of quotations," whether literal or nonliteral, and "any text is the absorption and transformation of another" text.[60]

Copyright scholars look to even more obvious examples of the pervasiveness of adaptation and transformation in literature and art. William Shakespeare extended and dramatized the metrical English translation of the Italian novella *Giuletta e Romeo*, and Plutarch's prose account of the life of Julius Caesar, which had been translated into English during his lifetime.[61] Mark Twain called all authors "thieves" and liberally took scenes and character types from other works.[62] The composers Bach, Beethoven, Brahms, Mozart, Schubert, and Wagner adapted melodies or themes from other formal compositions and/or from traditional songs.[63] Elvis Presley, the Beatles, the Rolling Stones, and Led Zeppelin imitated the styles of

---

[58] Travis (2007), note 56.

[59] Terry Eagleton, *Literary Theory: An Introduction* (Blackwell Publishers, 1983) at 138; Terry Eagleton, Marxism and literary criticism, in Charles Kaplan and William Anderson (Eds.), *Criticism: Major Statements* (St. Martin's Press, 2000) at 555–7.

[60] Julia Kristeva, Word, dialogue and novel, in Toril Moi (Ed.), *The Kristeva Reader* (Columbia University Press, 1986) [1966] at 37. See also Stanley Fish, *Is There a Text in This Class? The Authority of Interpretive Communities* (Harvard University Press, 1980) at 43, 94; Michel Foucault, *The Archaeology of Knowledge and the Discourse on Language* (A.M. Sheridan Smith trans., Pantheon, 1972) [1969] at 99.

[61] Shakespeare is said to have been born in 1564, while Sir Thomas North published an English translation of Plutarch's *Lives of Nobel Grecians [sic] and Romans* in 1759, Arthur Brooke published an English translation of Matteo Bandello's *Giulietta e Romeo* in 1764; and Francois Belleforest published a French translation of the Latin story *Vita Amlethi* (life of Hamlet) between 1564 and 1570. E.g. Laurie Johnson, *The Tain of Hamlet* (Cambridge Scholars Publishing, 2014) at 29–31; Margrethe Jolly, *The First Two Quartos of Hamlet* (McFarland, 2014) at 32–53; Amanda Mabillard, Romeo and Juliet: Sources, *Shakespeare Online* (November 21, 2009), www.shakespeare-online.com/sources/romeosources.html; Michael Perelman, *Steal This Idea: Intellectual Property Rights and the Corporate Confiscation of Creativity* (Palgrave, 2002) at 40; William Shakespeare, *Hamlet* (Horace Howard Furness, Ed., Courier, 2000) at 87–90; Hank Whittemore, "Romeus and Juliet" of 1562: Reason no. 83 why Edmund de Vere="Shakespeare," *Hank Whittemore's Shakespeare Blog* (January 25, 2014), https://hankwhittemore.com/2014/01/25/romeus-and-juliet-of-1562-reason-no-83-why-edward-de-vere-shakespeare/.

[62] Siva Vaidhyanathan, *Copyrights and Copywrongs: The Rise of Intellectual Property and How it Threatens Creativity* (New York University Press, 2001) at 56–7, 67–9.

[63] Arewa, note 27, at 607–10.

other rock n' roll and rhythm and blues performers; such famous artists also availed themselves of the right to record cover songs without having to run the gauntlet of a permissions-based musical culture.[64] Marvin Gaye wanted to be a powerful yet "silky" singer like Rudy West or Ray Charles, but also a romantic crooner like Frank Sinatra, Dean Martin, or Perry Como.[65] As a songwriter for some of the most famous female pop acts of the past two decades has observed, rock "n" roll songs often share melodies and riffs, because songwriters get inspired by other songs.[66] A guitarist and composer argues that a single "melodic pattern ... can be found in hundreds of musical excerpts" across various genres, because "a limited compositional palette makes periodic duplication inevitable ... ."[67]

Film historians are also comfortable with the reappropriation of imagery, character types, plotlines, and camera angles. The archetypal Hollywood blockbuster films, *Star Wars* and *The Empire Strikes Back*, weave together many elements of comic books and earlier films, including a helmeted overlord named Darkseid (now Darth Vader wielding the Dark Side) whose son challenges his rule over an evil empire from Jack Kirby's *New Gods* and *The Forever People* comics; a will-based force (now embodied in a green lightsaber) and a tiny gray (now green) wizard guardian from *Green Lantern*; the arc of a sword fighting hero's life from *King Arthur* and *The Hidden Fortress*; the wartime love triangle from *Gone With the Wind*; exciting shots of an aerial dogfight or an assault on an enemy base from World War II movies; and majestic shots of spacecraft overflying or approaching planets or moons and entering enormous hangars from *2001: A Space Odyssey*.[68]

---

[64] Ibid., at 616–19.

[65] Quoted in David Ritz, *Divided Soul: The Life of Marvin Gaye* (Omnibus Press, 2010), at https://books .google.com/books?isbn=085712160X&pg=PT44.

[66] NPR, On Point with Tom Ashbrook (March 17, 2015), www.wbur.org/onpoint/2015/03/17/blurred-lines-copyright-robin-thicke-marvin-gaye-pharell. See also Arewa, note 27, at 607–19.

[67] Matthew Cochran, Why Tom Petty should, but won't back down, *Vapor Trail from a Paper Plane Blog* (February 13, 2015), http://matthewcochranguitar.com/2015/02/13/why-tom-petty-should-but-wont-back-down/. See also About Matthew Cochran, http://matthewcochranguitar.com/about/.

[68] M. Keith Booker, *Alternate Americas: Science Fiction Film and American Culture* (Greenwood Publishing Group. 2006) at 113; Fievel Elliott, May the source be with you, *in* John Morrow (Ed.), *Collected Jack Kirby Collector* (TwoMorrows Publishing, 2004) at 87–9 (quoting Frank Miller, God save the king, 105 *The Comics Journal* 63 (1986)); *Green Lantern Vol 2 7*, Wikia (2017), http://dc.wikia .com/wiki/Green_Lantern_Vol_2_7; *Green Lantern Vol 2 22*, Wikia (2017), http://dc.wikia.com/ wiki/Green_Lantern_Vol_2_22; Dick Giordano et al. (Eds.), *The Green Lantern Archives*, vol. 1 (DC Comics, 1998); Kirby Ferguson, Everything is a remix remastered, *YouTube* (2015), www.youtube .com/watch?v=sx15aXjcDZg; Jeffrey Kripal, *Mutants and Mystics: Science Fiction, Superhero Comics, and the Paranormal* (University of Chicago Press, 2011) at 149–50; B. P. Opreza, *The Gospel According to Superheroes: Religion and Pop Culture* (Peter Lang, 2005) at 236; Jeff Rovin, *The Encyclopedia of Super Villains* (Facts on File, 1987) at 76; *Star Wars* influences: Behind the Force – chapter 1, YouTube (June 5, 2012), www.youtube.com/watch?v=gUM-4jbTybw; *Star Wars* influences: Behind the Force – chapter 2, YouTube (July 7, 2013), www.youtube.com/watch?v=uom2HwCaE6c; Visual Rhythm, 2001: *A Space Odyssey* and *Star Wars* – visual similarities, *YouTube* (May 9, 2017), www .youtube.com/watch?v=ffgQLcsjUxc.

In resolving one case, the court said "many Hollywood movies take their inspiration from other movies or works – or go even further – without running afoul of" copyright law.[69] Both the story and some visuals of films like Walt Disney's *Cinderella* were based on prior sources, although Disney licensed stories, musical compositions, and recordings that were still in copyright.[70] James Cameron's iconic blockbuster *Avatar* has faced two plot-based infringement claims, and allegations of potential visual influences particularly when it comes to the lush environment and related imagery.[71] Similarly, many musicians, songwriters, and producers acknowledge being inspired by, and using "building blocks" from, other musical compositions and recordings.[72]

Computer and video-game software history is replete with examples of influences that go beyond abstract ideas. Leading programmers imitate others' visual interfaces and the copying of small portions of computer code is widespread.[73] Similarly, popular video game layouts and dynamics reappear in many later games.[74] A norm has developed of allowing game "mechanics" and design to be copied, but not "assets" or graphics.[75]

With digital and social media, even infringers are creators, to an extent, of "user-generated content." They reformat existing works and send them to many other persons using digital technologies. They then tag, rate, link to, promote, and spread virally such user-modified or user-created work. This labor frequently makes useful that which was virtually invisible or unknown before.[76] Without this labor, some

[69] *Dean*, 53 F. Supp. 3d at 650.

[70] *Rip!: A Remix Manifesto* (DVD directed by Brett Gaylor, EyeSteelFilm/National Film Board of Canada, 2009).

[71] *Dean v. Cameron*, 53 F. Supp. 3d 641, 649 (S.D.N.Y. 2014) (dragon look-a-likes and airborne mountains featuring trees); *Moore v. Lightstorm Entertainment*, 992 F. Supp. 2d 543, 555–56, 558 (D. Md. 2014) (plot, "gargantuan" trees, upside down trees, 3D maps of trees and terrain, bioluminescence, and rainforest features), *aff'd*, 586 Fed. Appx. 143 (4th Cir. 2014); *Van v. Cameron*, No. 10cv1051, 2011 WL 13121346, at *3 (S.D. Cal. motion to dismiss granted September 26, 2011) (elaborate treehouses and plot). See also Eriq Gardner, Know your 'Avatar ' lawsuits: Meet three plaintiffs who hope to win billions, *Hollywood Reporter*, (December 20, 2011), www.hollywoodreporter.com/thr-esq/avatar-lawsuits-james-cameron-new-plaintiffs-275707.

[72] Briefs of Amici Curiae of 212 Songwriters, Composers, and Producers in Support of Appellants, at 13, *Williams* (9th Cir. brief filed August 30, 2016) (No. 15-56880).

[73] *Apple Computer, Inc. v. Microsoft Corp.*, 799 F.Supp. 1006 (N.D. Cal. 1992), *aff'd*, 5 F.3d 1435 (9th Cir. 1994); Hughes, note 1, at 579–80.

[74] Some examples include *Breakout, Space Panic, Donkey Kong, Doom, Quake, Super Mario Bros., Super Mario 64, Command & Conquer, The Sims*, and *Minecraft*. E.g. *First-person shooter*, Wikipedia (2017), https://en.wikipedia.org/wiki/First-person_shooter; *Platform game*, Wikipedia (2017), https://en.wikipedia.org/wiki/Platform_game; *Video game clone*, Wikipedia (2017), https://en.wikipedia.org/wiki/Video_game_clone; Jamin Warren, Attack of the clone attackers, *Killscreen* (February 12, 2012), https://killscreen.com/articles/attack-clone-attackers/.

[75] Simon Parkin, Clone wars: Is plagiarism killing creativity in the games industry?, *The Guardian*, (December 21, 2011), www.theguardian.com/technology/gamesblog/2011/dec/21/clone-wars-games-industry-plagiarism.

[76] Cf. Richard Stallman, Reevaluating copyright: The public must prevail, 75 *Oregon Law Review* 291 (1996) at 294.

works may as well never have existed, and user-generated content creators, by finding and displaying the works, have "invented" them.[77] The rise of fan works, vidding, mashups, and other forms of remix culture liberate the ordinary Internet user to profit, as Walt Disney did, from reworking the previous century of art and writing, or to profit, as others did, from reworking earlier music, novels, comic books, films, or TV shows.[78]

4.6. LEGAL CONTRADICTION AND THE SUPERSTRUCTURE THESIS

Copyright law has often been called "metaphysical" for the abstract and puzzling distinctions it draws.[79] Its core concepts of copying, similarity, independent creation, and fair use are malleable and generate haphazard precedents and numerous jurisdictional conflicts.[80] Copyright's plasticity opens the door wider for political economy to affect it.

The modern, sophisticated legal formalist's view is that decisionmaking is and should be determined by the application of established rules. Formalist legal theory posits a fundamental dichotomy between formal, cognitive, conceptual constraint and legislative discretion or political will.[81] In contrast, the legal idealist's position is that while formal rules may be unclear in wording and indeterminate in application, the gaps in formal rules are filled by principles, policies, and purposes. These ideals embodied in our law provide rational constraints on deciding officials, and even furnish us with the principled reasons for respecting rules at all.[82]

---

[77] A similar concept exists in patent law, whereby the rediscovery of a lost or forgotten "art," such as a way of making a safe, is treated as an "invention." *Gayler* v. *Wilder*, 51 U.S. [10 How.] 477 (1850); *Rich* v. *Lippincott*, 20 F. Cas. 672, 676 (C.C.W.D. Pa. 1853).

[78] Ferguson, note 68; *Rip!*, note 28.

[79] E.g. *Monge* v. *Maya Magazines, Inc.*, 688 F.3d 1164, 1171 (9th Cir. 2012), citing *Folsom* v. *Marsh*, 9 F.Cas. 342, 344 (C.C.D. Mass. 1841); Laura Lape, The metaphysics of the law: Bringing substantial similarity down to earth, 98 *Dickinson Law Review* 181 (1993).

[80] E.g. *VMG Salsoul, LLC* v. *Ciccone*, 824 F.3d 871, 886–7 (9th Cir. 2016) (describing varying rules across circuits as to whether sampling a sound recording constitutes copyright infringement); Paul Goldstein, *Goldstein on Copyright* (Aspen Publishers, 2005), at 9–8, 9–42 (differences in how circuits balance evidence of access to and similarity of works); Robert Osterberg and Eric Osterberg, *Substantial Similarity in Copyright Law* (Practicing Law Institute, 2003) (differing infringement standards across circuits). There may even be conflicts within circuits, as defendants from some industries – notably computer programs and fabric designs – encounter different standards than defendants from the music or film industries. E.g. Goldstein, ibid., at 9–9; Olufunmilayo Arewa, The freedom to copy: Copyright, creation, and context, 41 *University of California at Davis Law Review* 477 (2007) at 489–4.

[81] H. L. A. Hart, *The Concept of Law* (Oxford University Press, 2012) at 128, 274; Hans Kelsen, *The Pure Theory of Law* (University of California Press, 1978) at 245, 351; Hans Kelsen, *The General Theory of Norms* (Clarendon Press, 1991) at 380–426.

[82] Ronald Dworkin, *Justice in Robes* (Harvard University Press, 2006) at 248; Ronald Dworkin, *A Matter of Principle* (Oxford University Press, 1985) at 22–3, 96, 129, 313; Charles Fried, *An Anatomy of Values: Problems of Personal and Social Choice* (Harvard University Press, 1970) at 54–63; Charles

CLS rejects the theory that formal rules or legal ideals determine case outcomes, even in "easy cases" or most of the time. First, multiple potential rules with differing implications apply to any particular case, opening up several divergent outcomes from which a judge or judges may choose.[83] Families of legal concepts (such as copying, similarity, and fair use) may be read broadly or narrowly. "Easy cases" then appear not as a logical imperative but as a contingent outcome of judicial ideology and unequal ability on the part of litigants to shape legal determinations. Hence, we have the phenomena of "celebrity justice" and lack of "access to justice," when class shapes legal outcomes even more obviously than usual.[84]

Often, the thesis that there is one decision in each case that "best fits and justifies" an entire branch of legal doctrine is difficult to defend.[85] If it falls, the question remains of which constraints on judges are "law" as opposed to social pressures.[86]

Copyright infringement is a case in point. There are several rules and theories that war with one another in infringement disputes, and that open a space for divergent applications of law and seemingly arbitrary case outcomes.[87] Both the tests employed and the subject-matter involved in copyright approach closer to philosophy than in other branches of the law, and philosophy is notoriously debatable.[88] Table 4.1 illustrates several potentially contradictory rules and principles in copyright.

Fried, *Right and Wrong* (Harvard University Press, 1978)at 188; Charles Fried, *Saying What the Law Is: The Constitution in the Supreme Court* (Harvard University Press, 2006) at 63, 187.

[83] E.g. Joseph William Singer, The player and the cards: Nihilism and legal theory, 94 *Yale Law Journal* 1 (1984). Singer explains:

> Legal doctrines are always potentially indeterminate. Judges can move the line between rules and exceptions, or create new exceptions. They can nullify the application of a rule to a particular case by widening a legally enforceable standard so far that it eclipses the apparently applicable rule. Ultimately, judges always have the power to revise the rules. That judges may do these things, however, does not mean they will do them. Because judges participate in a legal culture that suggests how they are to act as judges, we can often predict how they will act (p. 22).

[84] Theodore Boutros Jr. and Michael Dore, Celebrity justice: A new double standard, 22 *Communications Lawyer* 3 (2004); Lieve Gies, Stars behaving badly: Inequality and transgression in celebrity culture, 11 *Feminist Media Studies* 347 (2011); Deborah Rhode, *Access to Justice* (Oxford University Press, 2004); Deborah Rhode, Whatever happened to access to justice?, 42 *Loyola Los Angeles Law Review* 869 (2008); Richard Zorza, The disconnect between the requirements of judicial neutrality and those of the appearance of neutrality when parties appear pro se: Causes, solutions, recommendations, and implications, 17 *Georgetown Journal of Legal Ethics* 423 (2003).

[85] Singer, note 83, at 12. See also Ronald Dworkin, *Law's Empire* (Harvard University Press, 1986) at 239; Ronald Dworkin, *Taking Rights Seriously* (Harvard University Press, 1977) at 83–130.

[86] As John Rawls put it, if there is no rule or principle according to which we can weigh competing rules or principles, "the means of rational discussion have come to an end." John Rawls, A *Theory of Justice* (Harvard University Press, 1971) at 41. To paraphrase Dworkin, treating like cases alike and respecting precedents is simply one principle (procedural fairness) to balance with others, including substantive fairness, economic efficiency, health, order, democracy, etc. Dworkin, note 85, at 113, 237.

[87] Singer, note 83, at 10 & n. 21, 12.

[88] Zechariah Chafee, Reflections on the law of copyright, in Los Angeles Copyright Society and UCLA School of Law (Eds.), *Copyright and Related Topics: A Choice of Articles* (University of California Press, 1964) at 1–13.

TABLE 4.1. Copyright infringement doctrine in the United States

	Differences do not matter	Differences matter
Pre-1976 act	"[N]o plagiarist can excuse the wrong by showing how much of his work he did not pirate."[a]	"Every book in literature, science and art, borrows, and must necessarily borrow, and use much which was well known and used before."[b]
Post-1976 act on dissimilarities	"It is entirely immaterial that in many respects plaintiff's and defendant's works are dissimilar if in other respects similarity as to a substantial element of plaintiff's work can be shown."[c]	"[A] defendant may legitimately avoid infringement by intentionally making sufficient changes in a work which would otherwise be regarded as substantially similar to that of the plaintiff's ... ."[d]
Contemporary jurisprudence on dissimilarities	"'[D]issimilarity between some aspects of the works will not automatically relieve the infringer of liability, for "no copier may defend the act of plagiarism by pointing out how much of the copy he has not pirated."'"[e]	"We have observed that 'numerous differences tend to undercut substantial similarity ... .' 'It is only when the similarities between the protected elements ... are of "small import quantitatively or qualitatively" that the defendant[s] will be found innocent of infringement.'"[f]
Post-1976 act on degree of similarity required	"'A use is insubstantial ... "only if it is so meager and fragmentary that the average audience would not recognize the appropriation."'"[g]	"The standard test for substantial similarity between two items is whether an 'ordinary observer, unless he set out to detect the disparities, would be disposed to overlook them, and regard [the]aesthetic appeal as the same.'"[h]

[a] *Sheldon v. Metro-Goldwyn Pictures Corp.*, 81F.2d 49, 56 (2d Cir.), cert. denied, 298 U.S. 669 (1936).
[b] *Micro Star v. Formgen Inc.*, 154F.3d 1107, 1111 (9th Cir. 1998) (brackets added), citing *Emerson*, 8F. Cas. at 619.
[c] *Warner Bros., Inc. v. American Broadcasting Companies*, 720F.2d 231, 241–242 (2d Cir. 1983) (quoting Melville Nimmer and David Nimmer, *Nimmer on Copyright*, vo. 3 (LexisNexis, 1983) at 13–38).
[d] Ibid., (quoting Nimmer and Nimmer, *Nimmer on Copyright*, vol. 3, above n. 625, at 13-38.1 to 13-38.2). See also *Herbert Rosenthal Jewelry Corp. v. Honora Jewelry Co.*, 509F.2d 64, 65 (2d Cir. 1974).
[e] *Porto v. Guirgis*, 659 F. Supp. 2d 597, 609 (S.D.N.Y. 2009) (quoting *Williams v. Crichton*, 84F.3d 581 588 (2d Cir. 1996) (emphasis added in original) (quoting *Rogers v. Koons*, 960F.2d 301, 308 (2d Cir. 1992))).
[f] Ibid. (quoting *Warner Bros.*, 720F.2d at 241–242, and *Williams*, 84F.3d at 588, 590).
[g] *Pryor v. Warner/Chappell Music, Inc.*, 111 U.S.P.Q.2d (BNA) 1221 (C.D. Cal. 2014) (quoting *Worth v. Selchow & Righter Co.*, 827F.2d 569, 570 n.1 (9th Cir. 1987) (citation omitted)).
[h] *Yurman Design, Inc. v. Paj, Inc.*, 262F.3d 101, 111 (2d Cir. 2001) (quoting *Hamil America, Inc. v. GFI*, 193F.3d 92, 97 (2d Cir. 1999)).

Table 4.1, and other scholars' analyses of these cases, suggest that courts have a great deal of discretion to disregard dissimilarities and enter judgments of infringement due to similarities at the level of what an ordinary person would call the works' "ideas" as opposed to their literal expression.[89] Decision-making in this area is even more "ad hoc" than is usual in court.[90]

Copyright's overlapping and often unclear rules stack the deck against the independent and resource-poor author. Large corporations, flush with cash, often find that copyright litigation is beneficial to them because they can seek multi-million-dollar attorneys' fees and statutory damages for their registered works, even if the works are dissimilar or if proof of actual damages or defendants' profits is lacking. Meanwhile, struggling artists and unknown authors who may be ripped off by big companies typically fail to register their copyrights in time to make litigation worthwhile for their potential attorneys.[91] Copyright law permits access to a protected work to be inferred from widespread distribution, even when the defendant denies copying it, so that infringement is more likely to be found with mass-produced works.[92] On the flip side, it is difficult to base a lawsuit on an unreleased or unpopular musical composition or recording, play or film screenplay, video game, or novel.[93] Even when some elite authors admit to taking from other work, contrived excuses are

[89] See also Mark Lemley, *Our bizarre system for proving copyright infringement*, 57 *Journal of the Copyright Society of the U.S.A.* 719 (2010), draft, at 27, (judgments of infringement in "dubious circumstances" are likely because law does not guide courts in ignoring "unprotectable elements"); Peter Menell, Adapting copyright to the mashup generation, 164 *University of Pennsylvania Law Review* 441 (2016) at 466 (arguing that "substantially similar" is "a notoriously vague standard").

[90] *Universal Athletic*, 511 F.2d at 907.

[91] John Tehranian, *Infringement Nation: Copyright 2.0 and You* (Oxford University Press, 2011), at 98–109.

[92] E.g. *Art Attacks Ink, LLC v. MGA Entertainment Inc.*, 581 F.3d 1138, 1144 (9th Cir. 2009) (sale of 2,000 copies would not justify inference of access); *Three Boys Music Corp. v. Bolton*, 212 F.3d 477, 480, 483–5 (9th Cir. 2000) (mass distribution of song on CD helped justify finding of access); *Jason v. Fonda*, 526 F. Supp. 774, 776 (C.D. Cal. 1981), *aff'd*, 698 F.2d 966 (9th Cir. 1982) (sale of 2,000 copies would not justify inference of access); *Bright Tunes Music Corp. v. Harrisongs Music, Ltd.*, 420 F. Supp. 177, 179 (S.D.N.Y. 1976) (presence of song on pop charts justifies finding of access), *aff'd on other grounds*, 722 F.2d 988, 998 (2d Cir. 1983) (access was close issue). See also *Loomis v. Cornish*, No. CV 12-5525, 2013 WL 6044345, at *10 (C.D. Cal. Nov. 13, 2013).

[93] E.g. *Jones v. Blige*, 558 F.3d 485 (6th Cir. 2009) (receipt of demo CD at record label that released allegedly infringing song did not adequately show access); *Armour v. Knowles*, 512 F.3d 147 (5th Cir. 2007) (receipt of demo tape by acquaintance of artist who released allegedly similar song did not adequately show access); *Jorgenson v. Epic/Sony Records*, 351 F.3d 46 (2d Cir. 2003) (receipt of song by same corporation that released allegedly infringing song did not adequately show access); *Selle v. Gibb*, 741 F.2d 896 (7th Cir. 1984) (receipt of demo tape and lead sheet by 11 recording companies did not adequately show access); *Scott v. WKJG, Inc.*, 376 F.2d 467 (7th Cir. 1967) (fact that script of play was not commercially distributed supported finding of no access); Goldstein, note 80, at 9-11–9-16; Marshall Leafer, *Understanding Copyright Law* (LexisNexis, 2010) at ch. 9. But see *Bouchat v. Baltimore Ravens, Inc.*, 241 F.3d 350 (4th Cir. 2001) (submission of drawing to close associates of infringer could show access); *Repp v. Webber*, 132 F.3d 882 (2d Cir. 1997) (degree of similarity between unpopular musical composition and popular musical play could result in infringement verdict, despite difficulties establishing that author of musical play had access to composition);

accepted which may not be available to the younger and less-well-connected artist, often branded a "pirate."[94]

The idea–expression distinction is supposed to salvage the rule of law in the copyright domain from the indeterminacies generated by infringement doctrine. Numerous cases illustrate that copyright protects what would be called "ideas" in ordinary language. Sam Smith had to settle with Tom Petty's representatives for using a similar chord progression. The words of the songs and the styles of singing are very if not completely different, with the similarities consisting of the notes la-sol-mi- ... mi-do-do.[95] Robin Thicke and Pharrell Williams used entirely different lyrics and a distinct melody from Marvin Gaye's *Got to Give It Up*, but were still found to infringe, initially, based on influences.[96] Led Zeppelin and Jay-Z have gone to trial over infringement of a few notes, many years after releasing songs that provoked few complaints at the time.[97]

4.7. COPYRIGHT THEORY AND THE QUESTION OF LITERARY FREEDOM

Critical theory refers to law as "superstructure" of the economy to indicate that law reflects and serves the balance of forces in the material economy, including the relative shares in which ownership of the means of production are distributed. In a small tribe with a dominant chief, or a large Stalinist state, there will be different laws than those in a capitalist or mixed democratic-socialist economy.[98] Some scholars see a contradiction in that law is supposed to be dictated by the mode of production, but law actually divides up the goods of the world into the property rights that make up productive capital.[99]

Smith v. Little, Brown & Co., 245 F. Supp. 451 (S.D.N.Y. 1965), *aff'd*, 360 F.2d 928 (2d Cir. 1966) (submission of manuscript to office of defendant's book editor could show access).

[94] Cf. Steven Jamar, Crafting copyright law to encourage and protect user-generated content in the Internet social networking context, 19 *Widener Law Journal* 843 (2010); James Griffin, 300 years of copyright law? A not so modest proposal for reform, 28 *John Marshall Journal of Computer & Information Law* 1 (2010).

[95] Ursula Smartt, *Media & Entertainment Law* (Routledge, 2017) at 402.

[96] Brief of Amici Curiae 212 Songwriters, note 72, at 2.

[97] Rory Carroll, Jay Z wins copyright infringement case over Big Pimpin' Egyptian song sample, *The Guardian*, (October 21, 2015), www.theguardian.com/music/2015/oct/21/jay-z-wins-copyright-infringement-case-big-pimpin-sample; *Skidmore*, No. 2:15-cv-03462-RGK , slip op.

[98] E.g. Raymond Belliotti, Marxist jurisprudence: Historical necessity and radical contingency, 4 *Canadian Review of Law and Jurisprudence* 145 (1991); Alan Hunt, The theory of critical legal studies, 6 *Oxford Journal of Legal Studies* 1 (1986); Karl Marx, *Capital: A Critique of Political Economy*, vol. 1 (Ben Fowkes trans. Vintage Books ed., 1977) at 175–6; Ira Katznelson, *Marxism and the City* (Oxford University Press, 1992) at 5–15; Akbar Rasulov, "The nameless rapture of the struggle": Towards a Marxist class-theoretic approach to international law, in Jan Klabbers (Ed.), *Finnish Yearbook of International Law* (Hart, 2010) at 243–94,; Alan Stone, The place of law in the Marxian Structure-Superstructure archetype, 19 *Law & Society Review* 39 (1985); Roberto Mangabeira Unger, The critical legal studies movement, 561 *Harvard Law Review* 570 (1983) at 570–2, 592–9, 663–9.

[99] Mark Tushnet, A Marxist analysis of American law, 1 *Marxist Perspectives* 96 (1978). See also Bob Jessop, *The Capitalist State* (New York University Press, 1982) at 11; Bob Jessop, *State Theory: Putting the Capitalist State in Its Place* (Wiley, 2013) at 49, 81–3.

Recognition of the role of law as superstructure to an economic base opens up, for some scholars, a space for transformation of the law. Ideas like "corporation" or "copyright" are dangerous because they may persuade judges and legislators of their reality, and foreclose efforts to make the law fairer. For example, corporate law may seem unfair when a corporation is difficult to sue because of the appearance of corporate "thinghood" in a country or place other than where the court is located, or where the plaintiff filed suit.[100] Realism about law, as an attitude and as a movement, is about using concepts to explain or summarize decisions that have been made about who owns what, etc., and not to dictate those decisions in a faux-deductive mode of reasoning.[101]

A copyright or trademark, if we are not careful, can be "thingified" into an entity that inherently leads to certain legal conclusions, dictating what others can do with their own pens, papers, computers, disks, businesses, careers, and communities.[102] A more realistic approach is to ask: Is society benefiting from greater trademark (or copyright) protection? Are consumers buying products that they prefer over those that they would buy with few or no such laws in force? Are IP owners gaining an unfair commercial advantage by snapping up language or imagery that appeals to particular cultural traditions or preferences?

A less realistic approach, which Cohen calls "transcendental nonsense," purports to discover facts about the world that are judge-made habits, norms, and guidelines.[103] In copyright, for example, a court might declare that a sculpture based on a photograph is illegal because the sculpture invaded the province of a "work" that already had an "author."[104] Every form, or work, can have only one author, the notion is. Any work reflecting inspiration by another work is superfluous, even if it was put to paper, canvas, or code by another natural person who was not the source of the inspiration. A better approach, some say, would be to assess each case as setting "information policy."[105] Policy analysis arguably looks at human needs, building rights from them.[106]

---

[100] Felix S. Cohen, Transcendental nonsense and the functional approach, 35 *Columbia Law Review* 809 (1935) at 811–12.

[101] Ibid., at 813.

[102] Ibid., at 815–19.

[103] Ibid., 815–17.

[104] Keith Aoki, Adrift in the intertext, 68 *Chicago-Kent Law Review* 805 (1993) at 813–14, citing *Rogers*, 960 F.2d 301 (2d Cir.), *cert. denied*, 113 S. Ct. 365 (1992); Peter Jaszi, On the author effect: Contemporary copyright and collective creativity, 10 *Cardozo Arts & Entertainment Law Journal* 293 (1992) at 301–14, 318–19.

[105] Aoki, note 112, at 813 n. 49 (quoting Jaszi, note 112, at 301).

[106] Cf. Alan Freeman, Legitimizing racial discrimination through anti-discrimination law: A critical review, in David Kairys (Ed.), *The Politics of Law: A Progressive Critique* (Pantheon Books, 1998) at 96–116; Mark Tushnet, An essay on rights, 62 *Texas Law Review* 1364 (1984) at 1386; Robin West, *Rights* (Ashgate/Dartmouth, 2nd ed. 2001) at 326.

Why not, then, imagine a situation in which characters and settings, like Batman, the Joker, and Gotham City, are placed on the "idea" side of the ledger along with a wizard college, the floating mountains of Pandora in *Avatar*,[107] and the like? Why not allow musicians to openly quote large passages from one another's work, as philosophers and legal scholars do?[108] Why not say that video game designers may reuse one another's imagery and sound effects in other games, especially if the plot or gameplay differs?

There are several arguments in favor of limiting the freedom of later authors in order to provide a benefit to initial authors. First, some authors want to be protected from the crass exploitation of altered versions of their works, especially those made by unscrupulous corporations and distributors.[109] Second, it may encourage more creativity overall if later authors have to come up with their own characters, subplots, settings, hooks, riffs, beats, and other trappings of a work that entertains.[110] Third, aggregate transaction costs may be lower if a corporation or brilliant author controls the expensive and labor-intensive process of creating improvements on a great and/or popular work. Centralized management may reduce rent-seeking "races" to claim improvements as property. Unified control may relieve initial authors of the burdens of overproduction and onerous security measures to keep works secret from imitators, and it may steer subsequent authors clear of potential litigation involving coincidental similarities.[111]

The argument from a moral right against modification arguably does not carry the weight it needs to, and if it does, it arguably proves too much. For one thing, reputational and control-related interests exist on both sides of the nonliteral infringement/derivative work equation. Later authors lose control over their works, and lose opportunities to develop their reputations, when initial authors

---

[107] *Dean*, 53 F. Supp. 2d 641 (S.D.N.Y. 2014).

[108] Menell, note 97, at 506–9.

[109] One of the "moral rights" of authors involves a legal entitlement to prevent the mutilation of a work in a way that harms one's reputation as a writer or artist. The United States is arguably bound to provide for such a right by law, although there is no ready way to punish it for failing to do so (outside of the derivative work right and the rights of integrity and attribution enjoyed by authors of limited-edition artworks). E.g. Berne Convention for the Protection of Literary and Artistic Works, art. *6bis* (Paris Text, 1971); Berne Convention Implementation Act of 1988, Pub. L. No. 100-568, 102 Stat. 2853; Visual Artists Rights Act of 1990, Pub. L. No. 101-650, 104 Stat. 5128 (1990) at 5128–9. See also Aoki, note 112, at 817; Phillip Infantino, Copyright wrong: The United States' failure to provide copyright protection for works of architecture, 47 *Washington & Lee Law Review* 1103 (1990) at 1119–121.

[110] Joseph Fishman, Creating around copyright, 128 *Harvard Law Review* 1333 (2014); Viktor Mayer-Schonberger and Lena Wong, Fan or foe: Fan fiction, authorship, and the fight for control, 54 *IDEA* 1 (2013); Emily Temple, Abusing the people of Westeros: Famous authors on fan-fiction, *Flavorwire* (April 19, 2012), http://flavorwire.com/281936/abusing-the-people-of-westeros-famous-authors-on-fan-fiction. See also *Ty, Inc. v. Publications, Ltd.*, 292 F.3d 512, 517–19 (7th Cir. 2002); and at 678, n. 56, 698 n. 163; *Castle Rock Entertainment, Inc. v. Carol Publishing Group, Inc.*, 150 F.3d 132, 145–6 (2d Cir. 1998).

[111] William Landes and Richard Posner, An economic analysis of copyright law, 18 *Journal of Legal Studies* 325 (1989) at 354–57.

prohibit imitation, inspiration, quotation, or paraphrase. Often, if later authors are unable to use words or themes that are too close to those of prior authors, their works may be judged lacking in some important respect, such as factual support or cultural context, damaging their reputations. These burdens hinder socially-useful investments in follow-on creative labor. Many infringers of the derivative work right should be entitled to copyright protection on their own behalf. For these reasons, among others, some courts have conceded that appropriation art that comments on social trends using copyrighted works of others, in the manner of Andy Warhol or contemporary art featuring repurposed Barbie dolls, should be lawful.[112]

The second argument is well-taken in that if copyright is to fulfill its purpose, judges and legislators will be keenly interested to prevent harm to authors' markets and income streams, including from such sources as foreseeable movie or video game deals, foreign translations, adaptations from prose to drama or vice versa, transformations from sheet music to recorded song or back the other way, etc. Nevertheless, it is not likely that the very uncertain and overbroad scope of copyright is required to achieve this purpose.

To conclude that copyright is not fulfilling its purpose, one would need an idea of how much income and how many markets are really needed to incentivize an adequate flow of newly-published informative and entertaining works. Perhaps all works that do "foreseeable" harm to the economic incentive to produce an initial work, due to being so similar yet produced in a different format, should be included within copyright regulation in order to achieve copyright's core purpose.[113]

It is difficult to know when copyright's purpose has already been fulfilled, and when society is overcorrecting for the absence of works by protecting copyright to a degree that does not result in more works in aggregate, because the growth of the authorial class is inhibited. When fans and remixers cannot become paid authors using their infringing works, there are fewer authors and works. Especially when a corporation has invested a modest amount to create a work that turned into a tremendous hit, did it really need the additional revenue from licensed derivatives to produce the work in the first place? Would it not be persuaded to make another one based on the income from the lucrative, non-derivative market? Once an author has already become a millionaire a hundred or several thousand times over, are additional markets and revenue streams really serving copyright's purpose, or are

[112] *Cariou v. Prince*, 714 F.3d 694, 706 (2d Cir. 2013); *Mattel Inc. v. Walking Mountain Prods.*, 353 F.3d 792, 806 (9th Cir. 2003).
[113] Christina Bohannan, Taming the derivative works right: A modest proposal for reducing overbreadth and vagueness in copyright, 12 *Vanderbilt Journal of Entertainment & Technology Law* 669 (2010) at 679, citing *Ty, Inc.*, 292 F.3d at 517–19; Christina Bohannan, Copyright harm, foreseeability, and fair use, 85 *Washington University Law Review* (2007) at 969, 1028–29.

follow-on authors and consumers being taxed for no good copyright-based reason? How do we know whether some authors made rich by copyright are resting on their laurels, and halting further creation?

Moreover, the squelching of many forms of pop art, appropriation art, postmodern writing, pastiche, satire, remix, etc. must be considered. Is copyright's "purpose" truly to fix and freeze creativity, once it is expressed? Why must a character or micro-work such as a magical weapon or a souped-up vehicle remain the exclusive province of one copyright conglomerate? Must a will-based force, which can be wielded with glowing laser swords, be portrayed only by those approved by Disney and Lucasfilm? Would copyright's "purpose" still be met if the owners of *Star Wars* earned billions by being able to restrain the full-length exhibition or reproduction in DVD or streaming format of the three trilogies, or perhaps a fourth and fifth trilogy as well, while allowing competing stories, like Bioware's *Knights of the Old Republic*, to be produced without restraint?[114] Would copyright's "purpose" still be achieved if pop stars, their labels, and their assignees or heirs control their musical recordings' duplication and sale in substantially complete forms, but not the sampling of them in new music or films by others?[115]

The insights of CLS and the base-superstructure model indicate that there is no natural or discoverable answer to these questions. Instead, the answer that we choose will be related to our vision of a creative and just economy and culture. Whether an artist or copyright purchaser has a "moral" right to prohibit this or that is precisely a "moral" question, or a question about how to use freedom to bring about "the good," which is a complex series of "higher ends" shaped by the state and its laws.[116] As with the law of bankruptcy or trespass, exceptions to property interests are allowed for the general welfare or for ends other than the secure enjoyment of property.[117]

The Chicago School theory of copyright scope in situations of sequels, adaptations, alterations, and remixes is that the law should maximize the incentive to

---

[114] Bioware licensed *Star Wars* in 2000 to make a role-playing game, the franchise's first. First-ever Star Wars RPG, *IGN* (July 25, 2000), www.ign.com/articles/2000/07/25/first-ever-star-wars-rpg. The result became one of the most cinematic video games ever made. Andrew Williams, History of Digital Games: Developments in Art, *Design and Interaction* (CRC Press, 2017) at 197. Since 2004, there has been no new game in the series released for consoles such as the Xbox or Playstation. There is an online PC game and its expansions, *Star Wars: The Old Republic*, however.

[115] Cf. *Cariou*, 714 F.3d 694 (some copying of photographs into transformative artworks may have infringed copyright by being too recognizable or complete); *Bridgeport Music, Inc. v. UMG Recordings, Inc.*, 585 F.3d 267, 272, 275–6 (6th Cir. 2009) (sampling of funk song performed by George Clinton's group infringed copyright despite sample being barely, if at all, recognizable to contemporary audiences); *Elvis Presley Enterprises, Inc. v. Passport Video*, 349 F.3d 622, 628–9 (9th Cir. 2003) (some Elvis performances included in a television or VHS/DVD biography lasted too long and were too prominent, so they infringed copyrights controlled by estate's management).

[116] G. W. F. Hegel, The philosophy [science] of right, in Mortimer Adler et al. (Eds.), *Great Books of the Western World, vol. 46: Hegel* (T.M. Knox trans., Encyclopedia Britannica, Inc., 1952) at 51.

[117] Ibid., at 45, 51. See also Sir William Blackstone, *Commentaries on the Laws of England*, vol. 2 (William Carey James ed., Bancroft-Whitney Co., 1916) at 1783, 1786–7.

produce new works by including all potential foreseeable uses or markets in the scope of the initial producer's copyright.[118] According to the Chicago School of law and economics, copyright politics attempt to balance the benefits generated by the increased incentives based on broad rights, against the costs of, for example, blocking competitors' efforts to reduce prices, make more copies more widely available, and improve their works' quality.[119] A natural-rights or "unjust enrichment" theory of copyright might achieve the same result by declaring it to be an injustice whenever a follow-on author takes advantage of another author's labors without compensation.[120] The theory here is that as a matter of corrective justice, an author must not reap what he or she has not sown, so that IP guarantees restitution for copyright infringement, as typified by the availability of the share of the infringer's profits attributable to the infringement as a remedy.[121]

Under the influence of Ronald Coase and his theory of transaction costs, the Chicago School and its progeny within the judiciary and the legal academy developed "market failure" accounts of various legal rules and principles. A market failure theory typically presumes that private ordering or "free-market" arrangements are more efficient than government-mandated ones, so that in the absence of a market failure such as natural monopoly, price fixing, or excessive transaction costs, the government should *laissez-faire*.[122] For example, if the law prohibited employers from firing employees except for "just cause" or a "good" reason, this would increase the cost of production, thereby increasing the cost of goods and reducing employment or wages and benefits, and reducing demand for other goods and impacting employment in those fields because consumers have paid more for other goods due to higher costs.[123]

In copyright, the market failure theory suggests that the law should maximize the incentive to create by forcing any imitator or subsequent author making

---

[118] E.g. William Landes and Richard Posner, Indefinitely renewable copyright, 70 *University of Chicago Law Review* 471 (2003) at 476.

[119] Felix Oberholzer-Gee and Koleman Strumpf, *File-sharing and copyright*, Paper for National Bureau of Economic Research's 2009 Innovation Policy and the Economy Conference (2010), www.scribd .com/doc/169830154/File-Sharing-Piracy-Paper-Felix-Oberholzer-Gee#scribd. See also Shyamkrishna Balganesh, Debunking Blackstonian copyright, 118 *Yale Law Journal* 1126 (2009) at 1137; Lawrence Lessig, *Code and Other Laws of Cyberspace* (Basic Books, 1999) at 131.

[120] E.g. Shyamkrishna Balganesh, Foreseeability and copyright incentives, 122 *Harvard Law Review* 1569 at 1603, n. 138; Shyamkrishna Balganesh, Rethinking copyright: Property through the lenses of unjust enrichment and unfair competition, 156 *University of Pennsylvania Law Review PENNumbra* 345 (2008) at 349–50; Wendy Gordon, On owning information: Intellectual property and the restitutionary impulse, 78 *Virginia Law Review* 149 (1992) at 238 and n. 337; Travis, note 56, at 795–803, 821, 826–44.

[121] Gordon, note 128, at 150–79.

[122] Richard Posner, Hegel and employment at-will: A comment, 10 *Cardozo Law Review* 1625 (1988–1989) at 1633–34. *Laissez-faire* means to leave alone, as in *laissez-faire la nature*. Lester Vernon Chandler, *A Preface to Economics* (Harper & Brothers, 1947) at 167.

[123] Posner, note 130, at 1633–5.

use of a copyrighted work to seek a license for the privilege unless the market fails, whether because the copyright owner regards the use as beneath its consideration or the market fails for some other reason.[124] One situation in which it is widely agreed that the market will fail is parody, because authors and their representatives are seen as precious little snowflakes whose "self-esteem" will not permit them to license their critics or those who openly mock their work.[125]

Economic harm is supposed to occur, according to the Chicago School, if copyrighted work is widely imitated or enters the public domain because it will suffer the fate of a frequently counterfeited currency, being "debased."[126] This threat explains the "adverse effects" test for infringement of the derivative right (and for its flip side, fair use). The test is for whether if the challenged use "should become widespread, it would adversely affect the potential market for the copyrighted work."[127] The effects test counts not only effects on the original work's market but also effects on the market for its derivatives.[128] Some courts have gone so far as to say that even if the copyright holder has openly announced its intention not to exploit a particular market, the imitation or use of its work in that market should be unlawful because people change their minds.[129]

This "incentives paradigm" is severely flawed, according to critical economic analyses of copyright and intellectual property. For one thing, it ignores the fact that if the incentive structure of copyright holders is artificially inflated by protection against free-riding infringers, resources will be inefficiently diverted away from other sectors of the economy characterized by more perfect competition, and less market power.[130] This is because expanding copyright protection to interfere with nonliteral

---

[124] *Harper & Row, Publishers, Inc.* v. *Nation Enterprises*, 471 U.S. 539, 568 (1985), citing Wendy Gordon, Fair use as market failure: A structural analysis of the Betamax case and its predecessors, 82 *Columbia Law Review* 1600 (1982) at 1615, and *Harper & Row v. The Nation*, Copyrightability and fair use, US Department of Justice Economic Policy Office Discussion Paper No. 13-17 (1984).

[125] *Campbell*, 510 U.S. 569, 592 (1994); 794 F.2d 432, 436–7 (9th Cir. 1986); *Henley* v. *DeVore*, 733 F. Supp. 2d 1144, 1154–5 (C.D. Cal. 2010).

[126] Michael Abramowicz, A theory of copyright's derivative right and related doctrines, 90 *Minnesota Law Review* 317 (2005) at 366–72; Landes and Posner, note 126, at 486–7; William Landes and Richard Posner, *The Economic Structure of Intellectual Property Law* (Harvard University Press, 2003), at 90–121. See also Dennis Karjala, Harry Potter, Tanya Grotter, and the copyright derivative work, 38 *Arizona State Law Journal* 27 (2006); Dennis Karjala, Congestion externalities and extended copyright protection, 94 *Georgetown Law Journal* 1065 (2006) at 1068–86.

[127] *Harper & Row*, 471 U.S. at 568, citing *Sony Corp. of America* v. *Universal City Studios, Inc.*, 464 U. S. 417, 451, 484, and n. 36 (1984).

[128] *Harper & Row*, 471 U.S. at 568.

[129] E.g. *Worldwide Church of God* v. *Philadelphia Church of God, Inc.*, 227 F.3d 1110, 1119 (9th Cir. 2000); *Salinger* v. *Random House, Inc.*, 811 F.2d 90, 99 (2d Cir.1987); *Henley*, 733 F. Supp. 2d at 1162; *Salinger v. Colting*, 641 F. Supp. 2d 250, 268 (S.D.N.Y. 2009), *rev'd*, 607 F.3d 68 (2d Cir.2010). See also *Castle Rock Entertainment, Inc.*, 150 F.3d 132, 145–6 (2d Cir. 1998).

[130] Glynn Lunney, Reexamining copyright's incentives-access paradigm, 49 *Vanderbilt Law Review* 483, (1996) at 655–6; Glynn Lunney, Trademark monopolies, 48 *Emory Law Journal* 367 (1999) at 446–7.

similarities will tend to make it relatively unprofitable to invest in non-copyright industries.[131]

In addition, overprotection of intellectual property results in a reduction of societal wealth to the extent that monopoly pricing results, causing deadweight losses. These losses occur when consumers would have benefited from purchasing a product, but they are priced out of the market for it (this costs the producer money as well, but the producer may accept this side-effect of higher prices).[132]

Neither the courts nor Chicago School scholars have any means of weighing the negative impact of these price hikes on consumers and subsequent authors against the higher prices' benefit to the initial authors and their business partners.[133] For example, books published many decades ago are much more likely to be available on Amazon.com for purchase by consumers if they are in the public domain, rather than still under copyright.[134] Despite costs of this kind, the Supreme Court seemingly counts only the benefits of copyright protection in its rudimentary economic analyses of fragmentary copyright infringement, conducted in the Chicago School style.[135] The Court does not describe or acknowledge the administrative costs or the transactions costs involved in recognizing expansive copyrights that treat identical republication and fragmentary quotation as equally infringing, leading to lawsuits over trifling similarities, like those against 2 Live Crew, Biz Markie, Jay-Z, Led Zeppelin, and Thicke/Williams.

Finally, the "deflation" or "dilution" theory of copyright's nonliteral infringement and derivative work doctrines is greatly undermined by practical experience of, and empirical work on, copyright industries. Works such as *Harry Potter, Jurassic Park, Lord of the Rings, Star Trek, Star Wars*, the Marvel and DC Comics universes, *Twilight, Fifty Shades of Grey, Attack on Titan*, and *Game of Thrones* are the subject of countless potentially infringing fanworks, downloads, acts of streaming "piracy," memes, video game modifications, smartphone apps, and other derivative works. Yet they seem to gain earning power as the level of infringement and imitation grows, rather than becoming unpopular or losing money due to the "dilution" of their "value."[136]

---

[131] Lunney (1996), note 138, at 640–1, 648.

[132] William Fisher III, Reconstructing the fair use doctrine, 101 *Harvard Law Review* 1659 (188) at 1700–17; Lunney (1999), note 138, at 367–8, 431, citing Edward Chamberlin, *The Theory of Monopolistic Competition* (1933); Lunney, note 138, at 564.

[133] E.g. Landes and Posner, note 134, at 90–121.

[134] Paul Heald, The public domain, in Richard Watt (Ed.), *Handbook on the Economics of Copyright: A Guide for Students and Teachers* (Elgar, 2014) at 98–100.

[135] *Harper & Row*, 471 U.S. at 558–9, 566–7, 569 (referring to benefit of copyright as encouraging more expression to be created, but dismissing benefit to public of greater public access to works as being unworthy of judicial recognition). See also *Campbell*, 510 U.S. at 592 (observing that "licensing of derivatives is an important economic incentive to the creation of originals," but not addressing whether unlicensed access to originals for purposes of creating derivatives would serve as economic incentive for derivatives' creation).

[136] E.g. Paul Carr, Book piracy: A non-issue, *Techcrunch* (August 23, 2011), https://techcrunch.com/2011/08/23/book-piracy-a-non-issue/ (works of Michael Crichton, author of *Jurassic Park*, widely

Perhaps the definitive study of this question was done using Girl Talk's album *All Day*, which sampled many albums; the sampled albums saw sales increase due to the "dilution" of having been "used."[137] Similarly, the CEO of Time Warner has suggested that unauthorized downloading of *Game of Thrones* episodes was "tremendous word-of-mouth" advertising, and "better than an Emmy."[138] The author Paulo Coelho had a similar experience with spreading free digital copies of his novels in Russian using BitTorrent and his website; sales exploded a thousandfold.[139]

infringed on file-sharing websites); Ernesto, Pirated 'Star Wars: The Force Awakens' Blu-Ray leaks online, *Torrent Freak* (March 23, 2016), torrentfreak.com/tag/star-wars/; Ryan Faughnder, 'Star Wars' breaks 'Jurassic World' global box-office record, *Los Angeles Times Envelope Blog*, (December 21, 2015), www.latimes.com/entertainment/envelope/la-et-ct-star-wars-jurassic-world-box-office-record-20151221-stort.html (*Star Wars: The Force Awakens* earned $528 million in first weekend, ten times more than *A New Hope* or *The Empire Strikes Back*, and a little more than *Jurassic World*, the previous record holder); Duncan Riley, The Latest Harry Potter book hits BitTorrent, *Techcrunch* (July 17, 2007), https://techcrunch.com/2007/07/17/the-latest-harry-potter-book-hits-bittorrent/ (last *Harry Potter* book was made available on bitTorrent, and torrents were indexed on Pirate Bay); see also All-Time Best-Selling Blu-ray Titles in the United States, *The Numbers* (2017), www.the-numbers.com/alltime-bluray-sales-chart (the following titles each earned more than $80 million in Blu-ray disc sales alone, since 2009: *Star Wars Ep. VII: The Force Awakens, The Avengers, Jurassic World, The Dark Knight Rises, Guardians of the Galaxy*, and *Star Trek* [2009], with *The Force Awakens* earning the most of these, at $145 million); Andy , CENSORED* Fifty Shades of Grey an HD BitTorrent hit, *TorrentFreak* (February 28, 2015), https://torrentfreak.com/censored-fifty-shades-of-grey-an-hd-bittorrent-hit-150228/ (*Fifty Shades* and *Taken* had HD-quality copies hit BitTorrent networks); James Hibbard, HBO: 'Game of Thrones' piracy is a compliment, *Entertainment Weekly* (March 31, 2013), http://ew.com/article/2013/03/31/hbo-thrones-piracy/ (*Game of Thrones* DVD sales broke records despite "rampant illegal downloading" including more than four million unauthorized downloads of one episode alone); Brett Lang, Box office: 'Batman v Superman: Dawn of Justice', *Variety*, (March 27, 2016), http://variety.com/2016/film/box-office/box-office-batman-v-superman-dawn-of-justice-shatters-records-with-170-1-million-debut-1201739978/ ('*Batman v Superman: Dawn of Justice*' had record-breaking March opening weekend with $170 million, which is just about twice as much, adjusted for inflation, as the first *Batman* film made in 1989, and about seventeen times what *Superman IV: The Quest for Peace* made two years before that); Kevin Melrose, With $60.5 million in sales, 'Attack on Titan' is its own media empire, *CBR.com* (December 30, 2015), www.cbr.com/with-60-5-million-in-sales-attack-on-titan-is-its-own-media-empire/ (*Attack on Titan* sold $60.5 million in manga, DVDs, Blu-ray discs, CDs, and novels in 2015); Motoko Rich, Record first-day sales for last 'Harry Potter' book, *The New York Times*, (July 22, 2007), www.nytimes.com/2007/07/22/books/22cnd-potter.html (last Potter book sold 8.2 million copies in first 24 hours of release, for one-day revenue of more than $160 million); *Top-selling DVDs in the United States* 2009 (2017), www.the-numbers.com/home-market/dvd-sales/2009 (*Twilight* made $186 million in DVD sales in 2009 alone); Andrew Trendell, The top 10 most pirated movies of 2016 revealed, *NME* (January 3, 2017), www.nme.com/news/film/top-10-pirated-movies-2016-revealed-torrent-download-deadpool-batman-1932469 (*Dawn of Justice* and *Force Awakens* among five most-downloaded on "torrent sites" in 2016).

137 W. Michael Schuster II, Fair use, Girl Talk, and digital sampling: An empirical study of music sampling's effect on the market for copyrighted works, 67 *Oklahoma Law Review* 443 (2013).

138 Quoted in Time Warner CEO says having Game of Thrones as 'most pirated' is 'better than an Emmy', *Techdirt* (August 8, 2013), www.techdirt.com/articles/20130808/02084524106/time-warner-ceo-says-having-game-thrones-as-most-pirated-is-better-than-emmy.shtml. See also Ed Krayewski, Piracy not really hurting Game of Thrones, most pirated TV show of 2012, says director, *Reason Hit & Run Blog* (February 28, 2013), http://reason.com/blog/2013/02/28/piracy-not-really-hurting-game-of-throne.

139 Paulo Coelho, Pirate Coelho (February 3, 2008), http://paulocoelhoblog.com/2008/02/03/pirate-coelho/.

Large-scale American and European studies of music and video-game purchases by real persons indicate that using unlawful sources to acquire music may sometimes be correlated with *more* purchases, controlling for other factors, and that some negative impacts may wash out in the end.[140]

Not only is the Chicago School paradigm questionable in its estimate of the benefits of maximal copyright scope, it wrongly neglects the cost to society of transfer payments from consumers to producers. In a perfectly competitive market, there are, as mentioned above, no consumers who are willing to pay for a product at a level above its marginal cost but who cannot afford it at its actual – higher – price. In addition, there is also no transfer of wealth from consumers to producers, or "rent."[141] This transfer may have negative effects on society that are not captured in an analysis solely focused on maximizing the incentives to produce new copyrighted works.[142]

For a start, many resource-poor creators find it difficult to offer valuable works, even at no charge, due to copyright protection against non-identical works, such as unauthorized sequels, remakes, translations, and the like.[143] Fans and creative people confront many burdens to becoming successful authors when images, sounds, art, film, and TV are locked down so that quoting and remixing are highly regulated.[144] Like collages or pop art prints like those of Andy Warhol, such fanworks are probably inefficient to prohibit, even though the copyright statute technically seems to bar them.[145]

---

[140] Martin van der Ende et al., Estimating displacement rates of copyrighted content in the EU, European Commission Chief Economist Team (2014) at 33–47, 119–35, 143, 149, https://tinyurl .com/vanderende2014, citing Irène Bastard et al., *L'impact du piratage sur l'achat et le téléchargement légal*, 65 *Revue économique* 573 (2014). See also Anne-Brit Gran and Audun Molde, Downloading music and CD purchases, Norwegian Business School (May 25, 2009), www.bi.edu/about-bi/ news/2009/05/Downloading-music-and-CD-purchases/.

[141] Lunney, note 138, at 489, 491, 556–8 (identifying rent as producer surplus or the difference between price and marginal cost, and arguing that in a competitive market, the price of a product approaches its marginal cost, leaving no rent or foregone purchases).

[142] "[A]s the law of diminishing marginal utility shows ... people on lower incomes feel the loss of small sums more than those on higher incomes feel the loss of large ones." Gordon Graham, *The Institution of Intellectual Values: Realism and Idealism in Higher Education* (Andrews, 2011) at https://books .google.com/books?isbn=1845402723&pg=PT146.

[143] Molly Shaffer Van Houweling, Distributive values in copyright, 83 *Texas Law Review* 1535 (2005) at 1569, citing Jed Rubenfeld, The freedom of imagination: Copyright's constitutionality, 112 *Yale Law Journal* 5 (2002) at 53–9.

[144] William Fisher III, Reflections on the Hope poster case, 25 *Harvard Journal of Law & Technology* 243 (2012); Lessig, note 27; Lessig, note 57; Rebecca Tushnet, Copy this essay: How fair use doctrine harms free speech and how copying serves it, 114 *Yale Law Journal* 535 (2004) at 566–81; Rebecca Tushnet, Legal fictions: Copyright, fan fiction, and a new common law, 17 *Loyola of Los Angeles Entertainment Law Journal* 651 (1997).

[145] William Landes, *Copyright, borrowed images, and appropriation art: An economic approach*, University of Chicago Law & Economics, Olin Working Paper No. 113 (2000) at 12–4, citing 17 U.S.C. 101, https://papers.ssrn.com/sol3/papers.cfm?abstract_id=253332,

Discussions of the welfare losses to consumers and to follow-on creators that the incentive paradigm might not recognize became more common after the Copyright Term Extension Act of 1998. A typical critique of the statute's impact on those who do not own large collections of copyrights explained that because royalties for follow-on works may be set at high rates, follow-on authors are unable to use the inputs they need. Society enjoys fewer works, and authors enjoy less income from projects that they feel would best employ their talents and serve the market in a timely way.[146]

4.8. SYNERGISTIC COPYRIGHT AS A SOURCE OF INEQUALITY

Publishing, film, music, and software have for the past three or four decades operated in a way that reminds scholars of conglomerates in other fields.[147] Copyright conglomerates such as Disney and Time Warner were behind the changes in copyright in the 1990s to cover more topics and impose more penalties, one theory goes.[148] They combine publishing, film, television production, and music arms within one corporation or series of affiliated corporations, such as News Corp., Sony, Viacom, and Vivendi in addition to Disney and Time Warner.[149] The leadership of these corporate families ensures that properties such as Batman or Gandalf (Time Warner), Iron Man or Darth Vader (Disney), James Bond or Spider-man (Sony), the X-Men (Fox/News Corp.), South Park (Viacom), or Warcraft's orcs (Blizzard/Vivendi) appear in film, TV shows, books, consumer goods, ads, and elsewhere.[150]

Vague and overbroad copyright infringement standards, and a reduced scope of fair use in cases of "derivative works" like sequels, are the legal superstructure of this "base." "Conglomerate Hollywood" relies upon these legal rules to operate in a way that exploits character and "film universe" franchises that earn a billion dollars or more at the box office around the world, and further enrich a parent conglomerate's

---

[146] Laurie Richter, Reproductive freedom: Striking a fair balance between copyright and other intellectual property protections in cartoon characters, 21 *St. Thomas Law Review* 441 (2009) (footnotes omitted) (quoting Richard A. Epstein, Constitutionality of copyright term extension: Congress's copyright giveaway, *The Wall Street Journal*, (December 21, 1998), http://homepages.law.asu.edu/~dkarjala/ OpposingCopyrightExtension/commentary/jhornAP.html).

[147] Arthur John Keefe, Current legal literature, *American Bar Association Journal*, December 1971, at 1238–40. See also Richard Herring and Robert Litan, *Brookings-Wharton Papers on Financial Services: 2003* (Brookings Institution Press, 2003); Reinhardt Krause, Meet the new digital conglomerates: Google, Facebook, Amazon, and ... Apple?, *Investor's Business Daily*, (June 11, 2016), www.investors .com/news/technology/google-facebook-amazon-apple-digital-conglomerates/.

[148] James Gaskin, *Corporate Politics and the Internet* (Prentice-Hall, 1997) at 208.

[149] William Kunz, *Culture Conglomerates: Consolidation in the Motion Picture and Television Industries* (Rowman & Littlefield, 2007), at 1–4, 28–34.

[150] James Gilmore and Matthias Stork, *Superhero Synergies: Comic Book Characters Go Digital* (Rowman & Littlefield, 2014); Patti McCarthy, *The Lucas Effect: George Lucas and the New Hollywood* (Tenco Press, 2014); Janet Wasko, *How Hollywood Works* (Sage, 2005).

DVD, digital download, video game, consumer product (merchandising), and music/book divisions.[151]

Scholars' fears of possible overinvestment in entertaining or informational works may have been sound. The "core copyright industries," basically entertainment and software/information, expanded at more than double the rate of the overall US economy between 1997–2001, and 70 percent faster than the economy's rate of growth in 2009–2013. The entertainment and information industries added 70,000 jobs and $500 billion in output between 2002 and 2013, while one of every seven US manufacturing jobs was lost between 2001 and 2007, and another one of every seven remaining manufacturing jobs was lost in the recession of 2008–2010.[152] This meant nearly five million such jobs lost, as well as 1.5 million construction jobs during the recession, as 70,000 American factories closed and 9.5 million homes went into foreclosure.[153] Meanwhile, the number of US musicians, singers, composers, actors, directors, and producers of music and film went from 354,000 in 2002 to 395,100 in 2008, and to about 435,300 in 2018.[154]

In his writing on the political economy of IP, Perelman linked expanded IP rights to the rise in income and wealth inequality, for as Lunney predicted, they erect bottlenecks that halt competition and regulate creativity in fine detail.[155] The private life of individuals, and not simply the public life of commodities, becomes regulated.[156] Robert Reich blames concentrated political influence for the rise in inequal-

[151] Thomas Schatz, New Hollywood, new millennium, in Warren Buckland (Ed.), *Film Theory and Contemporary Hollywood Movies* (Routledge, 2009) at 30.

[152] Congressional Record-Senate (2004) at S18894 (statement of Sen. Conrad) (daily ed., September 22, 2004), https://books.google.com/books?id=IxQjiH6EeOIC&pg=PA18894; Linda Levine, *Job Growth during the Recovery* (Congressional Research Service, 2011) at 6.

[153] Stephen Siwek, Copyright industries in the U.S. economy: The 2014 report, Economist Inc./ International Intellectual Property Association (IIPA) (2014) at 2, www.iipawebsite.com/ pdf/2014CpyrtRptFull.PDF; Stephen Siwek, Copyright industries in the U.S. economy: The 2004 report, Economists Inc./IIPA (Oct. 2004) at i, www.iipawebsite.com/pdf/2004_SIWEK_FULL.pdf. See also 153 Congressional Record-Senate 7672 (daily ed. March 26, 2007) (statement of Sen. Landrieu); Levine, note 160, at 6; Carolina Reid et al., Revisiting the subprime crisis: The dual mortgage market and mortgage defaults by race and ethnicity, 39 *Journal of Urban Affairs* 469 (2017); Bernie Sanders, *The Speech: On Corporate Greed and the Decline of Our Middle Class* (Nation Books, 2015), https://books.google.com/books?id=QbW6CgAAQBAJ&pg=PT93.

[154] E.g. US Department of Labor, *Bureau of Labor Statistics, Occupational Outlook Handbook 2010–2011* (2011) at 320, 329; US Department of Labor, *Bureau of Labor Statistics, Occupational Outlook Handbook 2004–2005*, www.umsl.edu/services/govdocs/ooh20042005/www.bls.edu/OCO/ocos095 .htm and www.umsl.edu/services/govdocs/ooh20042005/www.bls.gov/OCO/ocos093.htm.

[155] Michael Perelman, *The political economy of intellectual property*, 54 *Monthly Review* 29 (2003). at 32, 35.

[156] Ibid., at 29, 35. See also Annemarie Bridy, Graduated response and the turn to private ordering in online copyright enforcement, 89 *Oregon Law Review* 81 (2010); Sonia Katyal, Filtering, piracy surveillance and disobedience, 32 *Columbia Journal of Law and the Arts* 401 (2009) at 421–5; Sonia Katyal, The new surveillance, 54 *Case Western Reserve Law Review* 297 (2003) at 368; Ruth Okediji, The regulation of creativity under the WIPO Internet treaties, 77 *Fordham Law Review* 2379 (2009) at 2385–99.

ity, brought about by strengthened IP rights, as well as by relaxation of antitrust and telecommunications-neutrality laws, and new waves of legislation granting bailouts, bankruptcy protections, tax cuts, and contract and tort loopholes to corporations.[157]

Compared to cultural workers, manufacturing and construction firms and their workers find it more difficult to exclude competition.[158] In order to maintain its higher incomes, the copyright system imposes welfare losses on the society, due to consumers being priced out of the market for going to the movies, renting new-release films online, buying books or CDs, subscribing to music or ebook services, joining Netflix, etc. Many of these losses have no countervailing benefit, because they are occurring in the latter years of a copyright's term, which could have been much shorter while still motivating the author to produce and license the work.[159]

Moreover, the system that supports some authors' higher incomes suppresses other musicians' and authors' incomes, as their noninfringing and fair use works are rejected by publishers or studios as being infringing copies or derivatives (or are deleted from the Internet). The system imposes high administrative and transactions costs on society in order to obtain and enforce exclusive rights, including in massive class actions that are not allowed in other areas of the law such as gender discrimination or torture of suspected terrorists.[160] One lawsuit for relatively small damages in copyright terms, or less than $1 million, can exceed $300,000 in attorney time, filing fees, and other costs.[161] Policymakers have cited such costs to drastically rein in patents, as discussed in the previous chapter, but not to rein in copyrights.

Copyright industries' financials reveal occasionally supracompetitive profits. In other contexts, very high profit margins could be viewed as a reflection of monopoly power, or of very concentrated industries. Motion picture studios and music labels are much more profitable than Amazon or Netflix, with Disney earning a 32

---

[157] Robert Reich, *Corporate elite make rules on which the economy runs, San Francisco Chronicle,* October 4, 2015, at F8.

[158] E.g. 153 Congressional Record-Senate 7672.

[159] E.g. William Patry and Richard Posner, *Fair use and statutory reform in the wake of Eldred,* 92 *California Law Review* 1639 (2004) at 1658–9. In many cases, the earnings from copyrights flow to the grandchildren or the children of the author, whereas the salaries and pension benefits of many other professionals or blue-collar workers are difficult to pass down, although of course wages or pensions can be saved for a bequest in a will or for transfer to a trust. H.R. Rep. No. 105-452 (1998) at 4.

[160] Compare *Metro-Goldwyn-Mayer Studios Inc. v. Grokster, Ltd.,* 545 U.S. 913, 951 (2005) (Breyer, J., concurring) ("large class" of copyright owners allowed to sue software companies over copyright), *and Metro-Goldwyn-Mayer v. Grokster Ltd.,* 380 F. 3d 1154, 1158–59 & n.1 (9th Cir. 2004) (disclosing that class included more than 27,000 songwriters and music publishers and most of the major film and music companies in the United States), *with Wal-Mart Stores, Inc. v. Dukes,* 564 U.S. 277 (2011) (federal courts could not certify a class action to cover all women employed at Wal-Mart and subjected to alleged patterns of discrimination in promotion and compensation), *and Ashcroft v. Iqbal,* 556 U.S. 662 (2009) (Arab and Muslim man could not sue Attorney General of United States for discriminatory detention and torture despite his being a member of a group of 762 men allegedly subjected to such alleged mistreatment).

[161] Tehranian, note 99, at 99, citing American Intellectual Property Law Association, 2009 Report of the Economic Survey (2009) at I-100.

percent profit and Warner Bros. a 15 percent profit in the first quarter of 2017, and Warner Music nearly 10 percent profit in that quarter. Some cable television networks book a stunning 40 percent of their revenue as profit, compared to 3 percent at Amazon or Netflix, or perhaps 6 percent subtracting the international divisions of Amazon or Netflix. Due to content licensing and digital distribution costs, Netflix earned a third as much profit per US subscriber as HBO.[162] The world's largest music publisher, Sony/ATV, booked a 20 percent profit in 2015, which resulted in a combined music segment profit margin of about 14 percent for Sony Corp.[163] Films like *Star Wars: The Force Awakens*, *Rogue One: A Star Wars Story*, *Beauty and the Beast*, and *Zootopia* contributed to Disney making more profit per quarter in 2017 than the entire company made in revenue in fiscal 1985.[164] *Batman v. Superman: Dawn of Justice*, helped Warner Bros. hit $3.2 billion in revenue in the first quarter of 2016 and *Kong: Skull Island* propelled it to $3.4 billion in Q1 2017, more each time than the total box office for all studios in Q1 1989 or Q1 1999, adjusted for inflation.[165]

Of course, Apple, Facebook, and Google have even more dramatic numbers, with Apple at 28 percent net profit versus 10 percent cost of capital, Facebook at 41 percent versus 5 percent, and Google at 36 percent versus 8 percent.[166] Their businesses

[162] Jem Aswad, Warner Music posts double-digit growth in revenue, digital, *Variety*, (May 8, 2017), http://variety.com/2017/music/news/warner-music-double-digit-growth-earnings-report-1202411813/; John LaFayette, Time Warner reports higher Q1 earnings, *Broadcasting & Cable*, (May 3, 2017), www.broadcastingcable.com/news/currency/time-warner-reports-higher-first-quarter-earnings/165487; Daniel Sparks, 8 metrics show how Amazon.com, Inc. is crushing it, *The Motley Fool* (May 10, 2017), www.fool.com/2017/05/10/8-metrics-show-how-amazoncom-inc-is-crushing-it.asp; Matthew Ball, *The state and future of Netflix v. HBO in 2015*, *Redef* (Mar 5, 2015), https://redef.com/original/the-state-and-future-of-netflix-v-hbo-in-2015.
[163] Andrew Flanagan, Sony's 2016 financials show Adele dependency, streaming's ascent, *Billboard*, (Apr. 29, 2016), www.billboard.com/articles/business/7350230/sony-corp-music-2016-financials-adele-streaming; Sony/ATV, SONY/ATV Meeting of the Board of Representatives (October 21, 2014), Scribd (2014), www.scribd.com/document/252520203/SONY-ATV-Meeting-of-the-Board-of-Representative-October-21-2014&num=1&hl=en&gl=us&strip=1&vwsrc=0.
[164] Dave McNary, Disney tops earnings estimates, but revenues fall short, *Variety*, (May 9, 2017), http://variety.com/2017/film/news/disney-q2-2017-earnings-revenues-1202421361/. See also Joel Finler, *The Hollywood Story* (Wallflower, 2003) at 324.
[165] Brett Lang, HBO, Turner lift Time Warner earnings, *Variety*, (May 4, 2016), http://variety.com/2016/film/news/time-warner-earnings-hbo-1201766153/; Brett Lang, Time Warner earnings beat projections thanks to "Lego Batman Movie," "Big Little Lies," "*Variety*", (May 3, 2017), http://variety.com/2017/biz/news/lego-batman-big-little-lies-1202407837/. See also Box Office Mojo, *Yearly box office* (2017), www.boxofficemojo.com/yearly/.
[166] AAPL – NAS (USA), Gurufocus (2017), www.gurufocus.com/stock/AAPL; FB – NAS (USA), Gurufocus (2017), www.gurufocus.com/stock/FB; GOOGL – NAS (USA),Gurufocus (2017), www.gurufocus.com/stock/GOOGL; DIS – NYSE (USA), Gurufocus (2017), www.gurufocus.com/term/wacc/DIS/WACC-/Walt-Disney-Co; TWX - NYSE (USA), Gurufocus (2017), www.gurufocus.com/stock/TWX. See also Shira Ovide, Apple's glittering profit margins are golden handcuffs, *Bloomberg Quint* (June 7, 2017), www.bloombergquint.com/onweb/2017/06/05/apple-s-glittering-profit-margins-are-golden-handcuff.

are also robustly protected by copyright, which governs computer programs as sets of instructions for operating computers, including smartphones.[167]

Strong copyrights may cause economic damage by reducing the number of firms in a sector. Once the most valuable opportunities have been acquired by incumbent firms asserting IP, other firms may fail to gain a foothold, losing their meager market shares and confronting insolvency. Even worse, markets in which there are fewer companies after a merger, or a series of them, often see quite large price increases. This may happen, for example, if two of the five largest companies in an industry merge into one company, leaving four "majors" that control 70 percent of the market.[168] Abnormally high profits may result from large firms' access to capital and economies of scale.[169]

In response to concerns about industry concentration and profit margins in the entertainment industries, advocates for greater copyright protection often point to even greater concentration and higher margins among Internet and social media firms. Thus, Jonathan Taplin argues that Amazon, Facebook, and Google are the true monopolies, with single-firm market shares of 74 percent, 77 percent, and 88 percent, in ebooks, mobile social "traffic," and search advertising expenditures, respectively.[170] These monopolies were built by acquisition, he argues – notably of Audible (Amazon), Instagram (Facebook), and DoubleClick (Google) (YouTube, strangely, is not mentioned). He downplays the impact of copyrights, patents, trademarks, secrets, and contractual promises not to compete.[171]

There are at least two problems with pointing to Internet or social media companies' dominance as an argument for expanded copyright protection. First, these same companies could benefit from this alleged remedy by excluding competition with their own copyrighted algorithms and other computer programs. Previously permissible forms of imitation of Facebook's or Google's interfaces or algorithms could

[167] 17 U.S.C. § 101.
[168] US Department of Justice and Federal Trade Commission, Horizontal Merger Guidelines (June 25, 2015), www.justice.gov/atr/public/guidelines/horiz_book/toc.html. See also Nathan Miller, Marc Remer, Conor Ryan, and Gloria Sheu, Upward pricing pressure as a predictor of merger price effects, Economic Analysis Group Working Paper No. 16–2, US Department of Justice, Antitrust Division (March 2016), www.justice.gov/atr/file/829271/download.
[169] Mark Hirschey, *Managerial Economics* (Cengage Learning, 2015), 399–401; Laura Simon, Derek Youn, and Iain Pardoe, Lesson 1.5 – The coefficient of determination, r-squared, Penn State Eberly College of Science Department of Statistics (2017), https://onlinecourses.science.psu.edu/stat501/node/255. See also Jim Lee, Does size matter in firm performance? Evidence from U.S public firms, 16 *International Journal of the Economics of Business* 189 (2009).
[170] Jonathan Taplin, Is it time to break up Google?, *The New York Times*, (April 22, 2017), www.nytimes.com/2017/04/22/opinion/sunday/is-it-time-to-break-up-google.html. See also Jonathan Taplin, *Move Fast and Break Things: How Facebook, Amazon, and Google Cornered Culture and Undermined Democracy* (Little, Brown & Co., 2017) at 5–8, 21–22; Jonathan Taplin, Forget AT&T. The real monopolies are Google and Facebook, *The New York Times*, (December 13, 2016), www.nytimes.com/2016/12/13/opinion/forget-att-the-real-monopolies-are-google-and-facebook.htm.
[171] Taplin, note 178.

be unlawful as nonliteral infringement in a reformed copyright system.[172] Second, it is doubtful that mobile social traffic time or search engine advertisements qualify as antitrust markets.[173] A government official, private plaintiff, economist, or judge defending this position would have to explain why mobile social traffic does not compete with desktop, smart-television or game-console Internet traffic even though some of the same apps (Hulu, Netflix, YouTube, etc.) are accessible across these various devices. Likewise, while search engine advertisements may have special characteristics or different pricing structures, their similarity to other ads in content, purchasers, viewers, and cost per impression should be analyzed.[174] Antitrust economists working for the government suggested that despite higher subscription prices, satellite radio may be in the same market as other forms of digital music delivery and even with analog FM radio, probably due to overlapping listener bases, content, and ads.[175]

For these reasons, a ratcheted-up copyright system may contribute to economic and social inequalities in several ways. It may support prices and profit margins far above the cost of capital, which suggest monopoly power and losses to consumers as well as an inadequate level of production.[176] The relations of economic production would be serving as fetters on the means of production, generating a contradiction that may eventually be resolved by adopting relations better-suited to the evolving means of production. Also, copyright doctrine may be reducing the income of new

---

[172] E.g. Brief of the Computer and Communications Industry Association as Amicus Curiae in Support of Cross-Appellant and Affirmance, at 3–6, 12–18, *Oracle America, Inc.* v. *Google, Inc.*, Nos. 2013-1021, 2013-1022 (Fed. Cir. brief filed May 30, 2013), www.groklaw.net/articlebasic.php?story=20130531131357607.

[173] E.g. *Kinderstart* v. *Google, Inc.* No. C 06-2057 JF, slip op. at 8, 2007 WL 831806 (N.D. Cal. March 16, 2007) (search engine ads not a distinct market from other Internet ads). Cf. Katsiaryna Baran, Kaja Fietkiewicz, and Wolfgang Stock, Monopolies on social network services (SNS) markets and competition law, in ISI (Ed.), *Proceedings of the 14th International Symposium on Information Science (ISI 2015), Zadar, Croatia, 19th–21st May 2015* (Verlag Werner Hülsbusch, 2016) at 433.

[174] For an experiment that used the same video on Facebook and YouTube and calculated various differences in cost per view and per thousand impressions, see Toby Danylchuk, YouTube vs. Facebook video statistics: Two case studies, 39 *Celsius* (April 19, 2015), www.39celsius.com/youtube-vs-facebook-video-statistics-two-case-studies/.

[175] Although it did not adopt any definition of the market, the federal government, which employs economists for this purpose, basically accepted the argument of the Sirius and XM companies that "traditional AM/FM radio, HD Radio, MP3 players (e.g. iPods®), and audio offerings delivered through wireless telephones … offer many consumers attributes of satellite radio service." The government concluded that the "evidence developed in the investigation did not support" defining a satellite radio market that would be distinct from FM radio, iPods, music apps on iPhones or Android smartphones, etc. U.S. Department of Justice, Statement of the Department of Justice Antitrust Division on Its Decision to Close Its Investigation of XM Satellite Radio Holding Inc.'s Merger with Sirius Satellite Radio Inc., Release No. 08-226 (March 24, 2008), www.justice.gov/archive/opa/pr/2008/March/08_at_226.html.

[176] OFCOM, Assessment of Sky's Profitability and Cost of Capital; Annex 3, to Pay TV Statement (2010) at 12–14, www.ofcom.org.uk/__data/assets/pdf_file/0016/54070/annex3_statement.pdf; Gunnar Niels, Helen Jenkins, and James Kavanagh, *Economics for Competition Lawyers* (Oxford University Press, 2011), 160–2.

and poorly-financed creators, who cannot access the capital needed to buy into the market for permissions that characterizes our relations of creative production. Meanwhile, the high return on capital invested in the copyright industries may cause capital to be diverted from other forms of production, damaging both capital and labor in these sectors, typified by the losses of many US teaching and manufacturing jobs.[177] And copyright may not be an effective way to cut digital conglomerates down to size.

4.9. CAN THE STRUGGLE FOR LITERARY FREEDOM BE WON?

Between the seventeenth century and the early twentieth century, there was a rule that generally allowed literary and artistic appropriation, if it resulted in a "new, original and different work."[178] The collages and pastiches of Picasso, Dos Passos, and Eliot and the pop art of Warhol and others generally escaped copyright challenges, despite appropriating expression from others, and not merely general ideas.[179]

In the 1980s and 1990s, the freedom to make a fair use was eviscerated. These were boom times for the synergistic exploitation of copyrighted characters and themes, typified by Disney videotapes and merchandise, *Star Wars* films and merchandise, and Hasbro cartoons and merchandise. The Supreme Court repeatedly warned that fair use and the First Amendment confer no freedom to use substantial excerpts of copyrighted work, suggesting that "minuscule" and even clearly critical or parodic uses could be prohibited if they negatively affected a potential market for licensing literal or nonliteral portions of a work.[180] The Court denied that there was

---

[177] Lauren Carroll, Trump: Since China joined the WTO, U.S. has lost 60,000 factories, *Politifact* (March 24, 2017), www.politifact.com/truth-o-meter/statements/2017/mar/24/donald-trump/trump-china-joined-wto-us-has-lost-60000-factories/.

[178] *Columbia Pictures Corp.* v. *National Broadcasting Co.*, 137 F. Supp. 348, 352 (S.D. Cal. 1955); see also *Stowe* v. *Thomas*, 23 F. Cas. 201, 207 (C.C.D.E.D.Pa. 1853), citing *Millar* v. *Taylor*, 98 Eng. Rep. 201 (K.B. 1769); *Gyles* v. *Wilcox*, 26 Eng. Rep. 489, 490 (1740); *Folsom*, 9 F.Cas. 342, 345, 349 (C.C.D. Mass. 1841); Travis, (2000), note 56, at 819–25; Geri Yanover, The dissing of Da Vinci: The imaginary case of Leonardo v. Duchamp: Moral rights, parody, and fair use, 29 *Valparaiso University Law Review* 935 (1994).

[179] E.g. Shelley Fishkin, *From Fact to Fiction: Journalism & Imaginative Writing in America* (Johns Hopkins University Press, 1985) at 247; Thomas Rees, *The Technique of T. S. Eliot: A Study of the Orchestration of Meaning in Eliot's Poetry* (Mouton, 1974), at 174. Warhol or his entities settled at least two cases with paintings or prints and/or cuts of future royalties, but produced tens of thousands of works valued at $500 million or more upon his death. McLeod, note 27, at 137–40; Geraldine Newman, Art Market: Warhol: Famous for dollars 500m, *The Independent (U.K.)*, (July 2, 1994), www.independent.co.uk/arts-entertainment/art-market-warhol-famous-for-dollars-500m-seven-years-after-his-death-andy-warhols-work-is-still-1411418.html. These works would no doubt be worth even more today, possibly billions of dollars given their quantity. E.g., Andy Warhol Auction Price Results, *Invaluable* (2017), www.invaluable.com/artist/warhol-andy-gkwjvl6lvh/sold-at-auction-prices/.

[180] E.g. *Harper & Row, Publishers, Inc.*, 471 U.S. 539, 557–9 (1985). See also *Eldred* v. *Ashcroft*, 537 U.S. 186, 219–21 (2003); *Campbell* v. *Acuff-Rose Music, Inc.*, 510 U.S. 569, 590 (1994); In re Capital Cities/ABC, Inc., 918 F.2d 140, 143 n.6 (11th Cir. 1990).

a categorical or presumptive fair use when a speaker addressing an issue of public controversy copies a very small percentage of copyrighted work, claiming that this was necessary to ensure that authors are not "deprive[d] ... of their right in the property precisely when they encounter those users who could afford to pay for it ... ," or of "just compensation for their investment."[181]

The Supreme Court adopted a rudimentary Chicago School economics of the First Amendment,[182] whereby a narrow fair use right is deemed necessary to make copyright an "engine of free expression." The premise is that there will be nothing "worth reading" if copyright is brief or fair use is broad.[183] There would be no "economic incentive to create and disseminate ideas" without 100 or 150 years of copyright (life plus seventy terms).[184] Under an economic analysis informed by Chicago School concepts, courts should only recognize fair use where no "fully functioning market" exists to license a communication containing fragments of copyrighted work, even though the societal value of widely disseminating the fragments may outweigh any harm to the market for them.[185]

In the mid-twentieth century, a rule emerged that a partial use of another work to entertain, as opposed to for research or some forms of teaching, could not be a fair use.[186] Developing a new and meritorious work after being inspired by another's expression of an idea fell under a cloud of suspicion. Educators were frightened into using for classroom purposes no more than 250 words from a poem or 2,500 words from a fiction or nonfiction prose work, and excerpts from no more than one work from each author.[187] The (British) Society of Authors and the Publishers Association claimed, as some US publishers did in the past, that one work cannot quote another work unless the follow-on work is a criticism, a review, or the like, and quotes only

---

[181] *Harper & Row*, 471 U.S. at 557–9.

[182] See generally Eliot Disner, Antitrust law: The Chicago School meets the real world, *Los Angeles Lawyer*, March 2002, at 14–5, 17–8; Raymond Shih Ray Ku, The creative destruction of copyright: Napster and the new economics of digital technology, 69 *University of Chicago Law Review* 263 (2002) at 296–7, 304–5.

[183] *Eldred*, 537 U.S. at 219.

[184] *Harper & Row*, 471 U.S. at 558; *Eldred*, 537 U.S. at 207 n. 15, 217–9. For critiques of these conclusory accounts of economic incentives, in the context of copyright terms being too long, see *Eldred*, 537 U.S. at 254–5 (Breyer, J., dissenting). Justice Breyer pointed out that ...ercent chance of earning $100,000 per year in royalties for twenty years, seventy-five years after authorship, is not worth much.

[185] *Harper & Row*, 471 U.S. at 559–68, 566 n.9 (collecting authorities on economic analysis of fair use).

[186] E.g. *Harper & Row*, 471 U.S. 539; *Loew's, Inc. v. Columbia Broadcasting System, Inc.*, 131 F. Supp. 165 (S.D. Cal. 1955); see also *Rogers*, 960 F. 2d 301, 310–2 (2d Cir. 1992); *Maxtone-Graham v. Burtchaell*, 803 F.2d 1253, 1263–5 (2d Cir. 1986); *Walker v. University Books, Inc.*, 602 F.2d 859, 864 (9th Cir. 1979); *Walt Disney Productions v. Air Pirates*, 581 F.2d 751 (9th Cir. 1978); *Meeropol v. Nizer*, 560 F.2d 1061 (2d Cir. 1977); *Sheldon*, 81 F.2d 49, 56 (2d Cir.) (L. Hand, J.), *cert. denied*, 298 U.S. 669 (1936); *United Feature Syndicate, Inc. v. Koons*, 817 F. Supp. 370 (S.D.N.Y 1993); *Grand Upright Music*, 780 F. Supp. 182, 185 (S.D.N.Y. 1991).

[187] Marjorie Heins and Tricia Beckles, *Will Fair Use Survive? Free Expression in the Age of Copyright Control* (Brennan Center for Justice, 2005), at 6.

300 words at a time and only 800 words in total.[188] Emboldened, copyright owners hired software companies to fire off threatening letters to ISPs, often insisting that lawful digital content such as fair uses should be deleted from the Internet without judicial oversight or jury trial.[189]

Building on the existing copyright laws of other nations, and proposals by several scholars, it is possible to imagine a "fair use" regime that unleashes the productive forces of our computers, networks, and imaginations, while protecting the core economic rights of authors to earn an income from their unmodified work. For example, the right to use a work to create a new work under French or Canadian law could be transplanted to the United States, although the right is burdened in France by a requirement of "observing the rules" of "parody" or "pastiche," and in Canada by restrictions to (1) "solely" noncommercial uses (2) with "reasonable" credit given to the original (3) that do not "adversely effect" a "potential exploitation" of the original.[190]

The movement to defend "remixers" and fan creators from excessive copyright costs may culminate in a new law governing transformative work. Such a law might say: "In the following cases, a work may be exploited without the permission from, and without payment of remuneration to, the copyright owner: satire, caricature, parody, pastiche, and quotations relevant to criticizing or reviewing the work or to demonstrating a

---

[188] Katherine Lapworth, *Get Your Book Published* (Hachette, 2010) at https://books.google.com/books?id=f_szAgAAQBAJ&pg=PT70&; see also *Meeropol v. Nizer*, 417 F. Supp. 1201, 1201 (S.D.N.Y. 1976) (describing this as "alleged standard rule in the publishing industry"), *aff'd*, 560 F.2d 1061.

[189] One company was already sending out one million such deletion demands monthly by 2005. BayTSP Corp., Fighting online software piracy – what works in 2005 (2005), http://web.archive.org/web/20050305165944/ and http://www.baytsp.com/downloads2/SW_white_2005.pdf; BayTSP Corp., Trends relating to use of P2P file-sharing systems (2006), https://web.archive.org/web/20060618234308/ and http://www.ftc.gov/bcp/workshops/filesharing/presentations/ishikawa.pdf. See also Global File Registry, *Technical White Paper* (May 26, 2006) at 9, 19. The potential for restricting fair use and censoring lawful Internet speech became clear rather quickly, even before the YouTube Content ID controversies emerged. Katyal, note 164, at 368; Mark Lemley and R. Anthony Reese, Reducing digital copyright infringement without restricting innovation, 56 *Stanford Law Review* 1345 (2004) at 1380; Peter K. Yu, P2P and the future of private copying, 76 *University of Colorado Law Review* 653 (2005) at 661–2; Chris Morran, YouTube's Content ID system will take away your money if you dare sing "Silent Night," *Consumerist* (December 26, 2013), https://consumerist.com/2013/12/26/youtubes-content-id-system-will-take-away-your-money-if-you-dar-sing-silent-night. An early study of such letters sent to Google and other digital media firms concluded that nearly a third of the letters called for limiting access to noninfringing speech. *Internet study finds questionable use of cease-and-desist notices*, Faculty Footnotes [USC Gould School of Law], Fall 2006, at 2; Jennifer Urban and Laura Quilter, Efficient process or "chilling effects"? Takedown notices under section 512 of the Digital Millennium Copyright Act, Boalt Hall School of Law Working Paper (2005) at 2–3, https://papers.ssrn.com/sol3/papers.cfm?abstract_id=2210935.

[190] Sir Robin Jacob, Parody and IP claims: A defence? A right to parody, *in* Rochelle Cooper Dreyfuss and Jane C. Ginsburg (Eds.), *Intellectual Property at the Edge: The Contested Contours of IP* (Cambridge University Press, 2014) at 431–2; Peter K. Yu, Can the Canadian UGC exception be transplanted abroad?, 26 *Intellectual Property Journal* 177 (2014).

point in news reporting or scholarship."[191] The concept of "pastiche" should be sufficiently broad to cover remix, mashup, and machinima (the use of a video-game or other software engine and art library to create a new audiovisual work), as it refers to a work made up of fragments of other works (a medley), as well as to a work imitating the style of another work.[192] China's copyright law of 2010 suggests a path to this model, as do portions of Britain's quotation and parody law of 2014, and Hong Kong's similar proposal of 2014, both influenced by a European Union law of 2001.[193]

Lessig has proposed that noncommercial derivatives, or "remixes," could be excluded from the scope of copyright protection and litigation, rather than only excused as a "fair use." When a remix is commercially distributed or streamed, he suggests that a compulsory license, perhaps administered by a collecting society, ensure that fair compensation is paid for the inputs of the original authors of the remixed works.[194] This is already how the record labels operate with respect to some songwriters, paying a small share of the money made from cover songs.[195] A follow-on story by a fan or group of fans – or a remix with a whole new beat or tempo – differs even more dramatically from the original than a cover song does, and should not be more difficult to make.

France and Germany appear already to have legalized a great deal of remix and mashup by quotation of music or film/video in new music or video, although Germany distinguishes lawful musical quotation and quotation in film, video, or television for news reporting purposes, from risky quotations such as use of one

---

[191] This law combines the text of Britain's 2014 amendment with elements of the pre-amendment exception for quotations and reviews, Hong Kong's addition of satire to the list, and China's inclusion of "demonstration of a point" as a permissible purpose of quotation.

[192] Jonathan Griffiths, Fair dealing after *Deckmyn*: The United Kingdom's defence for caricature, parody, and pastiche, in Megan Richardson and Sam Ricketson (Eds.), *Research Handbook on Intellectual Property in Media and Entertainment* (Elgar, 2017) at 85; Machinima, *Wikipedia* (2017), http://en.wikipedia.org/wiki/Machinima. While the British and proposed Hong Kong amendments differ from my proposal in that they may exclude parodies or pastiches that harm the reputation of the author or lack attribution of source (Britain) or harm the potential market for or value of the work (Hong Kong), in my view including these carve-outs from the rule threaten its very functioning. In other words, we are free to quote from and imitate the styles of others, *unless* it is a fair use, which a quotation or imitation is *unless* it harms the market for the work or the reputation of the author, although no harm is likely *unless* the use has a significant or substantial effect on the value or reputation of the work, etc.

[193] E.g. The Copyright and Rights in Performances (Quotation and Parody) Regulations 2014 (United Kingdom of Great Britain and Northern Ireland), www.wipo.int/edocs/lexdocs/laws/en/gb/gb327en .pdf; Copyright Law for the People's Republic of China, art. 22, Second Revision 2010; European Communities, Information Society Directive 2001/29/EC; Norton Rose Fulbright LLP, Hong Kong government introduces Copyright (Amendment) Bill 2014, *Lexology* (July 16, 2014), www.lexology .com/library/detail.aspx?g=b42d0e1e-8f7c-4bf9-84f6-37fbc0e19c71. See also Hong Kong Free Press, Copyright owners, netizens fail to reach consensus in Copyright Bill talks (February 18, 2016), www .hongkongfp.com/tag/copyright-amendment-bill/.

[194] Lessig, note 57, at 255–7.

[195] Ibid., at 226; H.R. Rep. No. 94-1476 (Government Printing Office, 1976), at 108.

documentary or dramatic film clip in another form.[196] The right of the parodist or creator of pastiches or remixes to quote from existing music or video may override the reputational interests of the authors of quoted books, images, or songs.[197] While both France and Germany recognize the moral right of authors to preserve the integrity of works against changes "prejudicial" to their reputations,[198] a doctrine of "necessary evolution" of the economy and of human affairs has excused what would otherwise be unlawful mutilations of works.[199]

Authors and performers may object that replacing fair use with a right of quotation and other productive use would lose the protections for authors that are built into fair use. Moreover, international law arguably prohibits an open-ended right of quotation or imitation, a topic to which I return in Chapter 7.[200] Fair use currently requires, in most cases, consideration of commercial purpose, extent of use, provision of credit, and effect on the market for the original, including existing markets, actual effects, potential effects, and effects of a use in the aggregate once it is legalized.[201] In addition, moral rights as codified in Britain and elsewhere require giving credit, where feasible.[202]

A simplified version of "fair use" would mean that noncommercial or transformative uses would be "deregulated," rather than being seen as infringing works subject to a fair use defense.[203] As the First Senate of the Federal Constitutional

---

[196] E.g. French Intellectual Property Code of 2000, art. L. 122-5(4); German Law on Copyright and Neighboring Rights of 1965, as amended 1998, arts. 24(1), 49(2), 51; Bundesverfassungsgericht, Press Release, The use of samples for artistic purposes may justify an interference with copyrights and related rights, No. 29/2016 (31 May 2016), citing Bundesverfassungsgericht, Judgment of May 31, 2016, 1 BvR 1585/13; see also Belgian Law on Copyright and Neighboring Rights of 1994, art. 22(1)6.

[197] Neil Netanel, Why has copyright expanded? Analysis and critique, in Fiona Macmillan (Ed.), *New Directions in Copyright Law*, Volume 6 (Elgar, 2007) at 32.

[198] E.g. French Intellectual Property Code, art. L. 121-1 to L. 121-3; German Law on Copyright and Neighboring Rights of 1965, as amended 1993, arts. 12-14; Pascal Kamina, *Film Copyright in the European Union* (Cambridge University Press, 2002) at 284–6.

[199] W. W. Kowalski, A comparative law analysis of the retained rights of artists, 38 *Vanderbilt Journal of Transnational Law* 1141 (2005) at § IV.E (quoting Frederic Pollaud-Dulian, *Le droit moral en France a travers la jurisprudence recente*, 145 Revue Internationale Du Droit D'auteur [R.I.D.A.] 127 (1990) at 214).

[200] E.g. Information Society Directive 2001/29/EC, recital 44.

[201] E.g. *Harper & Row*, 471 U.S. at 557–68; *Keeling v. Hars*, 809 F.3d 43 (2d Cir. 2015); *Cambridge University Press v. Patton*, 769 F.3d 1232 (11th Cir. 2014); *Seltzer v. Green Day, Inc.*, 725 F.3d 1170 (9th Cir. 2013); *Authors Guild*, 721 F.3d 132; *Cariou*, 714 F.3d 694 (2d Cir. 2013); *Ty, Inc.*, 292 F.3d 512, 522 (7th Cir. 2002). The Hong Kong satire, parody, and pastiche bill would have incorporated the US fair use factors into the exception or defense. E.g. Nicola Kung and Eugene Low, Hong Kong: The Copyright (Amendment) Bill 2014, Mayer Brown JSM/*Mondaq* (July 4, 2014), www.mondaq .com/content/author.asp?article_id=325006&author_id=1209834.

[202] Griffiths, note 200, at 64, 74–5.

[203] Lessig, note 57, at 255; John Tehranian, Whither copyright? Transformative use, free speech, and an intermediate liability proposal, 2005 *Brigham Young University Law Review* 1201 (2005) at 1207. See also Debora Halbert, Mass culture and the culture of the masses: A manifesto for user-generated rights, 11 *Vanderbilt Journal of Entertainment and Technology Law* 921 (2008) at 958–9; Péter Mezei,

Court of Germany declared, the use of existing cultural influences is part of "artistic freedom."[204] Today, the noncommercial and/or highly creative purpose of a use only begins the analysis, although it frequently helps tip the scales in the user's favor. Other facts may lead to a conclusion of infringement, despite the creativity of the use, such as using the entire work of another, using a highly original work or its unique elements, or invading a potential licensing market of the initial author, reducing his or her income as a creative person. Several confusing and potentially circular inquiries remain, particularly in cases of parody, satire, pastiche, montage, remix, and mashup.[205] In the United States, many scholars have advocated for the simplifying fair use, lest creators stop relying on it.[206]

A mashup exclusion from copyright law, if we may call it that, would do several helpful things for creators. First, it would democratize creativity and place amateur creators on the same level as producers of television programs such as *Saturday Night Live* or *The Daily Show with Trevor Noah*, or less prominent users such as the musical group Green Day or the Baltimore Ravens, who make promiscuous use of fragments of others' works in a commercial context, with the benefit of copyright liability insurance, corporate licensing departments, and lawyers able to vigorously litigate fair uses.[207] Second, it would accelerate the production of high-quality mashups by removing legal uncertainty, reducing the impact of corporate censorship, and making wider collaboration possible across communities of creators. Third, it would implement the right that authors and artists have under international law to quote other works for "artistic effect." This right flows from both international copyright law and the international human right to engage in freedom of expression using all forms of information and communications media.[208] Finally, it would be a step towards harmonizing copyright law's free speech doctrines with those of US trademark and celebrity persona law, which

---

Fair use and culture: Comments on the Gowers Review, 39 *University of Toledo Law Review* 653 (2008) at 653.

[204] Bundesverfassungsgericht, note 204.

[205] E.g. Hannibal Travis, Google Book Search and fair use: iTunes for authors, or Napster for books?, 61 *University of Miami Law Review* 87 (2006)at 145–51.

[206] Hannibal Travis, Free speech institutions and fair use of copyrighted work: A new agenda for copyright reform, 33 *Cardozo Arts and Entertainment Law Journal* 673 (2016) at 712–15, 729–33.

[207] Jennifer S. Lee and Sewell Chan, Deep secrets of The Daily Show, *The New York Times City Room Blog* (November 10, 2008), https://cityroom.blogs.nytimes.com/2008/11/10/secrets-of-the-daily-show/.

[208] E.g., Tanya Aplin and Lionel Bently, Displacing the dominance of the three-step test: The role of global, mandatory fair use, in Wee Loon Ng, Haochen Sun, and Shyam Balganesh (Eds.), *Comparative Aspects of Limitations and Exceptions in Copyright Law* (Cambridge University Press, 2018); Sam Ricketson, WIPO Study on Limitations and Exceptions of Copyright and Related Rights in the Digital Environment, WIPO Standing Committee on Copyright and Related Rights Ninth Session, Geneva (June, 2003), www.wipo.int; Church of Spiritual Technology/Dataweb B.V., Arrondissementrechtbank [Rb.] [ordinary court of first instance and court of appeal to the Kantongerecht], Hague, March 12, 1996 (the Netherlands).

are more generous in many cases from the standpoint of the user's freedom of expression.[209]

The law in this area often operates to the disadvantage of creative people, suggesting that rewarding genius may be less of a motivator than concentrating rights and power in investable properties, which suits capitalism's purposes. The idea/expression distinction, which does a lot of work in this area, is arguably a "distinction that makes no sense," and one that confines the artist's freedom to "tell the truth" in a media-driven culture.[210] Copyright, as a norm enforced by private actors, accumulates "unseen deaths," inside of creators and their studios, even without an act by the State against Art.[211]

Ideas wither or disappear into paths not taken as creators encounter the uncertainty of broad derivative-work rights and judicial efforts to shrink the fair use privilege. When the law allows parody, but enjoins appropriation and pastiche, an artist may be manipulated into reaffirming societal norms by adopting parody's stance of outrage at the deviant and excessive, which is the wellspring of parody's humorous effect, rather than creating art in a decentered and multidimensional space.[212]

Netanel and others object, on the grounds of income losses for the original authors, to a First Amendment or "Free Culture" right to transform the novels or other works of others into new or better works. Novelists, for example in the fantasy or thriller genres, may find the film rights to their stories to be unmarketable unless a movie studio can be reassured that its version of the novel will be exclusive. Netanel suggests that the fair use doctrine should resolve the tension between the interests of initial authors and reusing authors by asking two questions: (1) whether the reusing author has added significant creative material or a new perspective, and (2) whether the initial author can prove harm to the market for or value of the work.[213] Simply assuming harm to the reuse license market, as some courts have been tempted to do,

---

[209] E.g., *Brown v. Electronic Arts, Inc.*, 724 F.3d 1235, 1244–8 (9th Cir. 2013); *The University of Alabama Bd. of Trustees v. New Life Art, Inc.*, 683 F.3d 1266 (11th Cir. 2012); *E.S.S. Entertainment 2000, Inc. v. Rock Star Videos, Inc.*, 547 F.3d 1095, 1100–1 (9th Cir. 2008); *Mattel*, 353 F.3d at 806; *ETW Corp. v. Jireh Publishing, Inc.*, 332 F.3d 915 (6th Cir. 2003); *Mattel, Inc. v. MCA Records, Inc.*, 296 F.3d 894 (9th Cir. 2002); *20th Century Fox TV v. Empire Distribution Inc.*, 161 F. Supp. 3d 902, 907–10 (C.D. Cal. 2016); *Medina v. Dash Films, Inc.*, No. 15-cv-2551, 2016 WL 3906714 at § III (S.D.N.Y. July 14, 2016); *Fortres Grand Corp. v. Warner Bros. Entertainment, Inc.*, 947 F. Supp. 2d 922 (N.D. Ind. 2013); *Lohan v. Perez*, 924 F. Supp. 2d 447 (E.D.N.Y. 2013); *Stewart Surfboards, Inc v. Disney Book Group, LLC*, No. CV 10-2982, 2011 WL 12877019 (C.D. Cal. May 11, 2011); *Caterpillar Inc. v. Walt Disney Co.*, 287 F. Supp. 2d 913 (C.D. Ill. 2003); *Ross v. Roberts*, 166 Cal. Rptr. 3d 359 (Cal. Ct. App., 4th Dist. 2013).
[210] Louise Harmon, Law, art, and the killing jar, *in* Richard Chused (Ed.), *A Copyright Anthology: The Technology Frontier* (Anderson Publishing Co., 1998) at 364, 371.
[211] Ibid., at 378.
[212] Fredric Jameson, *The Cultural Turn: Selected Writings on the Postmodern, 1983–1998* (Verso, 1998) at 4.
[213] Netanel, note 57, at 191–8.

or ruling that extensive use of a work cannot be excused, as others have, will chill creative speech.[214]

The law could aid imitative creators in other ways. Netanel advocates reducing the damages owed by authors of new works that are mostly original but are based in part on prior works. US law calls these mostly new creations "derivative works," and they are also known as adaptations, arrangements, reproductions, alterations, and (structural) transformations in American and British as well as French and German law.[215] Netanel and many others also endorse shortening the duration for copyright protection so that more characters and settings are available as inspiration without legal complications.

---

[214] Neil Weinstock Netanel, Locating copyright within the First Amendment skein, 54 *Stanford Law Review* 1 (2001) at 83–84.
[215] Netanel, note 57, at 196–9; Daniel Gervais, The derivative right, or why copyright law protects foxes better than hedgehogs, 15 *Vanderbilt Journal of Entertainment and Technology Law* 785 (2013) at 818, 830.

5

The Beijing Consensus

5.1. FROM WASHINGTON CONSENSUS TO BEIJING CONSENSUS[1]

In 2011 the actor Javier Bardem announced a new effort for actors to gain control of "the use of their performances on the Internet," including "non-commercial uses."[2] The effort was led by the World Intellectual Property Organization (WIPO), which launched a public campaign in which Bardem and other actors including Meryl Streep and Mei Baojiu argued in favor of adopting a treaty to protect actors' rights, and those of musicians.[3]

The World Intellectual Property Organization is an intergovernmental organization affiliated with the United Nations.[4] Along with the World Bank, International Monetary Fund (IMF), and World Trade Organization (WTO), it is part of a project of "international governance" based on a "Washington Consensus."[5]

The "Washington Consensus," in turn, is often associated with neoliberalism, or the reorientation of government's role towards facilitating market transactions rather than directly intervening to bring about fairness or overall utility. The World Bank and the IMF operate by linking compliance with Washington-driven legal

---

[1] Portions of this chapter are based on my article: WIPO and the American Constitution: Thoughts on a new treaty relating to actors and musicians, 16 *Vanderbilt Journal of Entertainment and Technology Law* 45 (2013).

[2] Statement by Javier Bardem to the High Level Copyright Dialogue on the Film Industry, WIPO (July 11, 2011), www.wipo.int/about-wipo/en/copyright_dialogue/statements/bardem.html.

[3] WIPO, WIPO Beijing Treaty on Audiovisual Performances is concluded (June 26, 2012), www.wipo.int/pressroom/en/articles/2012/article_0013.html.

[4] Jennifer Hanley, Note, ISP liability and safe harbor provisions: Implications of evolving international law for the approach set out in *Viacom v. YouTube*, 11 *Journal of International Business and Law* 183 (2012) at 190.

[5] Lawrence Busch, Quasi-states? The unexpected rise of private food law, *in* B. M. J. van der Meulen (Ed.), *Private Food Law: Governing Food Chains Through Contracts Law* (Wageningen Academic Publishing, 2011) at 54.

standards with access to foreign funds for reconstruction, development, and currency stabilization.[6]

WIPO, as part of the United Nations, operates with a more parliamentary-style system. Thus, most important IP standards, with the notable exceptions of performers' rights and laws prohibiting circumvention of digital rights management technologies, are promulgated and enforced under the authority of the faster and less democratic WTO, rather than by the quasi-legislative WIPO.[7]

WIPO has played an important role in promulgating international IP law.[8] In addition to binding states directly by persuading them to sign the WIPO Copyright Treaty, the WIPO Performance and Phonograms Treaty (WPPT), and other treaties,[9] the United States and its trading partners have entered into bilateral trade agreements that purport to obligate them to obey these treaties.[10] To comply, the United States enacted sections 1201–1204 of the Digital Millennium Copyright Act and a statute intended to outlaw the fixation of unfixed musical or dramatic performances on tape, disk, or film.[11]

In 2012, forty-eight countries signed WIPO's Beijing Treaty on Audiovisual Performances.[12] A few of its provisions promise to have significant impacts on consumers and creative freedom in the United States. The treaty provides performers in movies, music videos, television shows, or video games with the exclusive right to reproduce, distribute, or make available a performance.[13] It seems to grant a broad new right to restrict the "communication" of unfixed performances not already broadcast, with some exceptions.[14] It contemplates that additional royalties will paid to performers, irrespective of existing contracts governing performances embodied in works.[15]

The Beijing Treaty could represent an effort by the Global South, including China, Brazil, Nigeria, and other leading non-Western centers of cultural

[6] Ibid.
[7] Ibid.
[8] Pamela Samuelson, The copyright grab, *Wired*, (January 1996), www.wired.com/1996/01/whitepaper; Pamela Samuelson, Legally speaking: Why the anticircumvention regulations need revision, 42 *Communications of the ACM* 17 (1999) at 17.
[9] E.g. WIPO Performances and Phonograms Treaty, December 20, 1996, s. Treaty Doc. No. 105-17, 2186 U.N.T.S. 245.
[10] Implementation of US Bilateral Free Trade Agreements with Chile and Singapore: Hearing Before the Subcommittee on Trade of the House Committee on Ways and Means, 108th Cong. (2003) at 5; Shayerah Ilias and Ian Fergusson, Intellectual property rights and international trade, CRS Report No. RL34292, (2011) at 24, http://fpc.state.gov/documents/organization/159012.pdf.
[11] 17 U.S.C. §§ 1101, 1201–1202 (2012).
[12] US Department of State, Signing of Audiovisual Performances Treaty (June 26, 2012), www.state.gov/r/pa/prs/ps/2012/06/194101.htm.
[13] Beijing Treaty on Audiovisual Performances, arts. 5–12, June 24, 2012, WIPO Doc. No. AVP/DC/20 [hereinafter Beijing Treaty], www.wipo.int/edocs/mdocs/copyright/en/avp_dc/avp_dc_20.pdf.
[14] Ibid., art. 6.
[15] Ibid., art. 12.

production, to establish a norm of "fair culture," rather than "free culture," in the Internet age.[16] As Madhavi Sunder explains, "fair culture" could be a movement in which everyone enjoys "cultural rights" and is included in processes of "cultural signification, irrespective of their age, gender, ability, or ethnic, religious or cultural background."[17] In this theory, the Beijing Treaty could resemble efforts to "reclaim cultural identity" by asserting IP rights "defensively" against "misappropriation" in the form of "imperial" powers' digitization, commodification, and globalization. In this vein, the Chinese State Intellectual Property Office handed out more patents on traditional Chinese medicine, and India created a database of "traditional knowledge" to block Western patents on it.[18]

The Beijing Treaty has apparently yet to enter into force due to a lack of ratifications by signatory states. If all the original states that signed the treaty had ratified it, it would have almost immediately entered into force. Only 18 out of more than 47 signing states had ratified it by mid-2017.[19] Ratification or accession by China, Japan, and Russia means that the treaty could have a significant impact if it enters into force, however,[20] European countries, except for the Slovak Republic, have not ratified; nor has Brazil, Mexico, South Africa, South Korea, or the USA.

5.2. THE BEIJING TREATY AS LABOR LAW

The Screen Actors Guild and International Federation of Actors have led the way in seeking the conclusion and ratification of the Beijing Treaty.[21] According to the

---

[16] While Beijing is north of Washington, DC, and China is an economic superpower with major cities surpassing in "development" many of those in the Global North, and a middle-income country with the largest middle class in the world and possibly the most billionaires, it sees itself as a leader of the "South" especially when it comes to "South–South cooperation," with a former Chinese diplomat being named UN representative on that subject in 2014. E.g. Hu Mei and Liu Hongwu, Five decades of South-South cooperation between China and Africa, *China International Studies*, January/February 2012, www.cssn.cn/upload/2013/02/d20130227162622573.pdf; Secretary-General Designates Yiping Zhou of China Envoy on South-South Cooperation, U.N. Doc. No. SG/A/1472-BIO/4593-DEV/3097 (30 May 2014), www.un.org/press/en/2014/sga1472.doc.htm. See also Thomas Hylland Eriksen, What's wrong with the Global North and the Global South?, *Global South Studies Center* (January 2015), http://gssc.uni-koeln.de/node/454.

[17] Madhavi Sunder, From free culture to fair culture, 4 *World Intellectual Property Organization Journal* 20 (2012) at 23–4 (quoting Hannele Koivunen and Leena Marsio, Ethics and policy, *D'Art Topics in Arts Policy* 24 (2008), www.ifacca.org/topic/ethics-in-cultural-policy).

[18] Madhavi Sunder, IP3, 59 *Stanford Law Review* 257 (2006) at 267, 270–1.

[19] WIPO, WIPO-administered treaties (Aug. 2017), www.wipo.int/treaties/en/ShowResults.jsp?search_what=N&treaty_id=841.

[20] Ibid.

[21] E.g. International Federation of Actors, Sixteenth ratification and an ongoing worldwide campaign for the Beijing Treaty (July 28, 2017), http://beijingtreaty.com/news/news-details/article/sixteenth-ratification-and-an-ongoing-worldwide-campaign-for-the-beijing-treaty/; Screen Actors Guild-American Federation of Television and Radio Artists, SAG-AFTRA supports Senate approval of Beijing Treaty on Audiovisual Performances (February 10, 2016), www.sagaftra.org/sag-aftra-supports-senate-approval-beijing-treaty-audiovisual-performances/.

White House, the instrument would protect actors around the world, and encourage them to invest in their craft.[22] Along with the Motion Picture Association of America, the US government consulted with the Screen Actors Guild on the treaty's terms.[23]

The treaty may not do much to alter actor–producer relationships in Hollywood. WIPO and the USPTO promised that Hollywood would be protected because the transfer of rights from actors to producers will be automatic, making the AV Treaty more of a producers' and broadcasters' rights treaty.[24] Hollywood is protected by an Agreed Statement to Article 5, providing that "normal" changes to a performance would be lawful, "such as editing, compression, dubbing, or formatting, in existing or new media or formats."[25] Thus, actors' and directors' traditional objections to producers, directors, and studios engaging in unflattering editing, the cutting of performances, and translation to lower-quality images may still fail. This means that the principal selling point of the treaty is misleading, because power will not be shifted to actors and musicians and away from directors, producers, and studio heads. The main impact, as set forth below, will be on third parties, including social media users.

Within WIPO, a study emphasized one possibly significant potential change to actors' and other performers' rights as laborers for entertainment-industry capital. The Beijing Treaty could reshape the "intimate connection" between performers' intellectual property rights and labor law. A range of different collective management solutions are permissible under the terms of national labor law and practice.[26] In recent decades, labor action has been necessary to increase the performers' share of the income from collaborative projects uniting writers, performers, and directorial/technical creators.[27] In the United States, these include minimum daily and weekly wage rates, and percentages of "gross receipts" for showing film or TV shows on free or pay television or with the assistance of home videocassettes or DVDs.[28]

In addition, collective bargaining agreements for film and television address "the personality and reputation of the performer, including those governing credits … ."[29] Article 12 of the Beijing Treaty could be a bargaining chip during future strikes and negotiations, calling as it does for royalties to be paid to performers, regardless

---

[22] Pres. Barack Obama, Letter of transmittal (January 22, 2016), https://web.archive.org/web/20170511043010/http://www.congress.gov/114/cdoc/tdoc8/CDOC-114tdoc8.pdf.

[23] William New, WIPO lauded for new Beijing Treaty on Audiovisual Performances, *IP Watch* (June 29, 2012), www.ip-watch.org/2012/06/29/wipo-lauded-for-new-beijing-treaty-on- audiovisual-performances/.

[24] USPTO, Background and Summary of the WIPO Audiovisual Performances Treaty (June 2012), at 2, www.uspto.gov/news/WIPO_AVP_TREATY_FACT_SHEET.pdf; WIPO, note 1.

[25] Beijing Treaty, note 13, art. 5.

[26] Katherine Sand, Study on audiovisual performers' contracts and remuneration practices in Mexico, the United Kingdom and the United States of America, WIPO Doc. No. AVP/IM/03/3A (April 3, 2003), at 2, www.wipo.int.

[27] Ibid., at 1–2.

[28] Ibid., at 32–41.

[29] Ibid., at 33.

of existing contracts governing performances embodied in motion pictures, music, television shows, or video games.[30] Article 7 might bolster performers' efforts to control the use of their performances during the reproduction of works such as films, music videos, or games.[31]

As labor law, the impact of a treaty providing greater protections to performances would be unclear. It is conceivable that union heads are correct in that it would bolster efforts to obtain a greater share of media revenue for performers via collective bargaining. On the other hand, the strikes that benefited performers in this regard happened prior to the treaty, in an era in which film and television performers were not protected in this way. More importantly, the mandatory transfer of rights to producers by actors or musicians participating in audiovisual projects, and their inability to object to editing and similar treatments, might leave actors or musicians working on such projects with few additional rights.[32]

5.3. FREE SPEECH HYPOCRISIES

Two actors' unions and the lobbying arms of the motion-picture and television studios and of the music labels welcomed the Beijing Treaty.[33] The US actors' unions remarked that with "control over the use of our images and likenesses, actors will have important tools to protect themselves around the world."[34] WIPO warns: "Digital technologies make it easy to manipulate video images and may do so in ways that can harm an actor's reputation."[35] WIPO further states that "performers in some countries retain moral rights to object to … derogatory treatment of their performances."[36] Traditionally, the focus of audiovisual performers was advertising and merchandising rights, sloppy editing, and colorization, but the Beijing Treaty shifted the focus to social media, and would not do much for these purist performers due to language stating that editing, dubbing, or formatting performances in old or new formats is allowed.[37]

---

[30] Beijing Treaty, note 13, art. 12(3).

[31] Ibid., art. 7.

[32] USPTO, note 24; Travis, note 1, at 66–7.

[33] Phillip Merrill, ArtsWatch: Beijing Treaty protects actors, *Grammy.com* (July 2, 2012), www.grammy .com/news/artswatch-beijing-treaty-protects-actors.

[34] Nancy Tartaglione, Industry applauds Beijing Treaty on international actors' rights, *Deadline* (June 26, 2012), http://deadline.com/2012/06/industry-applauds-beijing-treaty-on-international-actors-rights-292151/.

[35] WIPO, Performer's Rights (2013), www.wipo.int/pressroom/en/briefs/performers.html.

[36] Ibid.

[37] E.g. Beijing Treaty, note 13, art. 5 (Agreed Statement); Travis, note 1 at 66–7. See also Michael Albano, Nothing to cheer about: A call for reform of the right of publicity in audiovisual characters, 90 *Georgetown Law Journal* 90 (2001) at 253; Joel Anderson, What's wrong with this picture-dead or alive: Protecting actors in the age of virtual reanimation, 25 *Loyola of LA Entertainment Law Review* 155 (2005); Lawrence Beyer, Intentionalism, art, and the suppression of innovation: Film colorization and the philosophy of moral rights, 82 *Northwestern University Law Review* 1011 (1987);

In other contexts, the US actors' unions and the entertainment industry including the record labels and movie studios have not been enthusiastic about laws protecting the reputations of ordinary persons. In one case, the American Federation of Television and Radio Artists joined the Writers' Guild West and other groups in persuading the Supreme Court that "regulation of public discourse is alien to our conception of free speech."[38] Likewise, the Motion Picture Association of America (MPAA) has urged that jury verdicts involving libels by book publishers or other creative firms should be thrown out because "'socially desirable speech'" may be impacted, at least where a jury's award is based on the unjust enrichment of an entertainment company that has profited by exploiting and then destroying another person's reputation.[39] Going even further, this group urged the virtual elimination of claims based on the uncompensated use of the name or picture of a celebrity or athlete in an expressive work such as a book, a film, or a piece of popular music.[40] The court hearing the dispute did not agree, expressing concern about "manipulation" of personalities, and "blatant acts of misappropriation."[41]

The court seemingly accepted the plaintiff's warning of a parade of "horribles":

> Life-like replicas of deceased musical artists are now "performing" live concerts. Deceased stars such as Sir Laurence Olivier are "acting" in new movies. It is not far-fetched to imagine a future action movie starring a "young" Tom Cruise, a future concert appearance by the "reunited" Beatles, or a news broadcast hosted by Walter Cronkite. Yet, under [a broad] interpretation of the First Amendment, all of these products could be marketed without licenses, consent, or payment to the individuals whose valuable personas have been appropriated solely to exploit their commercial value.[42]

Jane C. Ginsburg, Colors in conflicts: Moral rights and the foreign exploitation of colorized US motion pictures, 36 *Journal of the Copyright Society of the USA* 81 (1988); Michael Madow, Private ownership of public image: Popular culture and publicity rights, 81 *California Law Review* 125 (1993).

38 Brief of American Federation of Television and Radio Artists et al. as Amici Curiae in Support of Respondent, at 12, *United States* v. *Alvarez*, 567 U.S. 709 (U.S. brief filed No. 11-210), 2012 U.S. S. Ct. Briefs LEXIS 278, at *12.

39 Brief Amici Curiae of 33 Media Companies and Organizations in Support of Appellant Urging Reversal, at 19, *Ventura* v. *Kyle*, 825 F.3d 876 (8th Cir. 2016) (No. 14-3876) (quoting Dan Dobbs, *Law of Remedies: Damages – Equity – Restitution* (West Publishing 2nd ed., 1993), at § 7.2 (s14.23)).

40 Brief of Amicus Curiae the Motion Picture Association of America, Inc., at 3, *Hart* v. *Electronic Arts, Inc.*, 717 F.3d 141 (3d Cir. 2013) (No. 11-3750). See also Brief of Amicus Curiae the Motion Picture Association of America, Inc., In Re NCAA Student-Athlete Name and Likeness Litigation (*Keller* v. *Electronic Arts, Inc.*), 724 F.3d 1268 (9th Cir. 2013) (No. 10-15387).

41 *Hart*, 717 F.3d at 167 (quoting Brief of Amicus Curiae the Screen Actors Guild, at 21, *Hart*, 717 F.3d 141).

42 Reply Brief of Appellants, at 8, *Hart*, 717 F.3d 141 (3d Cir. brief filed July 19, 2012), citing Claire Suddath, How Tupac became a hologram (is Elvis next?), *Businessweek.com*, (April 16, 2012), www.businessweek .com/articles/2012-04-16/how-tupac-became-a-hologram-plus-is-elvis-next; Stuart Klawans, Dead stars, alive again, *The New York Times*, (August 1, 2004), at 44.

Actors, directors, producers, and the studios sometimes release motion pictures that prompt the people portrayed in supposedly "true stories" to sue for libel or misuse of their names or reputations.[43] For example, in 2010, an explosives disposal expert with the US Army in Iraq alleged that he was falsely portrayed in an Oscar-winning film as disdainful of human life, enamored with human mortality, and a bad father.[44] The court concluded, as the MPAA's brief suggested, that even if the film's portrayal was false, its makers could not be sued because the false suggestions did not satisfy libel law's high standard that the plaintiff suffer "'hatred, contempt, ridicule,'" or be "shunned[,] avoided, or ... injure[d] in his occupation."[45]

Long before the veteran's case was decided, George Clooney and Time Warner Entertainment allegedly portrayed a fishing vessel's captain as reckless in the film *A Perfect Storm*, which allegedly took dramatic license to depart from a nonfiction book on which it was based in several ways.[46] Whereas, in his family's view, the book portrayed the captain as successful and as taking no more risks than another captain was taking in the area, the motion picture immortalized him as "'an unprofessional ... and incompetent'" fisherman, and "'as having suffered a self-imposed death, abandoning his crew and any hope of survival.'"[47] An Atlanta federal court ruled that the portrayal was not "egregious" enough to justify a lawsuit.[48] Warner Bros. successfully argued that "fictional expression is entitled to the same First Amendment protection as fact," so that the subjects of films or their families may not "complain about the way an author or filmmaker chooses to express the story ... ."[49] Like the television broadcasters and the newspapers, the movie studios and the performers' unions would presumably object to a law stating that ordinary people have a "right of reply" when they are portrayed in a false or misleading way that is derogatory to their reputation or image.[50]

When an ordinary person such as a soldier sues for emotional distress arising out of a film, he or she typically will not have a claim, because being portrayed falsely to millions of people is not "extreme" enough.[51] But under the Beijing Treaty, a merely potential negative impact on an actor's or performer's reputation, or "prejudice," may give rise

---

[43] Brief of Amicus Curiae the Motion Picture Association of America, Inc. and Entertainment Merchants Association in Support of Defendants/Appellees, at 2–18, *Sarver v. Chartier*, 813 F.3d. 891 (9th Cir. brief filed Aug. 29, 2012) (No. 11-56986).

[44] *Sarver*, 813 F.3d at 895, 906.

[45] Ibid. (quoting *Nygard, Inc. v. Uusi-Kerttula*, 159 Cal. App. 4th 1027, 1047–8 (Cal. Ct. App. 2008)).

[46] *Tyne v. Time Warner Entertainment Co.*, LP, 336 F. 3d 1286, 1288–9 (11th Cir. 2003).

[47] John Aquino, *Truth and Lives on Film: The Legal Problems of Depicting Real Persons and Events in a Fictional Medium* (Jefferson, NC: McFarland, 2005) at 54–5.

[48] *Tyne*, 336 F.3d at 1292.

[49] Quoted in Aquino, note 47, at 56. Moreover, the film had a disclaimer in the closing credits to clarify its claim to being based on a true story. The disclaimer stated that: "Dialogue and certain events and characters in the film were created for the purpose of fictionalization." *Tyne*, 336 F.3d at 1289.

[50] Brief of the National Association of Broadcasters as Amicus Curiae, at 3–4, 8, *Miami Herald Publishing Co. v. Tornillo*, 418 U.S. 241 (1974) (No. 73-797), 1974 WL 185866.

[51] *Sarver*, 813 F.3d at 907 (quoting *Hughes v. Pair*, 209 P.3d 963, 976 (Cal. 2009)).

to legal claims.[52] It is not clear why the Congress or the courts should extend greater protection to actors and musicians against content damaging to their reputations than creative people and their employers extend to the ordinary people who are portrayed in films. The freedom of speech is implicated as much, or perhaps more so, when actors resist new versions or parodies of performances that become influential or iconic.[53]

The US Patent and Trademark Office ("USPTO") contends that the Beijing Treaty's new rights do not change existing law because US law already treats actors and musicians as "authors ... with copyright rights."[54] This is not entirely true with regard to traditional federal copyright law, which did not protect "unfixed performances."[55] An actor's performance is not separately copyrightable, even if fixed, due to the need to concentrate the rights in the movie as a "single integrated work." One court confirmed this rule in a difficult decision in a case where the actor received death threats due to the director's modification of dialogue she spoke. She believed she was filming an adventure called "Desert Warrior," but her dialogue was dubbed into a controversial video about Islam. Soon after it went viral on YouTube, it was falsely blamed by the Obama administration for the massacre of US personnel in Benghazi, Libya.[56]

By extending to performances the "moral right" to be protected from modification or distortion of one's work, Article 5 of the Beijing Treaty is a major change to US law. Under the US Copyright Act, moral rights only attach to limited edition, fixed "Writings" such as paintings and sculptures.[57] That was the outcome of a process in which various groups lobbied Congress for and against the Visual Artists Rights Act of 1990 (VARA). VARA may not protect unfixed works because they are not "Writings."[58]

5.4. THE THREAT TO SOCIAL MEDIA

The Beijing Treaty directly addresses itself to noncommercial speech by social media users. It controls all "communication[s]" of performances, and not merely

---

[52] Beijing Treaty, note 13, art. 5.
[53] Cf. Mike Masnick, WIPO is quietly signing an agreement to give Hollywood stars their own special version of copyright, *Techdirt* (June 26, 2012), www.techdirt.com/articles/20120625/20471219474/wipo-is-quietly-signing-agreement-to-give-hollywood-stars-their-own-special-version-copyright.shtml.
[54] USPTO, note 24, at 2.
[55] *Jarvis* v. *A&M Records*, 827 F. Supp. 282, 297 (D.N.J. 1993); H.R. Rep. No. 94-1476, above n. 88, at 52.
[56] *Garcia* v. *Google, Inc.*, 786 F.3d 733, 741–2 (9th Cir. 2015). See also *Garcia* v. *Google, Inc.*, at 738 (describing film's "purported connection to the September 11, 2012, attack on the United States Consulate in Benghazi, Libya"); *Garcia*, 786 F.3d 727, 730 (9th Cir. 2015) (Reinhardt, J., dissenting from denial of emergency hearing en banc); Teresa Welsh, Should Obama nominate Susan Rice for secretary of state?, *US News & World Report* (November 19, 2012), www.usnews.com/opinion/articles/2012 /11/19/ (attack later revealed to be planned before film controversy allegedly emerged).
[57] Cf. *United States* v. *Martignon*, 346 F. Supp. 2d 413, 421, 423 (S.D.N.Y. 2004) (holding that one of "central problems" with federal anti-bootlegging law is "that an unrecorded live musical performance is not a writing"), *vacated and remanded by* 492 F.3d 140 (2d Cir. 2007).
[58] *Kelley* v. *Chicago Park Dist.*, 635 F.3d 290, 293, 304–05 (7th Cir. 2011).

their copying or commercial use. It calls for civil remedies for communicating or making available to the public those "copies of performances fixed in audiovisual fixations knowing that electronic rights management information has ... altered."[59] This right could radically transform existing US law, not necessarily for the better. The derivative-work right in the United States does not extend to communicating the content of a work or to making it available without a fixed tangible item that contains a substantial amount of material from another fixed work and that uses the material for a similar purpose.[60]

Online streaming does not necessarily violate existing law.[61] Especially when an intermediary offers a service such as a list of hyperlinks to where videos may be streamed, the intermediary may not "publicly" perform the work.[62] When social media intermediaries cannot link to a performance or make it more available, then copyright will be more restrictive, and Internet services will be risker to offer.[63]

The Beijing Treaty tries to ban using a performance without including its original copyright information and credits.[64] This is common with many YouTube videos, political and other memes based on film or television scenes, pictures on blogs, and the like.[65] Existing US law has a copyright-management information provision (17

[59] Beijing Treaty, note 13, art. 16.
[60] E.g. *Ty, Inc. v. Publications International Ltd.*, 292 F.3d 512, 519–20 (7th Cir. 2002); *Lewis Galoob Toys, Inc. v. Nintendo of America, Inc.*, 964 F.2d 965, 968 (9th Cir. 1992); *RDR Books*, 575 F. Supp. 2d at 550.
[61] While it may be an infringement "to perform the copyrighted work publicly," 17 U.S.C. § 106(4), online streaming may be a private performance, such as when a subscriber to cable or satellite television performs the programming for himself or herself, without a decision or so-called "volitional" act of the cable or satellite provider. E.g. *American Broadcasting Cos., Inc. v. Aereo, Inc.*, 573 U.S., 134 S.Ct. 2498, 2513 (2014) (Scalia, J., dissenting); Ibid., at 2512 (Scalia, J., dissenting); *Perfect 10, Inc. v. Giganews, Inc.*, 847 F.3d 657, 666–9 (9th Cir. 2017); *Cartoon Network LP v. CSC Holdings, Inc.*, 536 F.3d 121, 131 (2d Cir. 2008); *Parker v. Google, Inc.*, 242 Fed. Appx. 833, 837 (3d Cir. 2007) (per curiam); *Fox Broadcasting Co. v. Dish Network LLC*, 160 F. Supp. 3d 1139, 1160 (C.D. Cal. 2015). But see *Aereo*, 134 S.Ct. at 2507–8 (streaming services that resemble traditional cable perform publicly even if viewers request shows).
[62] *Flava Works, Inc. v. Gunter*, 689 F.3d 754, 756, 758, 760–1 (7th Cir. 2012) (holding where streaming service embeds a video, but "video is being transmitted directly from the server on which the video is stored to the viewer's computer," that viewer rather than service infringes by public performance of video), citing *Perfect 10*, 494 F.3d at 797; *Cartoon Network*, 536 F.3d at 139 (streaming video is not a public performance when viewer decides when performance begins, potentially in the privacy of his or her home).
[63] Brief of Amicus Curiae Computer and Communications Industry Association and US Internet Industry Association, at 10–15, *Elektra Entertainment Group, Inc. v. Barker*, 551 F. Supp. 2d 234 (S.D.N.Y. 2008) (S.D.N.Y. brief filed February 24, 2006), www.ccianet.org/wp-content/uploads/library/CCIA_Barker_Amicus.pdf; Brief of Copyright Law Professors as Amici Curiae, *Capitol Records, Inc. v. Thomas*, 579 F. Supp. 2d 1210 (D. Minn. 2008) (D. Minn. brief filed June 13, 2008).
[64] Beijing Treaty, note 13, art. 16; Travis, note 1, at 54–6, 77–80.
[65] E.g. Nicholas Rodriguez, Trademark and copyright issues arising from memetic marketing on social media, *Association of Corporate Counsel* (July 16, 2014), http://webcasts.acc.com/handouts/ACC_264_EE69_109_Trademark_and_Copyright_Issues_Arising_from_Memetic_Marketing_on_Social_Media.pdf.

U.S.C. § 1202(a)), but it requires *intentional* removal or alteration of the information for purposes of infringement, not mere negligent failure to include the original credits.[66] Importing concepts of negligence into this area of copyright would mean that YouTube or Netflix is liable if it *should* have known that a documentary by Michael Moore, for example, uses an actor's voice without permission or without the credits from the original movie.[67] YouTube or Soundcloud could be liable for mashups or remixes containing either uncredited images or samples, or credited music soundtracks or music samples without the original copyright notices, liner notes, or terms of use information.[68] That is in addition to legal claims that a remix or mashup is bad for a performer's reputation by distorting or otherwise modifying the nature or impact of a filmed scene or a song.[69]

YouTube, according to many scholars, makes performances available to the public.[70] If the treaty were to be codified, YouTube might have to remove from its site all performances stripped of their original terms of use, for instance politicians' statements recorded from television or news sites.[71]

While YouTube may have licenses from some news organizations, it will not have them from many others, and the licenses it has may not cover unauthorized changes to the footage that political commentary requires. Further, a parody or lip-synching video could be at risk as a "copy" of a performance without its original credits and notices. A copy need not be literal or verbatim under many countries' laws.[72]

---

[66] *Gordon v. Nextel Communications & Mullen Adver., Inc.*, 345 F.3d 922, 927 (6th Cir. 2003); *Kelly v. Arriba Soft Corp.*, 77 F. Supp. 2d 1116, 1121–2 (C.D. Cal. 1999), *aff'd in part, rev'd in part*, 336 F.3d 811 (9th Cir. 2003).

[67] Fahrenheit 9/11, YouTube (June 19, 2012), www.youtube.com/watch?v=cYoOCdHICCo.

[68] 17 U.S.C. §§ 106, 106A, 512, 1202; cf. Robert Cookson, Songwriters' body sues SoundCloud over copyright, *The Financial Times* (August 27, 2015), www.ft.com/content/23ed1e50-4cc0-11e5-b558-8a9722977189; Kate Dries, How Soundcloud's corporate-friendly overhaul fucked over one small podcast, *Jezebel* (November 3, 2015), https://themuse.jezebel.com/how-soundclouds-corporate-friendly-overhaul-fucked-over-one-small-podcast; Peter Menell, Adapting copyright to the mashup generation, 164 *University of Pennsylvania Law Review* 441 (2016) at 484–6. For examples, see Brett Gaylor, *trailer* RiP: A remix manifesto, *YouTube* (October 27, 2008), www.youtube.com/watch?v=KykbPtRboK4&list=PL4B7CF46158341520&index=2; Morgan Spurlock, A day in the life, *CNN/YouTube* (September 7, 2011), www.youtube.com/watch?v=59UBB9Nukmc.

[69] *Gilliam v. American Broadcasting Cos.*, 538 F.2d 14 (2d Cir. 1976); Geri Yonover, Moral rights protections in the colorization of black and white motion pictures: A black and white issue, 16 *Hofstra Law Review* 503 (1988).

[70] *E.g.* Rebecca Tushnet, Scary monsters: Hybrids, mashups, and other illegitimate children, 86 *Notre Dame L. Rev.* 2133 (2011).

[71] Beijing Treaty, note 13, art. 16; Travis, note 1, at 54–6, 77–80.

[72] WIPO–OECS Colloquium for the Judiciary on the Protection of Intellectual Property Rights, July 28–29, 2006, Dominica Roseau, The Private Sector and the Enforcement of IP Rights: (B) Copyright Based Industries, 6, WIPO-OECS/IP/JU/ROS/06/5 (July 20, 2006), www.wipo.int/edocs/mdocs/lac/en/wipo_oecs_ip_ju_ros_06/wipo_oecs_ip_ju_ros_06_5.doc; Uma Suthersanen, Copyright in the courts: The Da Vinci Code, *WIPO Magazine*, (June 2006), www.wipo.int/wipo_magazine/en/2006/03/article_0004.html.

Again, YouTube may have licenses with most record labels or songwriters' organizations, but it may not be able to license the moral right of the performer to be identified as the performer and to object to any "prejudicial" modification of any performance from the standpoint of the performer's "reputation."[73]

Such changes to YouTube's collections would promote actor and musician control over recorded performances, but they would wreak havoc with competition and fair use. Copyright inquisitions against remixes and mashups could be toxic to user freedoms once excessive user censorship by social media platforms meets the proscriptions against communicating, hyperlinking to, and quoting from performances.[74] Performers and speech-giving politicians could take down memes, critical videos, parodies, artworks, and a variety of other lawful communications.

Copying a clip from a prior performance into a subsequent audiovisual work is essential to many forms of journalism, political speech, and parody.[75] Corporate newsrooms such as those of CNN or corporate-backed infotainment programs on Comedy Central or other channels may gather all the clips and images that they need from YouTube, Facebook, Instagram, cable television channels, and other sources.[76] Without expensive newsroom equipment, Internet users resort to "ripping" Web streams.[77] The use of media clips in noncommercial videos is often a fair use of a fixed copyrighted work, and there is no additional moral right for mass-market

---

[73] Beijing Treaty, note 13, art. 5.

[74] Organization for Transformative Works, Comments: In the Matter of Section 512 Study, U.S. Copyright Office/Library of Congress, Docket No. 2015-7 (April 2016), at 6–10, www.transformativeworks .org/wp-content/uploads/2016/04/512otw-submission.pdf; Organization for Transformative Works, Follow-Up Comments to Copyright Office Regarding DMCA Section 512, U.S. Copyright Office/ Library of Congress, Docket No. 2015-7 (February 2017), www.transformativeworks.org/wp-content/ uploads/2017/02/2016-NOI-Followup-OTW-comments.pdf.

[75] Patricia Aufderheide et al., Copyright, free speech, and the public's right to know: How journalists think about fair use, Center for Social Media Project Paper (July 30, 2012) at 5, http://papers.ssrn .com/sol3/papers.cfm?abstract_id=2119933; Sonia Katyal, Stealth marketing and antibranding: The love that dare not speak its name, 58 *Buffalo Law Review* 795 (2010) at 699; Collette Leland, All's fair in love and news: How the current application of the fair use doctrine favors the traditional media over amateur providers of news content, 8 *Wake Forest Intellectual Property Law Journal* 226 (2008) at 228; Daxton "Chip" Stewart, Can I use this photo I found on Facebook? Applying copyright law and fair use analysis to photographs on social networking sites republished for news reporting purposes, 10 *Journal of Telecommunications & High Technology Law* 93 (2012); Sunder, note 17, at 24; Tushnet, note 70, at 2135–6.

[76] ING, Social media has a growing impact on the news #SMING15 (8 October 2015), www.ing .com/Newsroom/All-news/Social-media-has-a-growing-impact-on-the-news-SMING15.htm; Bonnie Brennen and Scott Brennen, Taking our pictures: Citizen photojournalism in traditional US news media, in Stuart Allan (Ed.), *Photojournalism and Citizen Journalism: Co-operation, Collaboration and Connectivity* (Routledge, 2017) at 71.

[77] E.g. Christian Cawley, How to make a reaction video YouTube will love, MakeUseOf, www .makeuseof.com/tag/how-to-make-reaction-video/; Anthony King, How to rip streaming video, eHow, www.ehow.com/how_5028768_rip-streaming-video.html; Lindsay Pietroluongo, How to create a video mash-up, *eHow*, www.ehow.com/how_12167378_create-video-mashup.html.

photographs, films or television programs.[78] The Beijing Treaty, by contrast, would place the legality of films and shows that sample performances in severe doubt.[79]

5.5. TO STEAL A PERFORMANCE: AN INELEGANT OFFENSE

The Beijing Treaty seems to mimic the protection of performers in Chinese law, and to extend China's pro-performer around the world by consensus.[80] US law did not extend copyrights to performers, traditionally, because it focused on Writings and "works," which could contain or be infringed by performances, but which did not include performances as such. A performer may create a work, for example by utilizing the mechanical or technical assistance of a recording device or its operator, or co-authoring a work with a director, producer, or other compiler or editor of a series of performances on CD, film, disk, etc. Recognizing performances themselves as the subject of copyright may have been excluded from copyright law because this would multiply the overlapping rights that can be litigated, with a film or record being a derivative work of a performance that is itself a derivative work of a screenplay or musical composition, and so on.[81]

Giving performers and their producers strong protections from distorting or mutilating use of performances will require major changes to the framework governing US cultural production. The law of imitating performers' voices in advertisements is confusing and contradictory as it stands now.[82] In 1990, Congress observed that despite the resulting harm to the "dignity of the visual artist ... our copyright law allows distortion, modification and even outright permanent destruction of such efforts."[83] Nevertheless, Congress did not prohibit the destruction of recorded performances, let alone the modification of a performance detrimental to the reputation of the performer, director, producer, or movie studio involved in it. The belief at that time was

---

[78] E.g. *Bouchat* v. Balt. Ravens Ltd. Partnership, 737 F.3d 932 (4th Cir. 2013); *Fox News* v. *TVEyes, Inc.*, 43 F. Supp. 3d 379 (S.D.N.Y. 2014), *appeal pending*, 15-3885-cv (2d Cir. 2017); *Italian Book Corp.*, v. *American Broadcasting Co.*, 458 F.Supp. 65 (S.D.N.Y. 1978); 80 Fed. Reg. 65944 (2015). But cf. *Los Angeles News Service* v. *KCAL-TV Channel 9*, 108 F.3d 1119 (9th Cir. 1997); *Roy Export Co. Estab. of Vaduz* v. *Columbia Broadcasting System, Inc.*, 672 F.2d 1095 (2d Cir. 1982).
[79] E.g. Carolina Rossini, Mitch Stoltz and Yana Welinder, Beijing Treaty on Audiovisual, Performances: We need to read the fine print, *EFF Deeplinks Blog* (July 24, 2012), www.eff.org/deeplinks/2012/07/beijing-treaty-audiovisual-performances.
[80] Jingzhou Tao, *Resolving Business Disputes in China* (CCH, 2004) at 10,404, 10,601; Sun Xiaochen, Treaty to bump up IP protections, *China Daily*, (April 25, 2014), http://usa.chinadaily.com.cn/epaper/2014-04/25/content_17465588.htm. See also Masnick, note 53.
[81] E.g. *Garcia*, 786 F.3d 733, *panel opinion at* 743 F.3d 1258 (9th Cir. 2014); *Garcia*, 743 F.3d at 1270, (Smith, J., dissenting); Daniel Gervais, The protection of performers under U.S. law in comparative perspective, 5 *IP Theory* 116 (2015).
[82] John Tehranian, Guantanamo's greatest hits: The semiotics of sound and the protection of performer rights under the Lanham Act, 16 *Vanderbilt Journal of Entertainment and Technology Law* 11 (2013) at 29–34.
[83] H.R. Rep. No. 101-514, at 15 (1990).

that extending moral rights beyond fine art and photography would violate the First Amendment, because it would impact the fair use of published books and images.[84]

So, what has changed in the past two and a half decades? The implication of Bardem and others is that the Internet is harming performers, threatening their livelihoods. Perhaps, therefore, the White House decided to back the Beijing Treaty to save the class of audiovisual performers from an overwhelming tide of Internet-based piracy.[85] Another possibility is that Chinese law is influencing international law.

"To steal a book is an elegant offense," goes a Chinese saying quoted by William Alford in his 1995 on copyright in Chinese culture.[86] China did not develop some of the incidents of Western copyright law until relatively recently, whether this was due to political priorities of the imperial period in China, difficulties mass-producing printed works in bulk for the Chinese market prior to Western methods being imported, or beliefs that copying is a form of tribute that demonstrates the skill of the copied author.[87] The faithful copying of official culture was tolerated or rewarded.[88] In the socialist period, stronger copyright and patent enforcement could be seen as retarding economic growth and increasing Americans' income at the expense of Chinese consumers and firms.[89] Perhaps what changed, despite growing suspicion of private property after the Maoist transition, was the rise of a domestic constituency that could reap the rewards of stronger copyrights, despite the perception that infringement feeds economic growth.[90]

The road to the Beijing Treaty may have been paved with rhetoric expressing concern that the modern world trading system operates to the detriment of American producers and requires global reforms so that foreigners do not profit at US expense. The United States told its people that the World Trade Organization (WTO) agreements of 1994 contained strong IP protections, including "detailed civil, criminal, and border enforcement provisions" that its trading partners would respect, subject to WTO oversight. The agreements incorporated the WIPO treaties, requiring broader definitions of copyrightable subject matter, laws against burglarizing one's own computer files (anti-circumvention protections), and protections of performances and phonograms.[91]

---

[84] Travis, note 1.
[85] Tartaglione, note 34; US PTO, note 24; WIPO, note 35; Xiaochen, note 80.
[86] William Alford, *To Steal a Book Is an Elegant Offense: Intellectual Property Law in Chinese Civilization* (Stanford University Press, 1995) at 1.
[87] Ibid., at 17, 19, 29, 156.
[88] Ibid., at 18.
[89] Ibid., at 68, 103. See also Peter K. Yu, The second coming of intellectual property rights in China, Occasional Papers in Intellectual Property from Benjamin N. Cardozo School of Law, Yeshiva University, No. 11 (2002).
[90] Wei Shi, Cultural perplexity in intellectual property: Is stealing a book an elegant offense, 32 *North Carolina Journal of International and Commercial Regulation* 1 (2006) at 27.
[91] Paul Salmon, A short guide to international IPR treaties, in U.S. Department of State, Bureau of International Information (Ed.), *Focus on Intellectual Property Rights* (The editor, 2006) at 16.

Parts of corporate America hoped to get Chinese fans hooked on their products, even in an environment of widespread infringement of copyrights, and eventually convert these many fans into consumers paying full freight.[92] The Chinese market for luxury goods was on track to account for one in every three dollars spent on such goods globally by 2015.[93] The Chinese box office increased as fast as 50 percent per year in some years, rising in value from less than $250 million to nearly $7 billion.[94] The day may arrive when a single film or television series might earn $1 billion in China, in the box office, on home video, and through uses in advertising, video games, and merchandise.[95]

One less than elegant aspect of the Beijing Treaty lies in expanding the scope of a Chinese model of copyright that does not always fulfill what other countries would see as copyright's core functions. In 2001, China joined the WTO annex agreement requiring a wide variety of copyright, patent, trademark, and trade secret protections. It joined two WIPO treaties in 2006.[96] Even so, strict quotas on foreign films and television, and censorship of foreign books accompanied by favoritism of domestic publishing houses, kept most US cultural producers out, and undermined the value of their copyrights.[97] Despite a 2012 agreement to reduce infringement by increasing the quota, it remains very low, or 20 "foreign revenue sharing films per year" out of hundreds of foreign films, and various other laws made US ownership of Chinese television channels or streaming companies illegal.[98] For many years, China did

---

[92] Peter K. Yu, From pirates to partners (episode II): Protecting intellectual property in post-WTO China, 55 *American University Law Review* 901 (2006) at 982–3.

[93] Yu, note 92, at 981–2.

[94] *Markets*, Screen Digest, January 2005, at 25; Matt Pressberg, Even Hollywood can't save China's box office this year, *The Wrap* (December 20, 2016), www.thewrap.com/even-hollywood-cant-save-china-box-office-this-year/.

[95] The television series *Seinfeld* has already earned more than $3 billion around the world. Some video game franchises such as *Call of Duty* have earned more than $10 billion globally.

[96] Zhongnan University of Economics & Law, A Comparative Study on Criminal Protection of Intellectual Property in China and Europe 20 (January 2011), www.ipkey.org/en/ip-law-document/download/1565/1844/23, citing Agreement on Trade-Related Aspects of Intellectual Property Rights, signed April 15, 1994; WIPO Copyright Treaty, signed December 20, 1996, and WIPO Performances and Phonograms Treaty, signed December 20, 1996.

[97] For example, China allowed only a fraction of US films to be imported for exhibition, even many years after joining the WTO and its 1994 IP agreements. E.g. Aynne Kokas, *Hollywood Made in China* (University of California Press, 2017) at 19–28; see also Yu, note 89, at 23–4; Eric Smith, President, International Intellectual Property Alliance (IIPA), 'Intellectual Property Protection as Economic Policy: Will China Ever Enforce Its IP Laws?' (2005), www.gpo.gov/fdsys/pkg/CHRG-109hhrg21813/html/CHRG-109hhrg21813.htm; Eric Smith, President, International Intellectual Property Alliance, IIPA, Written Comments to the TPSC on China's WTO Compliance (September 22, 2009), at 6, www.iipawebsite.com/pdf/IIPAChinaTPSCwrittencomments092209.pdf; World Trade Organization, Dispute Settlement Panel, Panel report – Dispute 362, WTO Doc. No. WT/DS362/R (January 26, 2009), www.wto.org/english/tratop_e/dispu_e/362r_e.pdf.

[98] MPAA, Comments on the National Trade Estimate Report on Foreign Trade Barriers, USTR Docket No. USTR-2017-0013 (October 25, 2017), at 15–17, www.mpaa.org/wp-content/uploads/2017/10/mpaa-NTE-filing-Oct-25-2017.pdf.

not implement WTO recommendations regarding China's bans on the sale of some US films and music that violate international trade law.[99]

Legal protection for performances against imitations, transmissions, distortions, and fixations is inelegant for another reason. The frequency and social acceptability of such activities in the age of social media are such that the volume of disputes, and the statutory damages imposed under US law, could be astronomical. While Chinese law may have guaranteed performers the strong rights that their US counterparts lacked, this was in the context of the very modest remedies available in Chinese courts. Most importantly, the average copyright damages award in China is probably one-tenth or less of the US average.[100] The average patent damages award in China, similarly, was less than $80,000 at a time when it was in the millions in the United States.[101] Some scholars even describe China as generally a low-copyright environment.[102] In addition, China arguably has wider loopholes for ISPs to escape liability for copyright infringement.[103]

Transplanting broad performers' rights from China into the US system could be more costly than beneficial, due to high US damages awards on average, and doctrines of vicarious liability and inducement that heighten the exposure of online platforms. Streaming sites such as Netflix or Spotify that become embroiled in disputes between performers and producers could be facing overlapping claims from numerous performers, writers, and producers.[104] Background singers or extras might

---

[99] WTO, S363: China – Measures Affecting Trading Rights and Distribution Services for Certain Publications and Audiovisual Entertainment Products (2012), www.wto.org/english/tratop_e/dispu_e/cases_e/ds363_e.htm.

[100] Eric Priest, Copyright extremophiles: Do creative industries thrive or merely survive in China's high-piracy environment?, 27 *Harvard Journal of Law and Technology* 469 (2014) at 477. Assuming that the average in China was ten times higher in 2009 to 2016 than in 2006 to 2009, the last year for which I found data, the average in 2009–2016 would have been about $50,000, when the US average copyright damages award was $772,000 ($1.45 billion divided by 1,882 cases that led to judgment). Steve Brachmann, Copyright litigation in 2016 saw rise in textile plaintiffs, decline in file sharing cases, *IP Watchdog* (February 15, 2017), www.ipwatchdog.com/2017/02/15/copyright-litigation-textile-plaintiffs-decline-file-sharing, citing Lex Machina, 2016 Copyright Litigation Report, https://pages.lexmachina.com/CopyrightReport16_LP.html. Such an increase in China was unlikely because damages were trending lower, 2006–2009, so US awards may well have been hundred times higher, 2009–2016.

[101] Thomas Cotter, A comparative law and economics analysis of damages for patent infringement, *in* Theodore Eisenberg and Giovanni Ramello (Eds.), *Comparative Law and Economics* (Elgar, 2015) at 268–9; PriceWaterhouseCoopers, A closer look: 2008 Patent litigation study: Damages, awards, success rates and time-to-trial (2009) at 2, Priest, note 100, at 477. The US figure is a median, not an average, but the average may have been even higher due to large awards against Microsoft and other wealthy infringers.

[102] E.g. Jiarui Liu, Copyright for blockheads: An empirical study of market incentive and intrinsic motivation, 38 *Columbia Journal of Law and the Arts* 467 (2015).

[103] Xiao Ma, Establishing an indirect liability system for digital copyright infringement in China: Experience from the United States' approach, 4 *Journal of Intellectual Property and Entertainment Law* 2 (2015), http://jipel.law.nyu.edu/vol-4-no-2-3-ma.

[104] Brief of Amicus Curiae Netflix, Inc., *Garcia*, 786 F.3d 733 (9th Cir. brief filed November 25, 2014) (No. 12-57302); Ted Johnson, Netflix, Facebook, Twitter voice support for Google

even have claims for the contributions that their performances bring to a song, an action scene, or a tableau. Documentary filmmakers were particularly troubled by the possibility of combining the low standard for copyrightability in the United States with the copyrights in performances that would overlap with or override film-maker copyrights.[105] With US theories that allow stacking damages for each copyrighted work into one large multi-work damages calculation, online platforms could face billions of dollars in damages.[106]

5.6. WHAT WOULD JUSTICE FOR ACTORS AND MUSICIANS LOOK LIKE?

The fight against Internet giants on behalf of performers and writers has only intensified since the Beijing Treaty was negotiated. Alongside the perennial efforts of the copyright lobbying groups, tabloid media baron turned media conglomerate chief Rupert Murdoch was very public about Google's content "theft" and the need for media companies to join forces.[107] While seemingly assuming that each YouTube music video reduces the income of the musical artist portrayed in it, Taplin argues that $50 billion is taken by Google, Facebook, and other online platforms from "content creators."[108] Favorable press coverage of this argument followed in a variety of media.[109]

Comprehensive legislation for the benefit of musicians and songwriters is under consideration in Congress as a copyright omnibus, or "Musicbus." Advocates, including the Recording Academy behind the Grammy Awards, suggest that it could achieve fairness and evenhanded treatment for musicians and songwriters.[110]

in 'Innocence of Muslims' case, *Variety*, (November 26, 2014), http://variety.com/2014/biz/netflix-facebook-twitter-voice-suport-for-google-in-innocence-of-muslims-case-120165774/.

[105] Brief of Amici Curiae International Documentary Association et al. in Support of Rehearing en Banc or, Alternatively, Rehearing, at 2–3, *Garcia*, 786 F.3d 733 (9th Cir. brief filed April 14, 2014).

[106] Travis, note 1, at 84–5.

[107] E.g. Matthew Garrahan, Richard Waters, and Alex Barker, News Corp takes Google fight to Brussels, *Financial Times* (September 18, 2014), www.ft.com/content/82734430; Steven Perlberg and Mark Di Stefano, Rupert Murdoch is the media's unlikely hero in the war against Google, *Buzzfeed* (October 4, 2017), www.buzzfeed.com/stevenperlberg/rupert-murdoch-is-the-medias-unlikely-hero-against-tech/; Dirk Simmile, Murdoch wants a Google rebellion, *Forbes* (April 3, 2009), www.forbes.com/2009/04/03/rupert-murdoch-google-business-media-murdoch.htm.

[108] Peter Bart, Content creators robbed blind by Apple, Google, Facebook, *Deadline* (January 6, 2017), http://deadline.com/2017/01/content-creators-exploited-by-apple-google-facebook-taylor-swift-peter-bart-1201879413; Jonathan Taplin, *Move Fast and Break Things: How Facebook, Amazon, and Google Cornered Culture and Undermined Democracy* (Little, Brown & Co., 2017), at 6–7, 102–3. Taplin later concedes that "a big hit" might benefit from being at the "top of the search results."

[109] E.g. Matthew Rees, Whose song is it, anyway?, *The Wall Street Journal*, (April 19, 2017), www.wsj.com/articles/whose-song-is-it-anyway-1492642461.

[110] Neil Portnow, All aboard the Music Bus, *Roll Call*, (April 3, 2014), www.rollcall.com/news/all_aboard_the_music_bus_commentary-231873-1.html. See also Daryl Friedman, MusicBus gaining speed as members of Congress climb on, *Grammy News* (June 18, 2014), www.grammy.com/blogs/musicbus-gaining-speed-as-members-of-congress-climb-on; David Oxenford, What Washington has

There was growing sentiment on the House Judiciary Committee that FM radio is unfairly exempted from paying royalties per play to record labels and performers.[111] Empowering songwriters' groups such as ASCAP and BMI to extract a greater share of value from digital streaming services would be another objective. Harmonizing the disparate standards for calculating royalties for satellite radio, Internet streaming, and cable television music channels could also be included. Finally, ensuring payments to the copyright holders of sound recordings made prior to the 1972 federalization of sound recording copyrights, and to the performers to whom they pay royalties, would reduce the unfairness to the makers of America's classic hit music.[112]

Many of these reforms would lead to increased litigation, or at least the threat of it. With the RESPECT Act and other efforts to extend royalty obligations to more performers of America's classic tunes, class action lawsuits brought on behalf of classic music rightsholders could be revived.[113] New restrictions on playing songs online in exchange for modest payments, or on playing CDs and tapes over FM radio for even smaller payments, could present major issues for the industry.[114] The costs to the public and to those who exploit music could well be worth it, but members of Congress might demand a showing of some sort of problem, even a quite serious one, in order to disrupt music marketplaces in this way.

Is there really a unique crisis confronting actors or musicians that would justify radically expanding their rights to sue other people? One indication that there is not is the number of US musicians, singers, composers, actors, directors, and producers of music and film. That number rose from 354,000 in 2002 to 395,100 in 2008 and will be about 435,300 in 2018.[115] Copyright-related jobs seem to be

---

in store for broadcasters and digital media companies in 2015 – part 2, *Broadcast Law Blog* (February 2, 2015), www.lexology.com/16016/author/David_Oxenford.

[111] The House Judiciary Committee plans omnibus music licensing bill – the "Music Bus," *Broadcast Law Blog* (July 2, 2014), www.broadcastlawblog.com/2014/07/articles/the-summer-of-copyright-part-2-the-house-judiciary-committee-plans-omnibus-music-licensing-bill-the-music-bus/.

[112] Ibid.; see also Chris Israel, Congress, end a longstanding injustice for legacy music creators, *Washington Examiner* (May 11, 2018), https://www.washingtonexaminer.com/opinion/op-eds/congress-end-a-longstanding-injustice-for-legacy-music-creators. It has been estimated that most of the greatest songs in American history according to Rolling Stone and the GRAMMY Hall of Fame predated federal copyright protection for sound recordings. Nadiia Loizides, The RESPECT Act & Co.: Showing Some, but Not Enough, Respect to American Heritage Artists, 19 *Tulane Journal of Technology & Intellectual Property* 47 (2016) at 47.

[113] H.R. 4772, 113th Cong., 2d Sess. (2014); see also Eriq Gardner, Controversy over pre-72 sound recordings certified to New York Appeals Court, *The Hollywood Reporter Esq.* (April 13, 2016), www.hollywoodreporter.com/thr-esq/controversy-pre-1972-sound-recordings-883470.

[114] 17 U.S.C. §§ 106(6), 115; In Re Pandora Media, Inc., 12 Civ. 8035(DLC), 2013 WL 5211927, at *1 (S.D.N.Y. Sept. 17, 2013); Eriq Gardner, ASCAP pays $1.75 million to settle Justice Department probe, *The Hollywood Reporter Esq.* (May 12, 2016), www.hollywoodreporter.com/thr-esq/ascap-pays-175-million-settle-893162.

[115] The number of singers, composers, and music directors and producers grew from 215,000 in 2002 to 240,000 in 2008 and should grow to an expected 260,000 in 2018, while number of actors, producers,

growing at double the rate prevailing in other sectors of the economy. The 10 percent growth in such creative workers from 2008 through 2018 is double the rate of overall job growth in the twenty-first century, even excluding the agricultural sector.[116] Meanwhile, more than 300,000 schoolteachers lost their jobs between 2008 and 2013, even though America needed 400,000 more of them to serve the student population.[117] There is also a severe shortage of nurses and emergency rooms as the US population ages, which will compromise quality of care and dignity in old age and in cases of disability or illness.[118] Despite strong copyright-sector job growth, the male labor participation rate hit a post-World War II low, and the "out of the workforce" rate for men reached a postwar high (the female rates are not comparable due to feminism becoming more prominent).[119]

and directors grew from 139,000 in 2002 to 155,100 in 2008 and will probably grow by another 13 percent through 2018 assuming that employment of directors and producers grows at a similar rate to hiring of actors. E.g. U.S. Bureau of Labor Statistics, *Occupational Outlook Handbook 2010–2011* (Government Printing Office, 2010) at 320, 329; U.S. Bureau of Labor Statistics, *Occupational Outlook Handbook 2004–2005* (Government Printing Office, 2004), at www.umsl.edu/services/govdocs/ooh20042005/www.bls.gov/OCO/ocos095.htm and www.umsl.edu/services/govdocs/ooh20042005/www.bls.gov/OCO/ocos093.htm.

[116] Christopher Goodman and Steven Mance, Employment loss and the 2007–09 recession: An overview, *Monthly Labor Review*, (April 2011), at 4, www.bls.gov/opub/mlr/2011/04/art1full.pdf (nonfarm employment grew 5.3 percent, 2002–2008).

[117] Alexandra Hootnick, Teachers are losing their jobs, but Teach for America's expanding. What's wrong with that? *Hechinger Report* (April 21, 2014), http://hechingerreport.org/teachers-losing-jobs-teach-americas-expanding-whats-wrong/; see also Elise Gould, Disappointing jobs numbers and not enough teachers, *Economic Policy Institute* (October 2, 2015), www.epi.org/blog/disappointing-jobs-numbers-and-not-enough-teachers/.

[118] U.S. Bureau of Labor Statistics, Licensed practical and licensed vocational nurses (April 2012), https://web.archive.org/web/20120401235129/ and www.bls.gov:80/ooh/ healthcare/licensed-practical-and-licensed-vocational-nurses.htm; U.S. Bureau of Labor Statistics, Nursing aides, orderlies, and attendants (April 2012), https://web.archive.org/web/ 20120401213225/ and www.bls.gov/ooh/healthcare/nursing-assistants.htm. See also U.S. Bureau of Labor Statistics, Education, library, and training occupations (April 2012), https://web.archive.org/web/20120402060652/ and www.bls .gov:80/ooh/education-training-and-library/home; Institute for the Future of Aging Services, The long-term care workforce: Can the crisis be fixed? (January 2007), www.leadingage.org/sites/default/files/LTC_Workforce_Commission_Report_0. pdf. Approximately one in four US emergency rooms in hospitals closed between 1990 and 2009. Nicole Ostrow, Hospitals eliminate 1 in 4 U.S. emergency rooms since 1990, study finds, *Bloomberg News* (May 17, 2011), www.nationalnursesunited.org/news/entry/hospitals-eliminate-1-in-4-u.s.-emergency-rooms-since-1990-study-finds/. The number of beds in public US hospitals declined by 100,000 between 1994 and 2014. American Hospital Association, Trendwatch Chartbook 2016: Trends affecting hospitals and health systems (2016) at 23, www.aha .org/research/reports/tw/chartbook/2016/2016chartbook.pdf. Overcrowding and reduced access to care resulted from these trends. Ostrow, ibid. The poor, ethnic minorities, and uninsured Americans had to travel farther for care, or forego it. Jason Silverstein, The decline of emergency care, *The Atlantic*, (April 26, 2013), www.theatlantic.com/health/archive/2013/04/the-decline-of-emergency-care/275306/.

[119] Frank Lysy, There is no reason to expect increased labor force participation rates to be a source of spectacular growth, *An Economic Sense* (March 20, 2016), https://aneconomicsense .org/2016/03/20/there-is-no-reason-to-expect-increased-labor-force-participation-rates-to-be-a-source-of-spectacular-growth/; Mark Perry, Decline in labor force participation reflects demographics, may

Initial estimates that 40 percent of musicians' jobs had been lost due to Napster and other post-1998 infringement options turned out to be an artifact of using monthly data rather than annual comparisons. The figure was closer to 8 percent of jobs being lost, which is still not good, and is especially unnecessary because the US population grew by many millions, alongside rapid growth in broadcast and cable industry revenue and profits.[120] Between 2002 and 2016, perhaps 20 percent of employed musicians and singers had lost their jobs in aggregate, for a decline in some 43,000 jobs, some no doubt due to attrition.[121] More people may be working independently as musicians, because song production has increased.[122] Moreover, job losses have occurred in many fields, often to a worse extent than for singers and musicians, such as a decline of more than 500,000 for carpenters, or a decline of 100,000 for college professors and teachers.[123] In the 13–17 industries with above-average patent activity per 1,000 jobs, about 25 times as many jobs were lost as among musicians in the years leading up to 2015–2016, or nearly 1.1 million jobs.[124]

In hourly terms, actors, singers, and musicians made 50 percent to 300 percent more in 2016 than preschool teachers or nursing assistants, about 20 percent more than elementary and secondary school teachers, and about as much as registered nurses.[125] Directors and producers of audiovisual works earned about twice as much as preschool teachers, 15 percent more than elementary or high-school teachers,

---

not be as bad as reported, *American Enterprise Institute* (May 6, 2012), www.aei.org/publication/decline-in-labor-force-participation-reflects-demographics-may-not-be-as-bad-as-reported/.

[120] Michael Carrier, No, RIAA, it's not the end of the world for musicians, *Techdirt* (May 13, 2015), www.techdirt.com/articles/20150512/13343330980/no-riaa-not-end-world-musicians.shtml, citing Matthew Lasar, Have we lost 41 percent of our musicians? It depends on how you and the RIAA count, *Ars Technica* (October 2012), http://arstechnica.com/tech-policy/2012/10/have-we-lost-41-percent-of-our-musicians-depends-on-how-you-the-riaa-count/.

[121] U.S. Bureau of Labor Statistics, Musicians and singers (May 2016), www.bls.gov/ooh/entertainment-and-sports/musicians-and-singers.htm?view_full; U.S. Bureau of Labor Statistics, Musicians, singers, and related workers (2004), www.diversityworking.com/career/Arts_and_Entertainment/Musicians,_Singers,_and_Related_Workers/Musician.html.

[122] Felix Oberholzer-Gee and Koleman Strumpf, File-Sharing and copyright, in Josh Lerner and Scott Stern (Eds.), *NBER's Innovation Policy and the Economy*, Vol. 10 (University of Chicago Press, 2010) at 19–55, 47–8.

[123] U.S. Bureau of Labor Statistics, *Occupational Outlook Handbook* (May 2016), www.bls.gov/ooh/; U.S. Bureau of Labor Statistics, (2005) note 115; U.S. Bureau of Labor Statistics, *Occupational Outlook Handbook 2002–2003* (Government Printing Office, 2002).

[124] U.S. Bureau of the Census, 2015 business patterns (September 29, 2017), https://factfinder.census.gov; U.S. Economics and Statistics Administration and USPTO, Intellectual property and the U.S. Economy: Industries in focus (March 2012) at 8, www.uspto.gov/sites/default/files/news/publications/IP_Report_March_2012.pdf

[125] U.S. Bureau of Labor Statistics, Occupational employment statistics (May 2016), www.bls.gov/oes/current/oes_stru.htm. See also Barry Leonard (Ed.), Occupational employment and wages – May 2010, News Release No. USDL-11-0722, at 11, https://books.google.com/books?id=_nfno_kJMUUC&pg=PA11; U.S. Bureau of Labor Statistics, Musicians and singers (2017), www.bls.gov/ooh/entertainment-and-sports/musicians-and-singers.htm.

and 30 percent more than educators in general.[126] Licensed nurses often earned even less than teachers.[127]

The performers supporting the Beijing Treaty would possibly benefit from a measure of additional control over how their performances are used or reused. But it is not the kind of on–off switch for compensation that certain forms of patent reform are for many inventors and founders of startups. Actors and singers are not facing a situation, like that confronting many patent owners today, in which a work can easily be made and sold without any compensation for or consultation of them, while the infringer and its business partners make *all* the money. Instead, actors and musicians often have the power to decline to make films, shows, and records, and to use that leverage to earn dramatically higher pay or profits for reprising a role or taking on a new one.[128] In any event, the treaty would not necessarily grant performers any additional compensation from the corporations exploiting their work, due to the "transfer of rights" language in it.

It is often said by critics of the digital conglomerates and Internet pirates that musicians and singers, like book authors, cannot make money anymore. This does not seem to be true, given evolving compensation models and the growing fortunes of the top 1 percent of earners in creative industries. Musical performers and producers turned multiplatform entrepreneurs such as Sean Combs, Madonna, Dr. Dre, and Jay-Z approached billionaire status between 2008 and 2016, the supposed peak of music industry destruction, content monopolization by Google/YouTube, and unfairness to artists. Singer–songwriter Paul McCartney and actor–comedian Jerry Seinfeld are also probably worth more than two-thirds of a billion dollars.[129] Estimates put the value of the estates of Michael Jackson and Prince at as much as $800 million each, largely from ventures and income sources related to music.[130] By 2013, One Direction may have been the first boy band to generate a billion dollars in revenue in its first three years.[131] During the supposed crisis period

[126] U.S. Bureau of Labor Statistics, Labor force statistics from the current labor survey: Median weekly earnings of full-time wage and salary workers by detailed occupation and sex (2016), www.bls.gov/cps/cpsaat39.htm; U.S. Bureau of Labor Statistics, note 125, at 11–14; U.S. Bureau of Labor Statistics, (2010) note 115, at 320, 329–31.

[127] U.S. Bureau of Labor Statistics, (2016), note 126.

[128] For example, the pop stars Madonna and Prince signed contracts worth tens of millions of dollars after the strong sales of their previous albums, and the actors on the successful television show *Friends* earned a reported $20 million per year *each* in 2000–2002. E.g. Prince inks $100 mil. record contract with Warner Bros., *Jet*, (September 21, 1992) at 16; Hilary de Vries, Best friend, *Los Angeles Magazine*, (August 2000) at 112.

[129] Kathryn Vasel, The world's 10 richest recording artists, *CNN Money* (December 2, 2014), http://money.cnn.com/2014/12/02/luxury/richest-recording-artists/index.html.

[130] Top earning dead celebrities 2016, *Forbes* (2017), www.forbes.com/pictures/eeel45fhfim/1-michael-jackson-825/#4d891d3b1fdd; Prince dead: Who will inherit his $800m fortune?, *Stuff* (April 24, 2016), www.stuff.co.nz/entertainment/music/79263234/prince-dead-who-will-inherit-his-800m-fortune.

[131] Jesse Lawrence, One Direction could be worth $1 Billion, *Business Insider* (August 2, 2013), www.businessinsider.com/one-direction-worth-1-billion-2013-8.

for books and music between 2003 and 2012, J.K. Rowling nearly doubled her wealth to $750 million,[132] while Adele earned more than $100 million between 2012 and 2016, based in significant part on US album sales.[133]

5.7. PERFORMING CLASS STRUGGLE

In March 2015, Grammy-winning artist Alicia Keys led a gathering of pop music icons in declaring their intentions to save music by launching a fair, artist-backed digital streaming service called Tidal.[134] For some music executives, the goal of Tidal should be to eliminate low-paying, advertising-supported, nonsubscription streaming, like most streams on Spotify and YouTube.[135] It could pay $15,000 or more per million streams, as opposed to $5,000 or less for that many streams on Spotify or YouTube.[136]

Country music superstar Garth Brooks once remarked that the main question he had for YouTube was, how does he get his music taken down? Their response, according to his story: "silence."[137] Musicians are "treated like slaves," according to The-Dream, who composed Rihanna's hit "Umbrella" and released albums with Def Jam Records, perhaps because musicians find it difficult how to control how much "work" they do for others.[138] The-Dream, like Brooks and the Tidal group, launched his own business to capture some of the label's or distributor's share of album and single sales.

In 2014, Lee Thomas Miller participated in a rare hearing on the state of the music industry by a US congressional committee. Miller explained how it took him working in the Nashville music scene for eleven years, writing hundreds of songs,

[132] Harry Potter author richer than the Queen, *The Telegraph (U.K.)*, (April 27, 2003), www.telegraph .co.uk/news/1428496/Harry-Potter-author-richer-than-the-Queen.html; McCartney toppled from top of 'rich list,' *The Guardian (U.K.)*, www.theguardian.com/money/2004/apr/16/business.citynews; The millionaire authors' club, *The Telegraph (U.K.)*, (April 27, 2003), www.telegraph.co.uk/ culture/books/bookreviews/9272388/The-Millionaire-Authors-Club.html; Sunday Times Rich List 2012; UK's Richest People, *TheRichest* (May 15, 2012), www.therichest.com/rich-list/nation/ sunday-times-rich-list/.

[133] Shaun Kitchener, Rich List 2017, *The Daily Express (U.K.)*, (May 4, 2017), www.express.co.uk/ entertainment/music/799969/Rich-List-2017-music-Paul-McCartney-Adele-Mick-Jagger-Sunday-Times; *Sunday Times Rich List 2012*, note 132.

[134] Joe Lynch, Tidal live stream features slew of A-list artists, including Madonna straddling a table, *Billboard*, (March 30, 2015).

[135] Andrew Hampp, What Tidal means for the freemium vs. premium debate: The industry weighs in, *Billboard*, (Mar.ch30, 2015).

[136] Andrew Hampp, Behind the scenes of Tidal's stormy launch – and what's in store for the future, *Billboard*, (April 3, 2015).

[137] Garth Brooks on the state of digital music: YouTube is the devil, *Access Online* (November 17, 2014), www.accessonline.com/videos/garth-brooks-on-the-state-of-digital-music-youtube-is-the-devil/.

[138] Craig Marks, Singer–Songwriter The-Dream: 'Artists are treated like slaves', *Billboard*, (June 27, 2015), www.billboard.com/articles/columns/the-juice/6605182/the-dream-artists-aretreated-like-slaves-music-business-contra-paris.

to develop his first hit. Even so, he is paid nine cents or less per sale when other singers or bands record his songs, and thousandths of a penny when songs he wrote are digitally streamed.[139] Remarking on the operation of compulsory licenses, David Lowery of the band Cracker and the blog The Trichordist (#stopartistexploitation) remarked that singer–songwriters get paid less for a million plays, on a service like Pandora, than they would for selling a few t-shirts or CDs at a concert.[140] As a result, services such as Spotify and YouTube account for most streams but a small share of the revenue paid to artists, songwriters, and labels.[141]

According to a somewhat dated survey by the Pew Internet & American Life Project, two-thirds of songwriters and performers did not bring in 20 percent or more of their annual income from their work even before YouTube, Pandora, or Spotify launched.[142] Musical artists and groups often transfer their rights to record labels by contract, which then sometimes fail to account properly for royalties due, according to some musicians.[143] Lobbying by broadcasters resulted in no royalties being paid by radio stations to labels and their artists for the use of their tracks, even though songwriters do receive royalties from radio, and have received them for decades.[144]

Songwriters, musicians, and other music rights owners have come together repeatedly to seek reforms that would promise to increase their incomes at the expense of those exploiting their music. For example, Sheryl Crow and other songwriters and musicians fought the formal classification of musical tracks as works for hire.[145] Record labels try to claim musical albums as works made for hire, but they often decline to withhold employment-related income taxes or social insurance payments, pay salaries, guarantee regular employment, or

---

[139] Testimony on "Music Licensing Under Title 17, Part I" (June 10, 2014) at 19, https://judiciary.house .gov/wp-content/uploads/2016/02/113-105_88240.pdf.

[140] David Lowery, My song got played on Pandora 1 million times and all I got was $16.89, less than what I make from a single t-shirt sale! *The Trichordist* (June 24, 2013), https://thetrichordist.com/2013/06/24/ my-song-got-played-on-pandora-1-million-times-and-all-i-got-was-16-89-less-than-what-i-make-from-a-single-t-shirt-sale/. See also Roger Catlin, Singer David Lowery keeps the debate over streaming music services in your ear, *Washington Post*, (January 6, 2017), https://wapo.st/2iPQX6a.

[141] David Lowery, New math $.00666 : Billboard's new "consumption" chart, free streams and the end of meaningful metrics?, *The Trichordist* (November 24, 2014), https://thetrichordist.com/2014/11/24/ new-math-00666-is-billboards-new-consumption-chart-the-future-or-the-end-of-meaningful-metrics-for-music/.

[142] Mark Madden, Artists, musicians, and the Internet, *Pew Research Center* (December 5, 2004), www .pewinternet.org/2004/12/05/part-3-the-musicians-survey.

[143] Brief of Amicus Curiae the Motown Alumni Association, at 4–11, *F.B.T. Productions, LLC v. Aftermath Records*, 621 F.3d 958 (9th Cir. brief filed Jan. 4, 2010) (No. 09-55817).

[144] *BMI*, 444 U.S. at 5.

[145] United States Copyright Office and Sound Recordings as Works Made for Hire: Hearing Before the Subcommittee on Courts and Intellectual Property of the Committee on the Judiciary, U.S. House of Representatives (May 25, 2000).

provide office space. Therefore, many albums that they release could be owned by musical acts, album producers, and/or songwriters as the joint works of independent contractors.[146]

More recently, a coalition of groups claiming to represent 500,000 authors of diverse sorts of works asked the European Commission to relieve authors from clauses providing for the "forced transfer" of excessive rights from authors to companies, or other "unfair" license terms. They also seek transparency regulation in the form of mandatory reporting of sales and royalty accounts.[147]

The average musician in a four-person band may earn as little as 2.4 percent of the band's revenue from CDs and other sound recordings, because the label often takes nearly two-thirds of the money, the distributors one-fourth of it, and managers and lawyers one-fourth of the remaining slice of the pie.[148] These figures do not even account for the 20–40 percent of the retail price that is the retailer's mark-up on wholesale.[149]

With Internet streaming and downloads, musicians and songwriters should be earning closer to half of the revenue generated, at least. The labels' traditional deduction for plastic CD cases and cellophane wrappers should vanish.[150] The retailers do not need to cart around and display stacks and stacks of physical items, with all the payments that that entails to employees, landlords, utilities, and tax collectors. There are websites and apps that perform the tasks that used to be done by the managers, producers, and lawyers who claimed a significant share of the money paid by the label to the performers.[151]

Artists have complained, and empirical research has confirmed, that while a large share of revenue taken in by streaming or digital download services such as Pandora, Spotify, and iTunes goes to copyright holders, performers may receive as little as 7 percent of it.[152] Sometimes, this apparently happens despite contracts suggesting

---

[146] M. William Krasilovsky, and Sidney Schemel, with John Gross and Jonathan Feinstein, *This Business of Music: The Definitive Guide to the Business and Legal Issues of the Music Industry* (Billboard Books, 10th ed. 2007) at 185; see also Richard Schulenberg, *Legal Aspects of the Music Industry: An Insider's View* (Random House LLC, 1999) at 336–469.

[147] ECSA, EFJ, EWC, FERA and FSE Press Release, The Authors' Group welcomes the EU Directive proposal on copyright, European Writers Council (September 14, 2016), www.europeanwriterscouncil.eu/index.php?option=com_content&view=article&id=195:the-authors-group-welcomes-the-eu-directive-proposal-on-copyright&catid=7&Itemid=159.

[148] How much musicians really make in the industry - Part I, *Minority Fortune* (August 2010), http://minorityfortune.com/liabilities/how-much-musicians-really-make-in-the-industry-part-i/, citing How much do you musicians really make?, *The Root*, www.theroot.com/views/how-much-do-you-musicians-really-make?page=0,0.

[149] Ibid. (suggesting that CDs sold at wholesale for $10, but retailed for $16.98 on average in 2010).

[150] Brief of Amicus Curiae the Motown Alumni Association, note 143, at 11–12; How much musicians really make in the industry, note 148.

[151] Carrier, note 120.

[152] Mike Masnick, Yes, major record labels are keeping nearly all the money they get from Spotify, rather than giving it to artists, *Techdirt* (February 5, 2015), www.techdirt.com/articles/20150204/07310329906/yes-major-record-labels-are-keeping-nearly-all-money-they-get-spotify-rather-than-giving-it-to-artists

that bands should receive half of the revenue obtained by a label from a third party's sale or performance of master recordings.[153] When labels enter into direct licensing deals with third parties, the money often goes to them, and they decide how much performers are entitled to, which might be different than the amounts that attorneys for the performers or outside auditors would award them under the governing contracts and statutory provisions.[154] Music royalty disputes are popping up here and there, some alleging outright fraud.[155]

The ultimate class struggle may pit musical performers' case for royalties against FM radio broadcasters' insistence on being exempt from paying any to artists. Most of the money in music goes to FM and AM radio in the form of advertising dollars. Traditional radio brings in $20 billion per year, compared with less than $4 billion in streaming revenue in 2016, less than $2 billion in digital download and ringtone revenue, and even less than that in CD and other physical sales revenue.[156] This parallels the distribution of hours spent listening to musical radio and streams, which are lavished three to one on traditional radio, probably due to the greater ease of using it in cars.[157]

The Fair Play Fair Pay Act of 2017, H.R. 1836, would require commercial FM and AM radio stations to pay a royalty to record labels or other recording industry copyright holders, or seek a waiver of royalties from them. Five members of the US House of Representatives, at least four from districts with substantial numbers of musical acts (New York, San Diego, Nashville, and Detroit), argue that exempting FM radio in particular from royalty payments to performers "has disadvantaged music creators and pitted technologies against each other by allowing certain services to get away with paying little or nothing to artists."[158] These legislators faced an uphill battle because there are broadcasters in nearly every congressional district,

---

.shtml, citing Artists get 7% of streaming cash; Labels take 46%, *Music Business Worldwide* (February 2015), www.musicbusinessworldwide.com/artists-get-7-of-streaming-cash-labels-take-46/.

[153] *F.B.T. Prods., LLC v. Aftermath Records*, 621 F.3d 958, 965 (9th Cir. 2010).

[154] Greg Sandoval, Pandora wins court fight aimed at blocking music from internet radio services, *The Verge* (September 18, 2013), www.theverge.com/2013/9/18/4744494/attempts-to-block-pandora-from-accessing-ascaps-category-fail.

[155] *F.B.T.*, 621 F.3d 958; Complaint, ¶ 35, *James v. UMG Recordings, Inc.*, No. CV 11-1613 (C.D. Cal. complaint filed Apr. 1, 2011); Order Granting Plaintiffs' Motion for Final Approval of Class Action Settlement, ¶ 5, *James* (C.D. Cal. Apr. 13, 2016); Kat Greene, UMG only just begun to pay digital royalties, Carpenters say, *Law 360* (January 12, 2017), www.law360.com/articles/880138/umg-only-just-begun-to-pay-digital-royalties-carpenters-say.

[156] Patrick Koncel, Did copyright kill the radio star? Why the recorded music industry and Copyright Act should welcome webcasters into the fold, 14 *The John Marshall Review of Intellectual Property Law* 292 (2015) at 310; Marcel Boyer, The competitive market value of copyright in music: A digital gordian knot, TSE (France) Working Paper 17-844 (Sept. 2017), at 4, www.tse-fr.eu/sites/default/files/TSE/documents/doc/wp/2017/wp_tse_844.pdf.

[157] Boyer, note 156, at 4.

[158] Office of Darrell Issa, U.S. House of Representatives, Issa, Nadler, Blackburn, Conyers, Deutch and Rooney re-Introduce Fair Play Fair Pay Act (Mar. 30, 2017), https://issa.house.gov/news-room/press-releases/issa-nadler-re-introduce-fair-play-fair-pay-act.

and their friendship may be more helpful to a politician than the backing of a record label or rock band; as of this writing, Congress seem ready to pass a version of the Musicbus called the Music Modernization Act (S. 2823), which lacks the AM and FM radio provision of H.R. 1836.[159] A previous effort in this area failed to gain traction after broadcasters proposed lower digital royalty rates in exchange for higher FM and AM royalty rates; in 2018, Congress may raise some digital royalty rates without adjusting AM and FM radio's obligations.[160]

Finally, the Internet Radio Fairness Act (IRFA) would make digital music websites profitable, perhaps for the first time outside the confines of digital conglomerates like Apple or Google who have other income streams. The new Napster lost $200 million operating in a legal way after 2003 and had a smaller selection than the old Napster.[161] Perhaps Napster's true successor as a fully interactive service operating in a legal way is Spotify, which lost a dollar on every $10 in revenue in 2016.[162] By treating Internet radio like digital cable and satellite radio, IRFA would fix this.[163] Ultimately, the U.S. House of Representatives voted in 2018 to introduce parity between webcasters and digital cable or satellite radio providers but by making satellite radio rates more "fair" rather than reducing webcasting rates to make Pandora, Spotify, iHeart, and their competitors finally profitable.[164]

[159] The Future of What, The Future of What "The Fair Play, Fair Pay Act," *YouTube* (July 6, 2015), www.youtube.com/watch?v=AGA1mU_IQsg. David Philp, Music Modernization Act only goes half way, *Hypebot* (May 1, 2018), www.hypebot.com/hypebot/2018/05/halfway-modern-music-modernization-act.html.

[160] White House recommends performers share in copyright royalties, *Ratner Prestia* (April 15, 2011) www.ratnerprestia.com/2011/04/15/white-house-recommends-performers-share-in-copyright-royalties-2/; Soundexchange, Statement from SoundExchange President & CEO Michael Huppe on Introduction of Music Licensing Package in the U.S. Senate (May 10, 2018), www.soundexchange.com/news/statement-soundexchange-president-ceo-michael-huppe-introduction-music-licensing-package-u-s-senate/.

[161] Associated Press, Napster reports wider loss in 4Q but meets Wall St. estimates, *San Jose Mercury News*, (May 16, 2007), www.mercurynews.com/2007/05/16/napster-reports-wider-loss-in-4q-but-meets-wall-st-estimates/.

[162] Mark Mulligan, How Netflix can turn a profit while Spotify has not (yet), *Hypebot*, www.hypebot.com/hypebot/2017/01/why-netflix-can-turn-a-profit-while-spotify-cannot.html; Spotify Inc., Comments to the U.S. Copyright Office on Music Licensing Study, Docket No. 2014-3 (May 23, 2014), www.copyright.gov/docs/musiclicensingstudy/.

[163] Rick Marshall, The quest for "parity": An examination of the Internet Radio Fairness Act, 60 *Journal of the Copyright Society of the USA* 445 (2013).

[164] Most industry associations that take an interest in music law supported this bill. U.S. House of Representatives, What They're Saying about the Music Modernization Act (April 25, 2018), https://judiciary.house.gov/press-release/what-theyre-saying-about-the-music-modernization-act/; see also SoundExchange, note 160.

PART III

Pirates' Dilemmas

6

The Inquisitorial Internet

6.1. INTRODUCTION

This chapter will explore whether, in their haste to punish piracy and save jobs, legislators and some judges may be doing away with the public trial and vigorous defense methods that have distinguished the adversarial system. Are Internet services becoming Inquisitors? The Inquisitorial Internet is a concept that borrows a distinction – used in the sociology of law – between Anglo–American systems of justice by "public trial," which are known as "adversarial" because of the climactic contest of opposing counsel who put one another's evidence and theories to the test, and European and other civil law systems known as "inquisitorial" because they are based on Roman models of an administrative, bureaucratic investigation by a judge (Inquisitor) using an often scanty dossier of evidence.[1] Inquisitiorialism is a method of organizing decision-making power, and the procedures this method uses.[2] It vests a great deal of trust in the police, the prosecutors, and the judiciary, while seemingly distrusting the accused and defense counsel in matters of cross-examination of witness testimony, signed confessions, and negotiated verdicts.[3]

---

[1] E.g. Mirjan Damaška, *The Faces of Justice and State Authority* (Yale University Press, 1986); Robert A. Kagan, American and European ways of law, in Volkmar Gessner and David Nelken (Eds.), *European Ways of Law: Towards a European Sociology of Law* (2007) at 60–65; Nico Jörg, Stewart Field, and Chrisje Brants, Are inquisitorial and adversarial systems converging? in Phil Fennell, Christopher Harding, Nico Jörg, and Bert Swart (Eds.), *Criminal Justice in Europe* (Clarendon Press, 1995) at 41–47; Thomas Weigend, The decay of the Inquisitorial ideal: Plea bargaining invades German Criminal Procedure, in John Jackson and Maximo Langer (Eds.), *Crime, Procedure and Evidence in a Comparative and International Context* (Bloomsbury, 2008) at 60. For usage of the term "inquisitor," see Christoph Safferling, *Towards an International Criminal Procedure* (Oxford University Press, 2001) at 217.

[2] Damaška, note 1, at 16.

[3] James Sheptycki, Criminal investigation, in Alison Wakefield and Jenny Fleming (Eds.), *The SAGE Dictionary of Policing* (Sage, 2008) at 65; Goran Sluiter and Koen Vriend, Defending the

6.2. FACEBOOK DEAD?

In 2015, controversy erupted regarding Facebook's "freebooting" problem. YouTuber and Australian filmmaker Destin Sandlin dedicated an episode of his video blog to the topic in January 2015. Facebook was profiting from stolen videos uploaded by its users, he suggested, to the tune of five million views of a single viral video. One of Sandlin's videos had been viewed more than seventeen million times, but when Facebook finally removed it, he received none of the substantial money that may have been shared between Facebook and the user. "Drag it out, make it hurt, and hope that the offended party loses interest," is how he characterized Facebook's response to his complaints. Sandlin quoted *Hello Internet* as defining "freebooting" as taking someone else's video or other creation and passing it off as one's own for profit, e.g. by uploading it to Facebook. Stealing every day should be enough to "go to jail," he quoted a child as saying in his video.[4]

The online magazine *Slate* picked up the story, and it spread to other outlets, which published articles with titles like "Facebook Is Building an Empire on Stolen Video, and YouTubers Are Getting Screwed."[5] YouTubers were quoted as suggesting that Facebook was boosting its huge video viewcounts with false claims and misappropriation.[6] One commentator claimed that most of Facebook's billions of daily video views were of freebooted videos, which some data suggested included more than 70 percent of the 1,000 most popular videos on Facebook. YouTubers' plight was compounded by the fact that once they built Facebook groups and networks of followers, Facebook demoted their links to the YouTube videos in followers' feeds, alleging that users prefer to see videos on Facebook, so that freebooted versions of the videos often appeared.[7]

Of course, charges of theft against websites and Internet services are quite common. In the late 1990s, Motion Picture Association of America's Jack Valenti called illegal content the "dirty little secret" of the Internet, accounting for 80 percent of usage.[8] In early 2006, a YouTube product manager did an informal survey of "all the most viewed/ most discussed/top favorites/top rated" videos, and guessed that

---

undefendable? Taking judicial notice of genocide, in H. G. van der Wilt and Jeroen Vervliet (Eds.), *The Genocide Convention: The Legacy of 60 Years* (Martinus Nijhoff, 2012) at 82–3.

4   Destin Sandlin, Facebook Freebooting, *Smarter Every Day* 128 (January 2015), www.youtube.com/watch?v=L6A1LtokvMA (quoting Hello Internet, H.I. #5: Freebooting (2014), https://player.fm/series/hello-internet-62109/hi-5-freebooting).

5   Jack Smith IV, Facebook is building an empire on stolen video, and YouTubers are getting screwed, *MIC* (August 5, 2015), https://mic.com/articles/123368/facebook-video-vs-youtube.

6   Ibid., note 5, (quoting Hank Green, Theft, lies, and Facebook Video, *Medium* (August 2015), https://medium.com/@hankgreen/theft-lies-and-facebook-video-656b0ffed369).

7   Ibid.

8   Statement of Jack Valenti, MPAA, on On-line Copyright Liability Limitation Act and WIPO Copyright Treaties Implementation Act: Hearing on HR 2280 and HR 2281 Before the House Judiciary Committee, Courts and Intellectual Property Subcommittee, 105th Cong. (1997), quoted

more than 70 percent contained copyrighted material.[9] There were hundreds of thousands of clips from hit movies and television shows on the site, Viacom argued in its lawsuit against YouTube.[10]

Although the nuances of the YouTube litigation are beyond the scope of this chapter, critics of YouTube argued that the site "seems to have 'won' the early streaming-video market by using 'ubiquitous' piracy to marginalize law-abiding competitors," with the result being that "online markets for works belong to the amoral 'entrepreneur' most willing to break the law in order to use 'unlawfully expropriated property ... as part of the start up capital for his product.'"[11] Similarly, another streaming website, vimeo. com, became one of the most popular sites on the Internet by allowing copyrighted music but not copyrighted video to be used without authorization, with the result that up to 20 percent of its content contained unlicensed music, in more than 1,000 videos containing music owned or controlled by five labels alone.[12] Veoh Networks also saw a good deal of copyrighted content uploaded to its site without authorization, and its CEO has been characterized as admitting that "Veoh.com is host to a wide range of unauthorized and full-length copies of popular programs."[13]

Once courts had clarified that streaming websites are by and large not liable for creating a broad climate of infringement that serves as a draw for Internet users, the action shifted to Congress and the US Copyright Office. Lobbyists and trade associations highlighted the role of "rogue sites" such as The Pirate Bay, whose founders were convicted of copyright-related offenses by a Swedish court in 2010, and sentenced to pay $6.7 million in compensation to the site's entertainment-industry victims.[14] The Pirate

in Lilian Edwards, The fall and rise of intermediary liability online, *in* Lilian Edwards and Charlotte Waelde (Eds.), *Law and the Internet* (Hart Publishing, 2009) at 61.

[9] Plaintiff's Memorandum of Points and Authorities in Support of Its Motion for Summary Judgment, at 10, *Viacom International* v. *YouTube, Inc.*, 718 F. Supp. 2d 516 (S.D.N.Y. 2010) (No. 1:2007-CV-02103).

[10] Plaintiff's Memorandum, note 9, at 9–10. See also Robert Levine, *Free Ride: How Digital Parasites Are Destroying the Culture Business, and How the Culture Business Can Fight Back* (Anchor Books, 2011) at 273.

[11] Thomas Snydor, Why the *Viacom* v. *YouTube* summary-judgment ruling will be reversed, *The Progress & Freedom Foundation Blog* (July 29, 2010), http://blog.pff.org/archives/2010/07/print/006126.html (quoting Transcript of Oral Argument, at 36, *Grokster* (U.S. oral argument held March 29, 2005), www.supremecourt.gov/oral_arguments/argument_transcripts/04-480.pdf).

[12] Plaintiffs' Memorandum in Support of Motion for Partial Summary Judgment, *Capital Records, LLC* v. *Vimeo, LLC*, 972 F. Supp. 2d 500 (S.D.N.Y. 2013) (S.D.N.Y. January 4, 2013). The five labels include a group of affiliated EMI and Virgin labels, which would add up to more than five if they were counted separately.

[13] *UMG Recordings, Inc.* v. *Shelter Capital Partners*, 667 F.3d 1022, 1037–1040 (9th Cir. 2011) (quoting Brad Stone, Veoh's vexing visitor numbers, *The New York Times Bits Blog* (July 15, 2007), http://bits.blogs.nytimes.com/2007/07/15/veohs-vexing-visitor-numbers/, and Greg Sandoval, A new copyright battlefield: Veoh Networks, *CNET News* (February 21, 2007), www.cnet.com/news/a-new-copyright-battlefield-veoh-networks/).

[14] Associated Press, Pirate Bay founders lose appeal, *CBC* (November 26, 2010), www.cbc.ca/beta/news/technology/pirate-bay-founders-lose-appeal-1.923614.

Bay is a tracker that helps users find "seeders" of "torrents," which are deconstructed audio, video, or executable code files that can be reconstructed using the BitTorrent protocol; a hit film can have thousands of seeders at any one time.[15] Sweden attempted to shut down the site, and its founders were deemed criminally responsible for copyright infringement because they knew of a lot of infringing users, and connected these users with one another.[16] The court referred to this "awareness" as "complicity" in copyright infringement. This raised the question: what about the responsibility of Facebook and Google/YouTube for the infringement of which they were aware?[17]

6.3. DEDICATED TO THEFT

In the US House of Representatives, a notorious legislative proposal known as the Stop Online Piracy Act (SOPA) emerged in October 2011. It would have created a new type of copyright lawsuit against a website "dedicated to theft of US property," defined broadly as a site that "is taking, or has taken, deliberate actions to avoid confirming a high probability" that users employ it to commit copyright infringement.[18]

The Directors Guild, the MPAA, the TV production networks, actors of stage and screen, and other entertainment-industry employees told the Senate that IP theft was destroying hundreds of thousands of jobs per year, that the "blockage" of fair use and uncopyrighted material was an acceptable price to pay for halting infringement and that those harmed by blockage could repost noninfringing work elsewhere.[19] Judicial intervention would still be required before a domain name, advertisement, or payment account would be blocked, they added. The associations and unions repeated these arguments in another letter in support of SOPA.[20]

Many groups of writers, photographers, musicians, film studios, brand owners, professional sports leagues, and businesses endorsed SOPA, calling it necessary to prevent websites from earning money by intellectual property theft, which was

---

[15] CBC News, Can Sweden make the charges stick against The Pirate Bay?, *CBC.ca* (February 20, 2009), www.cbc.ca/news/business/can-sweden-make-the-charges-stick-against-the-pirate-bay-1.815813; Edwards, *The fall and rise,* above n. 927, 79–80.

[16] *The Prosecutor v. Fredrik et al.,* Verdict B 13301-06, Stockholm District Court, 17 April 2009, at 47–48, www.ifpi.org/content/library/Pirate-Bay-verdict-English-translation.pdf. See also Edwards, note 8, at 80.

[17] As one website pointedly argued, "[s]ites such as Google offer the same functionality [in terms of locating the seeders of torrents] as The Pirate Bay" but get off scot-free due to their "political and legal clout to defend themselves unlike small independent sites." Edwards, note 8, at 79 (quoting www .thepirategoogle.com).

[18] Stop Online Piracy Act, § 103(a)(ii), H.R. 3261, 112th Cong., 1st Sess. (2011).

[19] Floyd Abrams, Letter to Patrick Leahy, Chairman, Committee on the Judiciary, United States Senate, et al., (May 24, 2011), www.dga.org/~/media/Files/Internet%20Theft/110524ProtectIPActLetterFloyd Abrams.pdf, citing *United States* v. *Elcom Ltd.,* 203 F. Supp. 2d 1111, 1129 (N.D. Cal. 2002).

[20] Floyd Abrams, Letter to Lamar Smith, Chairman, Committee on the Judiciary, U.S. House of Representatives (November 7, 2011), www.dga.org/~/media/Files/Internet%20Theft/1110%20 SOPA%20Letter%20by%20Floyd%20Abrams.pdf.

destroying 2.5 million jobs in twenty developed countries.[21] As models for the enforcement of copyright law against search engines, streaming sites, and hyperlinks, the associations and unions pointed to US Department of Homeland Security seizures of the websites HQ-streams.com, Rojadirecta.com, and TVShack.net.[22]

One particularly powerful new legal action would not target the website directly, but would enable copyright holders to disconnect websites from the banking and credit-card processing systems, ending their revenue streams and driving them into bankruptcy.[23] Law professors called the provisions for extraordinary relief before trial an "Internet death penalty."[24]

The government would have been empowered, under the companion Senate bill to SOPA, to appear before a judge without an author's presence, and declare the author's content to be unlawful and blocked. This appeared to many as a prohibition of speech without due process of law, in violation of the Constitution. Massive quantities of lawful communication and opinion would be deleted when domains were targeted for some infringement.[25] There would be no trial, and the accusers and 'judges' doling out Internet death penalties would never meet the accused pirates, just as in the historic version of the inquisitorial system of criminal justice prior to the influence of Anglo–American conceptions of adversarial justice.[26] Elizabeth Thornburg observes that the Digital Millennium Copyright Act (DMCA) works in this way for individual files or pages:

> Unless the Web site owner files a lawsuit, the entire process takes place out of the public eye. It is commenced by a private party in a private setting and enforced by another private party. There is no court, no hearing, and no decision on the issue of copyright infringement.[27]

Sonia Katyal also explains that "piracy surveillance" would alter copyright law:

> [It] creates a world in which copyright owners can set the terms of use, police consumers, record and expose their personal information, and penalize potential infringers – all, to a varying extent, outside of the boundaries of state control … .

---

[21] 1-800-PETMEDS et al., Rogue Sites are Stealing American Jobs and Hurting Consumers! (February 15, 2011), www.ppa.com/files/pdfs/roguesite_letter.pdf.

[22] Abrams, note 20.

[23] SOPA, note 18, at § 103(a)–(b).

[24] E.g. Mira Burri, Controlling new media (without the law), in Monroe Price, Stefaan Verlust, and Libby Morgan (Eds.), *The Routledge Handbook of Media Law* (Routledge, 2012) at 337.

[25] Timothy B. Lee, Dozens of law professors: PROTECT IP Act is unconstitutional, *Ars Technica* (July 6, 2011), https://arstechnica.com/tech-policy/2011/07/dozens-of-law-professors-protect-ip-act-is-unconstitutional/.

[26] Mirjan Damaška, Evidentiary barriers to conviction and two models of criminal procedure: A comparative study, 121 *University of Pennsylvania Law Review* 506 (1973) at 551–77.

[27] Elizabeth G. Thornburg, Going private: Technology, due process, and Internet dispute resolution, 34 *U.C. Davis Law Review* 151 (2000) at 189.

Mere accusations of infringement can displace court-ordered determinations. In sum, piracy surveillance techniques also fail to consider two significant costs to non-offenders: overdeterrence of speech and evisceration of fair use.[28]

The anti-piracy legislation of 2011 would have been a super-DMCA in the sense that just as the DMCA immunizes YouTube from lawsuits filed by video creators who have their videos removed due to copyright issues, banks and payment processors would have been immune from lawsuits filed by entire websites that they starved of income.[29] This could overdeter platforms from hosting an account or website that quotes other another site (or a book, film, etc.), because the marginal benefit to the platform from one more account or site would be far outweighed by the catastrophic impact of being cut off from the financial system due to a number of infringing accounts or sites. This is consistent with the inquisitorial model of justice as a paternalistic endeavor for the greater good, in which due process and overdeterrence of the exercise of individual freedoms are not major concerns.[30]

The sponsor of SOPA, Rep. Lamar Smith of Texas, claimed that counterfeiting and piracy were costing the US economy $100 billion per year, as well as thousands of American jobs.[31] He added:

> Websites like Facebook and YouTube that host user content are not "dedicated to" illegal activity and they certainly do not make a business out of "facilitating" the illegal sale and distribution of counterfeit or pirated goods.
>
> Unfortunately, there are some critics of this legislation who are not serious about helping to protect America's intellectual property. That's because they've made large profits by working with and promoting rogue sites to U.S. consumers. Google recently paid a half billion dollars to settle a criminal case because of the search-engine giant's active promotion of rogue foreign pharmacies that sold counterfeit and illegal drugs to U.S. patients. Their opposition to this legislation is self-serving since they profit from doing business with rogue sites.[32]

At first glance, Rep. Smith's defense of the legislation was that (1) websites like Google are not covered by it, (2) but they are organizing opposition to it because

---

[28] Sonia Katyal, Piracy vs. privacy, 7 *Yale Journal of Law and Technology* 222 (2005) at 329, 332.

[29] Lee, note 25, at 104.

[30] Cf. Damaška, note 26, at 522, 527, 528, 568, 570–6; cf. also Lon Fuller, The adversary system, *in* Harold Berman (Ed.), *Talks on American Law* (Random House, 1961) at 30–45.

[31] Lamar Smith, Defending SOPA, *The National Review*, (December 1, 2011), http://webcache .googleusercontent.com/search?q=cache:ss4TQzvQTN8J:www.nationalreview.com/article/284535/ defending-sopa-lamar-smith, citing Frontier Economics, Ltd., Estimating the global economic and social impacts of counterfeiting and piracy, International Chamber of Commerce/Business Action to Stop Counterfeiting and Piracy (February 2011), https://cdn.iccwbo.org/content/uploads/ sites/3/2016/11/ICC-BASCAP-Global-Impacts-Full-Report-2011.pdf.

[32] Smith, note 31.

it might cover them.[33] One might reconcile this tension by distinguishing between occasionally or incidentally profiting from deals with rogue sites and being "dedicated" to that mission like The Pirate Bay. All large websites occasionally profit from infringement, so they unjustly (in Smith's view) jumped to the conclusion that they will be sanctioned as "rogue" sites even though the law was not meant for them.

There is a legal gray area between purposeful infringement and negligent toleration of it. SOPA's language did not draw such a clear distinction, because victims of Facebook or YouTube could argue that the high percentage of infringing videos in the top 100 or top 1,000 most-viewed lists proved that they were purposefully avoiding doing further research into their top videos so as not to "confirm" their copyright status, thereby justifying the 'Internet death penalty' against the site hosting those videos.[34] In addition to the verdict for "complicity" against The Pirate Bay's founders, this kind of theory had been successful against Napster clones, eBay, and some streaming sites.[35] A French decision against eBay involving counterfeit

[33] There is a plausible case that SOPA and the PROTECT IP Act did not cover Facebook or Google due to limitations on the liability of site owners and operators, including the requirement that the site be "primarily" made or used to infringe copyrights or trademarks (or, more loosely and in the alternative, that it is reckless in avoiding knowledge of such infringement, which would be more likely to apply to Facebook or Google, or that it has "limited purposes" other than infringement); the procedural requirement of a written, signed claim of infringement with specifics alleged under penalty of perjury; the ability of a site owner or operator to avoid some of the statute's penalties by sending a counternotification alleging noninfringement; the requirement of a personal lawsuit against the owner or operator by the complaining entities if it or they can be found; and a guarantee of judicial decisions on injunctions. SOPA, note 18; U.S. Copyright Office, H.R. 3261, the "Stop Online Piracy Act" (November 16, 2011), www.copyright.gov/docs/regstat111611.html.

[34] SOPA, note 18, at § 103(a)(ii). See also Parker Higgins, What's on the blacklist? Three sites that SOPA could put at risk, *The Electronic Frontier Foundation Deeplinks Blog* (November 15, 2011), www.eff.org/deeplinks/2011/11/whats-blacklist-three-sites-sopa-could-put-risk; Matthew Lasar, "Least restrictive means"? One way that SOPA could die in court, *Ars Technica* (January 18, 2012), https://arstechnica.com/tech-policy/2012/01/least-restrictive-means-how-sopa-could-go-the-way-of-copa/; Ryan Radia, Why SOPA threatens the DMCA safe harbor, *The Competitive Enterprise Institute* (November 18, 2011), https://cei.org/content/why-sopa-threatens-dmca-safe-harbor; Dana Smith, What Warner's recklessness says about SOPA, *Public Knowledge Blog* (November 11, 2011), www.publicknowledge.org/news-blog/blogs/what-warners-recklessness-says-about-sopa; David Sohn, House Copyright bill casts dangerously broad net, *The Center for Democracy and Technology Blog* (October 27, 2011), https://cdt.org/blog/house-copyright-bill-casts-dangerously-broad-net/.

[35] *A&M Records, Inc. v. Napster, Inc.* 239 F.3d 1004, 1020–1023 (9th Cir. 2001) (Internet service may lose its safe harbor from copyright liability if it "had knowledge or awareness of infringing activity on its system" or if infringement is a "draw" to its service, resulting in direct financial benefit to it, although such a "draw" is not inconsistent with the safe harbor "per se"); In Re Aimster Copyright Litigation, 334 F.3d 643, 655 (7th Cir. 2003) (noting that Internet service will lose its DMCA safe harbor if it does not "do what it can be reasonably be asked to do to prevent use of its service by 'repeat infringers'") (quoting 17 U.S.C. § 512(i)(1)(A)); *Arista Records, LLC v. Lime Group LLC*, 784 F. Supp. 2d 398, 424–433 (S.D.N.Y. 2011) (Internet service will lose safe habor if it contributes to infringement on large scale, and/or fosters it); *Arista Records LLC v. Usenet.com*, 633 F. Supp. 2d 124, 131–132, 143, 153–157 (S.D.N.Y. 2009) (where scale of user infringement was allegedly large, court noted that Internet service will lose safe harbor if infringement is a "draw" to its site or if it fosters

perfumes rested primarily on "serious faults" in eBay's trademark compliance system, just as YouTubers and some observers blame Facebook's system for not filtering out videos.[36] The websites Megaupload and Hotfile got shut down in part because they took down links to infringing files one by one, with other links remaining intact to provide access to the infringing file.[37] Copyright owners may well claim that major flaws in compliance should be equated with fostering or tacitly encouraging (i.e. being "dedicated to") piracy.

The advocacy surrounding SOPA may have heightened concerns that it could kill websites like Facebook. Two days after the blocking legislation was introduced, the Copyright Alliance invited the US Register of Copyrights, Maria Pallante, to a panel discussion and book signing with author Robert Levine.[38]

infringement, which occurs if infringement contributes to realization of service's "business model"), *superseded by* 784 F. Supp. 2d 398 (S.D.N.Y. 2011); *Capital Records, LLC* v. *Escape Media Group, Inc.*, No. 12-CV-6646, 2015 WL 1402049, at *53–54 (S.D.N.Y. Mar. 25, 2015) (Internet service may lose its safe harbor if it does not fully disassociate itself from infringing users and their activities); *Capital Records, LLC* v. *Vimeo, LLC*, 826 F.3d 78, 97–98 (2d Cir. 2016) (Internet streaming service could lose its safe harbor if based on the facts known to the service about a video, infringement was "'objectively obvious'" to a "'reasonable person'") (quoting 17 U.S.C. § 512(c)(1)(A)(ii)); *Columbia Pictures Industries, Inc.* v. *Fung*, 710 F.3d 1020, 1043–1044 (9th Cir. 2013) (Internet service will lose safe harbor if it "it would have been objectively obvious to a reasonable person that the material solicited and assisted [for upload and download] was both copyrighted and not licenses to random members of the public," or if its revenue is directly tied to advertising revenues from large-scale infringement which it could prevent by terminating user access or not "influenc[ing]" users who infringed); *Flava Works, Inc.* v. *Gunter*, No. 10 Civ. 6517, 2011 WL 3205399, at *10 (N.D. Ill. July 27, 2011) (Internet service loses safe harbor if it does not "determine whether a particular user had posted, on two or more occasions, a video that infringes ..."), *vacated on other grounds*, 689 F.3d 754 (7th Cir. 2012); *Grokster*, 454 F. Supp. 2d at 985 (Internet service loses safe harbor if it contributes to infringement on large scale, making it "more likely that [it] condoned illegal use" of the service).

[36] LVMH [Christian Dior Couture] v. eBay Inc., eBay International, Tribunal de commerce Paris, 1ère ch. B, 30 June 2008, No. 2006077799, 1 (Fr.); eBay Inc., eBay International/LVMH et autres, Cour de cassation Chambre commerciale, financière, et économique, Arrêt du 3 Mai 2012; Anne Debet, Épilogue judiciaire de l'affaire eBay contre LVMH: eBay n'est pas un hébergeur, *La Semaine Juridique*, 2 July 2012, www.lexisnexis.fr/droit-document/article/la-semaine-juridique-edition-generale/27-2012/789_PS_SJG_SJG1227CM00789.htm; Edwards, note 8 at 68; Danny Friedman, *Trademarks and Social Media: Towards Algorithmic Justice* (Elgar, 2015) at 254–7.

[37] U.S. Department of Justice, Office of Public Affairs, Press Release, Justice Department Charges Leaders of Megaupload with Widespread Online Copyright Infringement (January 19, 2012), www.fbi .gov/news/pressrel/press-releases/justice-department-charges-leaders-of-megaupload-with-widespread-online-copyright-infringement. See also Dominic Patten, MPAA wins Hotfile copyright lawsuit, *Deadline* (August 28, 2013), http://deadline.com/2013/08/mpaa-wins-hotfile-copyright-infringement-suit-573949; Todd Spangler, Hotfile shuts down after $80 mil MPAA piracy settlement, *Variety*, (December 4, 2013), http://variety.com/2013/digital/news/hotfile-shuts-down-after-80-mil-mpaa-piracy-settlement-1200918387. Moreover, the U.S. government alleged in the *Megaupload* case, and Disney Enterprises alleged in the *Hotfile* case, that the sites "conducted their illegal operation using a business model expressly designed to promote uploading of the most popular copyrighted works for many millions of users to download." U.S. Department of Justice, Office of Public Affairs, Press Release, above; see also, Plaintiffs' Motion and Memorandum of Law, at 18–34, *Disney Enterprises, Inc.* v. *Hotfile Corp.*, No. 1:11-cv-20427-a (S.D. Fla. brief filed March 5, 2012.

[38] Copyright Alliance, Copyright alliance – discussion, Washington Daybook/Westlaw Newsroom (October. 28, 2011), http://a.next.westlaw.com (search for document "2011 WLNR 22267449").

Levine argues that "the Internet" writ large has virtually destroyed the newspaper, publishing, and music businesses, and it will do the same for Hollywood movies.[39] Newspaper, movie, and music jobs were down, he wrote.[40] New rules were needed to seize the domain names of Russian and Swedish pirate sites, and to take lawsuits against US infringers out of federal court and into small claims court; these rules would also have to apply to Apple, Google, and Microsoft, he acknowledged (and, one might add, Facebook).[41] Along with Mr. Levine, Steve Bogard, President of Nashville Songwriters Association International, attended the meeting with Ms. Pallante after SOPA was introduced.[42] This association argued to the Supreme Court that any service is liable that benefits financially when users join the service to illegally upload and download copyrighted materials.[43] The MPAA and the Independent Film & Television Alliance claim that websites like YouTube should be liable for all copyright infringement that occurs when a profitable strain or nest of infringing use on their site comes to the site operators' attention, and the site allows it.[44]

6.4. HARD TIME FOR A FEW RHYMES

In 2011, the Obama administration called for a new felony crime of infringement by streaming.[45] SOPA and a Senate version of similar legislation known as PIPA would have fulfilled this wish, by criminalizing the willful public performance ten or more times of a work or works having a retail value of more than $2,500.[46] The administration repeated its call after the SOPA controversy died down.[47]

An ingenious campaigner against SOPA started the "Free Bieber" movement in response to all this. Along with clips of a young Justin Bieber publicly performing

[39] Robert Levine, How the Internet has all but destroyed the market for films, music, and newspapers, *The Guardian*, (August 13, 2011), www.theguardian.com/media/2011/aug/14/robert-levine-digital-free-ride; Levine, note 10, at 26–189.

[40] Ibid., at 253.

[41] Ibid. at 189, 245–9.

[42] Copyright Alliance, note 38.

[43] Brief of the American Society of Composers, Authors, and Publishers, BMI, Association of Independent Music Publishers, Church Music Publishers Association, Nashville Songwriters Association International, and the Songwriters Guild of America as Amici Curiae in Support of Petitioners, at 7, *Grokster* (U.S. brief filed Jan. 19, 2005), www.copyright.gov/docs/mgm/ASCAP.pdf.

[44] Brief of MPAA and IFTA as Amici Curiae Supporting Appellants, *Viacom International Inc.* v. *YouTube, Inc.*, 676 F.3d 19 (2d Cir. 2012) (No. 10-3270) (2d Cir. brief filed Sept. 27, 2012).

[45] Victoria Espinel, Concrete steps Congress can take to protect America's intellectual property, *The White House Blog* (March 15, 2011), https://obamawhitehouse.archives.gov/blog/2011/03/15/concrete-steps-congress-can-take-protect-americas-intellectual-property.

[46] SOPA, note 18, at § 201.

[47] U.S. Department of Commerce, Internet Policy Task Force, The "Green Paper" on Copyright Policy (2013), 100; Ben Isaacson, Obama administration revives SOPA proposal to make unauthorized streaming a felony, *The Huffington Post* (August 7, 2013), www.huffingtonpost.com/2013/08/07/unauthorized-streaming-felony_n_3720479.html.

copyrighted music such as Chris Brown's "With You," the website freebieber.org posted photoshopped images of a teenage Bieber languishing behind bars for five years of "brutal" confinement, an invitation for visitors to generate their own versions of the meme, and a petition against SOPA's provision making video use of copyrighted works a felony.[48] The campaign was featured on *The Daily Show*, generated 55,000 "Likes" on Facebook, and may have prompted Bieber to call for the legislation's sponsor to be hauled away in cuffs (before legions of YouTubers suffered such treatment).[49]

The question of criminal responsibility in copyright is a difficult one. Basic fairness as between physical and "virtual" thieves, for example shoplifters and downloaders or digital distributors, would seem to demand it. Indeed, the infrequency of criminal sentencing for music and movie uploading and downloading, as compared with shoplifting CDs, DVDs, or even staples such as food or cigarettes, could be seen as an example of class bias within the law, with Internet users generally being middle-class or above, at least until recently.[50] On the other hand, copyrights are very inexact concepts compared with physical books or discs.[51] It may be for this reason that there is no criminal accountability for patent infringement in the USA whatsoever. There is no clear analogue to considerations of abstract ideas, fair use, or nonliteral similarity when it comes to most cases of burglary, larceny, or embezzlement. Still, there are several crimes that make subtle distinctions based upon the legal status of an intangible thing or situation.

The consensus among American and European politicians, among others, is that criminal copyright law is here to stay. Moreover, the trend is to periodically expand its scope, potentially reaching ever-more common and routine uses of the Internet and copying technology, like Justin Bieber's alleged early YouTube performances.

---

[48] Free Bieber (2017), www.freebieber.org; see also Jonathan Zittrain, A close look at SOPA, *Harvard Blogs* (December 2, 2011), http://blogs.harvard.edu/futureoftheinternet/2011/12/02/reading-sopa.

[49] Free Bieber, note 48.

[50] Cf. James Grimmelmann, The ethical visions of copyright law, 77 *Fordham Law Review* 2005 (2009) at 2020–2021, citing MPAA, Piracy: It's a crime, YouTube (2004), www.youtube.com/watch?v=HmZm8vNHBSU. For example, men have been sentenced by federal judges to 24 months imprisonment for selling infringing movies and TV shows with a notional retail value of more than $10,000 or even $100,000, while a shoplifter who is a repeat offender might receive life in prison for stealing $34 in candy or $153 in VHS tapes. American Bar Association, Life in prison for shoplifting: Cruel and unusual punishment, *Human Rights Magazine*, Winter 2004, www .americanbar.org/publications/human_rights_magazine/; Cathy Itkowitz, Federal employee ran bootleg movie operation inside Labor Department, *The Washington Post*, (September 8, 2015), http://wapo.st/1ERXByX; Newser, Accused candy shoplifter faces life in prison, *USA Today*, (April 5, 2016), www.usatoday.com/story/news/2016/04/05/accused-candy-shoplifter-faces-life-prison; U.S. Attorney's Office, District of Connecticut, East Hartford man who pirated movies and television shows and sold them on eBay is sentenced to prison (September 26, 2008), www.justice.gov/criminal/cybercrime/singarellaSent.pdf.

[51] *Dowling v. United States*, 473 U.S. 207, 218 (1985) (infringement more "complex" than "run-of-the-mill theft").

After making commercial or financially-motivated infringement a felony following entertainment-industry lobbying, Congress criminalized the commercial distribution of recordings of performances that were recorded without a performer's
consent, for example during a concert, using decryption devices (descramblers)
and other hacks to obtain illicit access to copyrighted work, and making or using
a computer program or device that hacks technological locks that prevent a work's
copying, streaming, or remixing.[52]

Economic theories of criminal IP law range from the optimistic (some would say
naive) to the deeply critical. The optimistic theory is influenced by the Chicago
School of law and economics, like the theories of indirect liability and so much else in
copyright. It is possible, using such a theory, to advocate for the Bieber Incarceration
Act, aka section 201 of SOPA, on the basis that the harm from unauthorized performances of musical compositions and imitation of album tracks online will
be difficult to detect and to deter using actual and punitive damages, in part because
most infringers will lack the resources to satisfy a judgment, even if counsel could
be retained to sue them all.[53] The theory acknowledges that copyright may encourage
wasteful duplication of effort in a "race" to monopoly as well as deadweight loss due to
higher prices, but not that it transfers income from consumers to rightsholders.[54]
It simply assumes, without trying to measure the respective costs and benefits, that
the benefits of copyright are worth the costs of criminal remedies. Criminal law
typically achieves its benefits at high cost to the incarcerated person, as well as to
his or her family and the taxpayer.[55] Again, a Chicago School theory might see
these extreme costs as worth it because many violators of law are "judgment-proof,"
owning assets worth less than the damages they cause to others.[56] Thus, criminal law
"is designed primarily" for the poor.[57] Patent infringement, by contrast, is a game of
kings, with the richest companies in the world allegedly infringing patents daily.[58]

[52] 17 U.S.C. §§ 506, 1201; 18 U.S.C. § 2319A; *United States v. Martignon*, 492 F.3d 140 (2d Cir.
1997); Julie Cohen, Lydia Pallas Loren, Ruth Okediji, and Maureen O'Rourke, *Copyright in a Global
Information Economy* (Aspen Publishers, 4th ed. 2015) at 848; Neil Netanel, *Copyright's Paradox*
(Oxford University Press, 2005), at 16–17, 66–70.
[53] Jonathan Masur and Christopher Buccafusco, Innovation and incarceration: An economic analysis of
criminal intellectual property law, 87 *Southern California Law Review* 275 (2014) at 276–280.
[54] Ibid., at 282–3.
[55] Ibid., at 284.
[56] Ibid., at 285, citing Richard Posner, An economic analysis of criminal law, 85 *Columbia Law Review*
1193 (1985) at 1195.
[57] Masur and Buccafusco, note 53, at 286–9. It may be even more costly to incarcerate poor copyright
infringers than wealthy patent infringers, because the former may end up jobless and on the public
dole, and their children may grow up poor, inadequately educated, and at risk of pursuing a life of
crime..
[58] Cf. Brief of Amici Curiae Electronic Frontier Foundation and Public Knowledge in Support of
Remand, at 8–9, *CLS Bank Int'l v. Alice Corp. Pty. Ltd.*, 717 F.3d 1269 (Fed. Cir. 2013) (No. 2011-1301)
(Fed. Cir. brief filed December 7, 2012), www.eff.org/files/filenode/CLSBankEnBancAmicus_0.pdf;
Coalition for Patent Fairness, Comments on DOJ/FTC Workshop on Patent Assertion Entity Activities

As the Chicago School theory might therefore predict, there is no US criminal law on patent infringement.[59] Nevertheless, it is a crime in many other countries.[60]

Patent infringement may be too "white-collar" to be seen as a high-priority crime to prosecute, like hoarding (as in food), "touting" (as in stocks), "fixing" (as in prices), or polluting (as in air, water, food, or cosmetics).[61] Along with workplace accidents and the sale of cigarettes, such corporate and occupational crimes may be under-prosecuted because, Quinney argues, the ruling class may be committing them in business or as a byproduct of performing banking functions for businesses.[62] Here, again, the Chicago School has a defense for the system: white-collar crime is typically incidental to some legitimate business activity, and society will be harmed if it is overdeterred.[63] Copyright infringement, like shoplifting, is sufficiently unproductive to warrant hard time in the clink.[64] Still, intent and monetary thresholds are in the copyright statute, and are seen as necessary to avoid sweeping "ordinary business disputes" within the prohibition.[65]

(April 5, 2013), http://web.archive.org/web/20130919141746/ and www.ftc.gov/os/comments/pae/pae-0055.pdf; Selwyn Parker, Game of phones: Tech kings clash in smartphone patent wars, *The New Economy* (March 27, 2014), www.theneweconomy.com/technology/game-of-phones-tech-kings-clash-in-smartphone-patent-wars; Mario Trujillo, Tech CEOs press House leaders for patent vote, *The Hill*, (July 16, 2015), http://thehill.com/policy/technology/248213-tech-ceo-press-house-leaders-for-patent-vote. See also Zak Islam, Smartphone industry spent $20 billion on patents in 2011, *Tom's Hardware* (October 9, 2012), www.tomshardware.com/news/Patents-Smartphone-Apple- Google-Motorola,18231.htm.
[59] Irina Manta, The puzzle of criminal sanctions for intellectual property infringement, 24 *Harvard Journal of Law & Technology* 469 (2011) at 469. There is an argument, however, that the National Stolen Property Act as amended in 1988 or the federal conspiracy statute applies to patent infringement. Ibid., at 478–480, citing 18 U.S.C. § 2314, and *United States v. Alavi*, No. CR07-429-PHX-NVW, 2008 WL 1971391, at *2 (D. Ariz. May 2, 2008); John Boyle, Jr., May patent infringement be a criminal conspiracy?, 17 *Journal of the Patent Office Society* 529 (1935).
[60] E.g. Gibong Jeong, Why does Korea have so few criminal patent cases?, 30 *Bloomberg BNA World Intellectual Property Report* 37 (2016), http://news.bna.com/wiln/(South Korea); Jeremy, Patent infringement: is it a crime where you are?, *The IPKat* (June 6, 2012), http://ipkitten.blogspot.com/2012/06/patent-infringement-is-it-crime-where.html#comments (Europe); Kyushu University, Transparency of Japanese Law Project, Japanese Patent Law (2012), https://web.archive.org/web/20121123200154/ and www.tomeika.jur.kyushu-u.ac.jp/ip/index2.htm (Japan); Manta, note 59, at 471 (Thailand and Latin America).
[61] Lawrence Salinger, Introduction, in Lawrence Salinger (Ed.), *Encyclopedia of White-Collar & Corporate Crime*, Volume 1 (Sage, 2015) at viii–x.
[62] Drew Humphries, Book review, 3 *Crime and Social Justice* 78 (1975) at 78–80; Richard Quinney, *Class, State, and Crime: On the Theory and Practice of Criminal Justice* (David McKay Co. Inc., 1977) at 57–58, 84, 110–112, 142. See also Richard Quinney, *Critique of the Legal Order: Crime Control in Capitalist Society* (Transaction Publishers, 1974) at 59 ("[W]e find that the makers of criminal policy are members of or representatives of big business and finance, including the legal establishment which is tied to corporate and financial wealth."). See also p. 53 (defining ruling class).
[63] Masur and Buccafusco, note 53, at 287–8.
[64] E.g. Masur and Buccafusco, note 53.
[65] Manta, note 59, at 482 (quoting 138 *Congressional Record* 31,182 (1992)). See also Masur and Buccafusco, note 53, at 317–18, citing 17 U.S.C. § 506 (2012).

Criminal proceedings could be more efficient than civil ones in patent as well as in copyright law. Just like copyright owners, patent owners may take socially wasteful precautions to hide and protect their ideas, code, and documents in the absence of legal remedies for widespread infringement should they leak. It may be more efficient, due to economies of scale, for a Cybercrime Division or CSI: Patent Strike Force to prosecute and plea bargain with all patent infringers than for thousands of private parties to duplicate investigations and legal pleadings involving recidivist infringers.[66]

In the United States, SOPA probably came close to passing due to a lobbying push for it, which was halted by countervailing lobbying power of social-media and technology companies. According to the MapLight and SOPAtrack databases, legislators behind SOPA or something like it received four times as much campaign cash as those who opposed such a law at that time.[67] Google also spends millions on lobbying against laws like SOPA, and enjoys frequent access to US politicians.[68] In combination with the eyeballs reached by google.com and Google allies such as Wikipedia and Mozilla, the favorable television and newspaper coverage of SOPA did not have its desired effect, and the public and many politicians turned against the law.[69]

6.5. AN INQUISITORIAL INTERNET AND A FIRST AMENDMENT UNDERCLASS

Like the inquisitorial system in general, an Inquisitorial Internet might be more efficient from a court-costs perspective.[70] A civil action against a website's domain name and its owners' or operators' business partners or contractual ties, as called for by Senator Leahy, could be more efficient and less harsh than criminal prosecution of the owners or operators of a "rogue" website as individuals. There would be other harms that would be difficult to measure, on the other hand. Such lawsuits may inflict more collateral damage on protected speech and legitimate firms than the notice and takedown system. Operation In Our Sites, as a first foray into

---

[66] Masur and Buccafusco, note 53, at 290–2, citing William Landes and Richard Posner, *The Economic Structure of Intellectual Property Law* (Harvard University Press, 2003), at 119, Richard Posner, *The Economic Analysis of Law* (Aspen Publishers, 9th ed. 2014), at 1196, and A. Mitchell Polinsky, Private versus public enforcement of fines, 9 *Journal of Legal Studies* 105 (1980) at 107.

[67] Jay Costa and Darby Beck, Maplight: Revealing money's influence on politics, *in* Mickey Huff and Andy Lee Roth (Eds.), *Censored 2013: Dispatches from the Media Revolution* (Seven Stories Press, 2014) at 189.

[68] Jonathan Taplin, *Move Fast and Break Things: How Facebook, Amazon, and Google Cornered Culture and Undermined Democracy* (Little, Brown & Co., 2017), at 129–31.

[69] E.g. Protests against SOPA and PIPA, *Wikipedia* (2017), http://en.wikipedia.org/wiki/SOPA_blackout.

[70] Michael Asimow, Inquisitorial adjudication and mass justice in American administrative law, *in* Laverne Jacobs and Sasha Baglay (Eds.), *The Nature of Inquisitorial Processes in Administrative Regimes: Global Perspectives* (Routledge, 2016) at ch. 5.

enforcement by domain-name seizure, affected hundreds of thousands of potentially innocent users of Megaupload and Rojadirecta.[71] The founder of the World Wide Web, Tim Berners-Lee, referred to the Leahy legislation as a violation of the basic norm of due process of law going back to the Magna Carta.[72] Constitutional scholar Laurence Tribe argued that like Operation In Our Sites, raids could bring down entire sites with thousands or millions of pages based on one or a few instances of infringement on such a site.[73]

In patent law, despite potentially worse economic harm to individual companies than in copyright, the Justice Department typically does not delete entire businesses that may have infringed many IP rights, as called for by Senator Leahy.[74] It may well be more efficient to either treat unlicensed websites like a traffic infraction or a minor trespass in criminal terms, or to reform the existing mechanisms of civil lawsuits and DMCA takedowns to make them work better. Existing proposals to accomplish this suffer from the same defect as much of patent reform; they strip alleged infringers of their Seventh Amendment right to jury trial in cases seeking money damages.[75] The ouster of federal judges in favor of lawyers with industry ties or arbitration experience may tip the scales against the middle-class defendant sued by a major copyright concern.[76] In copyright, due process is even more important

[71] Anupam Chander and Uyên Lê, Free speech, 100 *Iowa Law Review* 501 (2015).

[72] Quoted in Sam Gustin, Web censorship bill sails through senate committee, *Wired* (November 18, 2010), www.wired.com/2010/11/coica-web-censorship-bill/.

[73] Laurence Tribe, The Stop Online Piracy Act violates the First Amendment, *Scribd* (December 6, 2011), www.scribd.com/document/75153093/Tribe-Legis-Memo-on-SOPA-12-6-11-1.

[74] Brief for the United States as Amicus Curiae in Opposition to Certiorari, at 20, *Samsung Electronics, Co., Ltd.* v. *Apple Inc.*, (U.S. brief filed Oct. 5, 2017) (No. 16-1102) (endorsing "narrowly tailored" approach to injunctions after finding of patent infringement); Cf. *Apple Inc.* v. *Samsung Electronics, Co., Ltd.*, 695 F.3d 1370, 1374–5 (Fed. Cir. 2012).

[75] Compare U.S. Copyright Office, Copyright small claims: A report of the Register of Copyrights (2013), http://copyright.gov/docs/smallclaims/usco-smallcopyrightclaims.pdf, with *Granfinanciera, S.A.* v. *Nordberg*, 492 U.S. 33, 50–1 (1989) (explaining why Congress may not assign a "private tort" or "property" claim to an administrative agency, because jury trial is required by the Constitution on the "common law side" of federal cases); *Pernell* v. *Southall Realty*, 416 U.S. 363, 383–4 (1974) (holding that action analogous to common-law claim could not be removed from jury's cognizance under Seventh Amendment); *EEOC* v. *Corry Jamestown Corp.*, 719 F.2d 1219, 1224–5 (3d Cir. 1983) (explaining why jury trial cannot be denied to individual sued under federal statute). Cf. also *Murray's Lessee* v. *Hoboken Land & Improvement Co.*, 59 U.S. (18 How.) 272, 284 (1856) ("[W]e do not consider congress can either withdraw from judicial cognizance any matter which, from its nature, is the subject of a suit at the common law ... "). The application of the Seventh Amendment and Article III of the Constitution to removal of issues traditionally tried to a jury to an administrative agency staffed by lawyers often with ties to industry was allowed by the Supreme Court (citing the availability when the Constitution was being drafted of a method of canceling patents by petition to the Privy Council rather than in the common law courts) in *Oil States Energy Services LLC* v. *Greene's Energy Group, LLC*, 639 Fed. Appx. 639 (Fed. Cir. 2016), *cert. granted*, 137 S. Ct. 2239 (U.S. June 12, 2017) (No. 16-712), affirmed, 584 U.S. ___, 139 S. Ct. ___, 2018 WL 1914662 (U.S. Apr. 24, 2018).

[76] E.g. Jeffrey Bils, David's sling: How to give copyright owners a practical way to pursue small claims, 62 *UCLA Law Review* 464 (2015) at 478–80.

than in patent law, due to the Copyright Office less aggressively examining applications for eligibility, and the disputed scope of rights.[77]

As at time of writing, the Directors Guild and the MPAA are seeking to enshrine website blocking in international law.[78] The US Register of Copyrights has testified before Congress that domain name registries and registrars know how to revoke domain names, and that search engines may likewise be able to filter rogue sites from appearing in their results, as they do with child pornography links.[79] Domain name blocking had become a standard response to sites like The Pirate Bay in Denmark, Ireland, and Italy.[80] Britain's Digital Economy Act calls for control of broadband use and selective disconnection of infringing users from the Internet.[81]

The European Commission is considering imposing an obligation for Internet platforms to filter out copyrighted material in order to redistribute value back to rightsholders.[82] The Brazilian Supreme Court has ordered YouTube to tame and control its proliferating video channels or face strict liability for any infringement on them.[83] SOPA's proposal for website blocking without a preliminary injunction hearing has been revived in private suits addressing Sci-Hub and other sites, and government enforcement actions against megaupload.com, sharebeast.com, and other sites.[84]

The Register of Copyrights has acknowledged concerns that website blocking would violate the First Amendment rights of other Internet users swept up in such orders, and that Internet engineers believed that it would damage the integrity of the domain name system while threatening the role of the United States as "steward" of Internet addressing systems through the Internet Corporation for Assigned Names

---

[77] Manta, note 59, at 495.

[78] Eriq Gardner, Entertainment industry sends U.S. trade office a NAFTA negotiation wish list, *The Hollywood Reporter THR Esq Blog* (June 20, 2017), http://www.hollywoodreporter.com/thr-esq/ entertainment-industry-sends-us-trade-office-a-nafta-negotiation-wish-list-1015056.

[79] Maria Pallante, Acting Register of Copyrights, Statement on Promoting Investment & Protecting Commerce Online: *Legitimate Sites v. Parasites*, Part I, U.S. House of Representatives, Committee on the Judiciary, Subcommittee on IP, Competition, and the Internet, (March 14, 2011), at 6–7, http:// judiciary.house.gov/_files/hearings/pdf/Pallante03142011.pdf.

[80] Pallante, note 82, at 8.

[81] Annemarie Bridy, ACTA and the specter of graduated response, 26 *American University International Law Review* 559 (2011) at 560, citing Digital Economy Act of 2010, c.24 (U.K.).

[82] Giancarlo Frosio, The death of 'no monitoring obligations': A story of untameable monsters, 8 *Journal of Intellectual Property, Information Technology and E-Commerce Law* 212 (2018), https://papers.ssrn .com/sol3/papers.cfm?abstract_id=2980786.

[83] Frosio, note 85.

[84] Mike Masnick, Judge ignores Congress, pretends SOPA exists, orders site blocking of Sci-Hub, *Techdirt* (November 6, 2017), www.techdirt.com/articles/20171106/17441638557/judge-ignores-congress- pretends-sopa-exists-orders-site-blocking-sci-hub.shtml; U.S. Department of Justice, Sharebeast .com owner pleads guilty to criminal copyright infringement (September 8, 2017), www.justice.gov/ usao-ndga.

and Numbers.[85] Her responses were that copyright infringement is not protected from injunctive relief by the First Amendment, and that "experts" could work out a technical response to threats copyright blocking orders posed to the domain name system.[86]

Relatedly, a coalition of "creative community organizations," running the gamut from capital to labor in the copyright sectors, asked the Obama administration to pressure websites such as YouTube to agree to a series of Principles for User-Generated Content Services.[87] YouTube has a ContentID system which permits it to uniquely identify specific copyrighted works when the holder provides reference data; Viacom and other copyright holders argued that even without such reference data, YouTube and other sites can find infringing files by audio fingerprinting and available software tools.[88]

YouTube video titles often contain the artist name, song title, album and track number of a commercially available CD or LP. The MPAA, Microsoft, and others maintained that YouTube's access to such metadata was adequate for it to develop a policy of proactively taking down user-uploaded videos or audio files, and prohibiting users from reuploading the files.[89] The Obama administration basically agreed on this point.[90] Nevertheless, requiring such proactive filtering does not reflect existing law. In 2010, groups of songwriters and the record labels, representing hundreds of thousands of creators and purchasers of music and music rights, pleaded with the Second Circuit to allow "representative lists" of infringing files to satisfy the DMCA's notice requirement, and to permit any information that may "indicate" infringement to trigger a duty on the part of ISPs to block or filter infringing content.

[85] Pallante, note 82, at 9 (quoting Open Letter from Internet Engineers to the Senate Judiciary Committee (September 28, 2010), www.eff.org/deeplinks/2010/09/open-letter).
[86] Pallante, note 82, at 9–10.
[87] American Federation of Radio and Television Artists et al., Letter to the Honorable Victoria A. Espinel, United States Intellectual Property Enforcement Coordinator, March 24, 2010, at 19, www.whitehouse.gov/sites/default/files/omb/IPEC/frn_comments/CreativeCommunityOrganizations.pdf.
[88] Taylor Bartholomew, The Death of fair use in cyberspace: Youtube and the problem with Content ID, 13 *Duke Law & Technology Review* 66 (2014); Amir Hassanabadi, Red flags of "piracy" online, in Hannibal Travis (Ed.), *Cyberspace Law: Censorship and Regulation of the Internet* (Routledge, 2013) at 117–18, 124, 134–35; Joe Karaganis and Jennifer Urban, The rise of the robo notice, 58 *Communications of the ACM* 28 (2015); Leron Solomon, Fair users or content abusers: The automatic flagging of non-infringing videos by Content ID on Youtube, 44 *Hofstra Law Review* 237 (2015); Hannibal Travis, Who controls the Internet? The Second Circuit on YouTube, in H. Travis (Ed.), *Cyberspace Law* (Routledge, 2013) at 137.
[89] Annemarie Bridy, Graduated response and the turn to private ordering in online copyright enforcement, 89 *Oregon Law Review* 81 (2010) at 124–5; Note also The Principles for User Generated Content Services: A middle-ground approach to cyber-governance, 121 *Harvard Law Review* 1387 (2008); User Generated Content Principles, The Principles for User Generated Content Services: Foster Innovation. Encourage Creativity. Thwart Infringement (2007), www.ugcprinciples.com.
[90] U.S. Department of Commerce, Internet Policy Task Force, Copyright policy, creativity, and innovation in the digital economy (2013), at 102, http://perma.cc/L7RS-YUQY.

The court disagreed, requiring complete lists of files.[91] Other courts have agreed that the Copyright Act does not contain a remedy that goes beyond enjoining infringing conduct, such as an injunction against any use of content or an order seizing a domain name, pretrial or otherwise.[92]

Michael O'Leary, Vice President for Global Policy and External Affairs at the MPAA, implored Congress to "follow the money" infringement earns in expanding copyright liability to intermediaries.[93] As Edwards points out: "It seems obvious to ask that if a [web]site is making a financial or other benefit from the hosting of illegal or infringing content, should it not be at least jointly responsible for that content?"[94]

Warner Music CEO Steve Cooper has argued for a policy denying a copyright defense or "safe harbor" at all to user-submitted online video sites such as YouTube. The statement came in the context of Warner Music receiving disadvantageous profit-sharing terms in a 2017 deal with YouTube.[95] Presumably the thinking is that YouTube has leverage to demand a higher share of profits from music streaming because it does not face a total blockade of major-label music from the service if deals fall through, in that users will upload CD tracks, concert footage, and cover songs.

The House Judiciary Committee is considering the establishment of a voluntary small claims procedure for lower-value infringements.[96] The US Copyright Office has been recommending this for many years, due to the difficulty and cost of bringing low-damages claims in federal court.[97] More than two-thirds of independent record labels report that songs that are taken down are later reposted to the same digital platform, or otherwise reappear on it. Nearly one-third of them give up tracking down infringements due to frustration with such issues.[98] If they could

[91] Brief of Amici Curiae Broadcast Music, Inc., the American Society of Composers, Authors and Publishers, SESAC, Inc., the Society of Composers and Lyricists, the Recording Academy, the Recording Industry Association of America, Inc., the Association of Independent Music Publishers, Songwriters Guild of America, the Nashville Songwriters Association International, Garth Brooks, et al. in Support of Appellants, at 1, 20–22, *YouTube*, (2d Cir. brief filed December 10, 2012), http://a2im.org/downloads/Amicus_Brief.PDF.

[92] E.g. *Righthaven, LLC* v. *Dibiase*, No. 2:10-cv-1343, 2011 WL 5101938 (D. Nev. Mar. 2011) (seizure); *Religious Technology Center* v. *Lerma*, 897 F. Supp. 260, 261–3 (E.D. Va. 1995) (any use).

[93] Michael O'Leary, Senior Executive Vice President, Global Policy and External Affairs, Motion Picture Association of America, Statement on the "Stop Online Piracy Act," 112th Cong., 1st Sess. (November 16, 2011), www.gpo.gov/fdsys/pkg/CHRG-112hhrg71240/html/CHRG-112hhrg71240.htm.

[94] Edwards, note 8, at 67.

[95] Jem Aswad, Warner Music posts double-digit growth in revenue, digital, *Variety*, May 8, 2017, http://variety.com/2017/music/news/warner-music-double-digit-growth-earnings-report-1202411813/.

[96] Jessica Marventano, Senior Vice President, Government Affairs, iHeartMedia, Letter to Hon. Bob Goodlatte and Hon. John Conyers, House Judiciary Committee (Jan. 31, 2017), https://judiciary.house.gov/wp-content/uploads/2017/02/iHeartMedia.pdf.

[97] U.S. Copyright Office, note 78.

[98] Future of Music Coalition, New survey documents independent labels' experience with notice & takedown (April 11, 2017), https://futureofmusic.org/filing/new-survey-documents-independent-labels-experience-notice-takedown.

represent themselves against infringers, large or small, they might stand a better chance of making each release of an album, single, or remix profitable. Large infringers may prove more difficult to sue, because the Office and any congressional action on small claims are likely to give savvy defendants the right to opt out of the small claims and into federal court.[99]

6.6. THE LAW AND ECONOMICS OF INTERNET CONTENT FILTERING

Copyright theory in the Chicago School tradition is supportive of Internet copyright filtering as an efficient public–private partnership to solve a costly legal problem by calibrating incentives, liabilities, and information-sharing. The Chicago School theory of indirect or secondary liability in copyright involves a somewhat ad hoc balancing of static costs and benefits generated by imposing copyright liability not only on the direct infringer, such as a user of a photocopier or file-sharing program, but also on the distributor of the copier or the program, which may have legitimate uses. If the savings to copyright owners outweigh the costs to the secondarily liable parties, the courts should impose the secondary liability, the theory seems to assume.[100]

The Chicago School theory of ISP liability and other forms of indirect liability in copyright should not persuade legislators or courts, in my view, for several reasons. For one thing, there is no practical way of balancing the benefits and costs of ISP liability.[101] Yet these costs are enormous. Due to copyright damages not being precisely measured in proportion to actual damages, as in patent law, the notional secondary liability of ISPs for copyright infringement could reach into the trillions of dollars.[102] Moreover, the attorney's fees in successful cases are high.[103] Such attorney's fees may be justifiable as protecting the value of copyright licensing deals from direct

---

[99] Copyright Alternative in Small-Claims Enforcement (CASE) Act, § 1405(g), H.R. 5757, 114th Cong., 2d Sess. (2016).

[100] Douglas Lichtman and William Landes, Indirect liability for copyright infringement: An economic perspective, 16 *Harvard Journal of Law & Technology* 395 (2003) at 397–398, 410; see also Doug Lichtman and Eric Posner, *Holding Internet service providers accountable*, University of Chicago John M. Olin Law & Economics Working Paper No. 217 (July 2004), at 5, 14, 22–26. One of the co-authors of these articles also takes a moral stand against the evil implied by willful blindness to copyright infringement. Douglas Lichtman, The case against YouTube, *Los Angeles Times*, (March 20, 2007), http://papers.ssrn.com/sol3/Delivery.cfm?abstractid=1472198.

[101] Glynn Lunney, Reexamining copyright's incentives-access paradigm, 49 *Vanderbilt Law Review* 483, (1996) at 486, citing, inter alia, William Landes and Richard Posner, An economic analysis of copyright law, 18 *Journal of Legal Studies* 325 (1989). See also H.R. Rep. No. 602222, 60th Cong., 2d Sess. 7 (1909).

[102] Brief of Amicus Curiae Consumer Electronics Association in Support of Appellees and Affirmance, at 4, 23–24, *Viacom* (2d Cir. brief filed April 4, 2011).

[103] *BMG Rights Management (US) LLC* v. *Cox Communications, Inc.*, Civil No. 1: 14-cv-1611 (E.D. Va. February 14, 2017), https://scholar.google.com/scholar_case?case=15797577648169022214 ($10 million); *Lotus Development Corp.* v. *Borland International, Inc.*, 140 F.3d 70, 72 (1st Cir. 1998) ($11 million); MATTEL INC: Hearing on appeal from damages award set for Dec. 10, Class Action Reporter, Nov. 8, 2012, http://bankrupt.com/CAR_Public/121108.mbx ($140 million); UMG's

infringement; it is doubtful that the burden of such fees is justifiable from the standpoint of those secondarily liable for providing the facilities with which copies can be made, such as the photocopier, the hard drive, the cable or telephone wires that connect computers, or the software services that provide interfaces for file transfers over wired or wireless networks.

In addition to difficulties balancing costs and benefits in the case of indirect copyright liability, there are other impediments to concluding that it is a more efficient rule than a rule remedying only the voluntary, direct infringement of a copyright. When, as typically happens, ISPs reap only a portion of fair use works' pecuniary and professional rewards, they will lack the incentive to preserve valuable fair use works to the same extent as their original authors.[104] Secondary liability threatens billions of dollars in damages to technology companies due to "unforeseen" user activities.[105] Therefore, ISPs may delete more lawful works than is socially optimal due to "overdeterrence."[106] Some ISPs will be deterred into leaving the market altogether, or disabling new technologies pending industry-wide deals.[107]

When it is more difficult to hold intermediaries secondarily liable, copyright law will discourage fewer innovative technologies and services from coming to market.[108] ISPs have argued for many years that it is not practical to review the trillions of bits that make up the Internet for compliance with the minutiae of copyright law.[109]

This overdeterrence and excessive censorship will be bad for cultural production. The theory of "efficient infringement" suggests that perfectly filtering out infringing works may not be the best way to promote creativity or creative output. Some degree of unauthorized use of copyrighted work is important as an input for new works, for personal noncommercial use, or for related purposes.[110] The analogy to other business decisions is obvious: if breaking a contract or making a false claim that a

---

Opposition to Veoh's Motion for Attorney's Fees and Costs, at i, 21–23, *UMG Recordings, Inc. v. Veoh Networks, Inc.*, No. CV-07-05744 AHM (C.D. Cal. brief filed Dec. 7, 2009) ($4 million).

[104] Neil Netanel, Impose a noncommercial use levy to allow free peer-to-peer file sharing, 17 *Harvard Journal of Law & Technology* 1 (2003) at 13. See also Lichtman and Posner, note 103, at 6 (criticizing this argument because it simply identifies a positive externality of Internet use).

[105] Brief of National Venture Capital Association as Amicus Curiae in Support of Respondents, at 17, *Grokster* (U.S. brief filed March 1, 2005).

[106] Assaf Hamdani, Who's liable for cyberwrongs?, 87 *Cornell Law Review* 901 (2002) at 918.

[107] Brief for Human Rights Watch et al. as Amicus Curiae in Support of Appellees, at 20, *Viacom* (2d Cir. brief filed April 7, 2011).

[108] *Grokster*, 545 U.S. at 957 (Breyer, J., Stevens., J., and O'Connor, J., concurring).

[109] Pamela Samuelson and John Browning, Confab clips copyright cartel, *Wired*, Mar. 1997, at 61, 63; Hannibal Travis, Pirates of the information infrastructure: Blackstonian copyright and the First Amendment, 15 *Berkeley Technology Law Journal* 777 (2000), at 833–5, 851. Technically, since 2012 Internet traffic has been measurable in the sextillions of bytes, or in the trillions of bytes multiplied by a billion. E.g. Jiajia Chen, Gong Yu, Matteo Fiorani, and Slavisa Aleksic, Optical interconnects at the top of the rack for energy-efficient data centers, 53 *IEEE Communications Magazine* 140 (2015).

[110] David Fagundes, Efficient copyright infringement, 98 *Iowa Law Review* 1791 (2013); Julian Azran, How *Cariou v. Prince* will revitalize sampling, 38 *Columbia Journal of Law and the Arts* 69 (2014) at 78–81.

product is great could lead to an enormously disproportionate fine or the zapping out of existence of part of a company, potentially valuable launches of new products of services would be halted.

Excessive ISP liability and other threats to fair use undermine the very foundations of the Chicago School theory of law, namely that courts and legislatures should promote wealth while leaving its redistribution to the tax and welfare systems.[111] As set forth above, imitation and quotation of the writings of others are part of free speech.[112] Once Internet copyright filtering chills and censors the portion of democratic discourse that has shifted online, the process of advocating changes to tax and the transfer system will be distorted.[113] The invasions of privacy involved when ISPs log Internet activity and open up the logs to copyright holders and government agencies further undermine the anonymity and uninhibitedness of democratic discourse.[114] Thus, secondary liability in copyright poses uniquely grave problems for economic analysis as compared with secondary liability in patent, which mostly does not concern "speech."

Class conflict is perhaps a more viable descriptive theory of why ISPs have been declared liable for their users' activities on many occasions since the late 1990s. In 1998, the European music label federation sought to impose liability on Internet companies that "should have been aware" that their customers were violating copyright. Its strategy was to give greater immunity to the powerful European telecommunications companies, so that they did not counter the music lobby's efforts to impose a strict Copyright Directive on everyone else, especially the non-European companies, e.g. the "American service provider[s]."[115] *Billboard* observed that the music "industry's contacts will be central to securing its interests in the Copyright Directive," which limited the quotation or remix of a work, even when it does not interfere with the normal licensing income or otherwise harm the original authors of the work. The federation promised to lobby using these "contacts" to change the directive to make it "tough."[116] Similarly, in the United States, the evolution of secondary liability has reflected the balance of forces between the telecommunications

---

[111] Cf. Daniel Benoliel, Copyright distributive injustice, 10 *Yale Journal of Law and Technology* 45 (2007), draft, at 15–16, http://papers.ssrn.com/sol3/papers.cfm?abstract_id=925132, citing, inter alia, Richard Posner, *Economic Analysis of Law* (Little Brown and Co., 2nd ed. 1977) at 10. See also p. 7–8 (collecting other sources).

[112] To paraphrase Justice Oliver Wendell Holmes, referring to use of the U.S. Postal Service, imitation is as much a part of speech "as the right to use our tongues." *Milwaukee Social Democratic Publishing Co. v. Burleson*, 255 U.S. 407, 437 (1921) (Holmes, J., dissenting).

[113] Cf. Brief for Human Rights Watch, note 110.

[114] Alberto Silva, Enforcing intellectual property rights by diminishing privacy: How the Anti-counterfeiting Trade Agreement jeopardizes the right to privacy, 26 *American University International Law Review* 601 (2011) at 622–625, 641.

[115] Jeff-Clark Meads, EU tackles copyright liability for online providers, telecoms, *Billboard*, (December 5, 1998), 117.

[116] Emmanuel Legrand, Copyright Directive to face "new" commission, *Billboard*, (July 31, 1999), 7.

and information industries on the one hand, and the publishing and entertainment industries on the other hand, including parts of the software industry.[117] Today, the hope is that newspapers or record labels will be able to micromanage other peoples' businesses, creating the sorts of barriers to access that protect conglomerates.[118]

Class-conscious accounts also provide reasons to oppose greater ISP liability, although it and other expansions of copyright may serve the interests of some authors and distributors who profit immensely from income streams threatened by the Internet. The populations of consumers and producers who benefit from copyright infringement are probably much larger than the populations of consumers and producers who are harmed by it. If the productive forces of creative people are restrained by copyright assertions, as studies on appropriation art and transformative works often conclude, then the heavy hand of expansive ISP liability may only make matters worse. Moreover, the users of copyrighted work will be, in many instances, less wealthy than those whose works they use, for example when an aspiring DJ or hip-hop artist samples a famous rock band. This means that the users will attach a higher utility to each incoming dollar than the owners of the IP that they want to use, so that a transfer would diminish aggregate well-being.

6.7. HOW MANY JOBS HAS THE INTERNET KILLED?

The critique of Internet capitalism seeks to halt the "disruption" practiced by Google against books and DVDs (and music), Facebook and Google against newspapers, Amazon against shopping malls and "Main Streets," Uber against taxis and car dealers, Airbnb against hotels and landlords, etc.[119] Creators' unions and guilds

---

[117] Samuelson and Browning, note 112, at 61, 63; Travis, note 112, at 834–5. See also *The Digital Millennium Copyright Act: Text, History, and Caselaw* (Pike & Fischer Inc., 2003) at 345 (President Clinton's statement on DMCA stated it was intended to protect copyright industries); also p. 10, 20 (Senate Report made similar observation, emphasizing importance of industries and Senate's aim of preserving "incentives" by ISPs to "cooperate" with copyright industries to "deal with … infringements").

[118] E.g. Taplin, note 68, at 272 (proposing windows for music that would restrict YouTube, for example, from streaming music until four weeks Timothy Vollmer, MEP Voss doubles down on worst elements of Article 11, Communia Association (Mar. 29, 2018), www.communia-association.org/2018/03/29/mep-voss-doubles-worst-elements-article-11/ (arguing that Article 11 of the proposed Copyright in the Digital Single Market directive may enable some journalistic organizations to claim copyright in "compilations of basic [factual headline] information"). Compare *Redbox Automated Retail LLC* v. *Universal City Studios LLP*, No. 08-766, 2009 WL 2588748 (D. Del. Aug. 17, 2009); Danny King, Court OKs Redbox suit against Universal, *Variety*, (August 9, 2009), http://variety.com/2009/biz/features/court-oks-redbox-suit-against-universal-1118007409/ (federal court in Delaware refused to dismiss claim that one movie studio threatened the freedom of commerce by imposing a "vending rental window" 45 days after DVD release).

[119] E.g. Joel Kotkin, How a few monster tech firms are taking over everything from media to space travel and what it means for the rest of us, *Daily Beast* (February 9, 2014), www.thedailybeast.com/articles/2014/02/09/how-a-few-monster-tech-firms-are-taking-over-everything-from-media-to-space-travel-and-what-it-means-for-the-rest-of-us.html; Legitimate Sites vs. Parasites: Hearing on Promoting

contended that YouTube was likely to contribute to declines in DVD sales, materially reducing the residuals to directors and performers that pay for pensions, retiree health care, and the like.[120]

Publishers, similarly, contend that software and Internet companies profit from actions that cause their sales to decline.[121] Advocates for the newspaper industry may seek an antitrust exemption to "unionize" in talks with Google or Facebook. Forming a sort of cartel, but blessed by law like a union of workers being exploited by capitalists, newspapers could then collectively bargain for better terms. Such terms might include more IP rights in the news, a greater share of digital subscription revenue sold through Facebook or Google Play, and better placement of content behind paywalls in feeds and search results.[122] Other cartel-like systems could emerge to control digital books, and online videos that quote other videos.[123] Analogous lobbying efforts at the federal level resulted in radio being commercialized, with denials of access to labor, the left, pacifists, and nonprofits.[124]

Investment and Protecting Commerce Online, Subcommittee on Intellectual Property, Competition, and Protecting Commerce, Committee on the Judiciary, U.S. House of Representatives, 112th Cong. (Statement of Maria Pallante, Register of Copyrights) (Government Printing Office, 2011) at 16; Levine, note 10at 115–116, 175–7; Levine, note 39; Taplin, note 68, at 21, 89–3, 102–6, 204; Hannibal Travis, Estimating the economic impact of mass digitization projects on copyright holders: Evidence from the Google Book Search litigation, 57 *Journal of the Copyright Society of the U.S.A.* 907 (2010) at 907, 921–922; Danny Yadron, World Bank: Silicon Valley tech firms are making inequality worse, *The Guardian (U.K.)/Business Insider* (January 16, 2016), www.businessinsider.com/world-bank-silicon-valley-exacerbates-inequality-2016-1.

[120] Brief of Amici Curiae AFM, AFTRA, DGA, IATSE, SAG, and Teamsters, at 15, *Viacom*, 676 F.3d 19.

[121] Paola Dubini, Francesco Saviozzi, and Maurizio Borghi, Liaisons dangereuses between legal and illegal industries in content consumption: The bridging role of information brokers, Paper presented to SERCIAC Conference (2007) at 6, www.gbz.hu-berlin.de/downloads/pdf/SERCIACPapers/Saviozzi.pdf.

[122] News Media Alliance, News Media Alliance calls for legislation to address impact of digital duopoly on news organizations (July 14, 2017), www.newsmediaalliance.org/release-digital-duopoly/; Jim Rutenberg, News outlets to seek bargaining rights against Google and Facebook, *The New York Times*, (July 11, 2017), www.nytimes.com/2017/07/09/business/media/google-facebook-news-media-alliance .html. The guild or union of newspapers would bargain for "stronger [IP] protections, better support for subscription models and a fair share of revenue and data," but they already have IP rights in full articles, so perhaps IP rights is sought for facts as opposed to expression of the facts. David Chavern, How antitrust undermines press freedom, *The Wall Street Journal*, (July 11, 2017), www.wsj.com/articles/how-antitrust-undermines-press-freedom-1499638532. Facebook and Google already support "subscription models," so other than revenue sharing, what may be at issue is better placement in search or feed results of conduct protected by a subscription paywall.

[123] Hannibal Travis, Free Speech Institutions and Fair Use of Copyrighted Work: A New Agenda for Copyright Reform, 33 *Cardozo Arts & Entertainment Law Journal*, 2, (2016), at 696–711, 717–19; *United States v. Apple Inc.*, 952 F. Supp. 2d 638, 691–94 (S.D.N.Y. 2013). See also PricewaterhouseCoopers LLP, Report of Independent Auditors [Movielink, LLC] (January 31, 2007), www.pwc.com/sg/en/illustrative-annual-report-2011/assets/9-IndependentAuditorReport.pdf.

[124] E.g. Jeff Cohen, Mainstream news coverage of economics, *Fairness and Accuracy in Reporting* (March 1, 2000), www.fair.org/index.php?page=254 (representatives of labor allowed on U.S. broadcast airwaves much less often than those of capital); One of ninety!, 9 *Life and Labor Bulletin* 1 (May 1931) (labor unions received one radio license out of 90 given to companies under Radio Act of 1927).

For Taplin, Facebook and Google have seized control of Americans' content consumption, "'eating'" journalism and record labels, in the words of venture capitalist, Netscape founder, and Facebook board member Marc Andreesen.[125] Nevertheless, Taplin undermines his own narrative by noting that *The Huffington Post* receives more than 20 million page views daily as a result of Facebook traffic.[126] To many Americans, a choice from among hyperlinks to thousands of news sources around the world in feeds and search boxes that are fairly easily to navigate may not feel like undue control over their reading.[127] As Taplin notes, *The Huffington Post* itself is an aggregator of news and opinion from many civic and journalistic organizations, such as Amnesty International or Pro Publica.[128]

Disruption has almost certainly been good for consumer choice, and for many content producers' profits. A newsstand or a news distributor to homes offered fewer choices in the past. To say that a great deal of traffic is fed by Facebook or Google to some online news and opinion websites, or that most Americans read articles linked to or posted on these platforms, means to Taplin that their choices have been reduced and that Facebook (Google here falls away) may soon dominate the news.[129] Not breaking down how many sources are included in Facebook or Google, or what the largest sources' market share is, is a little simplistic.[130] Moreover, downplaying in this context other options and their share of Web pageviews – such as Apple, Yahoo! news, Amazon Kindle magazines, or even torrent sites – makes the whole exercise questionable.[131] Was there more choice when most people subscribed to one newspaper and a few magazines, or when they were fed a few dozen news sites via portals such as AOL or MSN?

The explosion during the Bush and Obama administrations of news and opinion sites from left, right, and center suggests that the dominance of a few Big Media firms in the 1990s was tempered or broken. It is significant that sources such as *Buzzfeed* or *Vice* reach users of many different platforms, earning millions in profit and perhaps billions in capital gains. *The Huffington Post* might have sold in 2015

[125] Taplin, note 68, at 6–7. See also Todd Wasserman, The revolution wasn't televised: The early days of YouTube, *Mashable* (February 14, 2015), http://mashable.com/2015/02/14/youtube-history/.
[126] Taplin, note 68, at 163–4.
[127] E.g. Google News, *Wikipedia* (2017), http://en.wikipedia.org/wiki/Google_News.
[128] E.g. Amnesty International, *HuffPost* (2017), www.huffingtonpost.com/ topic/amnesty-international; Pro Publica, *HuffPost* (2017), www.huffingtonpost.com/topic/ProPublica?page=2.
[129] Taplin, note 68, at 93, 164–70.
[130] As of 2014, there was a robust Internet presence for five major US broadcast networks, three major US cable television news networks, one major UK broadcast network, four giant US newspapers, many non-US newspapers, several US magazines and television comedy or opinion shows, and eight primarily digital news sources. E.g. Pew Research Center, Political polarization and media habits (October 21, 2014), www.journalism.org2014/10/21/appendix-b-the-news-sources.
[131] E.g. comScore Video Metrix, Top U.S. online video content properties ranked by unique video viewers (February 2015); Melanie Hicken, Yahoo beats Google in traffic for the first time since 2011, *CNN Money* (August 21, 2013), http://money.cnn.com/2013/08/21/technology/yahoo-traffic-google/index.html.

for as much as $1 billion, if one of two reported offers submitted to its controlling entity AOL had been accepted.[132] Buzzfeed raised $200 million at a valuation of $1.5 billion in 2015.[133] The co-founder and CEO of Vice Media, Shane Smith, performed an even more impressive feat, becoming a billionaire on paper in 2017 as his company neared a $6 billion valuation, capping an expansion from a few magazines to a global news and entertainment giant.[134] All of this occurred after Google, Amazon, and Facebook had been accused of having monopoly market shares, built in part on the content of third parties such as magazine publishers.

The software industry today provides much of the entertainment value that books once did: stories, nonfiction works, sports statistics, guidebooks, and education or training. Authors, writers, and editors reportedly hold 145,000 fewer jobs than in 2008, but software applications writers and engineers hold 300,000 more jobs than back then.[135] The revenue and payroll of publishers of printed works or software increased strongly from 2002 to 2015, adjusted for inflation, even though the number of such publishers was down, as was the number of their employees, indicating that more people may be creating more works at fewer companies with larger or at least better-paid staffs. When it comes to the production of music, movies, and television, both the number of establishments in these industries and their collective payrolls have increased in the social media age. In fact, the payroll in these areas has risen by 10 percent, adjusted for inflation, and the number of jobs has risen by more than 50 percent, from 278,000 to 431,500.[136]

Despite the growing prominence of software and cable television, book sales have more than doubled since the early 1990s when far fewer people had computers, used the Internet, or subscribed to cable.[137] The number of titles published annually

---

[132] Paul Harris, Arianna Huffington's AOL deal sparks accusations of a political sell-out, *The Guardian*, (February 26, 2011), www.theguardian.com/media/2011/feb/27/arianna-huffington-post-aol-deal; David Segal, *Arianna Huffington's improbable, insatiable content machine*, *The New York Times*, (July 5, 2015), www.nytimes.com/2015/07/05/magazine/arianna-huffingtons-improbable-insatiable-content-machine.html.

[133] BuzzFeed buzzkill: Its stunning revenue miss goes viral, *CNN Money* (April 12, 2016), money.cnn .com/2016/04/12/media/buzzfeed-missed-projections/index.html.

[134] Natalie Robehmed, Vice Media's Shane Smith is now a billionaire, *Forbes* (June 20, 2017), www .forbes.com/sites/natalierobehmed/2017/06/20/vice-medias-shane-smith-is-now-a-billionaire.

[135] U.S. Bureau of Labor Statistics, *Occupational Outlook Handbook*, 2010–11 (Government Printing Office, 2012) at 336; Bureau of Labor Statistics, Software developers, applications (2017), www.bls .gov/oes/current/oes151132.htm; U.S. Bureau of Labor Statistics, Writers and authors, (2017), www .bls.gov/ooh/media-and-communication/writers-and-authors.htm; Jack Plunkett (Ed.), *Plunkett's Engineering & Research Industry Almanac 2006* (Plunkett Research, 2006), https://books.google.com/ books?id=ocNFM8TktVwC&pg=PT66

[136] U.S. Department of the Census, 2015 county business patterns, www.census.gov/programs-surveys/ susb/ and www.census.gov/programs-surveys/cbp/data/tables.html; U.S. Department of the Census, Statistical abstract of the United States 2005; www.census.gov/prod/2005pubs/06statab/infocomm .pdf.

[137] Hannibal Travis, Myths of the Internet as the Death of Old Media, 43 *American Intellectual Property Law Association Quarterly Journal* 1 (2015) at 13, 15.

more than tripled in the years leading up to 2012.[138] Sales of ebooks rose particularly rapidly, from 10 million in 2008 to 114 million in 2010 and 513 million in 2013; these figures are the number of ebooks, not the dollars generated.[139] Over some recent stretches of time, book sales have been flat, however, with adult titles lagging compared to children's books.[140]

In other words, more books are being sold for more money. However, fewer people are writing books professionally than at their peak level in 2002–2004, which incidentally was well before book sales peaked. Many Americans are writing for less money than they need to survive as authors. The head of the Authors Guild, former US Register of Copyrights Mary Rasenberger, claimed that Google Books contributed to US authors being "among the most poorly paid workers in America."[141] Yet there is good reason to question this conclusion as well: it may be based on a survey of fewer than 2,000 struggling authors, unhappy with their lot, seeking to organize into a form of labor union, namely the very Authors Guild that commissioned the survey.[142] Even if it does represent authors as a whole, this figure may reflect not so much availability on Google Books (from which publishers could opt out), but other competitive factors.[143] A more recent survey based on US Census data suggested that writers and authors who are actually employed in the field earn 10 percent more than the median salary or wage for Americans.[144] Many college professors with light teaching duties earn even more, based largely on their track record when it comes to writing and publishing.

Music is a much more troubling story than book publishing, with both jobs and sales down considerably. Shipments of recorded music and employment of musicians may have declined in self-reported terms by anywhere from 8 percent to 40 percent from 1999 through 2011.[145] Pre-recorded music and other audio sales went

[138] FLOOR64, The sky is rising 2014, at 16, www.ccianet.org/wp-content/uploads/2014/10/Sky-Is-Rising-2014.pdf.
[139] Julie Bosman, Publishing gives hints of revival, data show, *The New York Times*, (August 9, 2011), www.nytimes.com/2011/08/09/books/survey-shows-publishing-expanded-since-2008.html; Laura Owen, U.S. publishers' revenue from ebooks roughly flat in 2013, *but unit sales rose: Chart, Gigaom* (June 26, 2014), https://gigaom.com/2014/06/26/the-size-of-the-u-s-ebook-market-in-2013-chart/; Ahmad Takatkah, Blinkreads presentation, SlideShare (August 5, 2014), www.slideshare.net/ahmadtakatkah/blinkreads-presentation.
[140] E.g. Taplin, note 68, at 7.
[141] Carl Straumsheim, Supreme Court declines to hear Google Books case, *Inside Higher Ed*, (April 19, 2016), www.insidehighered.com/quicktakes/2016/04/19/supreme-court-declines-hear-google-books-case.
[142] The Authors Guild, The wages of writing: Key findings from the Authors Guild 2015 member survey (2015), at 5, 9, www.authorsguild.org/industry-advocacy/the-wages-of-writing/.
[143] Travis, note 122, at 8–89, 102–3.
[144] Gabe Habash, NEA studies writers statistics, *Publishers Weekly*, (November 4, 2011), www.publishersweekly.com/pw/by-topic/industry-news/trade-shows-events/article/49400-nea-studies-writers-statistics.html.
[145] Matthew Lasar, Have we lost 41 percent of our musicians? Depends on how you (the RIAA) count, *Ars Technica*, (October 7, 2012), http://arstechnica.com/tech-policy/2012/10/have-we-lost-41-percent-of-our-musicians-depends-on-how-you-the-riaa-count/; Travis, note 140, at 16–22, 27.

up more than $6 billion from 1991 to 1999, but fell $8 billion from 1999 to 2008, and another $3 billion from 2008 to 2015, for a total decline of $11 billion since 1999, not adjusted for inflation.[146] At the same time, music sales by unit regardless of format increased fewer than 800 million in 2001 to 1 billion in 2005 to 1.65 billion in 2012;[147] notably, these figures may ignore revenue earned by independent artists and labels.[148] Subscription and ad-supported streaming revenue surged, increasing by $1 billion between 2014 and 2015.[149]

Music sales in dollar terms may be down partly due to more efficient distribution methods. Digital downloads and streams do not require CD pressing plants, trucks full of CD or cassette boxes, retail shelves and cashiers to handle the product, or consumers to buy tracks they do not want.[150] The major music distributors may earn more profit than they did in the CD era, due probably to lower costs; the three labels that dominate more than two-thirds of the market had an operating profit of $1.1 billion in 2013, compared with only $695 million in 2004.[151] Assuming that the labels are valued at 16 times their forward earnings, as they would be on average in an efficient market, they anticipated (as of 2008–2012) to earn profits of more than $14 billion between 2013 and 2022.[152]

Overall entertainment industry sales and employment have increased much more rapidly than the general economy.[153] Total US home entertainment expenditures

[146] Shaun Nichols, Streaming now outsells downloads – Recording Industry Association of America, *The Register* (March 23, 2016), www.theregister.co.uk/2016/03/23/ riaa_streaming_music_outsold_downloads/; Recording Industry Association of America, 2000 Year-end shipment statistics (2001), https://web.archive.org/web/20090124040008/ and http://76.74.24.142:80/9C601D59-D955-CE22-6CC0-CF61CC8A829D.pdf; Recording Industry Association of America, 2008 Year-end shipment statistics (2009), https://web.archive.org/web/20090520234051/ and http://76.74.24.142:80/ 1D212C0E-408B-F730-65A0-C0F5871C369D.pdf. See also U.S. Copyright Office, Music Licensing Study (2015), at 72, https://web.archive.org/web/20150905081048/ and http://copyright.gov/policy/musiclicensingstudy/copyright-and-the-music-marketplace.pdf.

[147] Tim Arango, Digital shift dominates music sales, *New York Post*, (January 5, 2006), http://nypost .com/2006/01/05/digital-shift-dominates-2005-music-sales/; Chris Martins, America bought more music than ever in 2012, winners include vinyl and Adele, *Spin*, (January 4, 2013), www.spin.com/articles/music-sales-2012-adele-vinyl-taylor-swift-psy/; Steve Traiman, DVD saves the day, *Billboard*, (March 16, 2002), at 82.

[148] Michael Masnick and Michael Ho, *The sky is rising: A detailed look at the state of the entertainment industry* (2013), at 24, www.techdirt.com/skyisrising.

[149] Nichols, note 149.

[150] Chris Anderson, *The Long Tail: Why the Future of Business Is Selling Less of More* (Hyperion, 2006) at 89–97; Anita Elberse, Bye bye bundles: The unbundling of music in digital channels, 74 *Journal of Marketing* 107 (2010).

[151] E.g. Jonathan Band and Jonathan Gerafi, Still profitable after all these years, *Policy Bandwidth* (April 14, 2014), at 1.

[152] Band and Gerafi, note 154, at 3–4; see also Peter Ricchiuti, *Stocks Under Rocks: How to Uncover Overlooked, Profitable Market Opportunities* (Pearson, 2014) at 113.

[153] Stephen Siwek. *Copyright industries in the U.S. economy: The 2014 report*, Economist Inc./ International Intellectual Property Association (IIPA) (2014); Stephen Siwek, Copyright industries in the economy: The 2003–2007 report, Economists Incorporated/IIPA (2009), http://ei.com/wp-content/uploads/downloadables/IIPASiwekReport2003-07.pdf.

exceeded $18 billion in 2016, not counting video games or many Internet subscriptions, but including digital video on demand.[154] DVD and Blu-ray disc sales and rentals were more than $11.5 billion in 2013, up from $1.5 billion in 1999 (adjusted for inflation), while video downloading and streaming transactions reached a level of $6.5 billion in 2013 from virtually nil in 1999.[155] Films and TV programs on Blu-ray disc saw sales increase at an annual rate of eight percent in 2016. Video game software sales were $16.5 billion in 2015, up from about $3 billion in 1993 (adjusted for inflation).[156] Economic activity in the software industry rose by about $220 billion between 2000 and 2014.[157]

It is true that since 2006, a time when Facebook, YouTube, and Netflix had far fewer users, total video spending for home consumption is down more than $3 billion in nominal dollars, and down more than $6 billion once adjusted for inflation.[158] DVD and VHS retail transactions in 2002, adjusted for inflation, would have been worth nearly $30 billion in 2016.[159] However, given the lower costs of distributing books and video through Apple, Amazon, Comcast, Verizon, Google, or Netflix, and audio through Spotify, etc., the media conglomerates that sell DVDs have increased their profits and their market capitalizations by tens of billions of dollars, collectively (see Table 6.1).

Thus, home entertainment as an industry is not in a crisis state due to the Internet, although compact discs and DVDs may have benefited from a bubble in sales. The period of 1993–2008 saw extended periods of low unemployment, rising incomes, exploding asset prices, and growing US exports, driven in part by bubbles in technology and FIRE (financial, insurance, and real-estate) stocks

[154] Digital Entertainment Group, DEG 2016 year end home entertainment report (2017), www.degonline.org/portfolio_page/deg-year-end-2016-home-entertainment-report; Ryan Faughnder, Home video sales shrank again in 2016 as Americans switched to streaming, *Los Angeles Times*, (January 6, 2017), www.latimes.com/business/hollywood/la-fi-ct-home-video-decline-20170106-story.html.

[155] *US home entertainment market grows modestly for 2nd year; Disc sales resilient*, DVD and Beyond (2014), www.dvd-and-beyond.com/display-article.php?article=2018. Overall, home video entertainment rentals and sales were more similar, rising from $18 to $21 billion in 1999–2013. Split screens, *The Economist*, (February 23, 2016), www.economist.com/news/business/21572218-tale-two-tinseltowns-split-screens.

[156] Chris Morris, Level up! Video game industry revenues soar in 2015, *Fortune*, (February 16, 2016), http://fortune.com/2016/02/16/video-game-industry-revenues-2015/; Jeroen Binken, *System Markets, Indirect Network Effects in Action or Inaction?* (Erasmus Research Institute in Management, 2010) at 65.

[157] Robert Shapiro, The U.S. software industry: An engine for economic growth and employment, *SIAA and Sonecon* (2014), www.siia.net/Admin/FileManagement.aspx/LinkClick.aspx?fileticket=ffCbUo5PyEM%3D.

[158] Colin Dixon, 4K discs arrive, fail to stem disc sales losses in 2016, *nScreenMedia* (January 9, 2017), www.nscreenmedia.com/us-home-entertainment-spending-q4-2016/.

[159] August Grant and Jennifer Meadows, *Communication Technology Update* (Focal Press, 9th ed, 2004) at 34. Cf. Markets, *Screen Digest*, (January 2005), at 26. Note that $1 in 2004 would have been worth $1.27 in 2016.

TABLE 6.1. Profitability of media conglomerates, 2004–2014

	Operating income		Market capitalization	
	2004	2014	2005	2014
Time Warner	4.9	6.0	49	67
Disney/ABC	4.5	13.0	43	197
Fox/News Corp.	2.9	2.7	49	77
Viacom/CBS	2.3	4.1	54	51
Total	**14.6**	**25.8**	**195**	**392**
Per 1 Trillion GDP	1	2	15	23

Sources: Disney 2004 Annual Report; Disney Form 10-K Annual Report 2014; CSIMarket, Time Warner Inc. (2017), https://csimarket.com/stocks/income.php?code=TWX&annualuu; CSIMarket, Viacom Inc. (2017), https://csimarket.com/stocks/income.php?code=VIA&annual; Macrotrends.net (enter ticker symbol for DIS, NWS, TWX, and VIAB); News Corp. Form 10-K Annual Report 2005; Time Warner Inc., Time Warner Inc. Reports Results for 2005 Full Year and Fourth Quarter 2005, Business Wire (February 1, 2006), http://www.businesswire.com/news/home/20060201005432/ Time-Warner-Reports-Results-2005-Full-Year; Twenty-First Century Fox Inc. Form 10-K Annual Report 2015; Tom Von Alten, Top 100 companies by market capitalization, Fort Boise (July 31, 2005), http://fortboise.org/top100/top100-20050731.html.

that popped, respectively, in 2000–2001 and 2008–2009. For example, sales of new homes stood at about half their 1999 level from 2009 to 2013.[160] Contrary to Internet doomsayers' instincts, the home video market has more than doubled, adjusted for inflation, since the 1980s.[161] This means that sales were up long after the Internet was widely available to Americans.

[160] National Association of Home Builders, New-home sales are half-way back to normal (May 23, 2014), https://nahbnow.com/2014/05/new-home-sales-are-half-way-back-to-normal/.
[161] Eli Noam, *Media Ownership and Concentration in America* (Oxford University Press, 2009) at 118.

7

Why We Cannot Build Universal Digital Libraries

7.1. FROM SUMER TO STANFORD[1]

A universal digital public library would bring to fruition thousands of years of academic and archival labor. Ancient libraries dating back to the third millennium BCE recorded the religious and philosophical expressions of societies such as Egypt and Sumer.[2] Culminating in the 1,500-volume library of Assyria at Nineveh, these libraries recorded not only myths and legends but also the early history of education, commerce, law, and the sciences.[3] After the Enlightenment, the ideal of libraries that were open to anyone emerged with the concept of public libraries.[4]

Despite the promise of digitization and the Internet, the most sophisticated libraries remain closed to most people. Most people do not have library cards.[5] Especially in the medical and legal fields, access to the best secondary literature on important topics is not available to persons who are not able or willing to pay high per-article prices or join an institution that has some form of subscription-based access.[6]

---

[1] Portions of this chapter are based on Hannibal Travis, Estimating the economic impact of mass digitization projects on copyright holders: Evidence from the Google Book Search litigation, 57 *Journal of the Copyright Society of the U.S.A.* 907 (2010).

[2] Fayza Haikal, Private collections and temple libraries in ancient Egypt, *in* Mostafa el-Abbadi and Omnia Mounir Fathallah (Eds.), *What Happened to the Ancient Library of Alexandria?* (Brill, 2008) at 39–54; Samuel Noah Kramer, *History Begins at Sumer* (Thames & Hudson, 1956) at 289–300.

[3] Jane McIntosh, *Ancient Mesopotamia: New Perspectives* (ABC-CLIO, 2005) at 288–9.

[4] Michael Harris, *History of Libraries in the Western World* (Scarecrow Press, 4th ed. 1995) at 243; Ruth Rikowski, The corporate takeover of libraries, 14 *Information for Social Change* (2001/2002), www.libr.org/ISC/articles/14-Ruth_Rikowski.html.

[5] Hannibal Travis, Building universal digital libraries: An agenda for copyright reform, 33 *Pepperdine Law Review* 761 (2006) at 761–3.

[6] Hope Viner Samborn, In the land of the free: West's purchase of cult favorite Findlaw keeps pace with rival Lexis in bid to coax users onto paid sites, 87 *American Bar Association Journal*, April 2001, at 76; Jonathan Tennant et al., The academic, economic and societal impacts of Open Access: An evidence-based review, 5 *F1000Research* 632 (2016), http://europepmc.org/articles/pmc4837983; Travis, note 5, at 772–4.

Although for-profit digital libraries emerged in the 1990s and 2000s, limited offerings, high subscription prices, and varying restrictions on use reduced their impact.[7]

In 2004, Stanford University and Google Inc. announced an initiative to break
out of the limitations governing licensed digital libraries. They would attempt, in
the words of Stanford University librarian Michael Keller, to start "digitizing texts
for years ... to make them more accessible and searchable" on an "industrial" scale.[8]
"Within two decades, most of the world's knowledge will be digitized and available,
one hopes for free reading on the Internet, just as there is free reading in libraries
today," he added.[9] It was a step towards making all the information in the world
available on the Web.[10]

Copyright law, however, stands in the way of making information available to
all. Information scanned from books would be displayed only in compliance with
copyright, Stanford and Google explained. This meant that only "bibliographic"
information could be shown, which Stanford and Google read broadly as lines of
text from scans that are responsive to searches, as well as the author and title information, and the like.[11] Even when Google reached a settlement with the publishers
who filed suit against it over unauthorized scanning of their books in libraries, and
with representatives of an author's group as well, the terms of the settlement allowed
any copyright holder to withdraw their scans from view at any time.[12] Therefore, a
truly universal digital library, available to rich and poor, was always off the table in
contemporary America.

7.2. THWARTING DIGITAL LIBRARIES WITH IDEOLOGIES OF FREE COMPETITION

Even a much more modest version of Google Books, designed to win the approval
of book-scanning's most ardent critics in publishing, failed to get off the ground.

---

[7] Ann Bartow, Electrifying copyright norms and making cyberspace more like a book, 48 *Villanova
Law Review* 13 (2003) at 108; Lisa Guernsey, In lean times, e-books find a friend: Libraries, *The New
York Times* (February 21, 2002), at G3; Lisa Guernsey, The Library as the latest web venture, *The New
York Times* (June 15, 2000), at G1; Paula Hane, OCLC completes netLibrary acquisition, raises ebook
fees, *Information Today* (February 11, 2002), www.infotoday.com/newsbreaks/nb020211-2.htm; Lucia
Snowhill, E-books and their future in academic libraries, *D-Lib Magazine*, July/Aug. 2001, www.dlib
.org/dlib/july01/snowhill/07snowhill.html.
[8] Stanford and Google to make library books available online, *Stanford News* (December 14, 2004),
https://news.stanford.edu/pr/2004/pr-google-121404.html.
[9] John Markoff and Edward Wyatt, Google is adding major libraries to its database, *The New York Times*
(December 14, 2004), www.nytimes.com/2004/12/14/technology/google-is-adding-major-libraries-to-
its-database.html.
[10] Ibid.
[11] *Stanford News*, note 8.
[12] *Authors Guild, Inc.* v. *Google, Inc.*, 770 F. Supp. 2d 666, 672 (S.D.N.Y. 2011). See also Sergey Brin,
A library to last forever, *The New York Times* (October 8, 2009), www.nytimes.com/2009/10/09/
opinion/09brin.html?_r=1.

Although it covered an impressive twelve million digitized books, the digital library that Google proposed to the courts was designed to merge the visions of Google and academic libraries with those of publishers and authors' groups.[13] For this reason, any rightsholder could have opted out of inclusion at any time, unlike with a typical physical library, which could accumulate books for free reading and lending regardless of permissions.[14] Moreover, Google's scans of books still in copyright could only be previewed, and not read, without payment. Up to five adjacent pages could be read but not copied or printed prior to purchase, and even this modest preview could be removed by rightsholders, who would earn advertising revenue from the previews, incidentally.[15] To read beyond these brief previews, Internet users would have had to pay for the book, at a price set either by the rightsholder or by an algorithm devised by Google and author and publisher representatives in its absence.[16] There could also be public terminals with subscriptions to many of the scanned books, at public and other institutional libraries.[17]

The Google settlement would have spread knowledge around much more widely and at less cost than the system of buying, borrowing, and shipping books. This would "level the educational playing field," the largest association of US college and university students argued.[18] Although the major publishers would likely opt out of the settlement and never face competition from their back catalogs for their updated textbook offerings, textbooks and readers that had gone out of print would return to the marketplace, promising to save college and university students, and even high school students, hundreds of dollars per semester in book costs. Aside from considerations of book prices, a digital library on this scale would remove many geographic and socioeconomic barriers to accessing educational content that was formerly offered only to the "privileged few."[19] As described in Chapter 1, the National Federation for the Blind believed that considerable benefits would flow from Google's pledge to make the book

---

[13] *Authors Guild*, 770 F. Supp. 2d at 666–71. See also Motoko Rich, Google hopes to open a trove of little-seen books, *The New York Times* (January 5, 2009), at B1.

[14] See also Brin, note 12.

[15] Notice of Class Action Settlement, *Authors Guild* (S.D.N.Y. notice filed October 28, 2008), www .thepublicindex.org/wp-content/uploads/sites/19/docs/settlement/OriginalSettlementAttachments/ Attachment-I-Notice-of-Class-Action-Settlement.pdf.

[16] Settlement Agreement, *Authors Guild* (S.D.N.Y. notice filed October 28, 2008) at 48–51, 65, www .thepublicindex.org/wp-content/uploads/sites/19/docs/settlement/settlement.pdf.

[17] E.g. Ibid., at 40–8; Einer Elhauge, *Why the Google Books Settlement is Procompetitive*, Harvard Law School John M. Olin Center for Law, Economics and Business Discussion Paper Series, Paper 629, at 43 (2009), http://lsr.nellco.org/harvard_olin/629.

[18] E.g. Letter of United States Student Association in Support of Settlement, *Authors Guild* (S.D.N.Y. letter filed August 19, 2009), at 1–2, www.thepublicindex.org/wp-content/uploads/sites/19/docs/ letters/ussa.pdf.

[19] ibid., at 1–2.

excerpts it displays equally accessible to tens of millions of Americans with visual impairments.[20]

Various government officials and economic interests decried even this restricted and hobbled digital preview library as involving too much public access to formerly unavailable books. The head of the US Copyright Office argued that it violated copyright holders' "right to exclude," which as Chapter 3 explained, had already virtually been done away with for small patent holders by the *eBay* decision, a decision also applicable to copyright injunctions.[21] This argument persuaded the Justice Department to oppose the settlement, despite its massive benefits for the public.[22]

Microsoft predicted that Google would become too dominant. Instead, Congress should pass legislation on digital libraries, it suggested. "[M]onopolization is the wrong means to carry out the worthy goal of digitizing and increasing the accessibility of books."[23]

Google would have a monopoly over ebooks if it could not be sued for setting up search engines and digital bookstores, Amazon and Microsoft argued successfully.[24] Even if authors and publishers could opt out, the cost of scanning books and dealing with so many authors was too high for the other tech giants to incur, they said. There was no reason, however, why two companies with more than $65 billion in gross income between them in 2011, and almost 50 percent more than that in 2015 when the Google Books case was still pending, or $95 billion, could not spend a few billion on book scanning and copyright class action settlements, if their market positions were to be truly destroyed by Google's book scanning projects.[25] Google's

[20] Amicus Brief of Antitrust Law and Economics Professors, at 3, *Authors Guild* (S.D.N.Y. brief filed September 8, 2009).

[21] Hearing on Competition and Commerce in Digital Books: The Proposed Google Book Settlement Before the House Comm. on the Judiciary, 111th Cong., 1st Sess. (2009) at 3–8 (statement of Marybeth Peters, Register of Copyrights), https://web.archive.org/web/ 20100401000000*/ and http:// judiciary.house.gov/hearings/pdf/Peters090910.pdf.

[22] U.S. Department of Justice, Statement of Interest, *Authors Guild* (S.D.N.Y statement filed September 18, 2009) at 11.

[23] Objections of Microsoft Corp., at 5, *Authors Guild* (S.D.N.Y. brief filed September 8, 2009).

[24] Objections of Amazon.com to Proposed Settlement, at 1–5, *Authors Guild* (S.D.N.Y. objections filed September 1, 2009); Objections of Microsoft Corp., note 23, at 3, 5–6; Objections of Open Book Alliance to Proposed Settlement, at 22, *Authors Guild* (S.D.N.Y. objections filed September 4, 2009), www.thepublicindex.org/wpcontent/uploads/sites/19/docs/letters/open_book_alliance.pdf; Plaintiffs' Supplemental Memorandum Responding to Specific Objections, at 138, *Authors Guild*, (S.D.N.Y brief filed February 11, 2010).

[25] Marketwatch, Amazon.com Inc.: Annual Financials for Amazon.com Inc. (2016), www.marketwatch .com/investing/stock/amzn/financials; MarketWatch, Microsoft Corp.: Annual Financials for Microsoft Corp. (2016), www.marketwatch.com/investing/stock/msft/financials. On the ability of Amazon, Microsoft, and many others to scan in-copyright books, see Objections of Amazon.com, Inc., note 24, at 1, 5 (three million books scanned by Amazon); also p. 5 (Amazon made text of books available for searches inside books, which happened tens of millions of times each week); Objections of Microsoft Corp., note 23, at 3, 6; Marina Lao, The perfect is the enemy of the good: The antitrust objections to the Google Books Settlement, 78 *Antitrust Law Journal* 397 (2012), draft, at 23, www2 .it.luc.edu/media/lucedu/law/centers/antitrust/pdfs/events/lao.pdf.

investment in book scanning, by contrast, was in the hundreds of millions, and it faced $3 billion in copyright liability.[26]

Germany went further and claimed that Google would monopolize all information, with its digital library advantage, leading to an end to both freedom of speech and cultural diversity in the world.[27] A famous French librarian warned that other companies and even entire countries outside of the search or advertising markets could be subjected to liquidation from the historical record.[28] Some copyright scholars also expressed concerns that competitors such as Bing would go under if Google could sell digital excerpts of out-of-print books.[29]

There were several reasons why a Google platform to make chapters from out-of-print books available online would not have violated competition law. First, even if Google became the exclusive vendor of some books in conjunction with authors' and publishers' representatives, this would have made it part of an oligopoly at worst, and a vigorous participant in a competitive market at best, along with other ebook vendors such as Amazon, Apple iBooks, the Internet Archive working in conjunction with Microsoft and the Million Book Project, and the Sony-linked Kobo service.[30]

As late as 2015, Google Play, the company's authorized ebook platform outside the settlement, sold only one ebook for every thirty-seven that Amazon sold, and for every five sold on Apple iBooks for iPad, iPhone, and Macs.[31] The bundling of Google Play with every Android smartphone, or one out of every two smartphones sold in the United States as of 2012, did not prevent Google from being a minor and arguably a failing player in ebooks, potentially opening up another argument that the settlement was necessary to turn around a struggling business, and compete with earlier entrants.[32]

---

[26] Plaintiff's Memorandum of Law in Support of Motion for Final Settlement Approval, at 2, *Authors Guild*, No. 1:05-CV-8136-DC (S.D.N.Y. brief filed Feb. 11, 2010); see also Google defeats authors in US book-scanning lawsuit, *Reuters* (November 14, 2013), www.reuters.com/articles/us-google-books-idUSBRE9AD0TT20131114; Lao, note 25.

[27] Memorandum of the Federal Republic of Germany in Opposition to Proposed Settlement, at 14–16, The *Authors Guild* (S.D.N.Y. brief filed Sept. 1, 2009). Cf. U.S. Department of Justice, note 22.

[28] E.g. Jean Noël Jeanneney, *Google and the Myth of Universal Knowledge: A View from Europe* (Teresa Lavendar Fagan trans. University of Chicago Press, 2006).

[29] E.g. James Grimmelmann, How to fix the Google Book Search settlement, 12 *Journal of Internet Law* 1 (2009); James Grimmelmann, The Google Book Search settlement: Ends, means, and the future of books, *American Constitution Society Paper*, April 2009, at 1, 6.

[30] Scott Merrill, Kobo releases free Kobo desktop application, *TechCrunch* (September 8, 2010), https://techcrunch.com/2010/09/08/kobo-releases-free-kobo-desktop-application/.

[31] Michael Kozlowski, What market share do Amazon, Apple, B&N Kobo and Google have selling eBooks?, *Good Reader* (October 9, 2015), https://goodereader.com/blog/e-book-news/what-market-share-do-amazon-apple-bn-kobo-and-google-have-selling-ebooks.

[32] Geoff Duncan, One company, one store: Why Google axed Android Market for Google Play, *Digital Trends* (March 7, 2012), www.digitaltrends.com/android/one-company-one-store-why-google-axed-android-for-google-play.

Second, even if Google had a monopoly on out-of-print books, this would still be a more competitive environment than one in which there was no market whatsoever for these abandoned books.[33] The out-of-print books might undermine the market power of those in print. Again, the only books marketed to the public without written copyright licenses would be those that rightsholders did not opt out of being included in Google Books.

Third, there were several ways that Amazon, or Apple or Microsoft or Facebook for that matter, could respond to a Google monopoly brought about by a book-scanning settlement agreement. Amazon could use the vast sums spent by purchasers of its shares to gain market share in the ebook space from Google by subsidizing efforts to scan out-of-print books and pay copyright judgments. The user reviews contributed freely by Amazon's customers would reinforce the barriers to entry faced by other ebook sellers, and cement Amazon's pricing power online.[34] Further, Amazon could use transaction data to jump-start its advertising and cloud businesses.[35] Finally, the existence of a mechanism to bring rightsholders and digital scan distributors together could easily lead to entities other than Google being licensed to enter the market, just as many music services followed in the wake of Apple's iTunes or Yahoo!'s Launchcast.[36]

In fact, Amazon and Microsoft had a much greater likelihood than Google of developing monopoly power with the aid of an online retailing presence. It is much easier to switch from using Google to Bing for search, or from Android to iPhone for a cell phone, than for many consumers to abandon Microsoft Windows, or for publishers to stop selling on Amazon.[37] While Google has a large market share for general-purpose search engines, this figure does not account for searches on specialty sites, social networks, smartphone apps, and other alternatives.[38] When the government properly compares apples to apples, and includes all "functionally" similar services in defining monopoly market control, Microsoft and Amazon stand out for the power they wield over personal computer operating systems and ebook sales, respectively.[39] There are many more choices for placing an online ad or finding

---

[33] Elhauge, note 17; Lao, note 25, at 5; Mark Lemley, An antitrust assessment of the Google Book Search Settlement, *Social Science Research Network* (2009), at 3–9.
[34] Lina Khan, Amazon's antitrust paradox, 126 *Yale Law Journal* 710 (2016) at 712, 748–56.
[35] Khan, note 34. See also Lao, note 25, at 48–9.
[36] E.g. *Arista Records, LLC v. Launch Media, Inc.*, 578 F.3d 148 (2d Cir. 2009); *BMG Music v. Gonzalez*, 430 F.3d 888 (7th Cir. 2005); *In Re Pandora Media, Inc.*, 6 F. Supp. 3d 317 (S.D.N.Y. 2014); *Tucker v. Apple Computer, Inc.*, 493 F. Supp. 2d 1090 (N.D. Cal. 2006).
[37] E.g. *United States v. Microsoft*, 56 F.3d 1448 (D.C. Cir. 2001); Khan, note 34, at 715–16, 757, 760–1.
[38] E.g. Lao, note 25.
[39] Netmarketshare, Operating system share by version (2017), https://netmarketshare.com/operating-system-market-share.aspx; PublishDrive, Amazon Ebook Market Share 2017 – is it big enough? (January 4, 2017), https://publishdrive.com/amazon-ebook-market-share/. Compare this to Comscore, comScore Top 50 Multi-Platform Properties (Desktop and Mobile) (June 2017), www.prnewswire.com/news-releases/comscore-ranks-the-top-50-us-digital-media-properties-for-june-2017-300491305.html.

hyperlinks (Facebook, Twitter, etc.) than for adopting an operating system, or finding a place to buy or sell ebooks for a digital device. In the context of publishing digital content, Google is a drop in the Web's bucket. Unlike the old Microsoft Windows or Apple iPod cases, competition with Google.com is often free in out-of-pocket terms, and is "just a click away."[40]

Some critics of Google Books arguably overstated the reach of existing copyright law, neglected relevant precedents in terms of fair use, and erected a utopian alternative of a free public digital library. The Department of Justice selectively pointed to case law precedents in attempting to persuade Congress and/or the public that Google Books was a bad idea.[41] Cases involving the distribution of copyrighted works or excerpts thereof for profit, without a settlement or any opportunity to opt out, without any showing that the works were out of print, and without significant transformation of the contents into new research services in some cases, were cited as barring Google Books.[42]

A public library comparable to the Google settlement was proposed by some of those fighting the settlement, including the Copyright Office, but such a project

---

[40] Miguel Helft, Google makes a case that it isn't so big, *The New York Times* (June 28, 2009), www.nytimes.com/2009/06/29/technology/companies/29google.html. Compare *Microsoft*, 253 F.3d at 55–8 (barriers to entry in form of lack of applications compatible with non-Windows operating systems for PCs); *Tucker*, 493 F. Supp. 2d at 1094–5, 1099–102 (barriers to entry in form of iTunes music downloads not being compatible with non-Apple music devices). The Federal Trade Commission concluded in 2013 that evidence of anticompetitive behavior by Google would not hold up in court. Brian Fung and Andrea Peterson, The FTC's internal memo on Google teaches companies a terrible lesson, *Washington Post The Switch Blog* (March 20, 2015), www.washingtonpost.com/news/the-switch/wp/2015/03/20/the-ftcs-internal-memo-on-google-teaches-companies-a-terrible-lesson/?utm_term=.50427a50751a.

[41] Specifically, its statement claimed that all joint price-setting mechanisms are per se illegal and that Google's competitors would be harmed, but did not acknowledge case law to the contrary of these points. Compare, Statement of Interest of United States of America, at II.A.1-2., *Authors Guild* (S.D.N.Y. filed Sept. 18, 2009), with Brief for the United States as Amicus Curiae, *Texaco, Inc.* v. *Dagher*, 547 U.S. 1 (U.S. brief filed May 2005) (Nos. 04-805 and 04-814), https://web.archive.org/web/20150703023858/ and https://www.justice.gov/ osg/brief/texaco-v-dagher-amicus-invitation-petition (per se illegality does not apply to an "elimination of competition" that is "efficiency-enhancing"); Brief for the United States as Amicus Curiae, *American Needle, Inc.* v. *National Football League*, 560 U.S. 183 (U.S. brief filed May 2009) (No. 08-661), https://web.archive.org/web/20170511044308/ and www.justice.gov/atr/case-document/brief-united-states-amicus-curiae.

[42] E.g. Siva Vaidhyanathan, The Googlization of everything and the future of copyright, 40 *U.C. Davis Law Review* 1207 (2007) at 1225–30 (arguing that "Google cannot win" against publishers and authors on the legality of its book search functionality), citing *Tasini* v. *New York Times Co.*, 206 F.3d 161 (2d Cir. 2000), *aff'd*, 533 U.S. 483, 502–05 (2001); *American Geophysical Union* v. *Texaco, Inc.*, 37 F.3d 881 (2d Cir. 1994); *UMG Recordings, Inc.* v. *MP3.com, Inc.*, 92 F. Supp. 2d 349 (S.D.N.Y. 2000). See also Matt Williams, Recent Second Circuit opinions indicate that Google's Library Project is not transformative, 25 *Cardozo Arts & Entertainment Law Journal* 303 (2007), citing *Bill Graham Archives* v. *Dorling Kindersley Ltd.*, 448 F.3d 1 (2d Cir. 2006), and *Blanch* v. *Koons*, 467 F.3d 244 (2d Cir. 2006). Compare Travis, note 1, at 126–139 (including more cases in the analysis of fair use); Frank Pasquale, Copyright in an era of information overload: Toward the privileging of categorizers, 60 *Vanderbilt Law Review* 135 (2007) at 187–188 (same).

was never likely to materialize.[43] The Library of Congress and others had had many years and millions of dollars in funding to set up digital libraries, but had not done so effectively.[44] Despite scanning millions of files, the website is relatively little-used and remains difficult to navigate.[45]

Amazon proposed the Digital Audio Tape (DAT) recorders legislation as a model for digital libraries.[46] After the copyright holder for "Come Fly With Me," "High Hopes," and other popular songs sued Sony, the manufacturer of a DAT recorder, for enabling unauthorized high-quality copies of sound recordings to be made, Congress passed legislation regulating DATs in detail, but immunizing Sony for further such suits.[47] No one seemed to notice the problem with this model: the legally crippled DAT failed miserably, and Napster came along instead to enable sharing ripped CDs.[48] There has been little effort to achieve a statutory fix for digital libraries since the settlement was blocked.[49]

When it came to Google Books settlement, the Copyright Office would not go even as far as Amazon, which suggested a statutory reform to make mass digitization possible without ruinous copyright liability. The Office insisted that there should not be a statutory accommodation of Google Books absent a "market failure," without defining what would qualify.[50] Five million books had vanished from public view – how much greater of a failure was needed?

Overenforcement of copyright law against digital libraries often denies us access to works that should be in the public domain after many decades. Stored quietly on banks of computers or servers at Google are millions of books that no one is allowed to read, yet from which authors earn nothing.[51] Google erred on the side of "snippetizing" all books after a certain date because they might be in copyright,

[43] Objections of Microsoft, Inc., note 23, at 3–6; Office of the Register of Copyrights, Legal issues in mass digitization: A preliminary analysis and discussion document (October 20, 2011), at 1–2, 12, www.copyright.gov/docs/massdigitization/USCOMassDigitization_October2011.pdf.

[44] Travis, note 5, at 770–1.

[45] Office of the Register of Copyrights, note 43, at Appendix C at 1–3. The Library of Congress website appears to attract fewer than 10 million visits per month, as opposed to more than 87 million to books. google.com. E.g. SimilarWeb, books.google.com (November 2017), www.similarweb.com/websites/books.google.com; SimilarWeb., loc.gov (November 2017), www.similarweb.com/websites/loc.gov . The interface has been described as "outdated." Sally Stieglitz, The American Memory Project, in Janic Krueger (Ed.), *Cases on Electronic Records and Resource Management Implementation in Diverse Environments* (IGI Global, 2014) at 114.

[46] Objections of Amazon.com Inc., note 24, at 9, 11.

[47] *Cahn v. Sony Corp.*, No. 90 Civ. 4537 (S.D.N.Y. filed July 9, 1990); see also Audio Home Recording Act of 1992, Pub. L. No. 102-563, 106 Stat. 4237.

[48] Jimmy Guterman, How home taping fuels the record industry, *Forbes* (July 11, 1997), www.forbes .com/1997/07/11/taping.html; J. Gordon Holt and Alvin Gold, *Copycode: Diminishing DAT*, *Stereophile* (Aug. 2, 1987), www.stereophile.com/asweseeit/copycode_diminishing_dat/index.html.

[49] James Somers, Torching the modern-day library of Alexandria, *The Atlantic* (April 20, 2017), www .theatlantic.com/technology/2017/04/the-tragedy-of-google-books/523320.

[50] Office of the Register of Copyrights, note 43, at 2, 5, 30, 38; Statement of Marybeth Peters, note 21.

[51] Somers, note 49.

even though many of them are in the public domain due to failure to renew them or to include a copyright notice under the Copyright Act of 1909, or authorship by US federal workers.[52] This amounts to self-censorship of very beneficial efforts at cultural preservation and the memorialization of the history that is recorded in out-of-print books.[53]

Meanwhile, in the absence of a comprehensive legal marketplace, people simply downloaded ebooks from peer-to-peer networks or websites like library.nu or Sci-Hub.[54] As with the early days of digital music marketing, the unavailability of a comprehensive, competitively-priced, user-friendly, and ownership-based option for acquiring ebooks lawfully may be contributing to arguably unlawful downloads.[55] Although Apple iBooks and Amazon Kindle are widely used, many consumers may hesitate to adopt them given the vagaries of bestseller pricing, the absence of discounts for back catalog titles or used copies, privacy concerns with linking reading habits to credit cards, and concerns about proprietary formats and devices becoming inaccessible.

Denial of the Google Book Search settlement had a far more severe impact on the public domain, access to information, and literary freedom than the more-often decried Copyright Term Extension Act or Digital Millennium Copyright Act. While term extension pulled hundreds of thousands of works out of the public domain, most of them were published before 1964, so they are not much more up-to-date than public domain works from the 1910s or early 1920s.[56] The DMCA may erroneously remove millions of works from the Internet every year, but they may be reposted elsewhere.[57] Rejection of the Google Book Search settlement, based on to the false premise that information would be monopolized by allowing out-of-print books to be sold digitally, probably removed millions of books from public view for decades. Many of these books would have been very useful to students and engaged citizens attempting to learn more about their history, political situation, and environment.

7.3. GOOGLE BOOKS AS ANOTHER VICTIM OF THE WARS ON "PIRACY"

The Copyright Office had a somewhat better argument against the settlement, based on international law. While international copyright law is typically implemented by

---

52 Google Inc., Librarian Center (2006), www.google.com/librariancenter/articles/060603.html.
53 Cf. Office of the Register of Copyrights, note 43, at 13.
54 Balázs Bodó, Libraries in the post-scarcity era, in Helle Porsdam (Ed.), *Copyrighting Creativity: Creative Values, Cultural Heritage Institutions and Systems of Intellectual Property* (Routledge, 2016) at 82; George Delta and Jeffrey Matsuura, *Law of the Internet* (Aspen Publishers, 4th ed., 2016) at 10–103.
55 James Richardson, The Spotify paradox: How the creation of a compulsory license scheme for streaming on-demand music platforms can save the music industry, 22 *UCLA Entertainment Law Review* 45 (2014) at 48–9.
56 U.S. Copyright Office Circular 15, Renewal of Copyright (2017), www.copyright.gov/circs/circ15.pdf.
57 Jennifer Urban, Joe Karaganis and Brianna Schofield, Notice and takedown in everyday practice, SSRN (2016), https://papers.ssrn.com/sol3/papers.cfm?abstract_id=2755628.

Congress in amendments to the Copyright Act, there is an argument to construe existing statutes in such a way as to assume or promote compliance with international law.[58] Thus, the Register of Copyrights and some publishing industry associations argued that provisions of US copyright law against forced transfers and the like should preclude congressional or judicial approval of opt-out digital libraries, so as to prevent a potential violation of international authors' rights under the World Trade Organization (WTO) Agreement on Trade-Related Aspects of Intellectual Property (TRIPs).[59]

A little background may help illuminate this argument. During the Reagan administration, the United States, the European Economic Community, and Japan argued that limiting intellectual property rights to protect the public interest were simply a form of international "piracy." Intimidation of political elites in Brazil and India prompted their surrender to this notion in 1989, leading inexorably in to 1994's TRIPs Agreement, an annex to the Global Agreement on Tariffs and Trade, itself the basis of the WTO framework.[60] An arm of the United Nations described the TRIPs Agreement as "a premature strengthening of the intellectual property system ... that favors monopolistically controlled innovation over broad-based diffusion."[61] Treaties such as TRIPs or the North American Free Trade Agreement (NAFTA) arguably strengthen the quasi-monopolistic positions of dominant copyright holders by overriding freedom of speech online with copyright-based technicalities.[62] In this way, they privatize and reify what could be more fluid, public-interested, and open forms of communication and cultural exchange.[63]

TRIPs and other multilateral trade agreements are an obstacle to opening up knowledge to the masses, or so the Copyright Office and others believe. Article 13 of TRIPs purports to require WTO members to ensure that copyright extends to all

---

[58] E.g. Brief of Amici Curiae International Publishers Association, et al., *Authors Guild* (S.D.N.Y. brief filed Aug. 4, 2011), citing *Murray v. Schooner Charming Betsy*, 6 U.S. (2 Cranch) 64, 118 (1804).

[59] Office of the Register of Copyrights, note 43, at 1–3, 30, 38. See also Brief of Amici Curiae International Publishers Association (IPA), International Association of Scientific, Technical and Medical Publishers (STM), International Federation of Reproduction Rights Organisations (IFRRO), and Former U.S. Register of Copyrights Marybeth Peters in Support of Appellants, at 9, 16–28, *Authors Guild, Inc. v. HathiTrust*, 755 F.3d 87 (2d Cir. brief filed Apr. 14, 2014) (No. 13-4829-CV). While the Copyright Office was not very technical in discussing the right to exclude, 17 U.S.C. § 201(d)-(e) provides for a ownership and transfer of the exclusive rights comprised in a copyright, and prohibits involuntary seizure of transfer of those rights to others.

[60] S. P. Shukla, From GATT to WTO and beyond, World Institute for Development Economics and Research Working Paper 195 (August 2000), at 18, 21, www.wider.unu.edu/sites/default/files/wp195 .pdf.

[61] Quoted in Kevin Danaher and Roger Burbach, *Globalize This!: The Battle Against the World Trade Organization and Corporate Rule* (Common Courage Press, 2000) at 109.

[62] Christopher Marsden, Information and communications technologies, globalisation and regulation, in Christopher Marsden (Ed.), *Regulating the Global Information Society* (Routledge, 2005) at 18.

[63] Cf. Scott Prudham and William Coleman, Introduction, in William Coleman (Ed.), *Property, Territory, Globalization: Struggles over Autonomy* (UBC Press, 2011) at 24

"normal exploitation of the work and do not unreasonably prejudice the legitimate interests of the rights holder[s]."[64] Fair use or other statutory exceptions to copyright should not harm the "normal exploitation" or reasonable "interests" of rights holders, the argument goes. The United States Congress approved the TRIPs Agreement in 1994, although it did not codify the provision on the limits of copyright, and Congress was told that the WTO would have no power to modify US laws because of the 1994 agreements.[65]

Democratic input into the writing of legislation was expected to decline as trade agreements created law-making bureaucracies that could prompt nation-states to rewrite IP law, such as the TRIPs drafting committee or the NAFTA or WTO tribunals for trade disputes.[66] This was not surprising, as a key US negotiator was a former executive at Cargill, the eighth largest corporation or so by sales, which was "calling a lot of the shots" during the Reagan administration's push for TRIPs.[67] California's current Governor, Jerry Brown, as a failed US presidential candidate in 1993, remarked that trade agreements such as TRIPS and NAFTA go on for "thousands of pages in the most abstruse and technical language ... . So clearly the laws NAFTA imposes on us won't be understood except by that small group of trade insiders." He described the introduction of IP laws into the global trading regime as "subsidizing the growth of multinational companies [which] continues the trend toward greater inequality ... ."[68] Under TRIPs, paradoxically, the United States generated the fewest jobs in the three economic recoveries since 1993, among numerous recoveries from recessions since 1945.[69]

Despite some plausibility to the international-law case against the Google Books settlement, the Copyright Office failed to make several critical observations to the

---

[64] Agreement on Trade-Related Aspects of Intellectual Property Rights, Apr. 15, 1994, Marrakesh Agreement Establishing the World Trade Organization, Annex 1C, 1867 U.S.T. 154, 33 I.L.M. 81.

[65] 19 U.S.C. §§ 3511–3; Bernard Reams, Jr. and Jon Schultz, *Uruguay Round Agreements Act: A Legislative History of Public Law 103-465* (GATT and the WTO), Vol. 5 (William S. Hein & Co., Inc., 1995) at 1241. Congress drove the point home by clarifying that no one could file a lawsuit under TRIPs or WTO law except the United States.

[66] Robert Benson, Free trade as an extremist ideology: The case of NAFTA, 17 *University of Puget Sound Law Review* 555 (1994); Thomas R. Donahue, The case against a North American Free Trade Agreement, 26 *Columbia Journal of World Business* 93 (1991); Marci Hamilton, The TRIPS Agreement: Imperialistic, outdated, and overprotective, 20 *Vandeerbilt Journal of Transnational Law* 613 (1996); see also Public Citizen v. *Office of the United States Trade Representative*, No. 92-2102, U.S. Dist. LEXIS 8682 (D.D.C. June 30, 1993), rev'd, 5 F.3d 549 (D.C. Cir. 1993); Made in the USA Foundation v. *United States*, 242 F.3d 1300, 1305 (11th Cir. 2001).

[67] Brian Ahlberg, Cargill: The invisible giant, *Multinational Monitor* (July 1988), www.multinationalmonitor.org/hyper/issues/1988/07/mm0788_09.html.

[68] Noam Chomsky interviewed by Jerry Brown, *SPIN Magazine* (August 1993), www.wtp.org/archive/articles/chomsky_one.html.

[69] Jon Greenberg, Christie: The U.S. is in the worst recovery since WWII, *Politifact* (November 10, 2015), www.politifact.com/truth-o-meter/statements/2015/nov/10/chris-christie/christie-us-worst-recovery-wwii/; Ernest Hollings, Why GATT is a bad deal for Middle America, *The Christian Science Monitor* (November 3, 1994), www.csmonitor.com/1994/1103/03192.html.

Justice Department for relay to the court hearing the case, or the Justice Department failed to convey them to the court. First, the TRIPs Agreement is directed to legislators considering how to draft or amend exclusions from copyright, not to courts hearing class-action settlements about practices such as scanning library books.[70] Second, the WTO and TRIPs were not supposed to create private rights in court, or alter the Copyright Act. Third, even if the United States lost a dispute in the WTO about Google Books, it could simply have borne any retaliatory sanctions as a cost of massively increasing access to knowledge, or paid a modest settlement to other WTO members, as it did to resolve a dispute about the free use of music in small bars, restaurants, clubs, and stores.[71]

A law untethered from neoconservative trade agreements might create a statutory presumption that out-of-print works are in the public domain after many years. A less beneficial reform from the standpoint of consumers and follow-on authors than the Google Book Search settlement, but one that would be superior to denial of it with no real publicly-supported replacement in mind, is expansion of the library exemption under section 108 of the US Act. A broader 108 exemption could declare that out-of-print works "incidentally" included in a mass digitization project do not infringe copyrights.[72] Part of the rationale for an exclusion of incidental uses of works from copyright liability is the lack of market competition, which is apparent when a work is out-of-print.[73] Alternatively, those engaging in digitization while earning insignificant profits compared to a public company could pay a reasonable flat fee annually or a fair percentage of revenue or profits that would cover every out-of-print work that they might digitize, like college and university webcasters and public FM radio stations pay to US musical copyright holders.[74] Even highly profitable

[70] E.g. Brief of Amici Curiae Law Professors and Scholars, *HathiTrust*, 755 F.3d 87 (2d Cir. brief filed July 10, 2014).
[71] E.g. Office of the U.S. Trade Representative, Section 110(5) of US Copyright Act (2017), https://ustr.gov/issue-areas/enforcement/dispute-settlement-proceedings/united-states-%E2%80%94-section-1105-us-copyright-ac.
[72] British law provides a similar exception for incidental inclusion in a broader technologically-mediated project, such as a film or broadcast. E.g. Copyright Designs and Patents Act 1988, as amended by The Copyright and Related Rights Regulations 2003, s. 31, S.I. 2003/2498 (United Kingdom); *Fraser-Woodward Ltd v. British Broadcasting Corporation and another* [2005] EWHC 472(Ch).
[73] E.g. Elenora Rosati, Taking a selfie inside the National Gallery – a copyright infringement? *Legal Week* (24 August 2014), www.legalweek.com/sites/legalweek/2014/08/27/taking-a-selfie-inside-the-national-gallery-a-copyright-infringement/, citing Hugh Laddie, Peter Prescott, and Mary Vitoria, *The Modern Law of Copyright and Designs* (LexisNexis, 4th ed. 2011).
[74] E.g. 17 U.S.C. § 114; Assessing the Impact of the Copyright Royalty Rates on Recording Artists and Webcasters, Vol. 4: Hearing Before the United States. Congress, House Committee on Small Business (Government Printing Office, 2007) at 32. See also Susan Butler and Anthony Bruno, *Webcast woes*, *Billboard* (March 17, 2007), at 6; Cydney Tune and Christopher Lockhard, Licensing and royalty requirements for webcasters: Details and deadlines, *Pillsbury Law* (March 24, 2009), www.pillsburylaw.com/images/content/2/3/v2/2371/689FBDFD3B40B5495649A2DD84A50374.pdf, citing Digital Performance Right in Sound Recordings and Ephemeral Recordings: Final Rule and Order, 72 Fed. Reg. 24,084, 24,091, 24,096–100 (May 1, 2007); Noncommercial Educational

companies could pay no more than five percent of revenues, like some music streaming services do to songwriters.[75]

In 2012, the French parliament passed legislation allowing the original print publisher to release an ebook, six months after a book goes out of print according to a public database, on the condition that no author or other rightsholder objects within six months for any reason, or objects at any time in order to protect his or her authorial reputation. After ten years, libraries could distribute such titles noncommercially, further exposing them to new generations of readers.[76] With certain exceptions, any business could distribute the book after three years if its original publisher fails to make use of the exclusive window provided by the law, and any business may do the same after the six months if there was no contract as to the print rights. The law licensed more than 40,000 books for renewed release in 2013 and 2014 alone.[77]

The French experiment may be short-lived. Among other challenges, the European Court of Justice concluded that even with the law's many safeguards, it violated authors' right to prevent the reproduction and sale of their work absent their explicit notice and affirmative consent.[78] The ruling effectively means that little can be done in Europe to solve the problem of out-of-print books in a systematic way,

Broadcasting Statutory License: Notice of Proposed Rulemaking, 72 Federal Register 19,138 (April 17, 2007) at 19,140–1. Webcasters have proposed 4–5.5 percent of revenue as a standard. Digital Performance Right, ibid., at 24,087–88.

[75] Historically, the rate paid to stream music over cable television wires was as low as two percent of revenue. E.g. Comments of Music Choice, In the Matter of Music Licensing Study: Notice and Request for Public Comment, Docket No. 2014-03 (May 23, 2014), at 2, www.copyright.gov/docs/musiclicensingstudy/comments/Docket2014_3/Music_Choice_MLS_2014.pdf. The rate paid by satellite radio to musical composition owners was 2.35 percent at one point. Copyright Royalty Board, Library of Congress, Determination of Rates and Terms for Preexisting Subscription Services and Satellite Digital Audio Radio Services: Final Rule and Order, 73 Federal Register 4,080 (January 24, 2008) at 4,084.

[76] The law technically refers to out-of-commerce books, so as to exclude books out of print but in digital versions from the new licensing scheme, but this book uses out-of-print for clarity. David Hansen, Orphan works: Mapping the possible solution spaces, Berkeley Digital Library Copyright Project White Paper #2 (2012), at 17–18, http://ssrn.com/abstract=2019121, citing Loi no 2012-287 du 1er mars 2012 relative à l'exploitation numérique des livres indisponibles du XXe siècle (1) [Law 2012-287 of March 1, 2012 on the Digital Exploitation of Unavailable Books of the Twentieth Century], *Journal Officiel de la République Française* [J.O.] [Official Gazette of the French Republic], March 2, 2012, at 03986, www.legifrance.gouv.fr/jopdf/common/jo_pdf.jsp?numJO=0&dateJO=20120302&numTexte=1&pageDebut=03986&pageFin=03988#; Oleksandr Bulayenko, Permissibility of non-voluntary collective management of copyright under EU Law – The case of the French law on out-of-commerce books, 7 *Journal of Intellectual Property, Information Technology and E-Commerce Law* No. 1 (2016), www.jipitec.eu/issues/jipitec-7-1-2016/4402.

[77] Bulayenko, note 76.

[78] Case C-301/15, European Court of Justice, Judgment of 16 November 2016, *Marc Soulier and Sara Doke* v. *Ministre de la culture et de la communication and Premier ministre*; Brad Spitz, The ECJ condemns the French Act on digital exploitation of out-of-print books, *Kluwer Copyright Law Blog* (January 12, 2017), http://kluwercopyrightblog.com/2017/01/12/ecj-condemns-french-act-digital-exploitation-print-books.

given the difficulties locating and notifying authors of books that have fallen from the public view. It will be tough to find such authors or their heirs, and perhaps impossible to come to terms with them about licensing books for a permanent, global, digital library.[79]

7.4. A JURISPRUDENCE OF TECHNOLOGICAL POSSIBILITIES

The fate of the Google Books database is emblematic of the problem with copyright in the social media age. New technologies have emerged that enable Internet users to send one another copies of entire libraries at little to no additional cost. Services such as Google Book Search transport each interested user instantaneously into the stacks of dozens of research libraries built at tremendous cost to taxpayers, donors, and tuition-paying students. Along with services such as Facebook and Google Video, YouTube provides the imagery and sound for a truly universal digital library.[80] It is a portal into other places and times, like the magic mirror of Disney and the Brothers Grimm.

Humans born in any other era would be amazed; kings and emperors had no such powers. Yet the reaction of contemporary governments since the dawn of the Internet has been to subsidize Internet infrastructure, but to reign in the full potential of Internet search engines. The premise of governments seems to be that the law must preserve the concentrations of economic power that preceded search engines. (It must do much the same thing for political power, such as by aiming regulations and criminal prosecutions at the "fake news" and leaks upending the campaigns of politicians, or the wars of states.)

A digital library of out-of-print books could deliver the unique benefit of including books within the hyperlink structure that makes up the Web, linking outbound from scholarly references to source links, and inbound from the Web to book pages.[81] This is generally not true of many of the other digital library projects that were used to deny approval of the Google Books settlement on the pretext that licensed libraries existed.

The Internet was an opportunity to build a new economy free of the inherited inequalities of the past: the division of the land, the trading blocs, the central banks, the professional and occupational licensing systems, the regulatory agencies' heavy hand, etc. But, to paraphrase Robert McChesney, capital made the Internet less

---

[79] European Commission, Commission Staff, Working Document: Impact Assessment on the Modernisation of EU Copyright Rules, Accompanying the Document "Proposal for a Directive of the European Parliament and of the Council on Copyright in the Digital Single Market [Etc.]," EC Doc. No. SWD(2016) 301 final, part 3/3 (2016), at 125, 128–29.

[80] Steven Hetcher, Amateur creative digital content and proportional commerce, in Dan Hunter, Ramon Laboto, Megan Richardson, and Julian Thomas (Eds.), *Amateur Media: Social, Cultural and Legal Perspectives* (Routledge, 2013) at 47.

[81] Settlement Agreement, note 16, at 38–9.

democratic, and a tightly regulated Internet may return the favor by making capital less democratic.[82] Noting that the top one percent of earners is taking in a rising share of income growth, French economist Thomas Piketty sees a return to the super-elite or "rentier" class of the British manors. In the future, capital's returns will be so much higher than labor's that the top 10 percent will own 90 percent of society's wealth again, as in the nineteenth century.[83]

Visions of communal access to knowledge, in a manner unconstrained by the traditional relationship of consumer to capital, are taking hold. An expanded commons may dissolve the borders between monolithic corporations and the collaborative communities that forge a culture, according to Jimmy Wales and other pioneers of "Wikinomics." The light-touch of a self-organizing community can produce much more content, and disseminate it to many more people, than some traditional firms.[84]

Globalization and economic recessions transcending international borders renewed intellectual and popular interest in Marxist economic theory, which predicted that extreme inequality, ecological damage, and exploitative globalization would occur in late capitalist societies.[85] In globalized neoliberal capitalism, some theorized that the Internet would be redirected from a domain of scientific research and public-interested communication into one for the commoditization of persons and their data, with users "of the corporate web 2.0" being "exploited" and suffering surveillance and extraction of their creativity and communications as "free labor."[86] Communications, like other commons – open lands, the open seas, the air, underwater resources, and ideas – are disrupted and subverted by "corporate media power."[87]

Copyright and other IP stand in a contradictory (perhaps dialectical) relationship with corporate power in this debate. On the one hand, advocates for authors and especially for journalists and book writers look to copyright as a way of taming the digital and social media giants, and holding them accountable.[88] Jean-Noël Jeanneney, former director of the French National Library, argued that publishers must control

---

[82] Robert McChesney, *Digital Disconnect: How Capitalism is Turning the Internet Against Democracy* (The New Press, 2013).

[83] Thomas Piketty, *Capital in the Twenty-First Century* (Harvard University Press, 2014) at 514; Robert Antonio, Piketty's nightmare capitalism: The return of rentier society and de-democratization, 43 *Contemporary Sociology* 783 (2014) at 783–90, 787.

[84] Dan Tapscott and Anthony Williams, *Wikinomics: How Mass Collaboration Changes Everything* (Portfolio, 2007) at 76–7, 287–90.

[85] Christian Fuchs and Nick Dyer-Witheford, Karl Marx @ Internet Studies, 15 *New Media & Society* 782 (2012) at 784.

[86] ibid., at 788.

[87] ibid., at 789.

[88] E.g. Robert Levine, *Free Ride: How Digital Parasites Are Destroying the Culture Business, and How the Culture Business Can Fight Back* (Anchor Books, 2011); Jonathan Taplin, *Move Fast and Break Things: How Facebook, Amazon, and Google Cornered Culture and Undermined Democracy* (Little, Brown & Co., 2017).

the proliferating virus of digitized words and texts before it eats into citizens' capacity to think and to act, consuming culture in chaos.[89] These mechanisms for accountability, however, may revive the top-down production models of the past. Perhaps for this reason, Slavoj Žižek rejects theories of technological transcendence of prior economic relationships, arguing that ideologies of "participation, self-organization and cooperation" preserve exploitation by warping perception and thought.[90] IP plays a role because rights in algorithms, databases, methods of operating computer server farms and smartphones, and the like, preserve digital conglomerates' power.[91]

Philosophers and legal scholars have coined new terms for imagined alternatives to a hierarchical Internet, including "cybernetic communism," "dot.communism," and a "public-service Net." Themes that emerge include (1) harnessing the greater productivity of labor after computerization to produce more public goods and leisure time for all, (2) introducing more participatory ways of controlling the course of the economy, and (3) broadening the ownership of economic facilities.[92] The Internet is like the Wild West or a late medieval economy, in which scattered homesteaders coalesce with some difficulty to resist the robber barons and "land grabbers" of the upper classes. Cyber-communism is the resistance to the ongoing "cyber-spatial land grab."[93] There are similarities between organizing the yeomanry of England against enclosures of common lands and cyber-communists exhorting independent Internet users to guard little sites and posts against digital enclosures in the form of overbroad IP claims.[94]

Perhaps in cyber-communism or dot.communism, the Internet would eventually be a region free of property rights, contracts, payments, terms of use, and other capitalist demands. The Enlightenment critique of capitalism is that it views society as a mechanism "to spare those who are already the most fortunate the trouble of

---

[89] Jeanneney, note 28, at 65–81.

[90] Slavoj Žižek, *In Defense of Lost Causes* (Verso, 2009), at 6; Slavoj Žižek, *Demanding the Impossible* (Polity, 2013) at 58–65; Slavoj Žižek, *The Year of Living Dangerously* (Verso Books, 2012) at 9; Christian Fuchs, *Digital Labour and Karl Marx*, (Routledge, 2014) 12–3.

[91] Nuria Boot and Georgios Petropoulos, German Facebook probe links data protection and competition policy, *Bruegel* (March 14, 2016), http://bruegel.org/2016/03/german-facebook-probe-links-data-protection-and-competition-policy/; Ed Bott, Google's "highly proprietary source code": unfair edge for Motorola? *ZD Net* (August 17, 2011), www.zdnet.com/article/googles-highly-proprietary-source-code-unfair-edge-for-motorola; Foo Yun Chee and Eric Auchard, EU competition chief set to charge Google with Android abuse, *Reuters*, (April 18, 2016), www.reuters.com/article/us-eu-google-antitrust-idUSKCN0XF0PI.

[92] Fuchs and Dyer-Witheford, note 85, at 788–9, citing Richard Barbrook, *Imaginary Futures: From thinking machines to the global village* (Pluto Press, 2007); Eben Moglen, The dotCommunist Manifesto, *University of Columbia School of Law* (2003), http://emoglen.law.columbia.edu/my_pubs/dcm.html#tex2html2; Korinna Patelis, The political economy of the Internet, in James Curran (ed.), *Media Organisations in Society* (Arnold, 2000) at 84–107; Žižek, note 90, at 354, 429.

[93] Fuchs and Dyer-Witheford, note 85, at 787–8, citing J. W. Lindenschmidt, From virtual commons to virtual enclosures, 9 *The Commoner*, Spr.-Summer 2007, www.commoner.org.uk/?p=20.

[94] Hannibal Travis, Pirates of the information infrastructure: Blackstonian copyright and the First Amendment, 15 *Berkeley Technology Law Journal* 777 (2000), at 828–849, 851–6.

working"; a society seeking to spare as many as possible from unpleasant work might look to a minimum basic income.[95] If automation and ubiquitous connectivity could support a "basic minimum income," as Elon Musk of Tesla and Hyperloop One has predicted, will a gift economy emerge of complex production for noneconomic or semi-economic motives and rewards?[96] Mark Zuckerberg created a minor controversy when he called a basic income for all a "cushion to try new things" that could help create a society with more "meaningful" work.[97] In the form of "pirate parties," such visions play a role at the fringes of European politics.[98] Alaskan and Iranian law and experiments in Finland, Hawai'i, and India are making basic incomes a reality.[99] While funding the infrastructure for creating and distributing IP would be a challenge in a gift economy with minimum incomes, there are examples other than the traditional model of invest–distribute–earn, such as raising money using Kickstarter.[100]

One theory of how the Internet became so profitable and useful involves the transcendence of some venerable norms of copyright, trademark, and tax law. Richard Barbrook wrote that the digerati or entrepreneurial elite of the Internet age forged a "gift economy" of information, copied, and transmitted cheaply across a system in which "users always receive the results of much greater amounts of labour in return

---

[95] Paul-Henri d'Holbach, quoted in *Enlightenment Rationalism and the Origins of Marxism* (1998), www.marxists.org/history/etol/document/icl-spartacists/pamphlets/Enlightenement_Rationalism_Marxism.pdf.

[96] Catherine Clifford, Elon Musk: Robots will take your jobs, government will have to pay your wage, *CNBC* (November 4, 2016), www.cnbc.com/2016/11/04/elon-musk-robots-will-take-your-jobs-government-will-have-to-pay-your-wage.html.

[97] Quoted in Andy Kessler, Zuckerberg's opiate for the masses, *The Wall Street Journal* (June 18, 2017), www.wsj.com/articles/zuckerbergs-opiate-for-the-masses-1497821885?mod=trending_now_4.

[98] McKenzie Wark, Considerations on a hacker manifesto, in Trebor Scholzat (Ed.), *Digital Labor: The Internet as Playground and Factory* (Routledge, 2013) at 73; see also Pirate Party keeps a seat at the European Parliament, *Torrent Freak* (May 26, 2014), http://torrentfreak.com/pirate-party-keeps-a-seat-at-the-european-parliament-140526.

[99] Dom Galeon and Christianna Reedy, Mark Zuckerberg: The U.S. should learn from this state's basic income program, *Futurism* (July 5, 2017), https://futurism.com/mark-zuckerberg-the-u-s-should-learn-from-this-states-basic-income-program; Kansaneläkelaitos – The Social Insurance Institution of Finland, Universal basic income options to be weighed (November 19, 2015), www.kela.fi/web/en/press-releases/-/asset_publisher/LgL2IQBbkg98/content/universal-basic-income-options-to-be-weighed?_101_INSTANCE_LgL2IQBbkg98_redirect=%2Fweb%2Fen%2Fpress-releases; Guy Standing, India's experiment in basic income grants, *Global Dialogue* (December 12, 2017) http://isa-global-dialogue.net/indias-great-experiment-the-transformative-potential-of-basic-income-grants/; Chris Weller, Iran introduced a basic income scheme, and something strange happened, *World Economic Forum/Business Insider* (May 31, 2017), www.weforum.org/agenda/2017/05/iran-introduced-a-basic-income-scheme-and-something-strange-happened.

[100] Andrew Leysheon, *Reformatted: Code, Networks, and the Transformation of the Music Industry* (Oxford University Press, 2014) at 162.; Joseph Hogue, What Morrissey doesn't know about crowdfunding, *crowd101.com* (May 5, 2015), www.crowd101.com/morrissey-doesnt-know-about-crowdfunding/; De La Soul ... and the Anonymous Nobody (2017), www.kickstarter.com/projects/1519102394/de-la-souls-new-album.

from others."[101] This was in contrast to the system of early capitalism, in which the extraction of surplus value sometimes drove the wages of the worker down to a subsistence level, and often below it, even as he or she created vast wealth in the economic system.[102]

The developer of the World Wide Web and hypertext markup language, Tim Berners-Lee, argued that copyright made little sense in the new networked commons. Barbrook prefigured the rise of YouTube in explaining that television and film would be revolutionized by communities gifting downloads, remixes, and pirated works in relationships of friendship rather than alienation, of abundance rather than scarcity.[103] Aptly characterizing how many musicians and writers now operate, Barbrook wrote: "Since plagiarism will soon become ubiquitous, cyber-entrepreneurs must adopt other ways of commodifying the Net: real-time services, advertising, merchandising."[104]

[101] Richard Barbrook, Cyber-communism: How the Americans are superseding capitalism in cyberspace, 9 *Science as Culture* 5 (2007).
[102] James Caporaso and David Levine, *Theories of Political Economy* (Cambridge University Press, 1992) at 61; Simon Clarke, *Marx's Theory of Crisis* (Springer, 2016) at 132. Thus, nineteenth century novels dramatized how workers were alienated from the produce of their labor, the value created thereby being hoarded by capital due to laws and social norms against labor organizing or activism for wealth redistribution. Richard Lehan, *The City in Literature: An Intellectual and Cultural History* (University of California Press, 1998) at 70.
[103] Barbrook, note 101.
[104] Ibid. See also Barbrook, note 92, at 253–79.

8

Conclusion

In creative economies, the economic roles of persons with differential access to capital contribute to copyright class divisions. The blockbuster motion picture, often based on a comic book or other story told long ago, is one field of copyright struggle in our time. In some ways, the US Constitution's vision of copyright law has been abandoned, as corporate creativity has obtained priority treatment from Congress and the courts. Individual authors, who are supposed to be at the center of the copyright system, often lose the benefit of copyright reforms that are sold to Congress as helping them.

There are parallels between the disenfranchisement of some middle-class artists and authors under an increasingly corporate-focused copyright system, and the widespread stripping of patents from middle-class inventors in the name of "innovation." Just as doom was prophesied if the Constitution's preference for the individual author was respected, exaggerated claims that financial and technology companies will be devastated by the cost of patent suits has arguably warped legal doctrine in favor of the accumulation of corporate and great-family wealth. The ideology of innovation – that it will not continue unless capital gets its way – played a similar role in both cases.

Copyright conglomerates aggregate massive bundles of rights, with reduced accountability to the public and a tendency to accumulate great fortunes. Some advocates for authors contend that Hollywood studios enjoy a type of copyright immunity based on their economic prominence, with "Hollywood" being defined broadly to include both television networks and movie production studios. Most movie studios and television networks that have been sued for nonliteral copyright infringement and idea theft over the preceding twenty years, and then filed motions to throw out the claims, ultimately prevailed in court on final judgment. Alleged imitation of plot, style, or mood has escaped sanction in many instances, according to champions of authors. The trend in the law to prohibit or at least heavily regulate idea theft and derivative works has somehow evaded Hollywood firms.

The transition to synergistic exploitation of authors' creative output in the digital environment is taking place as legal stratagems subvert due process when authors litigate against multinationals. A two-track system of copyright justice may be emerging. Natural persons confront growing barriers to publishing their creative output, including widespread copyright censorship affecting the individual creator, and implemented by social media platforms. Automatic deletion of poor or middle-class creators' fair-use works occurs alongside proliferating fair-use works distributed by corporations or copyright aggregators. Even when claims of piracy are legitimate, due process falls by the wayside in a modern-day copyright inquisition. Meanwhile, the remedies enjoyed by corporations in cases of infringement have become more harsh, at least on paper.

Disparities in treatment also confront actors and musicians under the emerging international law of "performance rights." As performers complain of being shortchanged of royalties or of control over their own work, studios and labels are demanding and receiving sweeping expansions of their rights against unauthorized imitation, sampling, and mashup. The resulting changes in the law may pose a serious threat to the freedoms of Internet users and impecunious creators. Instruments such as the WIPO Treaty on Audiovisual Performances may transform the Internet's legal framework into one in which economic exploitation trumps civil and political rights.

Unforgiving applications of international copyright law could also cripple the most promising way to level the playing field of knowledge, the universal digital library. Even when publishers and authors' representatives agreed that Google should be able to create a competitively-priced ebook market using scanned library books and new pricing algorithms, the Obama administration opposed it in the name of protecting the interests of foreign publishers and Google's competitors such as Amazon.com and Microsoft.

Copyright systems may not be serving the interests of each class of persons equally. They may be suppressing the overall level of creative output, while accommodating the interests of follow-on authors and the general public just enough to blunt popular demands for more radical reforms. This development parallels accounts of late capitalism by authors such as Michael Hardt, Antonio Negri, Slavoj Žižek, and Thomas Piketty, whereby nation-states operate as councils of strategy for the owners of capital, who reform economic systems periodically to stave off broader mobilizations. It remains to be seen whether copyright will impose even tighter controls on follow-on creativity, and solidify the power of dominant creative firms by developing new regulatory structures. Critics of globalization predicted as much, in developing the theory of postmodern harmonized public–private governance by sovereigns and multinationals.

Index

income (*cont.*)
  incomes, of investors, i, 4–5, 8–10, 17, 56,
    77, 82–84, 126–127, 151, 163, 177, 186–187
  incomes, of manufacturing companies, 87
  incomes, of members of Congress, 9
  incomes, of performers of musical composi-
    tions or audiovisual scripts, 142–143, 154,
    159–162, 177
  incomes, of radio or television broadcasters or
    distributors/transmitters, 157, 162
  incomes, of software publishers, 58, 87–90
  incomes, of unemployed authors or
    performers, 210–11
inequality of incomes, 4–8, 14, 39–40, 63, 74,
    90, 92, 124–127, 130–131, 188–189, 205,
    208–209
infringement, *see* COPYRIGHTS or PATENTS
Instagram, 65, 72, 82, 129, 149
International Publishers Association, 205
Internet gift economy, *see* GIFT ECONOMY,
    OF INTERNET
Internet Radio Fairness Act, 163
Internet search engines, viii, 1–3, 16, 42, 47–48,
    52, 56, 59, 62, 65–73, 75, 80–83, 88–89,
    103, 106–107, 125, 128–130, 136, 146, 147,
    149, 153–154, 158, 163, 170–176, 179, 181,
    187–191, 193, 195–208, 213–215
  aol.com, *see* AOL, INC.
  bing.com, *see* BING
  Google.com, *see* GOOGLE, INC.
  yahoo.com, *see* YAHOO, INC.
investment theory, of politics, 7–8
inquisitorialism, 167, 171–172
iOs, *see* IPAD, IPHONE
iPad, 80, 199
iPod, 130, 201
iPhone, 14, 72, 81, 89, 130, 163, 189, 193,
    199–200
iTunes, 80, 189, 193, 200

Jackson, Michael, 103, 158
Jay-Z, 115, 121, 158
jobs, *see* EMPLOYMENT
journalism, 27–28, 35, 66, 73, 107, 131, 133–135,
    149, 187–189, 209

Kindle Reader, *see* AMAZON KINDLE
    READER
Kobo reader, 199
Kuznetz, Simon, 4

labor, laborers, viii, 4–10, 14, 17, 23, 25, 27, 29,
    35, 54, 65–66, 68–69, 72, 74, 82–84, 89–92,
    101, 110, 127, 133, 144, 154–156, 158, 160,
    188, 191, 209–210, 212

exploitation of labor, 5–6, 8, 14, 27, 133,
    144, 154–155, 158, 160, 188, 191,
    209–210, 212
labor statistics, 89–92, 126, 156–158, 190
labor unions, 8, 23, 66–67, 86, 88, 91,
    143–145, 170–171, 182, 187–188, 191
mobilizations of labor, 5–8, 23, 66–67,
    141–143, 160, 182, 191
Led Zeppelin, 103–104, 108–109, 115, 122
Lessig, Lawrence, 16, 76, 101, 106–107, 120, 124,
    134, 135
Levine, Robert, 11, 169, 174–175, 187–188, 209
Linkedin Corp., 61, 65, 71, 89
Litman, Jessica, 12, 16, 82
lobbying Congress, 8, 11–12, 61, 64, 72–76, 84,
    143, 154, 160, 169, 177, 179, 188
  for against provisions of Copyright Act of 1976,
    12, 51–52, 160
  for America Invents Act of 2011, 72, 75–77
  for or against provisions of Digital Millennium
    Copyright Act of 1998, 186–187
  for patent remedy reform, 61–62
  for patent venue reform, 61–62
  for or against Stop Online Piracy Act, 169,
    177, 179
  for WIPO Treaty on Audiovisual Performances,
    143
lobbying the European Commission, 186
Lowery, David, 160–161

Madonna (Ciccone), 158–159
market capitalizations, 44, 72, 88–89,
    189–195
  of Amazon.com, 89
  of Buzzfeed, 189–190
  of Disney/ABC, 194
  of entertainment conglomerates in United
    States, 193–194
  of Facebook, 88–89
  of Google, 89
  of Huffington Post, 189–190
  of Marvel Comics, 44
  of News Corp./Fox, 194
  record labels in United States, 192
  of Snapchat, 72
  of Time Warner, 194
  of Viacom, 194
  of Vice Media, 189–190
Marx, Karl, 7–8, 12, 13, 115, 210
Marxian theories, of societies/economies, 5–7, 13,
    16, 82–83, 85, 109, 209, 211
means of production, economic, 4–8, 16, 33, 37,
    44–45, 48, 72, 82, 104, 111–112, 115–116,
    119, 125–128, 130, 137, 142, 150, 160–161,
    185, 189, 210